Software & Technology

Laws, Principles & Paradoxes

Pocket Reference

1st Edition, 2025

This publication is designed to provide accurate and authoritative information in regard to the subject matter covered. It is sold with the understanding that neither the author nor the publisher is engaged in rendering legal, investment, accounting or other professional services. While the publisher and author have used their best efforts in preparing this book, they make no representations or warranties with respect to the accuracy or completeness of the contents of this book and specifically disclaim any implied warranties of merchantability or fitness for a particular purpose. No warranty may be created or extended by sales representatives or written sales materials. The advice and strategies contained herein may not be suitable for your situation. You should consult with a professional when appropriate. Neither the publisher nor the author shall be liable for any loss of profit or any other commercial damages, including but not limited to special, incidental, consequential, personal, or other damages.

Published by: Pebble Tree LLC
1st Edition: 2025

DEDICATION

To my wife and kids,
Thank you for all your daily support and encouragement – Q.S.

Introduction

I wrote this book mostly because a few months back I had read about the "Paradox Mindset" by the Marriott School of Business and the Center for Teaching and Learning at Brigham Young University - *https://learnstrategy.byu.edu/strategy-mindsets/paradox-mindset*

Effective strategists recognize the power of paradox in business. A paradox refers to two opposing realities or imperatives that, on the surface, cannot coexist at the same time. It often appears that pursuing one will inevitably hinder the other. In paradox language, we refer to these ends as the "poles" and we wrestle with the tension to push towards both poles at the same time.

Business leaders are continually confronted with paradoxes. For instance, should we prioritize innovation or operational efficiency? Should we focus on localizing our offerings for specific markets, or should we aim to create a universal, one-size-fits-all product? Should we invest in cutting-edge technology, or focus on improving current processes? Should we adhere strictly to industry standards, or challenge the status quo to disrupt the market?

Experienced leaders understand that choosing one pole of the paradox often means sacrificing the potential of the other. While people typically crave clarity and simplicity, it's tempting to choose one side of the paradox and commit to it fully. By choosing one pole, leaders can provide a clear, unified direction for their teams, allowing everyone to focus on a shared goal and create a predictable, straightforward work environment. However, this method is risky because it leaves organizations exposed to the negative consequences of neglecting the opposite pole.

Companies that fully embrace change at all costs might overwhelm employees, burn out or overextend their resources, and lose organizational stability. On the other hand, companies that cling too strongly to stability may struggle to adapt to shifting market conditions or emerging opportunities. Focusing only on efficiency may yield short-term profitability but limit the ability to innovate, while companies that focus solely on innovation might struggle to maintain consistent revenue streams in the present.

A paradox mindset encourages us to move from an "either-or" mentality to a more flexible "both-and" mentality. Instead of accepting the supposed trade-offs between opposing poles, great leaders challenge these dichotomies and look for ways to harness both at the same time. Rather than making high-level decisions to favor one pole, they craft more nuanced strategies that help them understand when it makes sense to prioritize one side over the other.

The best strategists embrace both sides of the paradox. They are uncomfortable when the path ahead appears too straightforward, always searching for the paradoxes that may be overlooked. They seek to identify these paradoxes, clearly define their opposing poles, and train themselves to leverage the strengths of both sides simultaneously, creating a more agile and resilient approach to business.

This Book's Approach

This book is meant to be a collection of knowledge about the laws, principles and paradoxes in software and technology. Feel free to read the book end-to-end or jump to a specific law, principle or paradox.

The book may at some points refer to "Software & Technology Laws, Principles & Paradoxes" in its short form as "LPP".

The break down for each law, principal or paradox is a follows

- Definition and Origin: Provide the reader with the LPP definition or description. Also to provide the reader with origins or history of the LPP.
- Context and Importance: Provide the reader with reasons why it is important and how it relates to software and technology.
- Best Practices and Guidelines: Provide the reader with some best practices and guidance.
- Misconceptions and Pitfalls: Provide the reader with some common misconceptions and pitfalls to watch out for.
- Related Concepts: Provide the reader with the associated or related concepts, so that the reader may conduct further research.

To keep each LPP focused on its origin, definition, best practices and related concepts I decided not to include any code samples. Since entire books could be written on single concepts it did not feel like the right fit for this book to also squeeze in any code samples.

Who This Book Is For

This book is intended for both software engineers and technical leaders.

The book may help software engineers by providing them with proven frameworks and techniques that guide their work, ensure better collaboration, improve the quality of their code, and ultimately lead to more robust, scalable, and user-friendly software. By adhering to these principles, engineers can make better design decisions, minimize errors, and develop software that meets both technical and business needs more effectively.

The book may empower technical leaders to make better strategic decisions, build high-quality systems, foster collaboration, and align technical efforts with business objectives. By applying these principles, leaders can improve not only the technical output of their teams but also the team culture and overall organizational success. These principles provide a strong foundation for guiding teams through complex technical challenges while ensuring continuous growth, efficiency, and alignment with business goals.

Software Development & Engineering

A. Core Programming

DRY: Don't Repeat Yourself

Definition and Origin

DRY (Don't Repeat Yourself) is a software development principle focused on minimizing code repetition and duplication. Coined by Andy Hunt and Dave Thomas in their book The Pragmatic Programmer: Your Journey to Mastery (1999), the principle asserts that every piece of knowledge or logic should only exist in one place within a system.

Context and Importance

The Don't Repeat Yourself (DRY) principle is a foundational concept in software development aimed at reducing redundancy within a codebase. It encourages developers to avoid duplicating logic, data, or functionality across multiple parts of a system. Instead, the idea is to centralize repetitive code into reusable functions, classes, or modules. By doing so, the codebase becomes more maintainable, as changes only need to be made in one place, reducing the risk of errors and inconsistencies. DRY is particularly important in large-scale applications, where duplication can lead to bloated and difficult-to-manage code. With a single source of truth, developers can ensure that all parts of the application reflect the same logic and behavior, improving the overall quality and efficiency of the software.

In addition to improving maintainability, adhering to DRY can also enhance collaboration and scalability within a development team. When code is modular and free from repetition, other developers can more easily understand and extend the system without having to navigate through redundant logic. This leads to faster development cycles and better long-term sustainability, as new features can be added or existing ones updated without having to rework multiple sections of code. In rapidly evolving technologies, maintaining a DRY codebase also facilitates refactoring and adapting to new requirements or platforms, helping teams keep pace with changing business needs and technology trends. Ultimately, DRY is crucial for optimizing code quality, reducing technical debt, and enabling more agile software development practices.

Best Practices and Guidelines

When applying DRY, consider these guidelines:

Think in terms of knowledge, not code. Ask yourself: "What knowledge does this code represent?" If the same knowledge appears in multiple places, that's a DRY violation.

Start by being specific, then generalize. Don't create abstractions preemptively. Wait until you see actual repetition before refactoring to remove it.

Consider the cost of change. If two similar pieces of code are likely to evolve differently, keeping them separate might be better than forcing them together.

Use composition over inheritance. When eliminating repetition, prefer composing smaller, focused pieces over creating deep inheritance hierarchies.

Common Misconceptions and Pitfalls

- DRY Means No Repetition at All: A common misconception is that DRY means there should be absolutely no repetition in the code. There are cases where repetition is acceptable, or even necessary. For example, small, repeated code snippets (like simple getters and setters) may not require abstraction into functions or classes. The goal is not to always eliminate repetition but to avoid unnecessary duplication.
- Over-abstraction: While DRY encourages reducing repetition, it can sometimes lead to over-abstraction. Developers might try to abstract every small piece of code, leading to a complex, convoluted design that's hard to understand and maintain. Striking a balance between abstraction and readability is crucial.
- Premature Optimization: Trying to apply DRY too early in a project can result in unnecessary complexity. It's better to first focus on getting the application working and then refactor the code later to eliminate duplication. Prematurely abstracting logic that doesn't need to be reused yet can make the code harder to read and understand.

- Inappropriate Generalization: Sometimes, developers may generalize a solution too much in an attempt to reduce repetition, creating a solution that works in many cases but is less efficient or harder to understand. Always evaluate whether the generalized solution really adds value before implementing it.

Related Concepts

1. SoC; Separation of Concerns
2. KISS; Keep It Simple, Stupid
3. YAGNI; You Aren't Gonna Need It

References

- Wikipedia, *Don't repeat yourself*, [pub: 14 Nov 2024, cited: 3 Jan 2025]

KISS: Keep It Simple, Stupid

Definition and Origin

The KISS principle is a design and problem-solving philosophy advocating for simplicity in both thought and implementation. In the context of software and technology, it emphasizes creating solutions that are straightforward, intuitive, and avoid unnecessary complexity. The term KISS (Keep It Simple, Stupid) was coined by Kelly Johnson, an engineer at the Lockheed Skunk Works, in the 1960s.

The philosophy can be summed up as: "Simple solutions are often the best solutions."

Context and Importance

In the context of software development, KISS advocates for avoiding unnecessary complexity, opting instead for straightforward, intuitive, and efficient solutions. This principle is rooted in the idea that systems should be designed in a way that minimizes the risk of errors, reduces maintenance overhead, and improves overall usability. By focusing on simplicity, developers can ensure that their software is not only easier to understand but also more adaptable to future changes, resulting in quicker updates and a smoother user experience.

The importance of KISS in software and technology lies in its ability to enhance both development efficiency and long-term sustainability. Complex code and convoluted designs often lead to bugs, performance issues, and high maintenance costs, as well as steep learning curves for new developers. By adhering to the KISS principle, teams can create software that is both reliable and scalable, reducing the potential for errors and making it easier to troubleshoot. Moreover, simpler systems are more likely to align with user expectations, as they tend to be more intuitive and accessible, which can directly lead to higher user satisfaction and adoption. In a rapidly evolving technological landscape, simplicity enables faster iterations, easier collaboration, and ultimately, more successful software products.

Best Practices and Guidelines

Write small, focused functions: Each function should do one thing and do it well. Avoid making functions do too many things at once.

Favor readability over cleverness: It's tempting to write complex, clever code, but it often reduces readability. Prioritize clarity and simplicity.

Use the simplest data structures: Choose the most straightforward data structures that meet the problem's requirements, like lists, dictionaries, and tuples, instead of overengineering with custom classes or structures unless necessary.

Avoid premature optimization: Focus on making your code simple and correct first. Only optimize when performance becomes an issue.

Refactor often: Regularly revisit and refactor your code to keep it clean and simple, especially when complexity starts to creep in.

Common Misconceptions and Pitfalls

- Misconception: "Simple Means Easy" A common misunderstanding is equating "simple" with "easy to create." Creating simple solutions often requires more thought and effort than creating complex ones. Albert Einstein captured this perfectly when he said, "Everything should be made as simple as possible, but no simpler."

- Misconception: Simplicity Means Lack of Features Simplicity does not mean removing important functionality. It means creating a solution that solves the problem efficiently and clearly without unnecessary complexity.
- Misconception: KISS Always Means Less Code Sometimes simplicity comes in the form of well-structured, legible code with appropriate abstractions. It doesn't always mean reducing the number of lines but rather focusing on clarity and purpose.
- Pitfall: Oversimplification While simplicity is key, oversimplifying a solution can lead to a loss of important functionality or flexibility. Strive for balance between simplicity and functionality.
- Pitfall: Avoiding Necessary Complexity Some problems inherently require complex solutions. KISS doesn't advocate for avoiding complexity at all costs, but rather for addressing complexity when it's necessary and managing it in a clean, understandable way.

Related Concepts

1. DRY; Don't Repeat Yourself
2. YAGNI; You Aren't Gonna Need It
3. Occam's Razor; Simplest explanation is usually correct
4. Bjarne Stroustrup's; Make Simple Tasks Simple!
5. Albert Einstein; Make everything as simple as possible, but not simpler

References

- Wikipedia, *KISS principle*, [pub: 19 Dec 2024, cited: 3 Jan 2025]

YAGNI: You Aren't Gonna Need It - Yet

Definition and Origin

YAGNI stands for "You Aren't Gonna Need It." It is a software development principle that advises against implementing features, functionality, or code optimizations until they are needed, emphasizing simplicity and avoiding unnecessary complexity or premature optimization.

The term YAGNI was coined by Ron Jeffries, one of the original proponents of Extreme Programming (XP), in the late 1990s, encouraging the idea of building software incrementally, focusing on the most urgent needs of the project and deferring speculative or hypothetical future requirements.

Context and Importance

YAGNI is a software development principle that encourages developers to focus only on the features or functionalities that are immediately necessary for the task at hand, rather than speculatively building out additional capabilities that may never be used. The core idea behind YAGNI is to avoid over-engineering by preventing the introduction of code or features that anticipate future needs or unknown requirements. By adhering to YAGNI, developers can ensure that they are spending time and resources only on the functionality that adds direct value in the present, thereby reducing complexity, minimizing technical debt, and improving overall software maintainability. This principle is often associated with Agile methodologies, which prioritize delivering incremental value with a focus on simplicity and responsiveness to user needs.

In the context of software development and technology, YAGNI is critical for maintaining a lean and efficient workflow. It helps prevent feature creep, where unnecessary or overly ambitious features are added without clear demand, potentially slowing down development and making the codebase more difficult to maintain. YAGNI also promotes a mindset of iteration and continuous improvement, where teams build just enough to meet current requirements and then refine or extend the product as new insights emerge. By embracing this principle, development teams can stay more focused on delivering high-quality, valuable software, reducing wasted effort and ensuring a faster, more flexible response to changes in user feedback or market demands.

Best Practices and Guidelines

Build for current needs: Focus on implementing features that provide immediate value or solve current problems. Avoid implementing speculative features.

Iterate: Make your software flexible and extensible by building iteratively. Add new features as real needs arise.

Keep it simple: Start with the simplest solution that works. Don't add complexity until it's absolutely necessary.

Avoid premature optimization: Prematurely optimizing or abstracting code often leads to wasted effort. Only optimize when you know it's required.

Minimize code duplication: Keep your code DRY (Don't Repeat Yourself) but avoid over-engineering generic solutions that might never be used.

Common Misconceptions and Pitfalls

- YAGNI means never planning ahead: YAGNI doesn't imply you should ignore future requirements entirely; it means don't build solutions for those requirements until you need them.
- YAGNI means ignoring refactoring: It's important to refactor your code when it becomes unmanageable but refactor only when there's clear value in doing so—not because you anticipate problems in the future.
- YAGNI means writing poor code: YAGNI isn't an excuse for writing sloppy or inefficient code. It's about avoiding over-complication and focusing on what's currently necessary.
- YAGNI means not planning for scalability: Scalability should still be a consideration, but don't preemptively over-engineer for extreme scalability before identifying if it's really needed.

Related Concepts

1. DRY; Don't Repeat Yourself
2. KISS; Keep It Simple, Stupid
3. Pareto Principle; Often, 80% of the value comes from 20% of the features.
4. Knuth's Optimization Principle; Premature optimization is the root of all evil

References

- Wikipedia, *You aren't gonna need it*, [pub: 2 Dec 2024, cited: 3 Jan 2025]

Big-O Notation: Algorithm efficiency measured by time and space complexity

Definition and Origin

Big-O notation is a mathematical concept used to describe the efficiency of an algorithm in terms of its time complexity (how long an algorithm takes to run) and space complexity (how much memory an algorithm requires) as the size of the input grows. It focuses on the behavior of an algorithm in the worst-case scenario, providing an upper bound on the growth rate of an algorithm's running time or space usage relative to the input size.

In essence, Big-O helps developers understand the scalability of an algorithm and whether it will perform well as input sizes increase.

Common Big-O Notations:

- O(1): Constant time – the algorithm takes the same amount of time regardless of input size.
- O(n): Linear time – time increases linearly with the input size.
- O(log n): Logarithmic time – time increases logarithmically as input size increases.
- O(n log n): Linearithmic time – a mix of linear and logarithmic growth, typical for efficient sorting algorithms.
- O(n^2): Quadratic time – time increases quadratically with input size.
- O(2^n): Exponential time – time doubles with each additional input element.
- O(n!): Factorial time – grows extremely fast, typical in algorithms that generate all permutations of a set.

Context and Importance

Understanding Big-O notation is fundamental for optimizing the performance of software applications. It allows developers to make informed decisions about which algorithms to use, ensuring that applications can scale effectively without unnecessarily consuming resources. As software deals with larger datasets, knowing the time and space complexities of algorithms becomes critical for maintaining performance and user experience.

Scalability: Big-O helps predict how an algorithm will perform as data grows, ensuring the system can handle large datasets efficiently.
Optimization: It aids in selecting the right algorithm for a given problem, particularly when time and space are limited.
Comparison: It provides a universal language for comparing algorithms regardless of implementation details or hardware.
Real-World Efficiency: It highlights potential bottlenecks that could severely impact performance in production systems.

Best Practices and Guidelines

Optimize for worst-case scenarios: Always consider the worst-case performance of your algorithm, especially for mission-critical or large-scale applications.

Use simpler algorithms when possible: A simple O(n) algorithm is usually better than an O(n log n) or O(n^2) algorithm, particularly when the data size is small.

Choose appropriate data structures: The choice of data structure (e.g., hash tables, arrays, trees) can significantly affect time and space complexities.

Avoid unnecessary computations: Use techniques like memorization or dynamic programming to avoid redundant calculations and reduce time complexity.

Benchmarking: While Big-O gives theoretical performance, always benchmark algorithms on actual data to understand real-world performance and trade-offs.

Common Misconceptions and Pitfalls

- Big-O is not about raw execution time: Big-O describes how the execution time scales with input size, not the actual time taken. Two algorithms with the same Big-O complexity might still have different constant factors, making one faster in practice.
- Big-O doesn't account for hardware: The actual performance can vary depending on the hardware (CPU speed, memory bandwidth, etc.), but Big-O helps compare algorithms in terms of scalability.

- All algorithms of the same Big-O are not equal: Two algorithms that both have O(n) time complexity may still have drastically different performance depending on their constant factors or the nature of the input data.
- O(1) does not mean fast: O(1) means constant time, but the constant factor might still be large. For example, a poorly designed O(1) algorithm may take a significant amount of time due to complex operations or high memory usage.
- Space complexity matters too: Focusing only on time complexity can lead to inefficiencies in memory usage. Always consider both time and space complexity when analyzing an algorithm.

Related Concepts

1. Amdahl's Law; Parallel speedup is limited by sequential portions
2. Amortized Analysis; Analyzes the average time complexity per operation over a sequence of operations.
3. Gustafson's Law; Suggests that for large problems, increasing the number of processors can yield near-linear speedup, emphasizing scalability for parallel algorithms.

References

- Wikipedia, *Big O notation*, [pub: 24 Dec 2024, cited: 3 Jan 2025]

First Principles: Breaking down complex problems into foundational concepts or truths

---

Definition and Origin

First Principles in the context of software and technology refers to breaking down complex problems or systems into their most fundamental, foundational concepts or truths. It involves understanding the core components, relationships, and constraints at the most basic level, and then building up solutions from scratch, rather than relying on assumptions or existing solutions. This approach encourages innovative thinking and problem-solving by challenging conventional wisdom and looking at problems from a fresh perspective.

The concept of First Principles originates from Aristotle, the ancient Greek philosopher. In his work on logic and philosophy, Aristotle introduced the idea of first principles as the fundamental, self-evident truths upon which all knowledge and reasoning are built. These principles are the starting points for understanding complex ideas or solving problems.

Context and Importance

In software and technology, applying first principles thinking is crucial because:

Innovation: By deconstructing a problem to its most basic components, new solutions can emerge that aren't limited by conventional approaches.

Optimization: Identifying inefficiencies in existing systems can lead to better performance, scalability, and resource usage.

Problem Solving: First principles help in overcoming cognitive biases and preconceived notions about how things work, leading to clearer and more effective solutions.

Fundamental Understanding: It encourages deep comprehension, not just surface-level knowledge, which leads to more maintainable, secure, and efficient systems.

By applying first principles thinking to software and technology, you can break free from conventional patterns and unlock novel, optimized solutions. Understanding the fundamental concepts, analyzing them critically, and iterating on solutions is a powerful strategy for developers and technologists seeking to innovate, optimize, and master their craft.

Best Practices and Guidelines

Deconstruct Problems: Break down complex problems into their most basic components. Analyze the fundamental rules that govern them before looking for solutions.

Focus on Efficiency: Always consider how an approach impacts performance. Efficiency is a key principle in software development, and it's often the first principle that gets overlooked.

Avoid Assumptions: Challenge existing norms and assumptions. Don't simply accept frameworks or libraries at face value without understanding how they work under the hood.

Keep It Simple: First principles thinking encourages simplicity. Solutions based on core principles are often simpler and more effective than those relying on complex abstractions.

Iterate and Improve: Start with a basic solution based on the first principles, then iterate on it to refine and improve as you discover more about the problem and possible optimizations.

Common Misconceptions and Pitfalls

- Overcomplicating the Problem: Some developers may think that deconstructing a problem into first principles requires solving everything from scratch. It's about understanding the basic components before leveraging pre-existing solutions when appropriate.
- Ignoring Abstractions: While it's important to understand the low-level workings, dismissing abstractions (like high-level libraries) completely can lead to reinventing the wheel unnecessarily. It's about balance.
- Failure to Optimize: First principles thinking doesn't always lead to immediate, practical solutions. While it's good to know the theory, always consider how practical your solution is in the real world.
- Disregarding Real-World Constraints: Often, first principles thinking is idealistic, but it's crucial to consider constraints like time, resources, and hardware limitations when implementing solutions.
- Reinvention without Purpose: Just because you understand a problem at the lowest level doesn't mean you should discard existing tools or libraries unless there's a clear and demonstrable benefit to doing so.

Related Concepts

1. DRY; Don't Repeat Yourself
2. KISS; Keep It Simple, Stupid
3. YAGNI; You Aren't Gonna Need It

4. DDD; Domain-Driven Design
5. Occam's Razor; Simplest explanation is usually correct
6. Design by Contract; Clear and formal agreements between software components

References

- Wikipedia, *First principle*, [pub: 21 Dec 2024, cited: 3 Jan 2025]

Knuth's Optimization Principle: Premature optimization is the root of all evil

---

Definition and Origin

Knuth's Optimization Principle states that "premature optimization is the root of all evil." It emphasizes that developers should avoid optimizing code or systems too early in the development process, before understanding the problem fully or identifying actual performance bottlenecks. Instead, focus on writing clean, correct code, and optimize only when necessary and based on real performance data.

Donald Knuth introduced the Optimization Principle in the early 1970s. He mentioned it in the context of his work on The Art of Computer Programming (specifically in Volume 1, Fundamental Algorithms, first published in 1968)

Context and Importance

This principle suggests that developers should focus first on writing clear, correct, and maintainable code before attempting to optimize performance. Often, early optimization efforts can lead to unnecessarily complex code, which may be difficult to maintain and debug, and can waste time on areas of the program that don't significantly impact overall performance. Knuth's insight encourages developers to initially prioritize problem-solving and readability, relying on profiling tools to identify true bottlenecks later in the development process.

In the context of software and technology, Knuth's principle is particularly important in a landscape where both the scale of software systems and the speed of hardware continue to evolve. Modern development practices emphasize agility and iteration, where code is frequently revised and optimized after user feedback and profiling data are collected. By focusing on correctness and maintainability early on, teams can ensure that their software is both efficient and adaptable in the long term. Once a clear understanding of performance issues is achieved through profiling, optimizations can then be applied in a more targeted, efficient manner, ensuring that resources are spent wisely, and that the system as a whole meets the needs of its users.

Best Practices and Guidelines

Profile first, optimize later: Always measure performance with tools like cProfile or timeit before making changes to optimize. Optimization should be data-driven, not assumption-based.

Prioritize readability and maintainability: Write clear, understandable code first. Optimization can often lead to harder-to-read code if applied prematurely.

Optimize only what matters: Focus your optimization efforts on areas that show up as bottlenecks in profiling or real-world usage.

Avoid premature abstraction: Don't add unnecessary complexity or abstraction until you know it will improve code reuse or performance.

Leverage built-in optimizations: Use language features, libraries, and data structures that are well-optimized for the task at hand (e.g., use sum() or join() in Python).

Common Misconceptions and Pitfalls

- Assuming optimization always leads to better performance: In many cases, prematurely optimizing can slow down development without providing real performance gains. Simple solutions may often be faster in practice.
- Premature optimization equals faster execution: Optimizing the wrong parts of the code (e.g., tiny operations that aren't bottlenecks) can make the program slower or harder to maintain without any measurable benefit.

- Favoring micro-optimizations over clarity: Small tweaks (e.g., changing variable types) often have negligible impact on performance but can reduce code clarity.
- Premature optimization is the same as avoiding optimization: The principle doesn't advocate avoiding optimization entirely but emphasizes when and where to focus optimization efforts.
- Using optimization techniques without understanding their trade-offs: Misusing techniques (like caching or concurrency) without a solid understanding of the problem context can introduce complexity and bugs.

Related Concepts

1. DRY; Don't Repeat Yourself
2. KISS; Keep It Simple, Stupid
3. YAGNI; You Aren't Gonna Need It
4. Occam's Razor; Simplest explanation is usually correct
5. Pareto Principle; 80% of the effects come from 20% of the causes.

References

- Wikipedia, *Program optimization*, [pub: 1 Dec 2024, cited: 3 Jan 2025]

The Rule of Three: Three strikes and you refactor

Definition and Origin

The Rule of Three suggests that you should only write a new piece of code (such as a function, class, or method) when you need it for the third time. The idea is that, after using or writing the same code twice, you may see a pattern or need for abstraction. This encourages developers to avoid premature abstraction or over-engineering and instead focus on solving actual, recurring problems. It helps to reduce complexity and ensures that code is only generalized when it's truly necessary.

The rule was popularized by Martin Fowler in the book "Refactoring: Improving the Design of Existing Code" in 1999 and attributed to Don Roberts.

Context and Importance

The Rule of Three emphasizes simplicity and helps prevent over-complicating code or systems before there's enough reason to do so. It encourages developers to only make changes or optimizations after seeing a problem arise multiple times. This avoids unnecessary work and keeps the codebase more maintainable, flexible, and less prone to bugs.

In the context of software design, the Rule of Three is often cited when considering:

Code duplication: Once code is repeated three times, it might be worth abstracting it into a reusable function, class, or module.
Optimizations: Don't optimize until performance bottlenecks are actually observed in real-world use.
Design patterns: Once a pattern becomes common in a project, it might be worth formalizing it into a reusable structure.
By adhering to the Rule of Three, software remains cleaner and easier to maintain, while ensuring that changes or optimizations are driven by actual need, not speculation.

Best Practices and Guidelines

Don't over-engineer: Avoid making complex abstractions or optimizations until the problem has arisen multiple times.

Refactor on repetition: If a pattern appears for the third time, consider refactoring it into a reusable structure (function, class, module).

Don't optimize prematurely: Focus on clear, functional code before worrying about performance optimizations.

Prioritize readability over premature efficiency: Ensure the code is easy to understand first and optimize later if necessary.

Avoid premature abstraction: Abstract only when the functionality has been implemented multiple times, and a common pattern emerges.

Common Misconceptions and Pitfalls

- Premature Abstraction: Some developers misinterpret the Rule of Three as a signal to abstract too early. This leads to over-complicated systems that are harder to maintain and understand. Refactoring after just one or two instances may lead to over-complicating your design prematurely. Ensure that you're refactoring for clear, recurring patterns, not just arbitrary code repetition.
- Ignoring Context: Some developers may strictly follow the Rule of Three without considering the context, leading to unnecessary complexity in simpler systems. Following the rule too rigidly can result in over-engineering for problems that do not require it. Use your judgment to decide whether refactoring is truly necessary for the current project.
- Performance Trap: Assuming that optimization should only happen after the third instance can delay necessary performance improvements that may have been obvious from the start. The Rule of Three should not delay necessary optimizations, particularly for known performance bottlenecks. Always profile and measure performance before assuming the code is optimal, and act on data, not assumptions.

Related Concepts

1. DRY; Don't Repeat Yourself
2. KISS; Keep It Simple, Stupid
3. YAGNI; You Aren't Gonna Need It
4. Knuth's Optimization Principle; Premature optimization is the root of all evil

References

- Wikipedia, *Rule of three (computer programming)*, [pub: 3 Sep 2023, cited: 3 Jan 2025]

Law of Demeter: Only talk to your immediate friends

Definition and Origin

The Law of Demeter (also known as the Principle of Least Knowledge) is a software design principle that states that a module should only communicate with its direct collaborators and not with the internal details of other objects. In simple terms, it suggests that an object should only talk to its immediate neighbors (e.g., objects it directly owns or is passed as parameters), rather than reaching through them to interact with other objects. This promotes loose coupling, making systems easier to maintain and less prone to errors.

The Law of Demeter was introduced by Ian Holland in 1987 while working at the Northeastern University in Boston, Massachusetts. Holland's goal was to reduce the complexity and interdependencies in software systems by promoting more modular and decoupled designs, making it easier to maintain and understand. The principle was later adopted and widely recognized in object-oriented software engineering and design patterns.

Context and Importance

The Law of Demeter (LoD), is a design guideline in software engineering that encourages a system to minimize dependencies and interactions between components. It was originally introduced in the context of object-oriented programming but has since become a general principle for building loosely coupled maintainable systems. The law stipulates that a module (or class) should only communicate with its immediate friends—meaning objects that are directly related to it or passed as parameters—rather than objects that are distant or nested within other objects. In simpler terms, a method should only call methods on objects it directly owns, objects passed to it, or objects it creates, avoiding calls to methods on objects that are further down the chain of relationships.

The importance of the Law of Demeter in software development lies in its contribution to creating systems that are more modular, easier to understand, and maintain. By reducing the interdependence between components, it encourages high cohesion and low coupling, two key principles of good software design. When components are loosely coupled, changes to one part of the system are less likely to ripple through and affect others, which makes the codebase more adaptable to changes and easier to refactor. In practice, adhering to the Law of Demeter reduces the likelihood of bugs, simplifies testing, and improves the overall scalability of a system. This leads to more resilient, maintainable software, which is especially crucial in complex or large-scale technology projects where managing interdependencies can become a significant challenge.

Best Practices and Guidelines

Limit method calls to the immediate "friends": An object should communicate only with objects that are directly related to it—either objects it owns, or objects passed to it as arguments.

Avoid "chained method calls": Example driver.car.engine.start(), this would be considered a violation of LoD. Instead, refactor the code to ensure each object has clear, well-defined responsibilities.

Use delegation when necessary: If an object needs to perform an action through another object, consider delegating that action rather than directly invoking it on nested objects.

Promote encapsulation: Ensure that objects expose only the methods that are necessary for interaction and keep their internal details private.

Refactor long method chains: If a method involves accessing properties across multiple objects, break it up into more manageable, cohesive parts.

Common Misconceptions and Pitfalls

- Overcomplicating the design: One common misconception is that following the Law of Demeter strictly requires a more complex design. While LoD promotes better modularity, it's important not to create unnecessary abstractions or over-engineered solutions. The goal is to reduce complexity, not add it.
- Ignoring convenience for theoretical purity: In some cases, you may be tempted to create a large number of intermediate objects or interfaces to avoid direct method calls. This can lead to a bloated design that complicates the codebase rather than simplifying it.
- Misunderstanding "immediate friends": Some developers mistakenly think that LoD means only objects that are directly instantiated within a class (i.e., properties defined in the constructor). However, it also applies to objects passed as arguments to methods, so these too should be considered "friends."

Related Concepts

1. High Cohesion: Reduce the need for them to interact with unrelated components.
2. Encapsulation: Limit the visibility of an object's internal state and behavior to the outside world.
3. Dependency Injection: Inject dependencies, promoting a more testable and maintainable codebase.
4. Single Responsibility Principle: Both LoD and SRP aim to keep components small, focused, and independent.

Reference

- Wikipedia, *Law of Demeter*, [pub: 7 Nov 2024, cited: 3 Jan 2025]

Postel's Law (Robustness Principle): Be conservative in what you send, liberal in what you accept

---

Definition and Origin

Postel's Law (also known as the Robustness Principle) states: "Be conservative in what you send, and liberal in what you accept." In the context of software and network protocols, it means that a system should be strict in adhering to the standards when sending data (conservative in what it does), but be flexible and tolerant when receiving data, accepting a wider range of inputs even if they are not perfectly formatted (liberal in what it accepts). This helps ensure systems are more robust and fault-tolerant in diverse, real-world environments.

Postel's Law was coined by Jon Postel, a pioneering computer scientist and one of the key figures behind the development of the Internet. Postel formulated the principle in the 1980s while working on Internet protocols, particularly the Transmission Control Protocol (TCP) and Internet Protocol (IP). It was first articulated in his work on the RFC 1122 (Requirements for Internet Hosts), published in 1989.

Context and Importance

In the broader context of software and technology, Postel's Law encourages systems to be resilient, promoting interoperability and flexibility. It helps prevent systems from failing completely due to unexpected or malformed inputs and allows them to continue functioning, even when the input deviates from what is strictly expected.

The principle is particularly important in network protocols, data serialization, web APIs, and situations where multiple systems or parties interact with each other in diverse ways. By embracing Postel's Law, developers can ensure that their systems handle real-world data variations without crashing, ensuring robustness and reliability.

Best Practices and Guidelines

Validate inputs before processing: Always ensure data is correctly structured before using it in your application to avoid errors.

Handle malformed data gracefully: Be flexible when receiving data and handle unexpected inputs with default values or meaningful error messages, not hard failures.

Follow standards, but tolerate deviations: When designing APIs or protocols, use well-defined standards but allow some flexibility in accepting data.

Provide clear error handling: Provide meaningful feedback to users or systems when encountering non-conforming data but avoid terminating processes unless absolutely necessary.

Test with real-world scenarios: Include test cases for unexpected, incomplete, or out-of-spec data to ensure robustness.

Common Misconceptions and Pitfalls

- Overly Lenient Acceptance of Bad Data: A common mistake is to be too lenient when accepting data, accepting any input without validation. This can lead to security vulnerabilities, data corruption, and unintended behavior.
- Assuming All Systems Are Forgiving: Just because one system is liberal in what it accepts doesn't mean all systems will behave the same way. Inconsistent data formats can lead to interoperability issues between different systems.
- Focusing Only on What You Receive: It's important to remember that Postel's Law applies to both what you send and what you accept. Being overly forgiving while not sending well-structured, validated data can cause problems down the line.
- Neglecting Security: Being too lenient in accepting malformed or unexpected data without proper validation can open doors to security vulnerabilities, such as injection attacks or buffer overflows.
- Inconsistent Error Handling: Failing to implement consistent and meaningful error handling when receiving unexpected data can lead to confusion and bugs. Developers may incorrectly assume that the system will always handle any input smoothly.

Related Concepts

1. Idempotence; operations that can be repeated without changing the result after the initial application.
2. Principle of Least Astonishment; a system should behave in a way that minimizes surprises for users or other systems.
3. Fault Tolerance: The ability of a system to continue operating properly even in the event of unexpected faults or errors.

4. Defensive Programming: A design philosophy where the developer anticipates potential failures or unexpected behavior and writes code to mitigate these issues.

References

- IETF, *DoD Standard Internet Protocol*, [pub: Jan 1980, cited: 3 Jan 2025]
- IETF, *Requirements for Internet Hosts*, [pub: Oct 1989, cited: 3 Jan 2025]
- Wikipedia, *Robustness principle*, [pub: 13 Aug 2024, cited: 3 Jan 2025]

Hollywood Principle: "Don't call us, we'll call you"

Definition and Origin

The Hollywood Principle is a design principle in software development that states, "Don't call us, we'll call you." It refers to the idea of Inversion of Control (IoC), where the control flow is inverted: instead of a program calling external components or services, the components are designed to be called by a higher-level framework or system. This principle is commonly applied in event-driven architectures, frameworks, and systems like GUI or web frameworks, where the system dictates when and how components are invoked.

The term Inversion of Control (IoC) was popularized by Martin Fowler, particularly in his 2004 book "Patterns of Enterprise Application Architecture". However, the concept itself dates back earlier to Johnson and Foote's paper Designing Reusable Classes, published by the Journal of Object-Oriented Programming in 1988. The term 'Hollywood Principle' seems to originate in a paper by Richard Sweet on Mesa in 1983.

Context and Importance

The Hollywood Principle, when applied to software architecture, it refers to a design pattern where components or modules of a system are structured so that lower-level components do not have to actively seek or depend on higher-level ones. Instead, the system is designed to delegate control to the higher levels, often through mechanisms like event-driven programming, inversion of control (IoC), or dependency injection. The key idea is that higher-level components manage the flow and control, simplifying dependencies and promoting more flexible, modular, and scalable system designs.

The Hollywood Principle plays a crucial role in improving the maintainability and extensibility of software systems. By ensuring that the control flow is inverted—meaning lower-level components are not tightly coupled to specific actions or workflows—developers can build more decoupled and reusable code. This leads to systems that are easier to modify or extend without introducing unintended side effects. Additionally, it allows for better testing and integration, as individual components can be tested in isolation without the need for knowledge of the higher-level orchestration. This principle supports modern software architectures, such as microservices and event-driven systems, by encouraging flexibility, loose coupling, and separation of concerns, which are foundational to achieving scalability and robustness in complex technology stacks.

Best Practices and Guidelines

Use Dependency Injection: Pass dependencies to classes rather than having classes create them themselves.

Leverage Frameworks: Use frameworks and libraries that implement IoC (e.g., Flask, Django) to simplify and abstract control flow.

Design for Extensibility: Build your software with the assumption that new modules or features will be added later, without needing to modify existing code.

Decouple Components: Ensure components interact with one another through well-defined interfaces rather than direct method calls.

Adopt Event-Driven Architectures: Use event handlers and queues to let components notify each other, rather than one component directly invoking another.

Common Misconceptions and Pitfalls

- Overuse of Frameworks: While frameworks that implement the Hollywood Principle are powerful, over-reliance on them can lead to systems that are difficult to debug or extend. Developers may become too abstracted from understanding the low-level mechanics of their code.
- Loss of Control: One misconception is that the Hollywood Principle makes the developer passive in their application. While control is inverted, developers still maintain control through proper design and architecture decisions.
- Complexity from Excessive Abstraction: Excessive reliance on inversion of control can introduce unnecessary complexity if not done thoughtfully. Using a framework to handle control flow is beneficial, but it may lead to "magic" or behavior that's hard to trace if the abstraction becomes too convoluted.
- Tight Coupling with Event Systems: Event-driven systems, which also use the Hollywood Principle, can lead to hidden dependencies and unintentional side effects if not managed properly. It's important to ensure that events are handled in a transparent and predictable way.
- Not Understanding the Control Flow: When applying the Hollywood Principle (especially in event-driven systems), it's easy to lose sight of the overall flow of control. This can result in confusion about when and why certain actions are triggered.

Related Concepts

1. Loose Coupling; allows components to work independently, minimizing dependencies between components.
2. Dependency Injection (DI); dependencies are injected into a class rather than the class creating them itself.
3. Event-Driven Architecture (EDA): A software architecture pattern where components communicate by emitting and reacting to events, and the flow of control is driven by event occurrence.

References

- Wikipedia, *Inversion of control*, [pub: 16 Nov 2024, cited: 3 Jan 2025]

Scout Rule: "Leave the code better than you found it"

Definition and Origin

The Scout Rule encourages developers to improve the codebase whenever they interact with it. This can involve refactoring, adding comments, simplifying complex logic, fixing bugs, or improving readability. The goal is to contribute to the overall health and maintainability of the code, ensuring that the next developer (or even your future self) who works on it benefits from the improvements.

The Scout Rule is attributed to Robert C. Martin (commonly known as Uncle Bob) in the book "97 Things Every Programmer Should Know: Collective Wisdom from the Experts".

Context and Importance

The Scout Rule is vital in environments where teams are collaborating on complex projects or when software is expected to evolve over time. This principle emphasizes that engineers should not just "get the job done" but also consider the following:

Sustainability: Systems should be designed for ease of maintenance, which minimizes future technical debt.
Collaboration: It encourages clear, understandable code that others can quickly comprehend and extend.
Proactive Planning: Instead of fixing problems as they arise, the Scout Rule encourages designing for future flexibility.
Refactoring and Iteration: By following this rule, engineers are more inclined to continuously improve the codebase, reducing complexity as new features are added.
As the scope of software projects increases, maintaining high-quality code becomes increasingly difficult. The Scout Rule supports long-term software health by embedding good practices in the initial stages of development.

Best Practices and Guidelines

Write Clear, Maintainable Code: Strive for readability and clarity in your code. Write comments where necessary and use meaningful variable names.

Refactor Regularly: Continuously improve your codebase by refactoring outdated or complex code to keep it clean and efficient.

Minimize Technical Debt: Avoid shortcuts or compromises that might solve a problem in the short term but create long-term issues.

Plan for Future Scalability: Design software with future requirements in mind. Use modular architectures, flexible data structures, and design patterns that allow easy changes and expansion.

Collaborate and Communicate: If working in teams, ensure that everyone understands the code. Use version control, write documentation, and follow consistent coding standards.

Common Misconceptions and Pitfalls

- Scout Rule is About Perfection, Not Pragmatism
- The Scout Rule is not about achieving perfect or over-engineered solutions. It's about balancing efficiency with sustainability. Don't get caught up in making everything flawless at the expense of progress.
- Overusing Abstractions
- While abstraction is important for maintainability, overusing it can lead to unnecessarily complex systems. Use abstractions wisely to avoid creating confusion or obfuscating logic unnecessarily.
- Ignoring Trade-offs
- Developers sometimes interpret the Scout Rule as always aiming for the "best" solution. However, some trade-offs are inevitable in software development. It's important to weigh the costs and benefits of your design choices, rather than adhering to a rigid ideal.
- Thinking Short-Term Fixes Are Enough
- Temporary fixes may seem like solutions in the short term, but they can lead to long-term problems if they don't align with the Scout Rule. Plan for the future and account for possible changes upfront.
- Assuming Someone Else Will Clean Up

- The Scout Rule encourages the idea that you should leave the code in a state that others (or your future self) can easily work with. Don't assume others will clean up your mess. Leave things better than you found them.

Related Concepts

1. Technical Debt: Accumulation of quick-and-dirty solutions that create more problems down the road. The Scout Rule is a way to minimize technical debt by writing maintainable code upfront.
2. Code Refactoring: Continuously improving the internal structure of the code without changing its external behavior. This aligns with the Scout Rule, as it keeps the codebase clean and manageable.
3. Clean Code: A set of principles for writing software that is easy to understand and maintain, closely related to the Scout Rule.
4. Sustainable Software Development: The idea that software should be designed with long-term maintenance in mind, making it easier to evolve as requirements change.
5. Modular Design: Creating software in small, independent components or modules that can be easily maintained and replaced, reflecting the principle of leaving the environment better than you found it.

References

- Wikipedia, *Robert C. Martin*, [pub: 5 Dec 2024, cited: 3 Jan 2025]

Principle of Least Astonishment: Software should behave in a way that users find intuitive and expected

---

Definition and Origin

The Principle of Least Astonishment (also known as the Principle of Least Surprise) states that a system should behave in a way that minimizes surprises for its users or developers. In other words, software should function in a manner that aligns with users' or developers' expectations, making the system intuitive and predictable. This principle helps enhance usability and reduces confusion by ensuring that actions lead to results that are consistent with what users anticipate.

In essence, if something is surprising or confusing, it likely violates this principle, leading to frustration and inefficiencies.

Context and Importance

The Principle of Least Astonishment plays a crucial role in software development and user interface design. Its main goal is to minimize cognitive load and improve usability by creating products that behave in expected ways. When users encounter unexpected behavior, it disrupts their mental model, leading to mistakes, dissatisfaction, and, in extreme cases, abandonment of the product.

In programming, it translates into clear, consistent code and intuitive APIs. For users, it translates into interfaces that "just work" in a way that feels natural.

Best Practices and Guidelines

Maintain Consistency: Consistent behavior and naming conventions reduce confusion. Functions and methods should do what their names imply.

Intuitive APIs: Avoid surprising side effects in functions. If a function modifies data, this should be clearly documented and expected.

Clear Documentation: Ensure that your code and APIs are well-documented, especially when the behavior deviates from common expectations.

Minimize Surprises in User Interfaces: In both graphical and command-line interfaces, make sure interactions are predictable and conform to standard conventions.

Follow Common Patterns: Leverage established design patterns and conventions in your language or framework. This reduces the learning curve for other developers.

Common Misconceptions and Pitfalls

- Overcomplicating Code for Flexibility: Striving for overly flexible or generalized code can lead to confusing or unexpected behavior. Sometimes, simplicity and predictability should take precedence over flexibility.
- Assuming Users Will Adapt: It's tempting to think that users or developers will adapt to surprising behavior, but it's always better to design with their expectations in mind.
- Ignoring Edge Cases: Not accounting for edge cases (e.g., passing None or invalid types) can lead to surprising results that go against the principle.
- Assuming Documentation is Enough: Just writing down expectations in documentation is not enough. The code should "speak for itself" through clear naming, structure, and behavior.
- Non-Intuitive Error Messages: An error message should provide information that helps users (or developers) understand what went wrong in a way that makes sense in the context of the application.

Related Concepts

1. Pareto Principle; The 80/20 Rule
2. Fitts's Law; Time to target depends on distance and size
3. Postel's Law (Robustness Principle); Be conservative in what you send, liberal in what you accept
4. Cognitive Load; mental effort required by users to understand and interact with a system
5. User-Centered Design; Involving real users in the design process and considering their expectations can help avoid surprises and ensure that software meets their needs.

References

- Wikipedia, *Principle of least astonishment*, [pub: 7 Sep 2024, cited: 3 Jan 2025]

GRASP Principles

Definition and Origin

GRASP (General Responsibility Assignment Software Patterns) is a set of nine principles used in object-oriented design to help assign responsibilities to classes and objects. These principles guide developers in creating clear, maintainable, and flexible systems by promoting appropriate assignment of responsibilities. The nine GRASP principles are:

1. Information Expert: Assign responsibility to the class with the necessary information to fulfill it.
2. Creator: Assign responsibility for creating an instance of a class to a class that has the necessary information or association.
3. Controller: Assign responsibility for handling system events to a class that represents a use-case or logical operation.
4. Low Coupling: Assign responsibility in a way that minimizes dependencies between classes, enhancing maintainability and flexibility.
5. High Cohesion: Assign related responsibilities to the same class to keep it focused and manageable.
6. Polymorphism: Assign responsibility for behavior to classes that can vary their behavior through polymorphism, enabling flexibility in response to different conditions.
7. Pure Fabrication: Assign responsibility to a class that doesn't represent a concept in the problem domain, but is created for technical reasons, such as a utility class or service.
8. Indirection: Assign responsibility to an intermediary object to mediate between other components to achieve flexibility or reduce coupling.
9. Protected Variations: Assign responsibility to protect elements of the system from variations in other elements, enhancing stability.

The GRASP (General Responsibility Assignment Software Patterns) principles were coined by Craig Larman, a software engineer and author, in his book "Applying UML and Patterns: An Introduction to Object-Oriented Analysis and Design and Iterative Development" (first published in 1997).

Context and Importance

GRASP is a set of nine design principles used in object-oriented software development to guide the allocation of responsibilities to classes and objects in a system. These principles help developers create software that is modular, maintainable, and easy to understand by ensuring that the responsibilities of each class are well-defined and appropriately distributed. GRASP includes principles such as information expert, which suggests assigning responsibility to the class that has the necessary information to fulfill it, and controller, which recommends assigning responsibility for handling system events to a controller class. The principles aim to promote high cohesion within classes and low coupling between them, resulting in more flexible and scalable software.

The importance of GRASP in software and technology lies in its ability to improve the design and quality of complex systems. By adhering to these principles, developers can create systems that are more robust, easier to maintain, and less prone to errors. GRASP helps to clarify the roles and interactions of different objects in a system, making the software more intuitive to work with and reducing the likelihood of miscommunication or flawed design. Additionally, following GRASP principles fosters better object-oriented design practices, supporting the creation of reusable components, efficient code refactoring, and a clearer system architecture. This is especially critical in large-scale or long-term projects, where maintainability and adaptability are key to the project's success.

Best Practices and Guidelines

Use Information Expert to assign responsibilities to the class that has the necessary data, reducing the need for excessive method calls between classes.

Favor Low Coupling by designing classes to interact with as few other classes as possible, promoting reusable components.

Maintain High Cohesion by ensuring that related methods and data are grouped together within a class, enhancing readability and maintainability.

Leverage Polymorphism for behaviors that change based on the object type, allowing you to avoid large conditional statements and promoting extensibility.

Protect Variations by encapsulating parts of the system that are likely to change, minimizing the impact on other components.

Common Misconceptions and Pitfalls

- GRASP principles are only for large systems.
- While GRASP principles shine in complex systems, they are valuable for smaller systems too. They help avoid bad design practices even in simple applications.
- GRASP always leads to more classes.
- Some developers mistakenly think GRASP principles will result in an over-complication of the system with unnecessary classes. However, it's about assigning responsibilities, not creating unnecessary entities. In some cases, this may reduce the number of classes by clarifying responsibilities.
- Overuse of Polymorphism.
- Polymorphism can be an excellent tool, but it's crucial to balance its use. Overuse can make the design overly complex and harder to debug.
- Misunderstanding of Controller Role.
- The Controller should be responsible for coordinating actions between objects, not performing business logic. It is a mediator, not the core logic holder.
- Ignoring Low Coupling in Favor of Convenience.
- It can be tempting to make objects depend on each other for convenience, but this creates tight coupling. This increases maintenance costs and reduces flexibility in the long run.

Related Concepts

1. SOLID Principles: GRASP shares common goals with the SOLID principles (especially Single Responsibility Principle, Open/Closed Principle) in promoting modular, maintainable code.
2. Design Patterns: Many GRASP principles align with design patterns. For example, Creator is similar to the Factory Method pattern, while Controller can resemble the Facade pattern in some contexts.

3. Separation of Concerns (SoC): GRASP encourages clear division of responsibilities within different classes, supporting the idea of separating concerns for better modularity and readability.

References

- Wikipedia, *GRASP (object-oriented design)*, [pub: 1 Jul 2024, cited: 3 Jan 2025]

SOLID Principles

Definition and Origin

The SOLID principles are a set of five object-oriented design principles that promote maintainable, flexible, and scalable software systems. They help developers write code that is easier to understand, modify, and extend. The SOLID acronym stands for:

- S - Single Responsibility Principle (SRP): A class should have only one reason to change, meaning it should have only one responsibility.
- O - Open/Closed Principle (OCP): Software entities (classes, modules, functions) should be open for extension but closed for modification, allowing behavior to be extended without changing existing code.
- L - Liskov Substitution Principle (LSP): Objects of a superclass should be replaceable with objects of a subclass without affecting the correctness of the program.
- I - Interface Segregation Principle (ISP): Clients should not be forced to depend on interfaces they do not use, meaning interfaces should be specific to the needs of the client.
- D - Dependency Inversion Principle (DIP): High-level modules should not depend on low-level modules. Both should depend on abstractions. Additionally, abstractions should not depend on details. Details should depend on abstractions.

They were introduced by Robert C. Martin (Uncle Bob) in his 2000 paper Design Principles and Design Patterns. Then later around 2004, the SOLID acronym was coined by Michael Feathers.

Context and Importance

The SOLID principles aim to improve the overall quality of software by encouraging better code organization and reducing the likelihood of problems like tightly coupled code, code duplication, and difficulty in adding new features. The SOLID acronym stands for: Single Responsibility Principle (SRP), Open/Closed Principle (OCP), Liskov Substitution Principle (LSP), Interface Segregation Principle (ISP), and Dependency Inversion Principle (DIP). Together, these principles provide a framework for designing object-oriented software that is easier to understand, modify, and extend without introducing unintended side effects.

The importance of SOLID principles in software and technology cannot be overstated, especially in today's fast-paced development environment. As systems grow in complexity, adhering to SOLID can significantly enhance code readability, reduce bugs, and simplify testing. By following SOLID principles, developers can create codebases that are more resilient to change, enabling teams to adapt to new requirements or technologies with less friction. These principles also promote better collaboration among team members, as the design patterns encouraged by SOLID make it easier for developers to work on different parts of a system without stepping on each other's toes. In an age where software is often built and deployed at a rapid pace, SOLID provides a solid foundation for maintaining long-term software health and sustainability.

Best Practices and Guidelines

Keep responsibilities clear: Each class should have one responsibility to ensure high cohesion and low coupling.

Prefer composition over inheritance: For extending behavior, use composition and polymorphism, rather than deep inheritance hierarchies.

Design for flexibility: Use interfaces and abstract classes to decouple dependencies and allow easier future changes.

Refactor regularly: Regularly review and refactor your code to ensure it adheres to SOLID principles, making it more maintainable.

Test your code: SOLID principles often lead to more modular code, which is easier to unit test and ensure quality.

Common Misconceptions and Pitfalls

- "SOLID is only for large applications": While SOLID principles are beneficial in large systems, they can improve code quality in smaller applications as well.
- "Over-engineering": Some developers over-complicate the design by adhering strictly to SOLID, even when the problem doesn't require such a level of abstraction. Use SOLID principles judiciously.
- "Inheritance is always the answer": While inheritance is a powerful tool, overusing it can lead to tight coupling and difficulties in extending your application. Favor composition where possible.
- "Single Responsibility means only one method": A class can have multiple methods, but they should all relate to the same responsibility.

Related Concepts

1. DRY; Don't Repeat Yourself
2. KISS; Keep It Simple, Stupid
3. YAGNI; You Aren't Gonna Need It

References

- Wikipedia, *SOLID*, [pub: 22 Nov 2024, cited: 3 Jan 2025]

B. Code Quality & Complexity

Cyclomatic Complexity Principle: Complexity based on independent paths

Definition and Origin

Cyclomatic Complexity is a software metric used to measure the complexity of a program's control flow. It counts the number of linearly independent paths through a program, with higher values indicating more complex and potentially harder-to-maintain code. As cyclomatic complexity increases, the program becomes more complex, making it harder to understand, test, and maintain.

Formally, it is defined as:

$$M = E - N + 2P$$

Where:

- M is the cyclomatic complexity.
- E is the number of edges in the control flow graph.
- N is the number of nodes in the control flow graph.
- P is the number of connected components (typically 1 for a single program).

In simpler terms, this formula counts the number of decision points (like if, while, for) and calculates the number of possible execution paths. A higher value indicates more complexity.

The Cyclomatic Complexity principle was introduced by Thomas J. McCabe in 1976.

Context and Importance

Cyclomatic complexity helps developers understand and manage the complexity of software systems. High cyclomatic complexity can indicate code that is difficult to maintain, test, and debug, potentially leading to more defects and higher development costs. Lower cyclomatic complexity often correlates with more maintainable, readable, and testable code.

In software development, complexity metrics like cyclomatic complexity are used during the code review process, to improve test coverage, and to guide refactoring efforts. It is especially important when determining the test coverage required for a given codebase, as it suggests the number of distinct paths that should be tested.

Best Practices and Guidelines

Aim for Low Cyclomatic Complexity: Keep cyclomatic complexity as low as possible. Complex code is harder to understand, test, and maintain.

Refactor Large Functions: Break large functions into smaller, simpler ones to reduce complexity.

Use Early Returns: Minimize nested conditions by using early returns or exits, which reduces complexity.

Limit Decision Points: Avoid excessive if, for, while, try/except, and case statements in a single function.

Focus on Testability: Use cyclomatic complexity to guide your unit testing efforts—higher complexity means more tests are needed to cover all paths.

Common Misconceptions and Pitfalls

- Cyclomatic Complexity Measures Functionality, Not Quality: While cyclomatic complexity can indicate how complex a function or module is, it does not directly measure how well the code performs its intended functionality or how robust it is.
- Higher Cyclomatic Complexity Is Always Bad: A high cyclomatic complexity value does not automatically mean the code is bad or buggy. Some complex tasks may require complex logic. However, it does mean the code is harder to maintain and test.
- Cyclomatic Complexity Alone Is Not Enough: Cyclomatic complexity should be used in conjunction with other metrics and practices, such as code coverage, readability, and coupling, for a more holistic approach to managing code quality.

- It's Not Always About Refactoring: While high cyclomatic complexity may signal a need for refactoring, some complex algorithms are inherently difficult to simplify without sacrificing performance or clarity. The goal should be to find a balance between simplicity and efficiency.
- Low Cyclomatic Complexity Doesn't Equal High-Quality Code: Low cyclomatic complexity is just one indicator of code quality. It doesn't mean the code is bug-free or optimized. It is important to consider other aspects, like performance and scalability, as well.

Related Concepts

1. DRY; Don't Repeat Yourself
2. KISS; Keep It Simple, Stupid
3. Dijkstra Observation; Complexity based on independent paths
4. Halstead Complexity Measures; Complexity metrics based on its operators and operands

References

- Wikipedia, *Cyclomatic complexity*, [pub: 29 Aug 2024, cited: 3 Jan 2025]

Dijkstra Observation: Complexity based on independent paths

Definition and Origin

Dijkstra's Observation states that a program's complexity is determined by the number of independent paths in its control flow, not just the number of lines of code. This insight led to the development of Cyclomatic Complexity, emphasizing that complexity arises from branching and decision points, rather than code length alone.

Dijkstra's observation about program complexity primarily comes from his influential paper "A Case against the Go To Statement" published in 1968.

Context and Importance

Dijkstra's observation arose in response to the complexity of control structures, particularly as programming languages evolved and became more expressive. He recognized that the true difficulty in understanding and testing a program comes from the number of independent paths through its control flow, rather than the sheer volume of code or the number of statements. In other words, a program's logical complexity—how its control flow branches and merges—was more important than just counting lines of code.

- Shift to Structured Programming: Dijkstra's insight was a key part of the structured programming movement, which advocated for breaking down code into well-defined, linear paths and avoiding unnecessary jumps (e.g., using goto statements). This led to the development of control flow structures like if, while, and for loops, which are simpler to follow and understand compared to unstructured jumps.
- Understanding Software Complexity: Dijkstra's observation helped shift focus from simple metrics like lines of code to more meaningful measures of complexity—such as Cyclomatic Complexity—that focus on decision points and independent paths in the code. This allowed developers to better understand the inherent complexity of a program's flow and manage it more effectively.
- Improved Testability: By recognizing that the number of independent paths was a critical measure of a program's complexity, Dijkstra's observation influenced testing practices. It emphasized the importance of path coverage and made it clear that testing should aim to cover all possible execution paths, rather than just verifying individual code statements. Cyclomatic complexity, which counts these independent paths, directly emerged from this insight, guiding software testing efforts.
- Enhanced Maintainability: The insight that complex programs have more branching paths also helped reinforce the idea that simpler code (with fewer paths) is easier to maintain. Code with fewer decision points tends to be less error-prone, easier to modify, and more straightforward for developers to understand.

- Guiding Software Design: Dijkstra's observation laid the foundation for better software design principles, emphasizing clarity and simplicity in program structure. It encouraged developers to aim for linear flow and modularization to reduce the number of independent paths, thereby improving both the quality and understandability of code.

Best Practices and Guidelines

Minimize Decision Points: Reduce unnecessary if, else, and switch statements to lower branching complexity and improve readability.

Use Early Returns: Simplify control flow by returning early from functions, avoiding deep nesting of conditions.

Limit Nested Loops: Avoid deeply nested loops, which significantly increase cyclomatic complexity and make code harder to test.

Refactor Long Functions: Break complex functions with many decision points into smaller, more focused functions to enhance maintainability.

Write Comprehensive Tests: Ensure unit tests cover all independent paths in the code, guided by cyclomatic complexity to assess test coverage.

Common Misconceptions and Pitfalls

- More Lines = More Complexity: Cyclomatic complexity measures branching, not the number of lines—short code can still be complex if it has many branches.
- Cyclomatic Complexity Equals Code Quality: High cyclomatic complexity doesn't necessarily indicate poor code quality; context, readability, and maintainability are also important.
- Refactoring Always Reduces Complexity: Refactoring code to reduce cyclomatic complexity can sometimes lead to over-complication if not done carefully.
- Complexity Equals Bugs: Higher complexity increases testing challenges, but it doesn't directly correlate with more bugs—effective testing is key.

- Low Cyclomatic Complexity Means Simple Code: A low cyclomatic complexity might overlook the subtle complexity of non-branching concerns, such as state management or algorithmic complexity.

Related Concepts

1. DRY; Don't Repeat Yourself
2. KISS; Keep It Simple, Stupid
3. Cyclomatic Complexity; Complexity based on independent paths
4. Halstead Complexity Measures; Complexity metrics based on its operators and operands

References

- Wikipedia, *Considered harmful*, [pub: 25 Dec 2024, cited: 3 Jan 2025]
- Edsger W.Dijkstra, *A Case against the GO TO Statement*, [pub: 8 Apr 2011, cited: 3 Jan 2025]

Gall's Second System Effect: Successful systems are succeeded by over-engineered systems

---

Definition and Origin

Gall's Second System Effect refers to the tendency of engineers or designers to overcomplicate a system after having gained experience with a simpler, first version. This often leads to excessive complexity, making the system harder to understand or maintain, as the desire to incorporate new ideas and features overwhelms practical usability.

Gall's Second System Effect phrase was first used by Fred Brooks in 1975 in his famous book The Mythical Man-Month.

Context and Importance

The importance of understanding the Second System Effect lies in the long-term health of software projects. Early systems tend to be more focused and simpler, reflecting an early stage of exploration and design. The second iteration is often where developers, having learned from the first system, attempt to "perfect" the system and add new features based on what they believe the product "should" have. This can result in:

- Increased complexity, leading to bugs and difficult debugging
- Increased development time and resources
- Poor scalability or performance issues due to overengineering
- Loss of focus on the core product goals
- A steeper learning curve for future developers and maintainers

Thus, recognizing this pattern can help guide development towards more sustainable, modular, and manageable software.

Best Practices and Guidelines

To avoid falling into the trap of Gall's Second System Effect, consider these best practices:

Keep It Simple: Start with a minimal, working version (MVP) and iterate based on user feedback and actual needs rather than theoretical ones.

Focus on Core Features: Add complexity only when it's necessary for meeting specific user needs, not just to "future-proof" the system.

Modularize: Break the system into smaller, manageable components that can evolve independently rather than trying to build everything at once.

Refactor Continuously: Instead of adding new features in bulk, refactor and optimize your code as you go, keeping it clean and efficient.

Adopt an Agile Mindset: Use an agile, iterative approach, where you focus on delivering small, incremental improvements, allowing flexibility for change.

Common Misconceptions and Pitfalls

- Misconception: More Features Equal Better Product: Adding more features in the second system doesn't necessarily improve the product. In fact, it can make it harder to use and maintain.
- Pitfall: Overcomplicating Solutions: Over-engineering in the second system can lead to convoluted code, making debugging and future development more difficult.
- Pitfall: Ignoring Technical Debt: Developers may prioritize new features and functionality while ignoring existing technical debt, which grows rapidly in complex systems.
- Misconception: Scale Early: Premature optimization and scaling can introduce more complexity and challenges before the product has even achieved product-market fit.
- Pitfall: Lack of User Feedback: Without incorporating user feedback early and often, developers may make assumptions about what features are necessary, leading to unnecessary additions.

Related Concepts

1. KISS; Keep It Simple, Stupid
2. YAGNI; You Aren't Gonna Need It

References

- Wikipedia, *Second-system effect*, [pub: 22 Sep 2024, cited: 3 Jan 2025]

Gilb's Laws of Unreliability: "Computers are unreliable, but humans are even more unreliable."

Definition and Origin

Gilb's Laws of Unreliable Programming are a set of principles proposed by Tom Gilb that highlight common pitfalls in software development. They emphasize that the more complex or larger a system becomes, the more likely it is to have bugs, and that adding features without proper attention to reliability can lead to increasingly unreliable software. Key aspects include the tendency for systems to fail unpredictably as they grow and the challenge of managing complexity while maintaining reliability.

Here are the key Gilb's Laws of Unreliability:

1. Law of Complexity: The more complex a system becomes, the more likely it is to become unreliable.
2. Law of Change: The more changes are made to a system, the more opportunities there are for introducing errors, reducing reliability.
3. Law of Incomplete Understanding: The less a team understands the system as a whole, the more likely they are to introduce bugs or make the system unreliable during development.
4. Law of Testing: The more features or code a system has, the less likely it is that every possible combination of interactions will be adequately tested, leading to unforeseen failures.
5. Law of Growth: As a system grows, the number of ways it can fail increases exponentially, making it harder to maintain reliability.

These laws highlight the challenges of maintaining software reliability as systems increase in complexity, scale, and change over time.

Context and Importance

Tom Gilb, a software engineer and pioneer in software engineering and systems design, proposed the Laws of Unreliability to illustrate the inherent challenges in software development. These laws emerged from his observations of real-world software projects and the tendency for systems to become unreliable as they grow, evolve, or undergo continual change. They are particularly relevant in contexts where software projects involve significant complexity, rapid development cycles, or frequent modifications.

Gilb's Laws are a critique of the common assumption that adding features or complexity automatically improves a system's value. Instead, they highlight that as systems increase in complexity or undergo frequent changes, they tend to become more error-prone and harder to maintain. This is critical in managing the long-term reliability and quality of software systems.

1. Emphasizes the Trade-Off Between Complexity and Reliability: Gilb's Laws underscore the importance of understanding that increasing complexity, especially without careful management, leads to greater risk of unreliability. This is vital for software architects, developers, and project managers to consider when designing systems or making decisions about adding features or capabilities.
2. Encourages Thoughtful System Evolution: The laws warn against mindlessly adding features or making changes without considering their impact on the system's stability. They advocate for a more deliberate, measured approach to software development, where reliability is maintained alongside progress.
3. Promotes the Need for Testing and Understanding: Laws like the Law of Testing and Law of Incomplete Understanding highlight the necessity of thorough testing, documentation, and comprehension of the system's architecture. A lack of these practices can lead to unpredictable failures and high maintenance costs.
4. Reinforces the Complexity of Maintaining Large Systems: As systems grow in size and scope, so do the number of potential failure points. Gilb's laws suggest that as complexity increases, the system's unreliability increases disproportionately, making it harder to keep systems functioning correctly over time.
5. Helps Manage Risk in Software Projects: Gilb's laws provide a framework for identifying potential risks early in the software development lifecycle. They encourage practices like incremental development, careful change management, and focusing on maintaining system reliability to prevent the "unreliability spiral" in large-scale projects.

In summary, Gilb's Laws of Unreliability serve as a cautionary guide for developers, engineers, and managers to think critically about the design, scaling, and maintenance of complex systems. They advocate for balancing new features with careful attention to the system's overall reliability and stability.

Best Practices and Guidelines

Minimize Complexity: Keep systems as simple as possible to reduce the risk of failure.

Limit Changes: Carefully manage changes to avoid introducing new errors.

Ensure Deep Understanding: Build a thorough understanding of the system before making modifications.

Prioritize Testing: Test all critical interactions and edge cases, especially as the system grows.

Control Growth: Scale systems incrementally to manage reliability and prevent exponential increases in failure risk.

Common Misconceptions and Pitfalls

- Overestimating Control: Belief that systems can be made entirely reliable through design. Gilb's laws emphasize that all systems will fail at some point—unpredictably or under certain conditions.
- Ignoring Real-World Conditions: Underestimating the complexity of real-world environments and assuming ideal conditions. Laws highlight how external factors often cause unexpected failures.
- Neglecting Human Error: Overlooking the role of human mistakes. Many failures stem from user errors or miscommunications, which Gilb's laws underscore.
- Misunderstanding Gradual Degradation: Assuming a system's reliability is binary (working or not) instead of a gradual decline over time or usage.
- Misapplying Reliability Metrics: Using simplistic or irrelevant metrics to measure reliability. Gilb stresses that reliability must be assessed in context and with dynamic real-world conditions in mind.
- Failure to Update Assumptions: Treating initial designs and assumptions as fixed, instead of evolving them based on new data or experiences.
- Assuming Linear Reliability Growth: Expecting improvements in reliability to follow a steady, linear trajectory rather than recognizing potential for sudden failure modes or non-linear degradation.
- Overreliance on Tests: Believing that passing tests guarantees long-term reliability. Testing can identify issues but cannot account for all potential real-world variables.

- Underestimating the Impact of Change: Failing to consider how even small changes in the system or environment can lead to unexpected reliability issues.
- Focusing on Failures Rather Than Prevention: Over-prioritizing post-failure analysis rather than proactively designing for reliability and understanding the underlying causes of failure.

Related Concepts

1. Murphy's Law; Anything that can go wrong, will go wrong
2. Lehman's Laws of Software Evolution; Software must constantly evolve to remain useful
3. Gall's Second System Effect; Successful systems are succeeded by over-engineered systems
4. Principle of Least Astonishment; Software should behave in a way that users find intuitive and expected

Reference

- Tom Gilb, *Gilb's Laws of Unreliability*, [cited: 3 Jan 2025]

Greenspun's Tenth Rule of Programming: Developers end up reinventing features already available in high-level languages

---

Definition and Origin

Greenspun's Tenth Rule of Programming was coined by computer scientist Philip Greenspun in the 1990s as a commentary on the inherent complexity and redundancy often found in software development. Specifically, it critiques how lower-level languages like C and C++ require programmers to implement complex features that are already present in more expressive, higher-level languages like Lisp.

This phenomenon arises because these languages, while powerful and flexible, lack many of the abstractions and built-in functionalities that higher-level languages provide. As a result, developers in C or C++ frequently recreate solutions to problems that have long been solved by language designers in Lisp, such as dynamic typing, garbage collection, and rich data structures. The rule serves as a reminder of how the process of software development often leads to the creation of unnecessary, ad hoc solutions that could have been avoided with a different choice of language.

Context and Importance

The importance of Greenspun's Tenth Rule lies in its broader implications for software design and choice of tools. It suggests that developers should be mindful of the trade-offs involved when selecting a programming language for a project. Using a language that lacks certain abstractions can lead to increased complexity, maintenance burdens, and potential bugs, all of which slow down development and make code harder to maintain. The rule emphasizes the value of higher-level languages that come with rich built-in features, which can help avoid reinventing the wheel. It also serves as a cautionary tale about the dangers of overcomplicated solutions when simpler, more elegant alternatives might exist. Ultimately, Greenspun's Rule encourages programmers to evaluate not just the immediate benefits of a language, but its long-term impact on development efficiency`and code quality.

Understanding this rule helps developers recognize when they're reinventing the wheel, building unnecessarily complex solutions, and making systems harder to maintain and extend. It emphasizes the importance of leveraging modern abstractions, tools, and paradigms.

Best Practices and Guidelines

Leverage high-level languages: Use languages with rich abstractions (e.g., Lisp, Python) to avoid reinventing complex features.

Minimize unnecessary complexity: Avoid overcomplicating solutions when simpler, built-in tools are available in other languages.

Focus on productivity: Choose languages that enable rapid development and maintainability rather than those that require extensive manual implementation.

Avoid premature optimization: Don't sacrifice readability and ease of maintenance for micro-optimizations that add unnecessary complexity.

Embrace modularity: Break down complex systems into reusable components instead of recreating functionality from scratch.

Common Misconceptions and Pitfalls

- Misconception: It's only about C/C++: Greenspun's Rule applies to any low-level language where developers tend to recreate high-level abstractions, not just C or C++.
- Pitfall: Overestimating performance benefits: Developers may wrongly believe that avoiding high-level languages leads to faster code, while in reality, the lack of abstractions can result in more bugs and maintenance overhead.
- Misconception: It's anti-C/C++: The rule is not a critique of C/C++ themselves but rather a caution about the tendency to overcomplicate solutions when using these languages.
- Pitfall: Ignoring long-term maintainability: Focusing on short-term efficiency by reinventing features can lead to long-term difficulties in maintaining and evolving the software.
- Misconception: All languages are equally expressive: Not all languages are designed to handle complex tasks with ease; failing to choose the right tool can lead to unnecessary work and inefficiency.

Related Concepts

1. DRY; Don't Repeat Yourself
2. KISS; Keep It Simple, Stupid
3. YAGNI; You Aren't Gonna Need It
4. Principle of Least Astonishment; Software should behave in a way that users find intuitive and expected

References

- Wikipedia, *Greenspun's tenth rule*, [pub: 12 Apr 2024, cited: 3 Jan 2025]

Kernighan's Law: Debugging is twice as hard as writing code

Definition and Origin

This principle highlights the difficulty of troubleshooting and fixing errors in code, emphasizing that the process of debugging often takes more time and effort than writing the initial code. It suggests that good design and careful coding can reduce the need for extensive debugging later.

Kernighan's Law was coined by Brian W. Kernighan, a computer scientist known for his work on the C programming language and the development of Unix. He made this statement to highlight the inherent challenges in debugging, emphasizing how much more effort is often required to fix mistakes than to write the original code.

Context and Importance

Kernighan's Law, underscores a critical reality in software development: debugging can be more time-consuming and complex than writing the original code. The statement emerged from the broader context of software engineering in the 1970s when computing was still relatively young, and programming tools were rudimentary. As software projects grew in complexity, developers found that after they wrote code, they would often encounter subtle bugs that could be difficult to trace and fix. The process of debugging requires not only understanding the code's logic but also diagnosing the underlying issues, which can involve tracing errors that may not be immediately obvious. This can involve delving into hardware interactions, memory management, or other system-level complexities that were less predictable in early computing environments.

The importance of Kernighan's Law lies in its practical implications for software development. It highlights the critical need for developers to allocate ample time for debugging in project timelines, and it suggests that the act of writing code should be approached with caution and foresight to minimize future issues. It also emphasizes the value of tools, such as debuggers, unit tests, and static analysis, in reducing the difficulties of debugging. Understanding this law helps developers maintain realistic expectations and encourages best practices, such as writing clean, well-documented code and conducting thorough testing throughout the development process, which can significantly reduce the debugging workload. By acknowledging that debugging is inherently challenging, developers can better prepare for the iterative nature of software development and the need for continuous refinement of their code.

Best Practices and Guidelines

Write Clear, Modular Code: Break code into smaller, well-defined functions to simplify debugging and isolate issues.

Test Early and Often: Implement unit tests to catch bugs early, reducing debugging complexity later.

Use Version Control: Track changes and easily revert to previous working versions to minimize debugging from new changes.

Leverage Debugging Tools: Use integrated debuggers, loggers, and profilers to efficiently identify and resolve issues.

Document Assumptions and Edge Cases: Clearly document your code to reduce misunderstandings and make it easier to pinpoint where bugs might arise.

Common Misconceptions and Pitfalls

- Underestimating Debugging Time: Assuming debugging will take the same amount of time as writing the code, leading to unrealistic project timelines.
- Blaming External Factors Too Quickly: Jumping to conclusions that external libraries or environments are causing the issue, without thoroughly checking the code itself.

- Ignoring Simple Solutions: Overcomplicating debugging by assuming the issue must be complex, missing simpler explanations like syntax errors or misconfigurations.
- Skipping Testing in Early Stages: Not writing tests or running them consistently, which leads to more extensive debugging when problems are discovered late.
- Overreliance on Automated Tools: Relying too heavily on debugging tools and missing the deeper understanding of code that comes from manually tracing issues.

Related Concepts

1. Kernighan's Principle (Controlling complexity is the essence of programming)
2. Brooks's Law; Adding manpower to a late project makes it later
3. Pareto Principle; The 80/20 Rule
4. Gall's Law; Complex systems that work evolved from simple systems
5. Spolsky's Law of Leaky Abstractions; All non-trivial abstractions, to some degree, are leaky

References

- Wikipedia, *Brian Kernighan*, [pub: 5 Dec 2024, cited: 3 Jan 2025]
- Wikipedia, *The Elements of Programming Style*, [pub: 30 Jan 2023, cited: 3 Jan 2025]

Reed's Law: The utility of large networks grows exponentially with size

---

Definition and Origin

Reed's Law states that the value of a network increases exponentially with the number of possible groups that can be formed within it. Specifically, it suggests that the value of a network grows as the square of the number of users, since each user can form connections with any subset of other users. This is particularly relevant for social networks and other collaborative platforms where groups of users are key to network value.

Formula (Reed's Law): If n is the number of participants in a network, Reed's Law suggests that the value of the network is proportional to 2^n, where n is the number of users and 2^n is the number of possible groups (sub-networks) they can form.

Reed's Law was coined by David P. Reed, an engineer and researcher, in the early 2000s. He introduced the concept in a paper where he extended Metcalfe's Law, which states that the value of a network grows with the square of the number of users. Reed argued that the value of a network increases exponentially not just with the number of individual users, but with the potential for users to form groups and sub-networks.

Context and Importance

Reed's Law emerged as an important extension to the earlier work on network theory, particularly Metcalfe's Law, which suggested that the value of a network is proportional to the square of its number of users. While Metcalfe's Law accurately captures the basic value generated from direct connections between users, Reed's Law introduces the idea that the true value of a network lies not only in the individual connections but in the groups and sub-networks that can form within it. These groups, which can be collaborative or social in nature, exponentially multiply the network's value because each new user contributes to a vast number of potential groupings and interactions. This perspective was especially relevant in the context of the rapid growth of the internet and social media platforms, where communities and shared interests are central to their success.

The importance of Reed's Law lies in its ability to explain the dynamics of large-scale networks such as social media platforms, collaboration tools, and online communities. It helps to understand why platforms that foster group interactions—like Facebook, LinkedIn, or Wikipedia—become exponentially more valuable as they scale. In business terms, this highlights the significance of not just growing a user base but also enabling and encouraging group formation, as these clusters of activity drive engagement, content creation, and ultimately the platform's success. Reed's Law emphasizes that for modern network-driven platforms, the value doesn't just grow linearly but accelerates as more users interact within the system and form multiple interwoven groups.

Best Practices and Guidelines

Encourage group formation: Design networks to facilitate the creation of sub-groups or communities, as they significantly increase network value.

Foster collaboration: Build features that enable users to easily collaborate, share, and create content within groups to maximize engagement.

Leverage user interactions: Recognize that the true value of a network comes from interactions among users, not just individual connections.

Focus on scalability: Ensure your platform can handle the exponential growth in group combinations and user interactions as the network expands.

Prioritize user retention: Retain users by continuously offering new group experiences and collaborative opportunities, enhancing the overall value of the network.

Common Misconceptions and Pitfalls

- Assuming value grows linearly: A common misconception is that network value increases simply with the number of users, ignoring the exponential value derived from group formation.
- Neglecting group dynamics: Focusing only on individual user connections and not facilitating group interactions can limit the network's true potential.
- Underestimating the complexity of group scaling: As networks grow, managing and supporting an increasing number of groups and interactions can become technically and socially complex.
- Overlooking user experience: Prioritizing growth without ensuring the platform supports meaningful group activities and collaboration can lead to user disengagement.
- Ignoring network diversity: Failing to foster diverse groups or niche communities within the network can restrict the variety of interactions and limit value creation.

Related Concepts

1. Metcalfe's Law; Network value grows with square of users
2. Sarnoff's Law; Network grows in proportion to the number of viewers
3. Zipf's Law**; The n-th entry is often approximately inversely proportional to n

References

- Wikipedia, *Reed's law*, [pub: 30 Jul 2024, cited: 3 Jan 2025]

Spolsky's Law of Leaky Abstractions: All non-trivial abstractions, to some degree, are leaky

---

Definition and Origin

Spolsky's Law of Leaky Abstractions states that all abstractions leak, meaning that no matter how simplified a system or interface is, users will eventually encounter the underlying complexity. As a result, abstractions that hide complexity will eventually fail to fully conceal it, forcing users to confront the details.

Spolsky's Law of Leaky Abstractions was coined by Joel Spolsky, a software engineer and writer, in a blog post titled "The Law of Leaky Abstractions," published in 2002. Spolsky's idea emphasizes that abstractions, while designed to simplify complex systems, will inevitably expose their underlying complexities when pushed to their limits or used in ways not anticipated by the abstraction's creators.

Context and Importance

Spolsky's Law of Leaky Abstractions emerged in the context of software engineering, where abstractions—such as APIs, frameworks, or higher-level programming languages—are commonly used to simplify interactions with complex systems. In his 2002 blog post, Joel Spolsky discussed how abstractions often fail to completely hide the complexities they are meant to shield from developers. He argued that when these abstractions are pushed beyond their intended use cases, the underlying complexity inevitably "leaks" through, forcing developers to deal with issues they were trying to avoid. This phenomenon can be seen when an abstraction doesn't fully account for edge cases, performance concerns, or low-level details, making the developer aware of the complexity behind the simplified interface.

The importance of Spolsky's Law lies in its recognition that no abstraction can be perfect. Understanding this principle helps developers approach abstractions with a more realistic mindset—acknowledging that while abstractions are useful for managing complexity, they aren't a panacea. By being aware of the inevitable "leakage" of complexity, developers are better prepared to deal with the underlying details when they emerge and can make more informed decisions about when and how to use abstractions effectively. This perspective also encourages the design of more robust and flexible abstractions that minimize leakage, ultimately leading to better software design and a deeper understanding of system architecture.

Best Practices and Guidelines

Expect complexity to emerge: Understand that all abstractions will eventually reveal their underlying details, especially under pressure or in edge cases.

Design with transparency in mind: Aim for abstractions that balance simplicity with flexibility, allowing users to access underlying functionality when needed.

Document limitations clearly: Provide users with explicit guidance on when and why they may encounter the complexities hidden by the abstraction.

Avoid over-reliance on abstractions: Use abstractions strategically but be prepared to work with lower-level details when performance or precision is critical.

Test thoroughly across use cases: Ensure that abstractions hold up in a variety of real-world scenarios, especially edge cases where leaks are most likely to occur.

Common Misconceptions and Pitfalls

- Abstractions can completely hide complexity: Many believe abstractions can fully shield users from the underlying system, but they will eventually "leak" when pushed beyond their design limits.

- More abstraction means less complexity: Over-abstraction can mask issues temporarily, but it can also introduce hidden complexity that becomes harder to manage in the long run.
- Abstractions are "set it and forget it": Assuming an abstraction will work flawlessly without needing adjustments or awareness of its limitations is a common pitfall.
- Only beginners struggle with leaks: Even experienced developers will encounter leaky abstractions, especially when working with intricate systems or performance-critical applications.
- Leaky abstractions are always a failure: While leaks are inevitable, they don't necessarily indicate a design failure; they often highlight areas where deeper understanding and optimization are needed.

Related Concepts

1. SoC; Separation of Concerns
2. Law of Demeter; Only talk to your immediate friends
3. Principle of Least Astonishment; Software should behave in a way that users find intuitive and expected

References

- Wikipedia, *Leaky abstraction*, [pub: 1 Oct 2024, cited: 3 Jan 2025]

Technical Debt Principle: Balance of delivery vs. Maintenance

---

Definition and Origin

The Technical Debt Principle refers to the trade-off between delivering software quickly and the cost of maintaining that software in the future. It describes the accumulated complexity, shortcuts, or suboptimal design choices made during development to meet immediate goals, which can lead to higher maintenance costs and reduced agility over time.

The Technical Debt Principle was coined by Ward Cunningham, one of the pioneers of Agile software development.

Context and Importance

The Technical Debt Principle emerged in the early 1990s, when Ward Cunningham used the metaphor to highlight the consequences of rushing software development. In an effort to meet deadlines or deliver features quickly, developers may cut corners or adopt less-than-ideal solutions. While these shortcuts might lead to immediate gains in speed or functionality, they create long-term liabilities—like debt—that accumulate over time. Just as financial debt incurs interest, technical debt increases the cost and complexity of future development. This principle helps developers and stakeholders understand that the choice to take on technical debt can lead to higher maintenance costs, reduced agility, and the need for frequent refactoring as the system grows and evolves.

Understanding and managing technical debt is crucial for maintaining a healthy codebase and ensuring sustainable development. While it can be tempting to accumulate technical debt to accelerate delivery, its importance lies in recognizing when it is appropriate to take on debt and when it becomes too costly to ignore. Properly managed technical debt allows teams to balance short-term goals with long-term maintainability. If left unchecked, however, technical debt can hinder progress, increase bugs, and make future changes more difficult. By addressing technical debt early and regularly, development teams can ensure that the software remains flexible, scalable, and capable of adapting to changing requirements over time.

Best Practices and Guidelines

Prioritize Debt Management: Regularly assess and prioritize technical debt alongside new features and bug fixes to prevent it from accumulating unnoticed.

Refactor Incrementally: Address technical debt in small, manageable chunks over time, rather than waiting for large, disruptive overhauls.

Balance Speed with Quality: Weigh short-term development speed against long-term maintainability, ensuring that shortcuts don't create unsustainable debt.

Document Debt: Track and document technical debt to provide visibility to the team and stakeholders, making it easier to plan for repayment.

Adopt Coding Standards: Establish and enforce coding standards and best practices to minimize unnecessary debt from the outset.

Common Misconceptions and Pitfalls

- Technical Debt is Always Bad: Not all technical debt is harmful; sometimes, taking on debt is necessary to meet deadlines or experiment with new features, as long as it's managed properly.
- Paying Down Debt Means Complete Refactoring: Paying down technical debt doesn't always require a full rewrite or massive refactoring; small, incremental improvements can make a significant difference.
- Only Developers are Responsible for Debt: Managing technical debt is a team effort; stakeholders, product owners, and managers should also understand and factor it into their decision-making.
- Technical Debt Can Be Ignored Until Later: Delaying the repayment of technical debt often leads to more complex problems down the line; it's best addressed proactively to avoid compounding issues.
- More Debt Means Better Short-Term Results: Excessive technical debt may offer short-term speed but will hinder long-term productivity, leading to more bugs, slower releases, and reduced flexibility.

Related Concepts

1. Scout Rule; "Leave the code better than you found it"
2. Pareto Principle; The 80/20 Rule
3. Spolsky's Law of Leaky Abstractions; All non-trivial abstractions, to some degree, are leaky
4. Conway's Law; Organizations design systems that mirror their communication structure

References

- Wikipedia, *Technical debt*, [pub: 11 Dec 2024, cited: 3 Jan 2025]

Wadler's Law: focus on reasoning, not on the syntax

Definition and Origin

Wadler's Law states that "The most important thing about a programming language is not its syntax, but its ability to help developers reason about code.". In essence, Wadler's Law emphasizes that the true value of a programming language lies not in its design or syntactic features, but in how it supports developers in understanding, reasoning about, and proving the correctness of the code, they write. This reasoning power leads to better reliability, easier debugging, and more maintainable software.

Wadler's Law was coined by Philip Wadler, a prominent computer scientist known for his work in functional programming. He is particularly recognized for his contributions to the development of the Haskell programming language and the study of type systems.

Context and Importance

The law underscores a fundamental principle in software engineering: simplicity leads to clarity. As software systems grow in size and complexity, maintaining readability and ease of understanding becomes crucial for development teams, especially when managing large codebases. Wadler's Law highlights the relationship between code brevity and its inherent complexity—suggesting that more concise code is generally easier to reason about and less prone to errors. This perspective has influenced not only Haskell but also broader programming practices, where minimizing unnecessary code is seen as a pathway to more maintainable and efficient software.

The importance of Wadler's Law lies in its ability to guide software developers toward writing clearer, more understandable programs. In a world where codebases often become bloated with excessive lines of code, the law serves as a reminder that verbosity is not always a sign of sophistication. By striving for minimalism—through techniques like functional decomposition, refactoring, and the use of high-level abstractions—developers can reduce cognitive load and make it easier to reason about the behavior of a program. This has far-reaching implications for debugging, testing, and collaboration, especially in teams where many developers work on the same project over time. In this way, Wadler's Law encourages a culture of simplicity and elegance, emphasizing that less can often mean more in terms of software quality.

Best Practices and Guidelines

Prioritize simplicity: Aim for concise code that is easy to understand and reason about.

Minimize unnecessary complexity: Avoid adding extra lines of code or features that don't contribute to the core functionality.

Refactor regularly: Continuously improve code to reduce verbosity and improve clarity.

Use higher-level abstractions: Leverage libraries and frameworks to avoid reinventing solutions with excessive code.

Focus on readability: Write code that is self-explanatory, using meaningful names and clear structure to enhance comprehension.

Common Misconceptions and Pitfalls

- Shorter code = better code: Simply reducing lines of code doesn't guarantee clarity; overly compact code can be harder to understand and maintain.
- All complexity is bad: Some complexity is necessary to solve complex problems; the key is managing it effectively, not eliminating it entirely.
- More concise code means faster execution: Code brevity doesn't always equate to performance gains; optimization should be guided by profiling and real-world needs.

- Avoiding all verbosity leads to obscure code: Striving for too much minimalism can result in overly abstract or cryptic code that is difficult for others to follow.
- Wadler's Law applies universally: While generally true, the law's application can vary depending on the context, language, and problem domain—some situations may require more explicit or verbose code.

Related Concepts

1. DRY: Don't Repeat Yourself
2. KISS: Keep It Simple, Stupid
3. YAGNI: You Aren't Gonna Need It - Yet
4. Law of Demeter: Only talk to your immediate friends
5. Occam's Razor: Simplest explanation is usually correct

References

- HaskellWiki, *Wadler's Law*, [pub: 26 Dec 2017, cited: 3 Jan 2025]

Wirth's Law: Software is getting slower more rapidly than hardware becomes faster

---

Definition and Origin

Wirth's Law states: "Software is getting slower more rapidly than hardware becomes faster."

This law, named after computer scientist Niklaus Wirth, in the 1990s, emphasizes the paradox that as hardware performance improves exponentially, software tends to become more complex and resource-hungry, ultimately negating the performance benefits of modern hardware. The idea is that software development often focuses on adding features and functionality without optimizing performance, leading to slower software despite the availability of more powerful hardware.

Context and Importance

The importance of Wirth's Law lies in its warning to developers and engineers about the dangers of feature creep and poor optimization in software development. It emphasizes the trade-off between adding functionality and maintaining or improving performance. In the context of modern software engineering, Wirth's Law highlights the need for careful design, optimization, and performance testing, especially as applications become more feature-rich and require more resources. The law serves as a reminder that the balance between functionality and efficiency is crucial for creating sustainable and high-performance software, particularly in resource-constrained environments like mobile devices or embedded systems.

Best Practices and Guidelines

Prioritize performance early: Optimize efficiency from the start to avoid performance degradation as features are added.

Avoid unnecessary complexity: Focus on simplicity in design and implementation to prevent bloated, inefficient software.

Implement regular performance testing: Continuously monitor and test performance as new features are added to catch inefficiencies early.

Refactor frequently: Regularly review and optimize code to ensure it remains performant as the software evolves.

Limit feature creep: Be cautious about adding features without evaluating their impact on performance and resource usage.

Common Misconceptions and Pitfalls

- Assuming hardware always compensates for software inefficiencies: Relying on increasing hardware power to mitigate poor software performance can lead to unsustainable bloat.
- Equating more features with better software: Adding features without considering their impact on performance or user experience can lead to diminished returns.
- Overlooking the long-term impact of small inefficiencies: Minor performance issues can accumulate over time, becoming significant bottlenecks in large systems.

- Assuming optimization is only for early stages: Optimizing should be an ongoing process, not just an initial step, to maintain efficiency as features grow.
- Neglecting maintenance and refactoring: Focusing too much on adding new functionality without revisiting and refining existing code leads to technical debt and inefficiency.

Related Concepts

1. Amdahl's Law; Parallel speedup is limited by sequential portions
2. Moore's Law; Computing power doubles approximately every two years
3. Brooks's Law; Adding manpower to a late project makes it later
4. Hofstadter's Law; It always takes longer than you expect

References

- Wikipedia, *Wirth's law*, [pub: 31 Jul 2024, cited: 3 Jan 2025]

Zawinski's Law: Every program attempts to expand until it can read mail

---

Definition and Origin

Zawinski's Law states that "Every program attempts to expand until it can read mail. Those programs which cannot so expand are replaced by ones that can." In other words, software tends to grow in complexity and feature set over time, often adding unnecessary functionality, particularly in the form of email handling, even when it's not central to the program's original purpose.

Zawinski's Law was coined by Jamie Zawinski, a software developer known for his work on the Netscape and Mozilla projects. He humorously observed that software projects often tend to grow and bloat over time, with email functionality being a common example of this expansion.

Context and Importance

Zawinski's Law emerged in the late 1990s as a tongue-in-cheek observation about the evolution of software development, particularly within the open-source community. Jamie Zawinski, who worked on the Netscape Navigator browser and later on Mozilla, noticed a recurring pattern in software projects: as developers added more features, they often veered into areas unrelated to the program's core purpose. The most common (and somewhat humorous) example he pointed out was the tendency for many applications to eventually include email-related functionality, even if it wasn't initially planned. Zawinski's Law served as a playful critique of software bloat, a phenomenon where programs become increasingly complex and cumbersome over time, often with a focus on adding features that are only tangentially related to the original goals.

The importance of Zawinski's Law lies in its reflection of a broader challenge in software design—balancing feature growth with usability and clarity. It highlights the risk of feature creep, where new additions can make software more difficult to maintain, slower, or less user-friendly. Zawinski's Law serves as a reminder for developers to stay focused on the primary purpose of their projects and be mindful of unnecessary expansions that can dilute the user experience or compromise the integrity of the original vision. In a sense, it underscores the need for intentional software design and thoughtful scope management to prevent software from growing uncontrollably.

Best Practices and Guidelines

Stay Focused on Core Functionality: Prioritize the primary goals of your software and avoid unnecessary feature creep.

Limit Scope Creep: Regularly assess whether new features align with the original mission and user needs.

Avoid Unrelated Features: Resist adding features (like email handling) unless they directly enhance the program's purpose.

Maintain Simplicity: Emphasize ease of use and performance over bloated feature sets.

Iterate Thoughtfully: Introduce new features only when they provide clear value, avoiding "just because" additions.

Common Misconceptions and Pitfalls

- Assuming More Features Equals Better Software: Adding features to make software "more useful" can lead to bloated, less intuitive applications.
- Overlooking User Needs: New features might not align with what users actually want or need, leading to wasted development effort.
- Neglecting Maintenance: Focusing too much on new features can detract from maintaining and improving existing functionality.
- Believing Email Integration Is Always Beneficial: Just because email functionality is common doesn't mean it's relevant or needed for all software.
- Ignoring Performance for Features: Adding features without considering performance can degrade the user experience.

Related Concepts

1. Murphy's Law; Anything that can go wrong, will go wrong
2. Brooks's Law; Adding manpower to a late project makes it later
3. Pareto Principle (80/20 Rule); "80% of the effects come from 20% of the causes."
4. Spolsky's Law of Leaky Abstractions; All non-trivial abstractions, to some degree, are leaky

References

- Wikipedia, *Zawinski's Law*, [pub: 5 Dec 2024, cited: 3 Jan 2025]

C. Software Evolution & Maintenance

Broken Windows Theory: visible signs of disorder and neglect in an environment encourage further disorder and more serious crimes.

Definition and Origin

The Broken Windows Theory suggests that visible signs of disorder and neglect in an environment (like broken windows in a neighborhood) encourage further disorder and more serious crimes. The theory emphasizes that small, seemingly insignificant problems can escalate into larger issues if not addressed promptly.

Broken Windows Theory was coined by social scientists George Kelling and James Q. Wilson in 1982. They introduced the concept in an article published in The Atlantic Monthly.

Context and Importance

In the context of software and technology, Broken Windows Theory can be applied to the maintenance of code quality and system integrity. Just as physical signs of neglect, like broken windows, can invite further disorder in urban environments, small, seemingly insignificant technical issues—such as poor coding practices, messy code, or unresolved bugs—can lead to more severe problems in software development. If developers or teams allow minor issues to persist, they may signal to others that attention to detail and code quality is unimportant. Over time, this can lead to a cycle of accumulated technical debt, making it harder to manage, scale, or fix the software, and ultimately reducing the system's overall stability and reliability.

The importance of Broken Windows Theory in software development lies in the proactive approach it advocates. By addressing small issues early—whether they be poor documentation, inconsistent naming conventions, or minor bugs—teams can prevent the growth of larger, more complex problems that might be harder to fix later. This philosophy encourages the creation of clean, maintainable code and fosters a culture of responsibility, where developers take pride in the quality of their work. By focusing on quality at every level of development, teams can ensure that software projects remain manageable, scalable, and resilient, reducing the risk of costly failures or security vulnerabilities down the line.

Best Practices and Guidelines

Maintain Code Quality: Regularly refactor and clean up messy code to prevent the accumulation of technical debt.

Address Small Issues Early: Fix minor bugs, warnings, or inconsistencies promptly to prevent larger problems from developing.

Implement Consistent Standards: Enforce coding standards, naming conventions, and documentation practices to ensure uniformity and readability.

Foster a Culture of Responsibility: Encourage all team members to take ownership of code quality and project health, promoting proactive problem-solving.

Automate Testing & Monitoring: Use automated tests and continuous monitoring to catch issues early, reducing the chances of "broken windows" going unnoticed.

Common Misconceptions and Pitfalls

- Overemphasis on Minor Issues: Focusing too much on trivial problems can divert attention from more critical issues that need urgent resolution.
- Punitive Approach: Misapplying the theory can lead to excessive policing or micromanagement, stifling creativity and innovation in teams.

- Ignoring Root Causes: Fixing surface-level problems without addressing underlying causes can lead to recurring issues and inefficiency.
- One-Size-Fits-All: The theory may not apply equally in all environments; in complex systems, a focus on minor details can be counterproductive.
- Neglecting Larger Context: Focusing solely on minor infractions or defects without considering broader strategic goals can hinder long-term progress.

Related Concepts

1. The Boy Scout Rule: "Leave the codebase cleaner than you found it." This principle encourages developers to improve the quality of the code, no matter how small the change, to prevent gradual degradation of the codebase.
2. Technical Debt: Just as broken windows accumulate into larger problems, technical debt results from quick fixes and shortcuts that accumulate over time, eventually leading to a bloated and unmanageable system.
3. The Law of Leaky Abstractions: Systems that hide complexity (via abstractions) will eventually reveal their flaws. Like broken windows, minor breakdowns in abstraction can lead to more visible and disruptive problems down the road.
4. Continuous Refactoring: Similar to maintaining a clean environment, continuous refactoring ensures that software remains easy to maintain and scale by addressing small issues and improving structure as part of the regular development process.
5. Fail Fast, Fail Early: This principle advocates for detecting and addressing issues early in the development process. Catching problems as they appear, instead of letting them fester, minimizes the risk of larger, more disruptive failures.

References

- Wikipedia, *Broken windows theory*, [pub: 18 Dec 2024, cited: 3 Jan 2025]

Cunningham's Law: To get the right answer is not to ask a question, but to post the wrong answer.

Definition and Origin

Cunningham's Law states: "The best way to get the right answer on the internet is not to ask a question, but to post the wrong answer." This principle suggests that people are more likely to engage and provide corrections when they perceive an incorrect statement than when a question is posed.

Cunningham's Law was coined by Ward Cunningham, the inventor of the Wiki and was a co-author of the Manifesto for Agile Software Development.

Context and Importance

Cunningham's Law holds particular relevance in the fields of software development and technology because it highlights the way users engage with collaborative and open-source platforms, which are key components of the modern tech ecosystem. In environments like Stack Overflow, GitHub, and various tech forums, individuals often seek to contribute by correcting mistakes rather than merely providing answers to questions. This creates a dynamic where knowledge is continually refined and verified through user interaction. In the fast-moving world of software, where new programming languages, frameworks, and tools emerge rapidly, the ability to quickly identify and correct inaccuracies—whether in documentation, code, or conceptual understanding—becomes crucial. Cunningham's Law essentially fosters a community-driven process that helps improve the quality of information in real-time.

Furthermore, the law underscores an important facet of technology's evolution: the collaborative nature of knowledge-sharing. In software development, open-source communities thrive on contributions from diverse individuals, many of whom join discussions not just to share what they know but also to correct missteps, whether in code or technical explanations. This process of correction and refinement is vital for building robust, reliable systems. It also reflects the self-correcting nature of the internet and online communities, where mistakes are often the catalyst for learning and improvement. Cunningham's Law, therefore, is not just an observation of human behavior but a principle that has helped shape how technology and software knowledge is distributed, debated, and refined in the digital age.

Best Practices and Guidelines

Encourage thoughtful correction: When correcting errors, do so constructively to improve understanding, not just to prove someone wrong.

Foster collaborative environments: Create platforms where users can safely and efficiently correct inaccuracies, helping to refine shared knowledge.

Prioritize clear documentation: Ensure that documentation is accurate and comprehensive to reduce the likelihood of confusion or misinformation.

Leverage community feedback: Use user contributions and corrections to continually improve code, designs, and technical resources.

Be open to mistakes: Acknowledge errors in your own work and use them as learning opportunities for both yourself and others.

Common Misconceptions and Pitfalls

- Assuming all corrections are helpful: Not every correction leads to a better answer; some may introduce confusion or be based on misconceptions.
- Overlooking the value of asking questions: Cunningham's Law suggests corrections come easily, but asking thoughtful questions still drives deeper understanding and discovery.

- Encouraging mistakes for the sake of engagement: Intentionally posting incorrect information to provoke corrections can degrade the quality of the discussion and mislead others.
- Assuming corrections are always accurate: Even well-intentioned corrections can be incorrect and blindly trusting them without verification can perpetuate errors.
- Focusing on speed over clarity: The rush to correct quickly can lead to shallow or incomplete fixes, rather than well-thought-out solutions that benefit the community in the long-term.

Related Concepts

1. Linus's Law: "Given enough eyeballs, all bugs are shallow." This principle suggests that open-source software benefits from a large community of contributors who can collectively identify and fix bugs, much like Cunningham's Law emphasizes correction through community engagement.
2. The Rule of Least Astonishment: This principle states that software should behave in a way that minimizes surprise for the user. It aligns with Cunningham's Law in the sense that incorrect or misleading information will be quickly corrected, ideally preventing confusion and ensuring clarity.
3. Boyd's Law of Iteration: "A good decision is based on good information, and good information comes from fast iteration." Similar to Cunningham's Law, Boyd's Law underscores the importance of rapid feedback and corrections to improve a system, whether that's in software or knowledge sharing.
4. The Law of Leaky Abstractions: This law highlights those abstractions in software, when flawed or incomplete, will inevitably "leak," exposing the underlying complexity. This mirrors Cunningham's Law in that errors or misconceptions in software (or documentation) are often exposed and corrected by the community.
5. The 80/20 Rule (Pareto Principle): "80% of the effects come from 20% of the causes." In the context of software, this means that most issues are often caused by a small subset of bugs or misinterpretations, which the community tends to focus on and correct first—just as Cunningham's Law suggests that mistakes drive the majority of corrections.

6. These principles all emphasize feedback, iteration, and community-driven improvement, which are central to the functioning of modern software development and the self-correcting nature of shared knowledge.

References

- Wikipedia, *Cunningham's Law*, [pub: 21 Nov 2024, cited: 3 Jan 2025]

Glass's Law: The complexity of a software system increases at an exponential rate as new features are added to the system.

Definition and Origin

Glass's Law states that the "The complexity of a software system increases at an exponential rate as new features are added to the system.". It emerged from observations regarding the challenges and inefficiencies that arise when additional features are added to software systems. Specifically, it suggests that adding features results in a greater increase in the complexity and effort required to maintain the software, often leading to diminishing returns in terms of functionality and usability.

Glass's Law was coined by Robert L. Glass, in the 1990s, in his "Measuring software design quality" publication.

Context and Importance

Glass's Law highlights a crucial challenge in software development: the exponential increase in complexity and cost as new features are added to a system. As software grows, the initial benefits of adding features often become outweighed by the increased difficulty in maintaining and integrating those features. This exponential growth is not just about adding lines of code; it encompasses a range of factors such as debugging, testing, user interface complexity, and the impact on performance. The law underscores a critical point for developers and project managers: the more features you incorporate, the more you risk introducing inefficiencies, conflicts, and potential failure points. This phenomenon can lead to diminishing returns, where additional features may not meaningfully improve the software and might even degrade its quality.

The importance of Glass's Law lies in its ability to guide software development practices and decision-making. It serves as a reminder to prioritize simplicity, focus on core functionality, and carefully evaluate the trade-offs of adding new features. The law also informs project management by emphasizing the need for strategic planning, rigorous testing, and iterative development to mitigate the complexities introduced by feature bloat. Understanding and applying Glass's Law can help avoid "feature creep," a common pitfall where projects spiral out of control, leading to higher costs and longer development times without proportional value added to the end product. As software systems continue to grow more complex, Glass's Law remains an essential principle for building maintainable, efficient, and user-friendly technology.

Best Practices / Guidelines

Prioritize core functionality: Focus on delivering a few essential features well rather than adding unnecessary extras.

Avoid feature creep: Regularly assess the impact of new features to ensure they align with user needs and project goals.

Simplify complexity: Strive for maintainable code and user interfaces by minimizing dependencies and avoiding unnecessary layers of complexity.

Iterative development: Implement features incrementally with frequent testing and feedback to prevent overwhelming the system.

Balance innovation with stability: Consider long-term maintenance costs and technical debt when adding new features to avoid diminishing returns.

Common Misconceptions and Pitfalls

- More features = better product: Adding more features doesn’t necessarily improve the product and may instead reduce its overall quality and usability.
- Feature addition is linear: Many assume the effort to add features is linear, but it grows exponentially, increasing complexity and maintenance burden.

- One-time development cost: Believing the cost of adding features is a one-time expense, when in reality, it leads to ongoing maintenance and support costs.
- Users always want more features: Focusing solely on feature expansion ignores the fact that users may prefer simplicity and stability over new, untested functionality.
- Neglecting scalability: Adding features without considering long-term system scalability and integration can lead to bottlenecks and system failures.

Related Concepts

1. Brooks' Law: "Adding manpower to a late software project makes it later." This principle emphasizes that increasing the team size to accelerate software development often leads to communication overhead, further delays, and inefficiencies—similar to how adding features can increase complexity and slow down progress.
2. Conway's Law: "Organizations which design systems are constrained to produce designs which are copies of the communication structures of these organizations." This suggests that the structure of a software system often reflects the communication patterns within the development team, which can become more complicated as more features are added, just like Glass's Law.
3. Pareto Principle (80/20 Rule): This principle asserts that 80% of a system's value comes from 20% of its features. It aligns with Glass's Law in that adding numerous features may result in diminishing returns, and focusing on the most impactful features leads to better results.
4. Lehman's Laws of Software Evolution: These laws describe how software systems evolve over time, particularly the idea that software must continuously evolve to remain useful, but also that adding new features can lead to a "preservation" stage where complexity increases without proportional benefit.
5. The Law of Diminishing Returns: In the context of software, this law suggests that after a certain point, the addition of new features results in smaller and smaller increases in value or user satisfaction, paralleling the concept of Glass's Law where complexity outpaces utility as features are added.

References

- Wikipedia, *Robert L. Glass*, [pub: 11 Nov 2024, cited: 3 Jan 2025]

Hyrum's Law: observable behaviors of your system will be depended on by somebody

---

Definition and Origin

Hyrum's Law states that "With a sufficient number of users of an API, it does not matter what you promise in the contract: all observable behaviors of your system will be depended on by somebody."

Hyrum's Law was coined by Hyrum Wright, a software engineer at Google. He introduced the concept to describe the challenges that arise in maintaining backward compatibility in widely used software systems, particularly APIs. Hyrum Wright observed that as an API gains more users, even unintended behaviors or undocumented features may become relied upon, making it harder to change the system without breaking existing functionality.

Context and Importance

Hyrum's Law emphasizes a crucial challenge in software development, particularly when dealing with public-facing APIs and large-scale systems. As more users interact with a software product, the scope of possible use cases and edge cases expands beyond the original design or intention of the developers. This means that even seemingly minor or unintended behaviors within an API can become essential to certain users or organizations. If these behaviors are inadvertently changed or removed in a future version, it can lead to unexpected breakages or malfunctions for those who have come to depend on them. This reality places a significant constraint on how developers can evolve and improve their systems without causing disruption.

The importance of Hyrum's Law lies in its reminder that software systems, especially those with broad user bases, must be designed with long-term stability and compatibility in mind. It underscores the need for careful planning when introducing new features, deprecating old ones, or making architectural changes. Developers must anticipate that their users might rely on things they didn't explicitly document or intend, which can make refactoring or upgrading systems more complex. The law has broader implications for versioning strategies, testing practices, and communication between developers and users, pushing the software industry towards more robust and considerate approaches to API design and version management.

Best Practices and Guidelines

Document all behaviors: Clearly document intended behaviors and edge cases in APIs to reduce reliance on undocumented features.

Version APIs carefully: Use semantic versioning to signal breaking changes and avoid altering existing functionality unless absolutely necessary.

Provide backward compatibility: Maintain compatibility with older versions as much as possible, especially for widely used public APIs.

Deprecate gradually: Deprecate features over time, offering users ample notice and alternatives before removing or changing functionality.

Test for unintended dependencies: Conduct thorough testing to identify and account for any unintentional dependencies or behaviors that could impact users.

Common Misconceptions and Pitfalls

- Assuming undocumented behavior won't be used: Developers may overlook the fact that even undocumented features or side effects can be relied upon by users.
- Underestimating the scale of users: Thinking that only a small subset of users will be impacted by a change, when in reality, even niche behaviors can have broad consequences.

- Believing that breaking changes are always obvious: Some breaking changes might not be immediately apparent, as reliance on subtle behaviors can be hidden or unnoticed until later.
- Neglecting backward compatibility during optimizations: Focusing on performance improvements or refactoring without considering the potential impact on existing functionality can lead to unexpected issues.
- Overestimating control over user behavior: Assuming that users will follow best practices and not exploit unintended behaviors, when in fact they often find and depend on them.

Related Concepts

1. Lehman's Laws of Software Evolution: These principles describe how software systems evolve over time, often in unpredictable ways. One key insight is that software must be continually adapted to meet user needs, and even small changes can have wide-reaching consequences, similar to Hyrum's Law's focus on the unintended reliance of users on existing behaviors.
2. The Law of Leaky Abstractions (Joel Spolsky): This law states that "all non-trivial abstractions are leaky," meaning that layers of abstraction in software (e.g., APIs, libraries) will eventually reveal their implementation details. This aligns with Hyrum's Law in that unintended or undocumented behaviors in an abstraction can still affect users.
3. The Principle of Least Astonishment: This principle suggests that software should behave in ways that least surprise the user. When changes or behaviors (documented or undocumented) violate this principle, it can cause disruptions, aligning with Hyrum's observation that users will depend on unexpected or unintended behavior.
4. Moore's Law: While Moore's Law specifically describes the doubling of computing power every two years, its indirect relevance to Hyrum's Law is in the exponential growth of software users and their interactions. As systems grow in scale, the probability of unexpected dependencies and behaviors increases.

5. Conway's Law: Conway's Law suggests that organizations design systems that mirror their own communication structure. This is related to Hyrum's Law in that misalignments in internal communication or assumptions about users' needs can lead to unintentional software behaviors that, once exposed to a large user base, become deeply ingrained and difficult to change.

References

- Obligatory XKCD, *Hyrum's Law*, [cited: 3 Jan 2025]
- Wiktionary, *Hyrum's Law*, [pub: 28 Sep 2024, cited: 3 Jan 2025]
- Recall, *Encountering Hyrum's Law in the Wild*, [pub: 20 Feb 2024, cited: 3 Jan 2025]

Lehman's Laws of Software Evolution: software must constantly evolve to adapt and remain useful

---

Definition and Origin

Lehman's Laws of Software Evolution are a set of principles that describe how software systems evolve over time. They were proposed by software engineer Manny Lehman in the 1970s. The key laws are:

1. "Continuing Change" (1974): Software systems must continuously evolve to remain useful and relevant in a changing technological, organizational, and user environment.
2. "Increasing Complexity" (1974): As software systems evolve, their complexity tends to increase unless deliberate efforts are made to manage or reduce it.
3. "Self-Regulation" (1974): The evolution of software systems is self-regulated through feedback loops, where the rate and nature of change are influenced by internal and external factors.
4. "Conservation of Organizational Stability" (1978): The rate of change in software is often regulated by the organization's processes, resources, and policies, resulting in stable development rhythms over time.

5. "Conservation of Familiarity" (1978): Software evolves in ways that preserve a level of familiarity for users and developers, preventing drastic changes that could disrupt usage or understanding.
6. "Continuing Growth" (1991): Software systems generally experience continuous growth, expanding in functionality and features as they adapt to meet new requirements or opportunities.
7. "Declining Quality" (1996): Without proactive efforts like refactoring, bug fixing, and maintenance, the quality of a software system deteriorates over time due to the accumulation of complexity and technical debt.
8. "Feedback System" (1996): Software evolution is governed by feedback loops, where changes in the system, user needs, and operational environment inform and guide further development.
9. Lehman's Laws of Software Evolution were coined by Manny Lehman, a British computer scientist, in the 1970s.

Context and Importance

Lehman's Laws of Software Evolution emerged in the 1970s when software development was transitioning from relatively simple systems to more complex, long-lived applications. At the time, many software systems were still in their infancy and were often discarded or rewritten after short lifespans. However, as software systems grew more intricate and began to serve critical roles in businesses, governments, and industries, Lehman observed a pattern: software is not static, and it needs continuous adaptation to stay relevant. He identified that software must evolve alongside changing user needs, hardware advancements, and regulatory requirements. Lehman's Laws offered a theoretical foundation for understanding the inevitable nature of software evolution and the challenges involved in maintaining and improving long-term software systems.

The importance of Lehman's Laws in modern software development cannot be overstated. As technology continues to advance rapidly, many software systems must support a growing array of features and handle increasing complexity over time. These laws highlight key phenomena such as the natural increase in complexity and the erosion of quality in software systems unless carefully managed. In practical terms, Lehman's Laws stress the need for ongoing maintenance, refactoring, and adaptation to prevent software from becoming obsolete or unmanageable. For organizations and development teams, the recognition of these laws has led to the adoption of software engineering practices like agile development, version control, and continuous integration, all aimed at keeping evolving systems functional and competitive in an ever-changing technological landscape.

Best Practices and Guidelines

Embrace Continuous Evolution: Software must be continuously updated and adapted to meet changing user needs, technology advancements, and environmental conditions.

Manage Complexity Actively: Recognize that software complexity will naturally increase over time, and actively refactor, modularize, and simplify to keep the system maintainable.

Plan for Long-Term Maintenance: Adopt practices that ensure ongoing software quality, such as regular updates, testing, and documentation, to prevent quality erosion.

Balance Innovation and Stability: Maintain a stable, regulated pace of change to avoid overwhelming development teams and ensure consistent system performance.

Monitor Feedback Loops: Pay attention to both user feedback and system metrics to guide the software's evolution and adjust priorities as necessary.

Common Misconceptions and Pitfalls

- Assuming Software Can Be "Completed": A common misconception is that software can be "finished" after the initial development phase. Lehman's Laws emphasize that software must evolve continuously to stay relevant.

- Ignoring Increasing Complexity: Believing that complexity can be eliminated or completely controlled leads to neglecting the inevitable growth of a system's intricacy over time, which can result in unmanageable code.
- Underestimating the Cost of Maintenance: Some teams focus too heavily on new features or innovation, neglecting the long-term maintenance costs and necessary updates, which can lead to software degradation.
- Overlooking Organizational Impact: Assuming that technical decisions are independent of organizational processes and resources can overlook the feedback loops that regulate the pace and scope of software evolution.
- Neglecting System Feedback: Failing to incorporate regular feedback from users, stakeholders, or system performance metrics can lead to missed opportunities for improvement and a disconnect between the software and its evolving needs.

Related Concepts

1. Brooks' Law (The Mythical Man-Month): "Adding manpower to a late software project makes it later." This principle emphasizes that as software projects grow in complexity and scale, adding more people does not necessarily speed up development and can even increase the system's complexity, aligning with Lehman's view of increasing complexity over time.
2. Conway's Law: "Organizations which design systems are constrained to produce designs which are copies of the communication structures of these organizations." This law highlights how the organization's structure influences the software design, mirroring Lehman's Law of self-regulation, where the software evolution is influenced by organizational factors.
3. Moore's Law: "The number of transistors on a microchip doubles approximately every two years, leading to increases in computational power." While primarily hardware-focused, this law impacts software evolution by creating new opportunities and challenges, often leading to increased system complexity (as described by Lehman's Laws).

4. Gall's Law: "A complex system that works is invariably found to have evolved from a simple system that worked." This principle supports Lehman's view that software must evolve iteratively, starting from simple systems that grow in complexity as they adapt and improve over time.
5. Pareto Principle (80/20 Rule): "80% of the effects come from 20% of the causes." In the context of software evolution, this can apply to the fact that a small portion of the code or features typically drive the majority of usage, emphasizing the need to focus on the critical parts of the software as it evolves to avoid unnecessary complexity.

References

- Wikipedia, *Lehman's laws of software evolution*, [pub: 14 Nov 2024, cited: 3 Jan 2025]

Linus's Law: Given enough eyeballs, all bugs are shallow

Definition and Origin

Linus's Law states that "Given enough eyeballs, all bugs are shallow." This principle suggests that when enough people have access to a software project, the collective scrutiny and contributions from the community can quickly identify and resolve most issues or bugs, regardless of their complexity.

Linus's Law was named in honor of Linus Torvalds, the creator of the Linux operating system. He articulated the idea to explain how open-source software, with its collaborative nature and large pool of contributors, tends to benefit from rapid bug detection and resolution. The law highlights the power of community-driven development.

Context and Importance

Linus's Law emerged from the open-source software movement, which emphasizes the collaborative development of software by a community of developers. The idea is rooted in the belief that open access to code allows many independent contributors—often with diverse perspectives and skill sets—to identify and fix issues more effectively than a small, closed group of developers could. Torvalds, through the development of Linux, demonstrated how allowing anyone to view, modify, and improve code leads to rapid detection and correction of bugs. This principle has since been central to the philosophy of open-source projects, where transparency and community involvement are seen as key drivers of innovation and quality.

The importance of Linus's Law in the realm of software and technology is profound. It highlights the value of collective intelligence and crowd-sourced problem solving, which can lead to faster and more reliable software development. With the ability to tap into a global pool of developers, open-source projects benefit from a broad range of expertise and perspectives, resulting in robust, well-tested solutions. As software has become increasingly complex, Linus's Law underscores how decentralized, collaborative models can not only enhance the speed of development but also improve the overall security and resilience of technology products. This model has had a lasting impact on industries beyond software, influencing the way technology solutions are created, maintained, and updated across various sectors.

Best Practices and Guidelines

Encourage open collaboration: Make code freely available to a wide range of contributors to harness diverse perspectives and expertise.

Foster community involvement: Actively involve users and developers in identifying, reporting, and fixing bugs to leverage collective problem-solving.

Prioritize transparency: Keep development processes and code changes visible to the community to facilitate faster detection of issues.

Promote continuous testing: Encourage extensive peer reviews and automated testing to ensure that bugs are spotted early and resolved quickly.

Leverage feedback loops: Act on user feedback promptly, as real-world usage often uncovers bugs that might not be found in isolated testing environments.

Common Misconceptions and Pitfalls

- More eyeballs don't guarantee immediate fixes: While many contributors may spot issues, resolving bugs still requires coordination, time, and expertise.
- Not all contributions are equal: The volume of contributions does not necessarily equate to quality or effectiveness in solving problems.
- Over-reliance on the community: Assuming the community will always catch all bugs can lead to neglecting proper testing, documentation, and initial development rigor.
- Focus on quantity over quality: Linus's Law may encourage large-scale participation, but without proper management, too many contributors can lead to chaotic or inconsistent code.
- Assumption that "open" equals "secure": Open-source code may be reviewed more often, but it still requires active oversight and security practices to ensure vulnerabilities are properly addressed.

Related Concepts

1. Raymond's Law (The Cathedral and the Bazaar): Coined by Eric S. Raymond, this law contrasts two models of software development: the "cathedral" (closed, centralized) and the "bazaar" (open, decentralized). Raymond argues that open-source development, like the bazaar, fosters greater creativity, innovation, and speed, much like Linus's Law suggests.
2. Metcalfe's Law: This principle states that the value of a network is proportional to the square of the number of its users (N^2). In the context of software, it suggests that as more contributors participate in an open-source project, the collective value and output of that project increases exponentially, similar to how more "eyeballs" help identify bugs faster.

3. Meyers' Law: This law asserts that "software is never done; it is always in a state of perpetual improvement." It aligns with Linus's Law by emphasizing continuous evolution through community-driven contributions, where bugs and features are iteratively improved over time.
4. The 90/10 Rule (Pareto Principle): In many open-source projects, 90% of contributions come from just 10% of the users. This highlights the importance of active, skilled contributors who can identify and address bugs or challenges, validating Linus's Law that a few expert "eyeballs" can make a significant difference.
5. Brooks's Law: "Adding manpower to a late software project makes it later." While seemingly opposite to Linus's Law, Brooks's Law emphasizes the complexities of scaling development efforts. In open-source projects, however, contributions are often self-directed and highly motivated, making additional contributors a force for rapid problem resolution rather than slowdowns.

References

- Wikipedia, *Linus's law*, [pub: 30 Jul 2024, cited: 3 Jan 2025]

Pesticide Paradox: same testing methods or tools become less effective at finding new bugs

---

Definition and Origin

The Pesticide Paradox in software and technology refers to the phenomenon where, over time, the same testing methods or tools become less effective at finding new bugs or issues. This concept is borrowed from the pesticide industry: if you use the same pesticide repeatedly, pests can develop resistance to it. In the context of software, it means that as you repeatedly run the same set of tests, new defects or bugs that didn't surface before may remain undetected, because the tests are not evolving in complexity or scope.

The Paradox of the Pesticides in software and technology was coined by Gary McGraw, a leading expert in software security. McGraw used this concept in his book "Software Security: Building Security In" (2006), drawing an analogy between the overuse of pesticides in agriculture and the over-reliance on security tools or techniques in software development. He explained that just as pests can become resistant to pesticides, software can become more vulnerable or resistant to traditional security measures when overused or applied without consideration of broader system dynamics.

Context and Importance

The Paradox of the Pesticides in software and technology is a cautionary concept that highlights the dangers of over-optimization or over-reliance on specific tools or techniques to solve complex problems, especially in the realm of security and debugging. In software development, the analogy stems from the agricultural phenomenon where the excessive use of pesticides eventually leads to pest resistance, making the pesticides less effective over time. Similarly, in software, relying too heavily on automated testing, static analysis tools, or predefined security measures can create systems that are not adaptive to new, evolving threats. Over-focusing on a single solution might lead to vulnerabilities or weaknesses that become harder to identify or mitigate as systems grow more complex.

This paradox is especially important in the context of cybersecurity, where the threat landscape constantly evolves. Security measures that worked in the past may not be sufficient for emerging threats, and the "pesticides" used to prevent security breaches could become ineffective or counterproductive. As software systems evolve, they become more intricate and interconnected, meaning that one-size-fits-all solutions or tools might only address symptoms rather than the root causes. Understanding and addressing the Paradox of the Pesticides encourages a more holistic and dynamic approach to software development, where flexibility, ongoing adaptation, and a combination of methods are used to maintain security and functionality without creating blind spots or future vulnerabilities.

Best Practices and Guidelines

Diversify Solutions: Avoid over-relying on a single tool or technique; combine various methods for security, testing, and debugging to address different types of issues effectively.

Embrace Adaptability: Continuously update and refine security practices, frameworks, and methodologies to stay ahead of evolving threats and technological changes.

Avoid Over-Optimization: Resist the urge to over-engineer solutions or apply overly restrictive measures that could stifle system flexibility or scalability.

Test in Real-World Scenarios: Ensure tools and solutions are validated in diverse, dynamic environments rather than in controlled, idealized conditions to reveal hidden vulnerabilities.

Encourage Ongoing Learning: Foster a culture of adaptability and learning to recognize and respond to new threats or inefficiencies in the system as they emerge.

Common Misconceptions and Pitfalls

- Overconfidence in Automation: Relying too heavily on automated tools (e.g., static analysis or test suites) can lead to false security and overlook nuanced issues or edge cases.
- Fixation on Compliance: Prioritizing adherence to established standards or regulations can result in a false sense of security, ignoring the need for adaptive and proactive approaches.
- One-Size-Fits-All Solutions: Assuming that the same security practices or debugging methods will work universally across all systems can lead to ineffective protection and unaddressed risks.
- Ignoring System Complexity: Focusing solely on eliminating specific vulnerabilities without considering the system's broader architecture may introduce new risks or create inflexible designs.
- Stagnation in Approach: Failing to evolve security strategies or development methodologies based on emerging trends and threats can lead to outdated defenses and missed opportunities for improvement.

Related Concepts

1. The Law of Leaky Abstractions (Joel Spolsky)

2. This principle asserts that no abstraction is perfect; flaws and complexities always "leak" through, revealing limitations. Just as pesticides can have unintended side effects, reliance on high-level abstractions (like security tools) can obscure underlying issues, leading to blind spots or vulnerabilities.
3. The Principle of Least Astonishment
4. This principle suggests that software should behave in a way that minimizes surprises for users and developers. Over-optimization or over-reliance on specific techniques (like security frameworks or static analysis) can lead to unexpected behavior or false assumptions, making systems harder to maintain or adapt.
5. The Mythical Man-Month (Fred Brooks)
6. Brooks' law highlights the counterproductive nature of adding more resources to a late project, which can cause more delays rather than solve problems. Similarly, applying more tools or measures (pesticides) to fix software issues without a holistic strategy can make the system more complex and harder to manage.
7. The Second System Effect (Fred Brooks)
8. This principle posits that the second version of a system is often more complex than it needs to be due to overengineering, adding unnecessary features in an attempt to solve all potential problems. Over-optimizing a system with too many tools or layers of security can lead to fragile, hard-to-manage systems.
9. Conway's Law
10. Conway's Law suggests that software systems tend to mirror the communication structures of the organizations that develop them. Over-relying on specific tools or frameworks to solve problems without considering the broader context can create systems that are less adaptive and more difficult to evolve, similar to the way pesticides fail when applied indiscriminately.

References

- InformIT, *The Pesticide Paradox*, [pub: 20 Nov 2000, cited: 3 Jan 2025]
- Wikipedia, *Paradox of the pesticides*, [pub: 4 Mar 2023, cited: 3 Jan 2025]

Richardson Maturity Model: resources, http verbs, and hypermedia controls.

Definition and Origin

The Richardson Maturity Model (RMM) is a framework proposed by Leonard Richardson in 2008 for evaluating the quality and sophistication of web APIs, particularly RESTful APIs.

1. Level 0: The Swamp of POX: APIs at this level use HTTP as a basic transport protocol but do not leverage HTTP's features. They often use a single endpoint with a non-RESTful approach (e.g., XML or JSON payloads), making them essentially "Plain Old XML" (POX) or "Plain Old JSON" (POJ). There's little or no distinction between resources.
2. Level 1: Resources: At this level, the API introduces distinct resources, each represented by unique URIs (Uniform Resource Identifiers). The server starts to model entities in the system as individual resources but still lacks full utilization of HTTP methods and status codes.
3. Level 2: HTTP Verbs: APIs at this level use standard HTTP methods (GET, POST, PUT, DELETE) to represent actions on resources. This improves the expressiveness of the API and better adheres to REST principles, allowing for CRUD-like operations (Create, Read, Update, Delete) through HTTP verbs.
4. Level 3: Hypermedia Controls (HATEOAS): At this highest maturity level, the API fully embraces HATEOAS (Hypermedia as the Engine of Application State). The server provides links (hypermedia controls) within responses, guiding clients on available actions and transitions. This allows the client to navigate the API dynamically without prior knowledge of the structure, making the API more self-descriptive and flexible.

Context and Importance

The Richardson Maturity Model plays a crucial role in helping developers assess and improve the design of RESTful APIs, which are foundational to modern web and mobile applications. As more systems become distributed and interact via APIs over the internet, ensuring that these APIs are designed to be scalable, efficient, and maintainable is vital. The model provides a structured approach to evaluate how well an API adheres to REST principles, helping developers move from basic, minimal implementations (Level 0) to more sophisticated and robust designs (Level 3). By following this model, developers can ensure that their APIs are not only functional but also follow best practices for performance, scalability, and ease of integration, which are critical for long-term software success.

In the broader context of software and technology, the Richardson Maturity Model serves as a benchmark for modern API design, encouraging a shift away from simple HTTP-based communication to more powerful, self-descriptive, and stateless web services. APIs that operate at higher maturity levels (such as Level 2 or Level 3) are easier to maintain, evolve, and scale, which can lead to better user experiences and reduced technical debt. Moreover, it helps ensure that the API design can take advantage of HTTP's full potential, including its verbs, status codes, and hypermedia capabilities, promoting a more standardized and interoperable ecosystem. This model is particularly significant in the era of microservices, cloud computing, and the growing need for systems that communicate seamlessly and efficiently across various platforms.

Best Practices and Guidelines

Start Simple, Then Evolve: Begin with a basic API (Level 0), then progressively adopt RESTful principles like resource-oriented design and HTTP methods as your API matures (Level 1 and 2).

Use HTTP Methods Correctly: Leverage HTTP verbs (GET, POST, PUT, DELETE) for their intended purposes to model resource interactions and ensure clear, intuitive API behavior.

Implement Statelessness (Level 2): Ensure each request is independent and contains all necessary information, avoiding server-side session storage to improve scalability and reliability.

Embrace Hypermedia (HATEOAS) (Level 3): At higher maturity levels, implement hypermedia links in responses to guide clients on possible actions, making the API more self-descriptive and dynamic.

Ensure Consistency in Naming: Follow clear, consistent conventions for endpoint naming, resource URIs, and status codes, fostering simplicity and usability for API consumers.

Common Misconceptions and Pitfalls

- Level 3 Is Always the Goal: Not all APIs need to reach Level 3 maturity; depending on use case, a simpler Level 1 or 2 design may be sufficient, balancing complexity with needs.
- Just Using HTTP Methods Doesn't Make It RESTful: Properly implementing HTTP methods is essential, but REST is more than just using GET, POST, PUT, and DELETE—it requires a resource-oriented architecture and stateless communication.
- Hypermedia Is Not Always Practical: Implementing HATEOAS (hypermedia as the engine of application state) can be complex and may not always be necessary, especially for smaller APIs or those with limited interactions.
- REST Is Not Synonymous With HTTP: REST is an architectural style, not a strict protocol—it's possible to use RESTful principles while still supporting multiple protocols or data formats beyond HTTP.
- Level 0 Can Be Mistaken for RESTful: APIs at Level 0 that just expose raw HTTP endpoints without using REST principles (such as resource-oriented design) are often misclassified as RESTful, even though they don't fully align with REST standards.

Related Concepts

1. Roy Fielding's REST Constraints: REST (Representational State Transfer) is based on a set of architectural constraints outlined by Roy Fielding, such as statelessness, cacheability, uniform interface, and layered system architecture. The Richardson Maturity Model builds on these constraints, helping developers design APIs that adhere to the full scope of REST principles.

2. Law of Demeter (LoD): Also known as the "Principle of Least Knowledge," this principle encourages minimal knowledge and tight coupling between components. In the context of the Richardson Maturity Model, a higher maturity API (Level 3) aligns with LoD by limiting dependencies and interactions between client and server to the bare minimum, reducing complexity and improving maintainability.
3. Separation of Concerns: This principle advocates for dividing a system into distinct sections, each responsible for a specific aspect of the system's functionality. In the context of the Richardson Maturity Model, properly separating resources (using meaningful URIs) and their interactions (via correct HTTP methods) helps manage complexity and fosters modular, scalable systems.
4. Interface Segregation Principle (ISP): A key SOLID principle, ISP suggests that clients should not be forced to depend on interfaces they don't use. This aligns with higher maturity levels of the Richardson Model, where APIs are designed with clear, focused endpoints, allowing clients to interact only with the relevant parts of the system without unnecessary exposure to other resources or methods.
5. Fail-Fast Principle: This principle encourages systems to detect and handle errors as soon as possible to avoid cascading failures. In the context of RESTful API design, Level 3 maturity—particularly through proper use of HTTP status codes and error messages—aligns with the fail-fast principle by providing clear feedback to clients about invalid requests or system errors, enabling quicker troubleshooting and resolution.

References

- Martin Fowler, *Richardson Maturity Model*, [pub: 18 Mar 2010, cited: 3 Jan 2025]
- Wikipedia, *Richardson Maturity Model*, [pub: 8 Aug 2024, cited: 3 Jan 2025]

Semantic Versioning Rule: communicate the nature of changes through the versioning

---

Definition and Origin

Semantic Versioning (SemVer) is a versioning system that defines how version numbers should be assigned and incremented based on changes to a software project. The version number is composed of three segments: MAJOR.MINOR.PATCH.

- MAJOR version increases when incompatible API changes are made.
- MINOR version increases when functionality is added in a backward-compatible manner.
- PATCH version increases for backward-compatible bug fixes.

Additionally, pre-release or build metadata can be included using hyphens or plus signs, respectively. The goal is to communicate the nature of changes through the version number itself, helping developers understand the potential impact of upgrading.

Semantic Versioning (SemVer) was introduced by Tom Preston-Werner, co-founder of GitHub, in 2009. He published the specification in a document called "Semantic Versioning 2.0.0", which provided a clear, standardized approach to version numbering for software projects. The system was designed to address the need for more predictable and meaningful versioning, making it easier for developers to understand the impact of updating dependencies based on version numbers.

Context and Importance

In the context of software and technology, managing dependencies is a critical part of modern development. As software ecosystems grow, multiple projects and libraries interact, often relying on specific versions of one another. Without a clear and standardized versioning system, developers might struggle to manage compatibility between different versions of libraries, tools, or APIs. This is where Semantic Versioning (SemVer) plays a pivotal role. By providing a structured way of communicating changes in software, SemVer helps developers quickly understand the potential impact of upgrading or downgrading dependencies. It provides a clear signal about whether an update introduces breaking changes, adds new features, or simply fixes bugs, thus allowing for better decision-making when managing software updates.

The importance of SemVer lies in its ability to mitigate the risks and complexities of dependency management, which has become more critical as the use of open-source libraries and third-party packages has grown. By adhering to SemVer, developers can ensure that updates to a software package won't unintentionally break dependent systems, especially when upgrading to newer versions. For example, an increment in the MAJOR version number indicates a breaking change that could require code modifications, while a MINOR update signifies a backward-compatible feature addition. This transparency is crucial for fostering trust in both open-source and proprietary software ecosystems, ensuring that projects can scale and evolve without the constant fear of compatibility issues.

Best Practices and Guidelines

Increment MAJOR version for breaking changes or incompatible API modifications.

Increment MINOR version for backward-compatible feature additions or improvements.

Increment PATCH version for backward-compatible bug fixes and minor improvements.

Avoid incrementing the version if changes are internal or do not affect the public API.

Use pre-release labels (e.g., 1.0.0-alpha) for unstable or beta versions to indicate non-stable software.

Common Misconceptions and Pitfalls

- Treating PATCH as for minor features: PATCH should only be used for bug fixes, not for adding new features or functionality.
- Incrementing MAJOR for minor changes: MAJOR should only be incremented for breaking changes that require user code modifications, not for small updates.
- Not using pre-release versions: Failing to mark unstable or experimental versions with labels like -alpha or -beta can lead to confusion about the stability of the software.

- Assuming backward compatibility is guaranteed with MINOR: MINOR updates should add features without breaking existing functionality, but developers should still carefully review changes to avoid accidental compatibility issues.
- Ignoring build metadata: Build metadata (e.g., 1.0.0+20130313144700) is often neglected, but it can be useful for distinguishing versions built from the same source code in different environments or times.

Related Concepts

1. The Law of Leaky Abstractions (Joel Spolsky): This law suggests that software abstractions, like APIs, inevitably leak implementation details to users. In the context of SemVer, it emphasizes the importance of clear versioning to signal when changes in the underlying implementation (or API) may require users to modify their code.
2. The Principle of Least Astonishment: This principle states that software should behave in a way that is least surprising to its users. In versioning, it translates to making sure that MAJOR version bumps indicate breaking changes, so users are not surprised by disruptions after an update.
3. The Law of Software Evolution (M. Lehman): This principle posits that software systems evolve over time, and as they do, their structure becomes more complex. Semantic versioning supports this idea by ensuring that version numbers communicate the evolutionary path of software, helping developers track how updates relate to previous versions.
4. The Principle of Backward Compatibility: This is a fundamental software engineering concept that emphasizes maintaining compatibility with older versions of the software. SemVer enforces this principle by distinguishing MINOR and PATCH updates as backward-compatible changes, thus reducing the risk of breaking functionality when upgrading.
5. The Law of Demeter (Principle of Least Knowledge): While not strictly about versioning, this law encourages minimal knowledge between components. In SemVer, it implies that developers should make breaking changes (i.e., MAJOR version updates) only when absolutely necessary, preserving stable interfaces and avoiding unnecessary interdependencies that could force consumers to adopt major changes.

References

- Spec, *Semantic Versioning*, [pub: 19 Dec 2023, cited: 3 Jan 2025]
- Wikipedia, *Tom Preston-Werner*, [pub: 5 Oct 2024, cited: 3 Jan 2025]
- Wikipedia, *Semantic versioning*, [pub: 2 Jan 2025, cited: 3 Jan 2025]

D. Testing & Debugging

Heisenbug Uncertainty Principle: Bugs that vanish when you try to study them

Definition and Origin

A Heisenbug is a type of software bug that seems to disappear or alter its behavior when you try to observe or debug it. The term is derived from the Heisenberg Uncertainty Principle in physics, which states that the act of measurement affects the system being observed. Heisenbugs are often difficult to reproduce consistently and can be tricky to diagnose because they appear or vanish depending on the environment or debugging methods used.

The term Heisenbug was coined by Jim Gray, a computer scientist and Turing Award winner, in the late 1980s. Gray used the term to describe bugs in software that seemed to disappear or change behavior when developers attempted to debug or observe them, much like the Heisenberg Uncertainty Principle in physics, where the act of measuring a system affects its state.

Context and Importance

In the context of software development, a Heisenbug represents a particularly elusive and frustrating type of software defect that behaves unpredictably when developers attempt to debug or observe it. The name comes from the Heisenberg Uncertainty Principle in quantum mechanics, which suggests that the act of measuring a system can affect its state. In software, when a developer adds logging, sets breakpoints, or runs diagnostic tools to track down the bug, it might vanish or change its manifestation, making it exceedingly difficult to pinpoint the root cause. These bugs are often environment-dependent, appearing only under specific conditions or interactions that are hard to reproduce consistently. They can be triggered by timing issues, race conditions, memory corruption, or complex system interactions, all of which are notoriously hard to simulate or debug.

The importance of understanding Heisenbugs lies in the challenge they present to software reliability and development efficiency. Since these bugs are difficult to observe and reproduce, they can significantly slow down the debugging process, increasing the time and resources required for software testing. For developers, Heisenbugs can be particularly maddening because their transient nature means they may only occur intermittently or under very specific conditions, often after the system has been deployed or during complex use cases. Addressing these types of bugs requires sophisticated debugging techniques, such as careful logging, advanced static and dynamic analysis tools, and sometimes even modifications to the environment to reproduce the issue. Recognizing Heisenbugs helps in managing development expectations and focusing on robust testing strategies to minimize their impact.

Best Practices and Guidelines

Reproduce the issue consistently: Try to isolate the bug by creating a minimal, controlled environment or test case that triggers the issue reliably.

Use logging extensively: Add detailed, strategic logging to capture system state and flow without relying on a debugger, as breakpoints may alter behavior.

Leverage non-intrusive debugging tools: Use tools like profilers, memory analyzers, and static code analyzers that minimize interference with the system's behavior.

Test in varied environments: Ensure tests cover different configurations, hardware, and system states to account for the specific conditions that might trigger the bug.

Consider race conditions and timing issues: Be mindful of concurrency problems, as Heisenbugs often relates to issues like race conditions or thread synchronization.

Common Misconceptions and Pitfalls

- Assuming the bug is gone when it doesn't appear in debugging sessions: The bug might still exist but only manifests under certain conditions that aren't captured during normal debugging.
- Relying solely on breakpoints: Breakpoints or stepping through code can change timing and memory states, potentially hiding the bug or making it behave differently.
- Overlooking environmental factors: Heisenbugs often depend on specific hardware, configurations, or external systems, so testing in a single environment can be misleading.
- Believing the bug is fixed because it's not reproducible: Just because a bug doesn't appear during testing doesn't mean it's resolved; it might still be lurking under different circumstances.
- Blaming third-party libraries or external dependencies without full investigation: While external dependencies can contribute, the root cause may lie within the software itself, such as race conditions or improper handling of system resources.

Related Concepts

1. Murphy's Law: "Anything that can go wrong, will go wrong."
2. Heisenbugs often embody this law because, even in well-tested code, unexpected bugs can appear under seemingly unpredictable or rare conditions, adding complexity to debugging.
3. Heisenberg Uncertainty Principle (in Software):
4. The act of observing or debugging a system can alter its behavior, making it difficult to reproduce or diagnose certain types of bugs, especially timing-dependent issues like race conditions.
5. Lehman's Laws of Software Evolution: "A program that is constantly evolving will always accumulate more and more bugs."
6. As software evolves with new features or refactoring, Heisenbugs may arise due to unintended side effects of code changes, complicating the process of maintaining stable software.
7. The 90-90 Rule: "The first 90% of the project takes 90% of the time; the remaining 10% takes the other 90%."

8. Heisenbugs often appear late in the development process, making debugging and resolving them much more time-consuming, especially when they are elusive and hard to reproduce.
9. Conway's Law: "Organizations which design systems are constrained to produce designs which are copies of the communication structures of these organizations."
10. Complex communication and interaction between teams or components may lead to Heisenbugs, where defects arise from subtle interactions that are hard to observe and fix without understanding the larger system.

References

- Wikipedia, *Heisenbug*, [pub: 11 Mar 2024, cited: 3 Jan 2025]

Kaner Non-Symmetry: Acknowledge the differing perspectives and knowledge bases of developers and testers

---

Definition and Origin

Kaner Non-Symmetry in software and technology refers to a principle from the field of software testing and quality assurance, attributed to Cem Kaner. It highlights the inherent asymmetry between developers and testers. Specifically, developers typically have detailed knowledge of the system's design, code, and intended behavior, while testers often work with incomplete or less detailed information, relying on exploration and heuristics. This asymmetry can lead to differences in how each group identifies and approaches issues, with testers focusing on user experience, potential failure points, and edge cases, while developers focus on technical correctness and functionality.

This concept emphasizes the challenges in communication and collaboration between these two groups, as well as the need for effective testing strategies that account for this imbalance.

Context and Importance

Kaner Non-Symmetry, as introduced by Cem Kaner, is a critical concept in the field of software testing because it acknowledges the differing perspectives and knowledge bases of developers and testers. Developers typically have deep insights into the inner workings of the software, including its architecture, code, and design decisions. This gives them an advantage when it comes to troubleshooting and debugging technical issues. Testers, on the other hand, often work with limited or incomplete knowledge of the system's inner mechanisms, focusing instead on how the software behaves from an external, user-centric perspective. They may lack access to the code or have limited understanding of the system's internal logic, but their strength lies in exploring the software's functionality and identifying unexpected behaviors or usability issues. The non-symmetry between these two roles becomes significant in highlighting the unique challenges each faces in ensuring software quality.

Understanding Kaner Non-Symmetry is important because it shapes how software testing is conducted and the strategies employed for collaboration between developers and testers. The recognition of this asymmetry fosters more effective communication, as developers and testers must bridge their knowledge gap through documentation, knowledge-sharing, and collaboration. It also influences the tools and techniques testers use, encouraging them to adopt exploratory testing, heuristic evaluation, and other methods that rely on the tester's creativity and user-centric perspective. By acknowledging the differences in knowledge and approach, teams can better align their efforts to uncover potential defects, improve usability, and ensure a more comprehensive testing process. Moreover, it encourages a shift from viewing testing as a purely technical task to one that also requires an understanding of user experience, further enhancing the overall quality of the product.

Best Practices and Guidelines

Foster Collaboration: Encourage open communication between developers and testers to bridge the knowledge gap and align on goals, ensuring a shared understanding of the software's intended behavior and potential risks.

Leverage Exploratory Testing: Since testers often lack detailed knowledge of the code, they employ exploratory testing techniques that allow testers to uncover unexpected issues by focusing on user experience and edge cases.

Document Assumptions and Knowledge Gaps: Developers and testers should document key assumptions and areas where knowledge is incomplete, helping testers focus on areas with higher uncertainty and reducing potential blind spots.

Utilize Heuristics: Testers should rely on heuristics and domain knowledge to guide testing efforts, especially when lacking full access to the system's design or code, improving the efficiency of uncovering defects.

Shift Focus to Usability and User Experience: Testers, with their external perspective, should focus on usability, user interactions, and potential failure modes that may not be obvious to developers, ensuring a comprehensive quality assessment.

Common Misconceptions and Pitfalls

- Assuming Testers Know the System as Well as Developers: One common misconception is that testers should have the same deep understanding of the code or design as developers, which overlooks the inherent knowledge asymmetry between the two roles.
- Expecting Testers to Find All Bugs: There's a pitfall in expecting testers to catch every issue despite working with incomplete information; this ignores the fact that some bugs may only be apparent with access to internal design or code insights.
- Overlooking the Value of Exploratory Testing: A misconception is that testing should always follow predefined scripts or automated checks, neglecting the critical role of exploratory testing in discovering unforeseen issues due to the tester's external perspective.
- Underestimating Communication Gaps: Failing to address the communication challenges between developers and testers can lead to misalignment in priorities, assumptions, and expectations, affecting the overall quality assurance process.
- Assuming Automation Can Fully Replace Manual Testing: Some teams mistakenly believe that automated testing can entirely replace manual, exploratory testing, ignoring the fact that automation often lacks the flexibility to identify issues that testers with limited system knowledge might uncover.

Related Concepts

1. Pesticide Paradox (Gerald M. Weinberg): This principle states that running the same set of tests repeatedly will eventually stop finding new bugs. It aligns with Kaner Non-Symmetry by emphasizing that a tester's perspective, different from that of the developer, is necessary to discover new and unforeseen issues—especially when the tester has limited access to the system's internal knowledge.
2. Dunning-Kruger Effect: This cognitive bias suggests that people with limited knowledge tend to overestimate their ability in that domain. In the context of Kaner Non-Symmetry, it highlights the risk of developers overestimating their ability to predict how end-users will interact with the software, leading to potential gaps in testing from a user-centric perspective.
3. Testing Context Principle (Cem Kaner): A core idea in Kaner's own work, this principle stresses that testing is heavily dependent on the context, including the level of knowledge testers have about the system. It underscores the importance of understanding the differences in expertise between developers and testers, as well as adapting testing strategies accordingly.
4. The Law of Leaky Abstractions (Joel Spolsky): This law suggests that abstractions (like software APIs or systems) often fail to completely hide underlying complexity. In the context of Kaner Non-Symmetry, it reinforces the idea that developers have a clearer view of these abstractions, while testers may encounter unexpected issues or limitations when those abstractions "leak" into the user experience.
5. Fagan Inspection (Michael Fagan): This inspection method involves peer reviews where developers examine each other's code. While it focuses on the developer's role, it complements Kaner Non-Symmetry by emphasizing that external perspectives, such as those from testers or users, are essential for identifying quality issues that might be overlooked by those with deep technical knowledge of the system.

References

- Wikipedia, *Cem Kaner*, [pub: 19 Mar 2023, cited: 3 Jan 2025]

Law of Diminishing Returns: More resources yield smaller improvements

Definition and Origin

The Law of Diminishing Returns in software and technology refers to the principle that, as more resources (e.g., time, money, or effort) are invested in a project or system, the incremental benefits or improvements gained from each additional unit of input decrease after a certain point. Initially, adding resources can significantly enhance performance or efficiency, but beyond a certain threshold, the gains become smaller and may eventually plateau or even decline.

The concept of the Law of Diminishing Returns was first introduced by David Ricardo, a British economist, in the early 19th century. It was part of his work on economic theory, particularly in relation to agriculture. Ricardo observed that, as more labor and capital are applied to a fixed amount of land, the additional output (or yield) produced by each new unit of input tends to decrease after a certain point. This principle later became a foundational concept in economics and was expanded to other fields, including technology and software.

Context and Importance

In the context of software and technology, the Law of Diminishing Returns highlights the point at which adding more resources—such as developers, hardware, or time—yields progressively smaller improvements in output or performance. In software development, for example, increasing the number of developers on a project can initially speed up progress, but after a certain threshold, adding more developers can lead to inefficiencies due to communication overhead, coordination problems, and diminishing collaboration effectiveness. Similarly, upgrading hardware or increasing computing power can enhance system performance up to a point, but beyond that, the performance gains per unit of investment begin to shrink. This law emphasizes the need for optimizing resource allocation and managing complexity as projects scale.

The importance of the Law of Diminishing Returns in technology and software development lies in its practical implications for decision-making and resource management. Recognizing this law helps companies avoid wasteful overinvestment in areas where additional input no longer provides proportional benefits. It encourages a focus on efficiency, balance, and strategic innovation rather than simply increasing resources in an attempt to boost performance. Understanding when diminishing returns set in allows organizations to make smarter choices about scaling infrastructure, improving software, and managing teams—ensuring that resources are deployed where they will have the most impact, and preventing stagnation or inefficiency as projects grow in complexity.

Best Practices and Guidelines

Optimize resource allocation: Prioritize quality over quantity when adding resources (e.g., developers or hardware), ensuring each addition maximizes efficiency and output.

Monitor performance thresholds: Regularly assess system performance and development progress to identify when incremental improvements begin to diminish.

Balance scaling and complexity: Scale infrastructure or teams gradually, ensuring systems and workflows can handle growth without causing bottlenecks or inefficiencies.

Emphasize incremental innovation: Focus on smaller, continuous improvements rather than large-scale overhauls that may offer diminishing returns.

Streamline collaboration: Avoid over-expanding teams, as large teams can introduce coordination overhead and reduce overall productivity.

Common Misconceptions and Pitfalls

- Assuming more is always better: Believing that adding more resources (developers, time, hardware) will always lead to proportionally greater results, ignoring the point where returns begin to diminish.

- Overlooking hidden costs: Failing to account for inefficiencies like increased communication overhead, management complexity, or system bottlenecks as resources grow.
- Neglecting optimization: Focusing solely on adding resources instead of improving existing processes or technologies, which could yield better results with fewer inputs.
- Over-investing in outdated technology: Continuing to pour resources into improving older systems or infrastructure, even when the marginal gains are negligible or unsustainable.
- Ignoring diminishing returns in team dynamics: Expanding teams without considering the diminishing effectiveness of collaboration, which can lead to slower decision-making and lower productivity.

Related Concepts

1. Brook's Law: "Adding manpower to a late software project makes it later."
2. This principle highlights how adding more people to a project that is behind schedule can increase complexity, communication overhead, and inefficiency, rather than speeding up progress, which reflects diminishing returns in team scaling.
3. Pareto Principle (80/20 Rule):
4. This principle asserts that roughly 80% of the effects come from 20% of the causes. In software, it suggests that a small portion of code or features delivers the majority of value, meaning that adding more features or complexity beyond that point yields progressively less value.
5. Conway's Law: "Organizations which design systems are constrained to produce designs which are copies of the communication structures of these organizations."
6. This law points out that as teams grow or become more complex, the design and communication structure of the team can directly influence system efficiency, leading to diminishing returns in performance when scaling poorly organized teams.
7. The Law of Leaky Abstractions:
8. This law suggests that all abstractions leak, meaning that adding more layers of abstraction in software design can ultimately lead to inefficiency and complexity. As systems scale, these leaks can cause diminishing returns in terms of performance and maintainability.

9. The Mythical Man-Month:
10. Coined by Fred Brooks in his famous book, this principle states that tasks do not scale linearly with the number of people involved. It underscores the diminishing returns when trying to scale software development by adding more personnel, as the added complexity can outweigh the benefits.

References

- Wikipedia, *Diminishing returns*, [pub: 7 Dec 2024, cited: 3 Jan 2025]

Murphy's Law: Anything that can go wrong, will go wrong

Definition and Origin

Murphy's Law is the adage that suggests "Anything that can go wrong will go wrong", often at the worst possible moment. It reflects the inevitability of errors, failures, or mishaps in situations beyond one's control.

Murphy's Law is attributed to Edward A. Murphy Jr., an American aerospace engineer. The law originated in the late 1940s during a project at Edwards Air Force Base in California, where Murphy was working on experiments involving the safety of rocket sleds.

Context and Importance

In software and technology, Murphy's Law serves as a reminder of the inherent unpredictability and complexity of systems. Software development is a highly intricate process, often involving multiple layers of code, hardware, and external dependencies. Despite meticulous planning and testing, unexpected bugs, system failures, or configuration issues can arise, sometimes at the most critical juncture. Murphy's Law in this context underscores the necessity for thorough testing, error-handling protocols, and contingency planning. Developers are encouraged to anticipate that things will go wrong, even with the best-laid plans, and to design systems with the resilience to recover from unexpected failures.

The importance of Murphy's Law in the technology sector also extends to project management and risk assessment. It drives home the point that no matter how detailed the specifications or how optimized the solution, the unexpected will happen. This principle influences the adoption of best practices such as redundant systems, comprehensive logging, and failover mechanisms in critical applications. It encourages a culture of caution and continuous improvement, where engineers are proactive in identifying potential pitfalls before they occur. By acknowledging that things can and will go wrong, teams are better equipped to build robust, reliable software that can withstand unforeseen challenges and minimize disruptions.

Best Practices and Guidelines

Expect the Unexpected: Always plan for failures, bugs, or unforeseen issues in both development and production environments.

Automate Testing: Implement comprehensive automated tests to catch issues early, reducing the risk of undetected problems.

Design for Resilience: Build systems with redundancy, failover capabilities, and graceful error handling to mitigate potential failures.

Prioritize Monitoring: Set up real-time monitoring and logging to quickly identify and resolve problems when they occur.

Plan for Contingencies: Have a clear disaster recovery and rollback plan in place to minimize downtime and data loss.

Common Misconceptions and Pitfalls

- Overconfidence in Testing: Believing that thorough testing guarantees no failures, ignoring the possibility of edge cases or unforeseen issues.
- Underestimating Complexity: Assuming that simple projects won't encounter major problems, leading to inadequate preparation or oversight.
- Neglecting Risk Management: Failing to plan for potential failures or assuming they won't happen, which can lead to disaster when they do.

- Assuming One-Size-Fits-All Solutions: Relying too heavily on a single solution or approach without considering its limitations or adaptability in real-world conditions.
- Ignoring Human Error: Overlooking the potential for mistakes in code, configuration, or deployment, assuming everything will go as planned.

Related Concepts

1. Conway's Law: "Organizations which design systems are constrained to produce designs which are copies of the communication structures of these organizations."
2. This highlights how the structure and communication within development teams can shape the software they build, often leading to unexpected outcomes based on organizational limitations.
3. Brooks' Law: "Adding manpower to a late software project makes it later."
4. This emphasizes that despite good intentions, interventions or changes (like adding more people to a project) can often make things worse, akin to Murphy's Law predicting that things will go wrong despite efforts to improve them.
5. Parkinson's Law: "Work expands to fill the time available for its completion."
6. This suggests that software development tasks can take longer than anticipated, often spiraling into delays or unforeseen issues, much like Murphy's Law's expectation of things going wrong.
7. The Law of Leaky Abstractions: "All abstractions leak."
8. This law states that no matter how well an abstraction is designed, the underlying complexity will eventually surface, often causing issues that developers didn't anticipate—similar to Murphy's Law's unexpected failures.
9. Law of Demeter: "Only talk to your immediate friends."
10. Also known as the principle of least knowledge, it encourages minimizing dependencies in software. If adhered to poorly, it can cause hidden interdependencies, which can lead to bugs or unexpected behaviors, reminiscent of Murphy's Law.

References

- Wikipedia, *Murphy's law*, [pub: 17 Dec 2024, cited: 3 Jan 2025]

Fallacy of Complete Code Coverage

Definition and Origin

The Fallacy of Complete Code Coverage refers to the mistaken belief that achieving 100% code coverage (i.e., every line of code being executed by tests) guarantees that the software is fully tested and free of defects. In reality, high code coverage does not necessarily ensure thorough testing, as it may miss edge cases, logic errors, or scenarios that aren't covered by the test cases. Quality testing involves both coverage and the effectiveness of the tests themselves.

The Fallacy of Complete Code Coverage doesn't have a single, widely recognized inventor. However, the concept emerged organically from the software testing community as awareness grew about the limitations of using code coverage as the sole indicator of test quality. While no single individual can be definitively credited with coining the term, it reflects a broader understanding of the nuances of software testing and the limitations of automated coverage metrics.

Context and Importance

In software development, code coverage is often used as a metric to gauge the extent to which a program's source code is exercised by automated tests. A high level of code coverage, typically 100%, is frequently seen as a sign of thorough testing, and many developers and teams treat it as a benchmark for test quality. However, this assumption can be misleading. The Fallacy of Complete Code Coverage highlights that just because every line of code is executed during testing, it doesn't necessarily mean the software is free from bugs or that the tests are meaningful. Tests may cover code paths but still fail to check for edge cases, unexpected inputs, or integration problems that might arise in real-world usage. Code coverage tools typically measure only how much of the code is run, not the depth or quality of the test cases themselves.

This fallacy is significant in the context of software development and technology because it encourages a focus on metrics rather than true test effectiveness. A team might be misled into thinking that achieving 100% coverage guarantees software quality, which is far from the case. For example, a test suite could cover all code paths without considering important aspects like error handling, performance, security vulnerabilities, or user behavior under unusual conditions. As software systems become more complex, relying solely on coverage metrics can lead to complacency and missed opportunities for deeper, more insightful testing. The key to effective testing is not just about covering every line of code but ensuring that the tests are designed to uncover bugs and validate the system's behavior in real-world scenarios.

Best Practices and Guidelines

Focus on Test Quality, Not Just Quantity: Prioritize writing meaningful tests that check for edge cases, unexpected inputs, and real-world behavior rather than striving for 100% code coverage.

Complement Code Coverage with Other Metrics: Use additional testing metrics such as defect density, test effectiveness, and code complexity to gauge software quality more accurately.

Risk-Based Testing: Focus testing efforts on the most critical, high-risk areas of the codebase, even if they are not fully covered by automated tests.

Use Code Coverage as a Guideline, Not a Goal: Treat high code coverage as an indicator of test reach, not a guarantee of comprehensive testing or bug-free software.

Regularly Review and Refine Test Cases: Continuously evaluate and improve test cases based on feedback, new requirements, and observed software behaviors, rather than just increasing coverage percentages.

Common Misconceptions and Pitfalls

- 100% Coverage Means No Bugs: Achieving full code coverage does not guarantee that the software is bug-free or behaves as expected in all real-world scenarios.

- All Code Paths Are Equally Important: Covering every line of code doesn't necessarily mean testing the most critical or high-risk paths effectively.
- Automated Tests Are Enough: Relying solely on automated tests with high coverage can miss issues related to user experience, integration, or complex system interactions.
- Code Coverage Tools Identify Quality Tests: High code coverage doesn't equate to well-designed, meaningful tests—tools only measure execution, not the depth of testing.
- Higher Coverage Always Improves Quality: Aiming for 100% coverage can lead to diminishing returns, where additional tests cover trivial or unimportant code without adding real value to the overall quality.

Related Concepts

1. Law of Diminishing Returns (or Pareso Principle):
2. The value of adding more tests decreases as code coverage increases. After a certain point, the effort to achieve higher coverage may not yield meaningful improvements in software quality or defect discovery.
3. The Pesticide Paradox (by Edsger Dijkstra):
4. Just like using the same pesticide repeatedly leads to resistance in pests, running the same set of tests (even with high coverage) repeatedly will eventually stop finding new defects, limiting the effectiveness of the test suite.
5. The 80/20 Rule (Pareto Principle):
6. In testing, 80% of defects are often found in 20% of the code. Focusing on achieving 100% coverage can distract from testing the most critical or error-prone parts of the system.
7. Brooks' Law (from Fred Brooks, The Mythical Man-Month):
8. "Adding manpower to a late software project makes it later." Similarly, adding more tests to increase code coverage doesn't necessarily improve test quality or catch more bugs and may even increase the complexity without meaningful benefit.
9. The Law of Software Entropy (also known as Lehman's Laws of Software Evolution):
10. Software systems naturally evolve into more complex and less maintainable states over time. Merely achieving high coverage without addressing overall system complexity or maintainability may miss long-term quality concerns that automated tests alone cannot uncover.

References

- Martin Fowler, *Test Coverage*, [pub: 17 April 2012, cited: 3 Jan 2025]
- Wikipedia, *Code coverage*, [pub: 14 Nov 2024, cited: 3 Jan 2025]

Project Management & Development Process

E. Time Estimation & Planning

Cone of Uncertainty: Early project estimates have inherent unpredictability

---

Definition and Origin

The Cone of Uncertainty is a concept used in project management, particularly in software development, to describe the evolving level of uncertainty in project estimates over time. It suggests that the accuracy of estimates improves as a project progresses, with the range of uncertainty being broad at the beginning and narrowing as more information becomes available. This is often visualized as a cone, where the wide end represents the high uncertainty at the start, and the narrow end represents more refined estimates as the project moves forward.

The foundational concept of the Cone of Uncertainty was first developed in the 1950s by the founders of the American Association of Cost Engineers (now AACE International) for engineering and construction projects in the chemical industry. In 1958, they introduced a proposed standard classification system for estimates, which included uncertainty ranges, and used "cone" illustrations in industry publications. Later, the concept was adapted for the software industry by Barry Boehm.

Context and Importance

In the context of software development and technology projects, the Cone of Uncertainty serves as a critical framework for understanding and managing the inherent unpredictability of project estimates, particularly during the early stages. At the outset of a project, there is often limited information available about the requirements, technologies, and potential challenges, leading to a wide range of possible outcomes. This high level of uncertainty can result in initial estimates that are overly optimistic or pessimistic, making it difficult for stakeholders to have a clear view of the project's scope, timeline, and costs. As the project progresses and more data is gathered—such as user feedback, testing results, and design iterations—the estimates become more precise and reliable, helping teams make better-informed decisions. The Cone of Uncertainty illustrates this evolution by showing how the uncertainty narrows over time, providing a visual representation of the increasing confidence in the estimates as the project matures.

The importance of the Cone of Uncertainty in software and technology projects lies in its ability to set realistic expectations for project stakeholders, including managers, clients, and developers. By acknowledging that estimates are likely to be imprecise at the beginning, teams can focus on refining their predictions rather than relying on early numbers that might not be reflective of actual outcomes. This mindset helps prevent unnecessary stress or frustration caused by initial estimate discrepancies and fosters a more flexible, adaptive approach to project planning. Additionally, the concept emphasizes the value of iterative development processes, such as Agile, where feedback loops and continuous improvement help reduce uncertainty over time. Ultimately, the Cone of Uncertainty encourages transparency and proactive risk management, making it easier to navigate the complexities of software and technology projects.

Best Practices and Guidelines

Acknowledge early uncertainty: Recognize that initial estimates are likely to be imprecise and will evolve as more information becomes available.

Iterate and refine estimates: Continuously update estimates based on new data, progress, and feedback throughout the project lifecycle.

Communicate risks transparently: Share the range of uncertainty with stakeholders to manage expectations and encourage flexibility.

Use Agile or iterative methodologies: Break down the project into smaller chunks to reduce uncertainty progressively through frequent releases and reviews.

Track and learn from deviations: Regularly assess estimation accuracy and use past project data to improve future forecasting.

Common Misconceptions and Pitfalls

- Assuming early estimates are reliable: Believing that initial estimates are accurate, rather than acknowledging that they will likely change as the project progresses.
- Expecting linear progress: Assuming that uncertainty will decrease steadily, when in reality, it can fluctuate based on unforeseen challenges or new discoveries.
- Ignoring the Cone's range: Focusing too heavily on a single estimate rather than understanding the broader range of possibilities and potential risks.
- Overestimating accuracy too soon: Relying on more precise estimates too early in the project, without enough data to justify them.
- Failing to update estimates regularly: Not revising estimates based on changing circumstances or new information, leading to outdated projections and unrealistic expectations.

Related Concepts

1. Parkinson's Law: "Work expands to fill the time available for its completion." This principle suggests that the more time allocated to a task, the more likely it is that complexity and uncertainty will increase, which is why initial estimates are often overinflated and need continuous refinement.
2. Brooks' Law: "Adding manpower to a late software project makes it later." This principle highlights the complexity of software development and how uncertainty around timelines and effort increases as more people are involved, especially without clear requirements and early understanding.

3. The Mythical Man-Month: Coined by Fred Brooks, this principle suggests that large software projects often suffer from unrealistic time and resource estimates, which ties into the uncertainty seen in early project planning and the challenge of refining those estimates over time.
4. Cone of Uncertainty Principle (Steve McConnell): As directly related to the original concept, McConnell's principle asserts that the range of uncertainty in software estimates starts wide and narrows as development progresses, reflecting the importance of iterative refinement and information gathering.
5. Law of Diminishing Returns: This principle states that after a certain point, the effort spent to reduce uncertainty or improve accuracy in estimates leads to progressively smaller gains. In software, it underscores the need to balance effort spent on estimation with the practical limitations of refining the Cone of Uncertainty.

References

- Wikipedia, *Cone of uncertainty*, [pub: 2 Oct 2024, cited: 3 Jan 2025]

Hofstadter's Law: It always takes longer than you expect

Definition and Origin

Hofstadter's Law states that "It always takes longer than you expect, even when you take into account Hofstadter's Law." It highlights the tendency for tasks to take longer than anticipated due to unforeseen complexities, even when we consciously try to account for delays.

Hofstadter's Law was coined by cognitive scientist and author Douglas Hofstadter. It first appeared in his 1979 book Gödel, Escher, Bach: An Eternal Golden Braid. The law reflects Hofstadter's exploration of self-referential and recursive phenomena, illustrating the difficulty of predicting the time required to complete complex tasks.

Context and Importance

Hofstadter's Law is particularly relevant in the fields of software development and technology because it encapsulates the inherent unpredictability of complex projects. Software development often involves a multitude of variables — from the intricacies of coding to unforeseen bugs, system integrations, and evolving requirements. Despite the best planning, developers and project managers consistently underestimate the time required to complete tasks. This phenomenon, highlighted by Hofstadter's Law, is a key reason why software projects often run over budget or miss deadlines. As tasks become more complicated or interact with other parts of a system, new challenges arise that were not initially anticipated, leading to delays even after accounting for potential setbacks.

The importance of Hofstadter's Law in technology lies in its influence on project management and the expectations set within software teams. It encourages a realistic, flexible approach to time estimation, emphasizing that tasks often require more time than expected, no matter how thorough the initial planning might be. Acknowledging Hofstadter's Law can lead to better risk management, more conservative time estimates, and greater resilience when delays occur. It also underscores the need for agile methodologies, which allow for iterative progress and adaptation to unforeseen challenges, ultimately improving the likelihood of successful project completion. In this way, the law serves as a reminder to balance optimism with caution in the fast-evolving and often unpredictable world of technological development.

Best Practices and Guidelines

Overestimate Time: Add buffer time to project estimates, acknowledging that tasks will take longer than initially anticipated.

Plan for Uncertainty: Expect unforeseen complexities, bugs, and changing requirements that could delay progress.

Iterate Frequently: Use agile methodologies to adapt to new information and adjust timelines as necessary.

Document Risks: Identify potential challenges early and track them to manage delays proactively.

Stay Flexible: Be prepared to adjust expectations and deliverables if projects start to fall behind schedule.

Common Misconceptions and Pitfalls

- Underestimating Complexity: Assuming tasks will be linear or straightforward without accounting for unexpected complications.
- Ignoring Buffer Time: Failing to add extra time for potential delays, leading to overly optimistic deadlines.
- Overconfidence in Early Estimates: Believing initial estimates are accurate, even when previous experience suggests otherwise.
- Neglecting Dependencies: Overlooking how tasks or systems interconnect, which can amplify delays across the project.
- Assuming Past Successes Predict Future Results: Relying too heavily on past projects for time estimates, without considering new or unique challenges.

Related Concepts

1. Parkinson's Law – "Work expands to fill the time available for its completion." This law highlights how tasks can stretch to fit the amount of time allocated, often leading to delays if time estimates are too generous.
2. Murphy's Law – "Anything that can go wrong, will go wrong." In software development, this is a reminder that unexpected problems, bugs, or system failures are inevitable, often causing delays even when tasks seem manageable.
3. The Peter Principle – "In a hierarchy, every employee tends to rise to their level of incompetence." In tech projects, this can manifest when team members are assigned tasks beyond their expertise, leading to inefficiency and missed deadlines.
4. Brooks' Law – "Adding manpower to a late software project makes it later." This principle suggests that adding more developers to a delayed project can actually slow it down due to coordination overhead and the time needed for new team members to get up to speed.
5. Conway's Law – "Organizations design systems that mirror their communication structure." In software development, this can lead to inefficiencies and delays if the organizational structure isn't aligned with the needs of the project, complicating communication and decision-making.

References

- Wikipedia, *Hofstadter's law*, [pub: 17 Jul 2024, cited: 3 Jan 2025]

Lewis's Law of Project Planning: No project plan survives first contact with reality.

Definition and Origin

Lewis's Law of Project Planning states that no project plan, no matter how carefully crafted, can withstand the unexpected challenges and complexities that arise once the project is executed. Essentially, it highlights the unpredictability of real-world conditions, suggesting that initial plans will inevitably require adjustments as the project unfolds.

Helmuth von Moltke the Elder – The famous Prussian military strategist is often credited with a similar quote: "No plan survives contact with the enemy." This reflects the idea that even the best military strategies must adapt when faced with unforeseen challenges.

Context and Importance

In the context of software and technology development, Lewis's Law of Project Planning underscores a fundamental truth about the inherent unpredictability of real-world execution. While planning plays a critical role in outlining the scope, resources, and timelines for a software project, the dynamic and complex nature of technology often renders these plans obsolete or impractical once the development process begins. Factors such as evolving user requirements, unforeseen technical challenges, shifting market conditions, and the inherent difficulty of estimating time and resources lead to significant deviations from initial plans. In software development, particularly in agile methodologies, this unpredictability is acknowledged and managed through iterative cycles, continuous feedback, and a focus on adaptability. The law highlights the need for flexibility in project management and emphasizes that no matter how detailed or thorough a plan might seem at the outset, reality will inevitably impose changes and adjustments.

The importance of Lewis's Law in the tech industry lies in its reminder that the best-laid plans are often just a starting point. Recognizing this reality helps teams adopt a mindset of continuous learning, improvement, and adaptation. In software development, this often translates into agile practices where teams are encouraged to pivot, refine, or re-scope based on new insights or shifting goals. This mindset helps mitigate risks such as scope creep, missed deadlines, and resource misallocation. By accepting that plans will evolve, software teams can better allocate their resources, communicate with stakeholders, and ultimately deliver products that are more aligned with real-world needs and conditions. Lewis's Law fosters a culture of resilience, where change is not viewed as a failure but as an inevitable and necessary aspect of successful project execution in the fast-paced, ever-evolving world of technology.

Best Practices and Guidelines

Embrace Flexibility: Be prepared to adapt plans as new information and challenges emerge throughout the development process.

Iterate Frequently: Use agile methodologies to break projects into manageable increments, allowing for regular feedback and adjustments.

Prioritize Communication: Maintain open communication with stakeholders to manage expectations and align on evolving goals.

Focus on Risk Management: Identify potential risks early and develop contingency plans to address unforeseen challenges.

Document Learnings: Continuously capture lessons from deviations and incorporate them into future planning to improve overall project outcomes.

Common Misconceptions and Pitfalls

- Overconfidence in Initial Plans: Believing that detailed, upfront plans can be rigidly followed without considering the inevitable need for changes.
- Ignoring Uncertainty: Failing to account for the unpredictable nature of software development, such as scope changes, technical challenges, and evolving user needs.

- Lack of Contingency Plans: Not preparing for potential setbacks or unexpected issues, assuming the project will proceed as initially planned.
- Over-reliance on Estimations: Relying too heavily on initial time and resource estimates, which often prove inaccurate as the project progresses.
- Resistance to Change: Viewing changes to the plan as failures rather than necessary adjustments, which can hinder progress and innovation.

Related Concepts

1. Murphy's Law – "Anything that can go wrong, will go wrong." This law highlights the inevitability of unexpected challenges and failures, reinforcing the need for flexibility and preparedness in project planning.
2. Brooks's Law – "Adding manpower to a late software project makes it later." This principle underscores that increasing resources in response to delays often exacerbates problems, as new team members require time to integrate, further disrupting the project.
3. Parkinson's Law – "Work expands to fill the time available for its completion." This law suggests that project scope often expands or becomes more complex over time, which can lead to delays or the need for continual adjustments to the plan.
4. The Iron Triangle (Triple Constraint) – Scope, Time, and Cost are interdependent. The principal stresses that any change in one of these constraints (such as increased scope or tighter timelines) will require adjustments to the others, which frequently happens as projects unfold.
5. The Law of Leaky Abstractions – "All abstractions are leaky." In software development, this means that high-level plans or abstractions often fail to capture all the complexities of implementation, leading to unexpected challenges that disrupt the initial plan.

References

- Wikipedia, *Project management triangle*, [pub: 1 Nov 2024, cited: 3 Jan 2025]

Parkinson's Law: Work expands to fill the time available for its completion.

Definition and Origin

Parkinson's Law states that "work expands to fill the time available for its completion." In other words, the more time you allocate to a task, the longer it will take to complete, often due to inefficiency or unnecessary complexity.

Parkinson's Law was coined by British naval historian and author Cyril Northcote Parkinson. He first introduced it in a 1955 essay published in The Economist and later expanded on it in his book Parkinson's Law: The Pursuit of Progress (1958). Parkinson formulated the law as a satirical observation on bureaucracy and the inefficiencies in organizations.

Context and Importance

In the context of software development and technology, Parkinson's Law is particularly relevant when considering project management, timelines, and resource allocation. Software projects often suffer from scope creep, where the complexity of a project increases as the deadline or resources are extended. Developers and teams may expand the functionality of a system, add unnecessary features, or over-engineer solutions when given more time, resulting in delays and inefficiencies. As deadlines stretch, the perceived need for perfection increases, which can lead to diminishing returns in the quality of the product. Parkinson's Law thus highlights the danger of giving excessive time or resources to a project without clear, well-defined objectives and constraints.

Understanding and applying Parkinson's Law can be crucial for improving productivity and efficiency in the tech industry. By setting tighter, more realistic deadlines or limiting the time allocated to certain tasks, teams can avoid over-engineering and focus on delivering essential features in a timely manner. Agile methodologies, for example, often embrace time-boxed iterations or sprints, aligning with Parkinson's observation that work will expand to fill the available time. By recognizing the tendency to expand tasks unnecessarily, software developers and technology managers can counteract inefficiency, fostering a more focused and results-driven approach to development.

Best Practices and Guidelines

Set Clear, Time-Boxed Deadlines: Establish fixed timelines for tasks and projects to prevent unnecessary expansion of work.

Prioritize Core Features: Focus on delivering the most essential functionality first, avoiding feature creep and excessive complexity.

Break Projects into Smaller Tasks: Use agile methods like sprints to create smaller, manageable chunks of work with defined goals.

Minimize Scope Creep: Limit changes to project scope during development to prevent the task from growing beyond its original purpose.

Embrace Iteration and Incremental Progress: Focus on delivering working solutions quickly and improve iteratively, rather than waiting for a "perfect" final product.

Common Misconceptions and Pitfalls

- Assuming All Work Is Inefficient: Not all tasks expand unnecessarily; some genuinely require time and effort for quality results.
- Overlooking Quality for Speed: Focusing too much on tight deadlines may lead to rushed work, compromising the quality of the final product.
- Underestimating Task Complexity: Some tasks may take longer due to inherent complexity, and strict deadlines may ignore these factors.
- Mistaking Parkinson's Law for Procrastination: Parkinson's Law is not about avoiding work; it's about how work expands when time is too generous.
- Ignoring the Need for Buffer Time: While Parkinson's Law emphasizes efficiency, it overlooks the necessity of buffers for unexpected challenges or risks.

Related Concepts

1. The 80/20 Rule (Pareto Principle): This principle suggests that 80% of the results come from 20% of the efforts. In software development, it often means that a small portion of features or tasks deliver the majority of the value, which encourages prioritization and avoiding unnecessary complexity (aligned with Parkinson's Law).
2. Brooks's Law: "Adding manpower to a late software project makes it later." This law highlights how additional resources (like developers) can increase the complexity and coordination overhead of a project, often leading to inefficiencies, similar to Parkinson's observation of work expanding to fit the available resources.
3. The Law of Leaky Abstractions: Proposed by Joel Spolsky, this law states that all abstractions leak—meaning that hidden complexities inevitably surface as systems grow. It relates to Parkinson's Law by suggesting that the more time you allocate to a project, the more you may discover inefficiencies and complexities that weren't initially apparent.
4. Conway's Law: "Organizations which design systems are constrained to produce designs which are copies of the communication structures of these organizations." This law implies that inefficiencies in team structure or communication can lead to bloated, inefficient systems, mirroring Parkinson's Law where the scope or complexity of a project expands based on organizational factors.
5. The Mythical Man-Month: Coined by Fred Brooks in the same book as Brooks's Law, it suggests that software projects often take longer than expected, and adding more developers to a project doesn't always speed it up and may even slow it down due to overhead. This aligns with Parkinson's Law in that more time or resources can lead to inefficiencies rather than progress.

References

- Wikipedia, *Parkinson's law*, [pub: 22 Oct 2024, cited: 3 Jan 2025]

Planning Fallacy: Tendency to underestimate time, costs, and risks, while overestimating ability to complete tasks.

Definition and Origin

The Planning Fallacy is a cognitive bias where people tend to underestimate the time, costs, and risks of future tasks, while overestimating their ability to complete them. This leads to overly optimistic predictions and often results in delays or budget overruns.

The Planning Fallacy was coined by psychologists Daniel Kahneman and Amos Tversky in 1979. They discovered this bias while studying how people make predictions about future events, particularly in the context of planning projects and estimating time and costs.

Context and Importance

In the context of software development and technology projects, the Planning Fallacy is particularly relevant because it often leads to underestimation of project timelines and costs. Developers, managers, and teams tend to be overly optimistic about the amount of time and resources required to complete software projects. This bias can result in unrealistic schedules, missed deadlines, and budget overruns. For example, in software engineering, the complexity of coding, testing, and integrating different systems can often be overlooked or simplified during the planning phase. As a result, developers might underestimate the challenges they will face or the potential for unforeseen issues, like bugs or integration problems, leading to project delays and compromised quality.

The importance of recognizing the Planning Fallacy in technology lies in its impact on project management, resource allocation, and stakeholder expectations. By understanding that over-optimism can skew predictions, teams can adopt more realistic planning practices, such as incorporating buffer time for unexpected delays or using historical data to improve estimates. Techniques like Monte Carlo simulations, Parkinson's Law (work expands to fill the time allotted), and Agile methodologies (which break work into smaller, more manageable tasks) can help mitigate the effects of the Planning Fallacy. Recognizing this cognitive bias is crucial for ensuring that software projects are completed on time, within budget, and to the expected quality standards, ultimately leading to better decision-making and more successful outcomes.

Best Practices and Guidelines

Use Historical Data: Base estimates on past projects and similar tasks to improve accuracy and avoid overly optimistic predictions.

Break Projects into Smaller Tasks: Decompose large projects into manageable parts to better assess time and resource needs.

Include Buffer Time: Add contingency time to account for unforeseen challenges and risks, especially in complex or innovative projects.

Engage in Realistic Risk Assessment: Continuously evaluate potential risks and their impact on timelines and resources throughout the project.

Regularly Reassess Estimates: Adjust timelines and budgets as the project progresses to reflect new insights and emerging challenges.

Common Misconceptions and Pitfalls

- Overconfidence in Initial Estimates: Believing that initial optimistic predictions are accurate without accounting for unforeseen complications or challenges.
- Underestimating Task Complexity: Simplifying tasks or ignoring potential obstacles, leading to significant underestimation of required time and resources.
- Ignoring Past Failures: Failing to learn from previous projects or experiences, and assuming this time will be different, despite similar conditions.
- Overlooking External Factors: Neglecting the impact of external dependencies, such as team availability, stakeholder changes, or third-party integrations.
- Relying Too Heavily on Ideal Scenarios: Planning based on the best-case scenario without factoring in typical delays, bugs, or other common issues.

Related Concepts

1. Parkinson's Law: "Work expands to fill the time available for its completion." This highlights how tasks often take longer than expected because people tend to use all allocated time, regardless of the original estimate.

2. Brooks' Law: "Adding manpower to a late software project makes it later." This underscores how project delays can be exacerbated when teams are expanded in an attempt to speed up delivery, due to communication overhead and ramp-up time.
3. The Law of Continuing Change (also known as Conway's Law): "Organizations which design systems are constrained to produce designs which are copies of the communication structures of these organizations." This principle can contribute to the Planning Fallacy by leading teams to underestimate how organizational complexity and communication inefficiencies impact timelines.
4. Hofstadter's Law: "It always takes longer than you think, even when you take into account Hofstadter's Law." This principle, often humorously cited in software development, emphasizes the inherent unpredictability and underestimation of the time required for complex tasks.
5. The Iron Triangle (or Project Management Triangle): The trade-off between scope, time, and cost. Planning Fallacy often leads to overestimating the ability to meet deadlines or budgets without adjusting scope, leading to unrealistic project expectations.

References

- Wikipedia, *Planning fallacy*, [pub: 25 Aug 2024, cited: 3 Jan 2025]

Student Syndrome: Tendency to procrastinate starting tasks

Definition and Origin

Student Syndrome refers to the tendency of students (or individuals) to procrastinate and delay starting a task until the last possible moment, often underestimating the time required and only beginning to work intensively when the deadline is imminent. This behavior typically leads to unnecessary stress and suboptimal performance.

The term "Student Syndrome" was indeed coined by Eliyahu M. Goldratt in his book Critical Chain (1997). Goldratt used it to describe the tendency of students (and workers in general) to procrastinate, delaying the start of a task until just before the deadline, only to rush through the work under pressure. This behavior, Goldratt argued, applies not just to students, but to anyone facing a project or task with a clear deadline, especially in complex environments like project management and software development.

Goldratt introduced the concept as part of his broader work on Theory of Constraints (TOC), which focuses on identifying and addressing the limiting factors that hinder the performance of systems, including the inefficiencies caused by procrastination and unrealistic task management in project timelines. The term is now widely applied to project management and software development to highlight the negative impact of delaying work until the last minute.

Context and Importance

In the context of software development and technology projects, Student Syndrome is particularly relevant because these fields are often deadline-driven and require substantial planning and effort to meet complex requirements. Developers and engineers, much like students, might delay the start of a task or underestimate how long it will take, especially when there are no immediate pressures or milestones in sight. As deadlines approach, the pressure to deliver leads to a rush of activity, often resulting in subpar quality, overlooked bugs, and a lack of proper testing. This tendency is common in agile environments where sprint deadlines might encourage short-term focus, but if not managed well, it can lead to a recurring cycle of "crisis-mode" work that undermines long-term project stability and quality.

Understanding Student Syndrome is crucial for improving productivity and team performance in technology fields. Teams that recognize this behavior can take proactive steps to address it, such as adopting better time management techniques, setting intermediate milestones, or using more robust estimation methods to avoid the last-minute scramble. By breaking work into smaller, more manageable pieces and encouraging regular progress checks, teams can avoid the pitfalls of procrastination. Additionally, fostering a culture of early planning and continuous testing can prevent the "rush" phase that typically leads to technical debt and burnout, ultimately ensuring higher-quality software delivery and a more sustainable work environment.

Best Practices and Guidelines

Break tasks into smaller chunks: Divide large projects into manageable pieces with clear, achievable milestones to avoid last-minute rushes.

Set realistic deadlines: Estimate task durations accurately and build in buffer time for unforeseen challenges to reduce the temptation to procrastinate.

Prioritize early testing: Begin testing and validation early in the development cycle to catch issues before they snowball.

Encourage incremental progress: Focus on continuous, steady progress rather than waiting until the deadline to start full-scale work.

Foster accountability: Implement regular check-ins and progress reviews to ensure that tasks stay on track and aren't delayed until the last moment.

Common Misconceptions and Pitfalls

- Procrastination is only a time management issue: It's often rooted in a lack of awareness about task complexity or a fear of failure, not just poor scheduling.
- Rushing at the last-minute leads to better results: Crunched work typically sacrifices quality, leading to more bugs, incomplete features, or rushed testing.
- Deadlines are the only motivator: Without breaking tasks into smaller, manageable goals, even looming deadlines can't prevent procrastination and stress.

- Multitasking helps avoid procrastination: Switching between tasks can actually reduce focus and prolong task completion, increasing the likelihood of a last-minute rush.
- Student Syndrome only affects beginners: It can impact experienced developers too, especially when they feel overconfident in their ability to complete tasks quickly under pressure.

Related Concepts

1. Parkinson's Law: "Work expands to fill the time available for its completion." This principle is closely related to Student Syndrome, as it highlights how tasks often take longer than expected when deadlines are distant, leading to procrastination.
2. The Pareto Principle (80/20 Rule): In the context of software development, 80% of the work may often be completed in the final 20% of the time, reflecting how procrastination delays the initial effort until there's little time left to finish.
3. Brooks' Law: "Adding manpower to a late software project makes it later." This law demonstrates how the pressure of a looming deadline, often exacerbated by Student Syndrome, can result in inefficiencies, despite the increase in resources or effort.
4. Hofstadter's Law: "It always takes longer than you expect, even when you take into account Hofstadter's Law." This principle captures the inherent underestimation of time that contributes to procrastination and rushed work in software projects.
5. The Law of Diminishing Returns: In the context of software development, this law suggests that as developers work under tight deadlines (often caused by Student Syndrome), their productivity and work quality degrade, especially as stress increases near the end of a project.

References

- Wikipedia, *Student syndrome*, [pub: 29 Apr 2024, cited: 3 Jan 2025]

The Ninety-Ninety Rule: First 90% of a project takes 90% of the time, and the last 10% takes the other 90%

Definition and Origin

The Ninety-Ninety Rule is a humorous concept in project management that suggests: "The first 90% of a project takes 90% of the time, and the last 10% takes the other 90%." It highlights how tasks often take longer than expected, especially when nearing completion, due to unforeseen challenges or details that were initially overlooked.

The Ninety-Ninety Rule is generally attributed to Tom Cargill, a researcher at Bell Labs, in the early 1980s. He coined the rule to humorously describe the tendency of software development (and by extension, other projects) to encounter delays, particularly during the final stages of a project. Cargill's insight was meant to highlight how progress often appears to be faster at the beginning, but the final 10% can be unexpectedly time-consuming and complex.

Context and Importance

In the context of software development and technology projects, the Ninety-Ninety Rule highlights a common phenomenon where the initial stages of a project progress quickly, leading teams to believe they are on track to meet deadlines. However, as the project nears completion, the remaining 10% of the work often requires much more effort and time than anticipated. This can be due to the discovery of bugs, unforeseen technical complexities, integration challenges, or the need to fine-tune and optimize various components. The rule underscores the unpredictable nature of software projects, where initial optimism often gives way to frustration in the final stretch. The final 10% typically involves debugging, user testing, and meeting various compliance or performance standards, all of which are frequently more time-consuming than anticipated.

The importance of the Ninety-Ninety Rule in the software and technology industries lies in its ability to set realistic expectations for project timelines and resource allocation. Developers, managers, and stakeholders can use this rule to anticipate the potential for delays in the final stages and plan accordingly. Acknowledging this phenomenon helps teams prepare for the hard work involved in finishing a project, encouraging better time management and contingency planning. The rule also serves as a reminder of the inherent complexity in technology projects, where the last phase is often more difficult than it appears at first glance, despite the seemingly straightforward nature of the remaining tasks. By internalizing this principle, teams can mitigate risks, avoid surprises, and increase the chances of successful project completion.

Best Practices and Guidelines

Anticipate Delays: Plan for the possibility that the final 10% of a project will take longer than expected, factoring in testing, debugging, and integration challenges.

Allocate Buffer Time: Include extra time in schedules for unforeseen issues, particularly in the last stages of development.

Prioritize Testing Early: Start testing and bug fixing as soon as possible to avoid bottlenecks during the final phase.

Monitor Progress Regularly: Track progress throughout the project, adjusting expectations and resources as needed to stay on track for completion.

Prepare for Scope Creep: Stay vigilant against feature creep or last-minute changes that can extend the time needed for completion.

Common Misconceptions and Pitfalls

- Assuming Fast Start = Fast Finish: Mistaking early progress as a sign that the project will remain on schedule, leading to unrealistic expectations for the final stages.
- Underestimating Final Complexity: Overlooking the fact that the last 10% often involves complex debugging, integration, or compliance work that wasn't anticipated earlier.

- Neglecting Contingency Planning: Failing to allocate sufficient buffer time for unexpected challenges in the final phase, leading to rushed or incomplete delivery.
- Overconfidence in Early Milestones: Celebrating early completion of milestones without acknowledging that they may not reflect the challenges of finishing the full project.
- Ignoring Team Fatigue: Assuming that the team will maintain the same pace throughout the project, ignoring potential burnout or diminishing productivity in the final stretch.

Related Concepts

1. Brook's Law: "Adding manpower to a late software project makes it later." This principle emphasizes that rushing to complete a project by adding resources can cause more complexity and delays, particularly in the final stages where the bulk of the work remains.
2. Murphy's Law: "Anything that can go wrong will go wrong." This law reflects the unpredictable nature of software development, where unforeseen issues (especially in the last 10% of a project) are common and can lead to delays.
3. Parkinson's Law: "Work expands to fill the time available for its completion." This principle suggests that tasks often take longer than expected because the allocated time is fully consumed, regardless of the amount of work remaining, echoing the tendency for the final stages to stretch unexpectedly.
4. The Law of Leaky Abstractions: This principle suggests that when building complex systems, lower-level details inevitably "leak" through the abstraction layers, creating unforeseen problems in the final stages, similar to the hidden challenges in the last 10% of a project.
5. The Second System Effect: This law posits that a developer's second attempt at designing a system often becomes unnecessarily complex due to over-engineering, which can lead to the same pitfalls seen in the final stages of a project as anticipated in the Ninety-Ninety Rule.

References

- Wikipedia, *Ninety–ninety rule*, [pub: 9 Oct 2024, cited: 3 Jan 2025]

Three F's of Priority Management: Focus, Finish, Freedom

Introduction

The Three F's of Priority Management refer to a framework for effectively managing tasks by focusing on:

1. Focus: Concentrate on high-priority tasks that align with your goals.
2. Finish: Complete tasks before moving on to new ones to avoid unfinished work.
3. Freedom: Create time and space to address unexpected opportunities or challenges by managing priorities efficiently.

This approach helps prioritize what matters most, ensuring productivity and goal alignment.

According to Google The "Three F's of Priority Management" concept was popularized by Brian Tracy, a well-known author and motivational speaker specializing in time management and personal development. Tracy introduced this framework as part of his broader teachings on how to prioritize effectively, manage time, and boost productivity. While he may not be the sole originator of the idea, he is widely recognized for bringing the concept into mainstream time management discussions.

Context and Importance

In the fast-paced world of software and technology, effective priority management is crucial due to the constant influx of new tasks, features, updates, and urgent deadlines. The Three F's of Priority Management—Focus, Finish, and Freedom—serve as a strategic approach to help software developers, engineers, and tech teams navigate this complexity. Focus ensures that teams concentrate on the most critical tasks, such as fixing high-priority bugs, delivering key features for a release, or addressing customer feedback, rather than being distracted by less important issues. By maintaining focus on what aligns with the project's goals or company objectives, teams can avoid wasted effort on low-impact tasks that might not contribute directly to the product's success.

Finish and Freedom are equally significant in the tech industry. "Finish" encourages teams to complete tasks before moving on to new ones, which is essential in software development to prevent the "start-stop" cycle that leads to unfinished features or incomplete bug fixes. This principle ensures that every task or project reaches a functional and deployable state, reducing technical debt and enhancing overall product quality. "Freedom," on the other hand, emphasizes the importance of leaving room for unforeseen challenges, such as urgent bug fixes, technical debt management, or the adoption of new technologies. By managing priorities with flexibility and a clear focus, tech teams can more effectively navigate deadlines, shifting requirements, and unexpected changes, ultimately leading to more efficient project delivery and innovation.

Best Practices and Guidelines

Focus on High-Impact Tasks: Prioritize critical features, bugs, or technical debt that directly contribute to the project's goals or user experience.

Finish What You Start: Complete tasks or sprints before moving on to new ones to maintain momentum and avoid unfinished work.

Balance with Flexibility: Allow room for urgent, unforeseen tasks (e.g., critical bug fixes or urgent security patches) without losing sight of major priorities.

Break Down Large Tasks: Split complex tasks into manageable chunks to ensure consistent progress and minimize overwhelm.

Regularly Reevaluate Priorities: Continuously assess and adjust priorities based on evolving project needs, user feedback, and market changes.

Common Misconceptions and Pitfalls

- Misconception: Focusing on everything is effective: Trying to focus on all tasks at once can lead to burnout and reduced quality; prioritizing helps avoid spreading efforts too thin.
- Pitfall: Prioritizing urgency over importance: Mistaking urgent tasks (e.g., minor issues or distractions) for important ones can derail long-term goals and key project objectives.

- Misconception: Completing tasks quickly is always better: Rushing to finish tasks can lead to poor quality or incomplete work, ultimately creating more problems in the future.
- Pitfall: Overlooking flexibility in planning: Rigidly sticking to a plan without considering new urgent priorities (like critical bugs) can hinder a team's responsiveness to real-time needs.
- Misconception: Freedom means ignoring priorities: Leaving too much unstructured time for unexpected tasks can lead to a lack of direction and inefficiency.

Related Concepts

1. Pareto Principle (80/20 Rule): This principle suggests that 80% of results come from 20% of efforts. In the context of priority management, it emphasizes focusing on the critical few tasks (those that provide the most value) rather than spreading efforts across all tasks.
2. Law of Leverage: In software development, leverage refers to focusing on tasks that provide the highest impact with the least effort. By concentrating on high-priority tasks (Focus) and completing them efficiently (Finish), teams can maximize their productivity and outcomes.
3. Parkinson's Law: This law states that work expands to fill the time available for its completion. To counteract this, teams should focus on defining clear, prioritized tasks with specific deadlines, avoiding the trap of overelaborating low-priority work.
4. The Eisenhower Matrix: A decision-making tool that divides tasks into four quadrants based on urgency and importance. This aligns with the "Focus" aspect of the Three F's, helping teams prioritize tasks that are both important and urgent, while minimizing time spent on less impactful work.
5. Technical Debt: This principle refers to the cost of choosing quick or easy solutions in the short term, which can accumulate over time and require more effort to fix. Managing technical debt by prioritizing finishing important work (Finish) and addressing key issues (Focus) helps prevent the accumulation of problems that slow down future development.

References

- Wikipedia, *Task management*, [pub: 26 Nov 2024, cited: 3 Jan 2025]

F. Team Dynamics & Productivity

Amdahl's Law: Parallel speedup is limited by sequential portions

Definition and Origin

Amdahl's Law is a formula used to predict the theoretical maximum speedup of a computational task when only part of the task can be parallelized. It states that the overall speedup of a system is limited by the portion of the task that remains sequential.
The law is expressed as:

$$S = \frac{1}{(1 - P) + \frac{P}{N}}$$

Where:

- S is the speedup,
- P is the parallelizable portion of the task ($0 \leq P \leq 1$),
- N is the number of processors.

As the number of processors increases, the speedup gains diminish due to the non-parallelizable portion of the task.

Amdahl's Law was coined by Gene Amdahl, a computer scientist and IBM fellow, in 1967. He introduced the law in a paper titled "Validity of the Single Processor Approach to Achieving Large-Scale Computing Capabilities", where he discussed the limitations of parallel processing and how the speedup of a system is constrained by the sequential portion of a task.

Context and Importance

Amdahl's Law is crucial in the context of software development and technology because it highlights the inherent limitations of parallelism in computational tasks. As hardware advances with more cores and processors, the temptation to parallelize applications for increased performance grows. However, Amdahl's Law reminds developers and engineers that not all parts of a program can be parallelized. Even if a program has a large parallelizable portion, the remaining sequential code becomes a bottleneck, ultimately capping the performance improvements achievable with additional processors. This understanding forces software architects to carefully consider which aspects of their systems are worth parallelizing and which might provide diminishing returns, especially as hardware capabilities expand.

In technology, Amdahl's Law also plays a significant role in shaping decisions around system design and optimization. It emphasizes the importance of balancing parallel processing with the efficiency of sequential code, as well as understanding that adding more resources (like additional processors) may not always yield proportional performance gains. This insight is critical in fields such as cloud computing, big data processing, and supercomputing, where parallelism is often used to handle large-scale computations. The law serves as a benchmark for evaluating the cost-effectiveness of scaling systems and is foundational for understanding the limits of performance improvement in multi-core and distributed computing environments. It encourages a holistic view of performance optimization, blending hardware, software, and algorithm design.

Best Practices and Guidelines

Prioritize Parallelization of Computation-Intensive Sections: Focus on parallelizing the parts of the code that will yield the highest performance gain, as limited by the sequential portion.

Optimize Sequential Code: Minimize the time spent on sequential operations, as Amdahl's Law shows that improvements in parallelism are constrained by the non-parallelizable code.

Evaluate Diminishing Returns: Understand that adding more processors yields smaller performance gains as the parallelizable portion of the task increases, making the incremental benefits less significant.

Balance Hardware and Software: Consider both hardware capabilities (e.g., multi-core processors) and software optimization (e.g., efficient algorithms) to achieve the best performance.

Test Scalability: Continuously measure the performance of parallelized systems to assess scalability and determine the point at which additional resources no longer provide meaningful speedup.

Common Misconceptions and Pitfalls

- Overestimating Parallelizable Potential: A common misconception is assuming large portions of a program can be parallelized, leading to unrealistic expectations of performance improvement.
- Ignoring Sequential Code Impact: Focusing too heavily on parallelism without optimizing the sequential code can result in minimal performance gains, as the sequential portion limits speedup.
- Assuming Perfect Scalability: People often believe that adding more processors will always yield linear performance improvements, but Amdahl's Law shows that performance gains decrease as the sequential portion becomes more significant.
- Neglecting System Overheads: The overhead introduced by managing parallel tasks (e.g., synchronization, communication) can reduce the effectiveness of parallelization, often overlooked when estimating potential speedup.
- Underestimating the Cost of Parallelization: The complexity and cost of making code parallel (e.g., debugging, testing, synchronization) can outweigh the benefits, especially for tasks with small parallelizable portions.

Related Concepts

1. Gustafson-Barsis's Law: Unlike Amdahl's Law, which assumes a fixed problem size, Gustafson-Barsis's Law suggests that scaling up the problem size with more processors can lead to greater overall performance. It emphasizes that performance improvement can be achieved by increasing the workload, thus overcoming Amdahl's Law's constraints on fixed-size problems.

2. Moore's Law: Moore's Law predicts that the number of transistors on a chip doubles approximately every two years, leading to exponential growth in computational power. This trend influences Amdahl's Law because as hardware improves, the theoretical performance limits for parallel systems may be pushed higher, though still constrained by sequential tasks.
3. Amdahl's Law vs. Strong vs. Weak Scaling: This principle distinguishes between strong scaling (fixing the problem size and adding processors) and weak scaling (increasing both problem size and processors). Amdahl's Law primarily addresses strong scaling, while weak scaling is more aligned with the ideas in Gustafson-Barsis's Law.
4. The Law of Diminishing Returns: This principle applies to the performance benefits of adding more processors or resources. As seen in Amdahl's Law, adding resources (e.g., processors) results in progressively smaller performance improvements as the parallelizable portion of the task becomes saturated.
5. Little's Law: In the context of parallel processing, Little's Law connects the average number of tasks in a system, the arrival rate of tasks, and the time a task spends in the system. It is relevant in understanding system bottlenecks, such as those that might arise when trying to parallelize a task and manage its components efficiently.
6. Each of these principles either provides an extension of or context for Amdahl's Law, helping to shape our understanding of system performance, scalability, and optimization.

References

- Wikipedia, *Amdahl's law*, [pub: 17 Dec 2024, cited: 3 Jan 2025]

Brooks's Law: Adding manpower to a late software project makes it later

---

Definition and Origin

Brooks's Law states that "adding manpower to a late software project makes it later." This is because the time needed for new team members to get up to speed and the overhead of communication among a growing team can outweigh any potential productivity gains.

Brooks's Law was coined by Fred Brooks in his 1975 book The Mythical Man-Month: Essays on Software Engineering. Fred Brooks was a computer scientist and project manager who worked on the development of IBM's System/360 and its OS/360 operating system.

Context and Importance

Brooks's Law emerged from Fred Brooks' experience managing large-scale software projects, particularly during the development of IBM's System/360. The law highlights a counterintuitive phenomenon in software development: adding more people to a project that is already behind schedule does not necessarily accelerate progress and may, in fact, lead to further delays. This is primarily due to the increased complexity in communication and coordination as the team grows, as well as the time required for new members to become productive. In the context of software development, where tasks are often interdependent and require deep collaboration, the influx of new personnel can disrupt existing workflows, introduce more bottlenecks, and complicate decision-making.

The importance of Brooks's Law lies in its insight into the dynamics of project management, particularly in the technology and software industries. Many software teams still struggle with the temptation to "throw more resources" at an overrun project, believing that additional workers will help. Brooks's Law teaches that success in software projects depends more on proper planning, efficient use of existing resources, and clear communication than on simply adding more personnel. The law has had a lasting impact on software engineering practices, influencing modern agile methodologies and the focus on smaller, more manageable teams that are better equipped to collaborate and iterate efficiently. Understanding and respecting Brooks's Law helps organizations avoid common pitfalls in scaling development efforts and promotes smarter, more sustainable approaches to complex software projects.

Best Practices and Guidelines

Limit team size: Keep teams small and manageable to enhance communication, collaboration, and productivity.

Plan realistically: Avoid the assumption that adding people will speed up a delayed project; focus on refining existing workflows.

Prioritize training: Onboard new members efficiently to minimize the disruption caused by the learning curve.

Optimize communication: Foster clear and frequent communication to reduce overhead and misunderstandings as team size increases.

Use agile methodologies: Emphasize iterative development and incremental progress to adjust quickly to challenges without relying on adding more resources.

Common Misconceptions and Pitfalls

- More people = faster progress: Believing that adding resources to a late project will accelerate completion, despite Brooks's Law stating the opposite.
- Overlooking communication overhead: Ignoring the fact that as team size grows, the complexity of coordination and communication increases significantly.
- Underestimating ramp-up time: Assuming new team members will immediately contribute at full capacity without accounting for onboarding and training delays.
- Neglecting team dynamics: Failing to recognize that adding more people can disrupt existing team chemistry and hinder collaboration.
- Ignoring project scope and planning: Relying on resource augmentation rather than addressing fundamental issues in project scope, planning, and management.

Related Concepts

1. Conway's Law: "Organizations which design systems are constrained to produce designs which are copies of the communication structures of these organizations." This highlights the impact of team structure and communication on software design, emphasizing that team size and organization affect the quality and complexity of the system.
2. Parkinson's Law: "Work expands to fill the time available for its completion." This law suggests that tasks will grow in complexity or time consumption to match the allocated schedule, similar to how project timelines can stretch as more people are added, which may further delay completion.

3. The Mythical Man-Month Principle: Closely tied to Brooks's Law, this principle explains that software development cannot be easily divided into discrete, parallel tasks, and adding more people does not linearly decrease the time required for completion.
4. Little's Law: "The average number of items in a system equals the arrival rate multiplied by the time an item spends in the system." In software development, this emphasizes the importance of managing work-in-progress (WIP) and minimizing bottlenecks, rather than relying on additional resources to speed up delivery.
5. The Law of Diminishing Returns: This principle states that after a certain point, adding more resources (such as personnel) leads to progressively smaller gains in output. In software projects, this applies when more developers are added but the productivity gains are insufficient to offset the coordination costs.

References

- Wikipedia, *Brooks's law*, [pub: 10 Jul 2024, cited: 3 Jan 2025]

Bus Factor: Measures how many key people need to be unavailable before a project is at risk.

Definition and Origin

The Bus Factor is a measure of the risk to a project or organization if key individuals were suddenly unavailable, for example, due to an accident (hence the "bus" metaphor). It refers to the number of people who would need to be incapacitated before the project or team would be seriously hindered or unable to function effectively. A low bus factor indicates a high risk, as too much knowledge or responsibility is concentrated in too few people.

Context and Importance

In the context of software development and technology, the Bus Factor refers to the degree of risk associated with the loss of key team members, particularly those holding critical knowledge about a project or its infrastructure. In many software projects, especially smaller teams or startups, a handful of developers may hold disproportionate amounts of technical expertise, whether in core codebases, system architecture, or proprietary tools. If one of these individuals were to suddenly become unavailable—whether due to illness, departure, or other unforeseen circumstances—the project could face significant setbacks or even become unsustainable. This is particularly concerning in technology companies where continuous development, maintenance, and innovation are vital for staying competitive.

The importance of the Bus Factor in software and technology cannot be overstated. A low Bus Factor (i.e., a project relying heavily on one or two people for key decisions or knowledge) introduces a serious risk to a project's long-term success. It can lead to bottlenecks, delays, and potentially even project failure if those individuals are unavailable. To mitigate this, teams are encouraged to build more collaborative environments where knowledge is shared, documentation is comprehensive, and expertise is distributed across multiple members. Higher Bus Factors reduce dependency on any single individual and help ensure the resilience and sustainability of the project, as well as the ability to continue operations even in the face of unexpected changes.

Best Practices and Guidelines

Promote Knowledge Sharing: Ensure team members regularly share knowledge through documentation, code reviews, and collaborative discussions to avoid knowledge silos.

Cross-Training: Encourage team members to learn and contribute to different parts of the project, reducing dependency on any single individual.

Create Comprehensive Documentation: Maintain clear, up-to-date documentation for critical systems and processes to make onboarding easier and mitigate the impact of key personnel departures.

Distribute Key Responsibilities: Avoid concentrating critical tasks or decision-making power in one or two individuals; spread responsibilities across the team.

Foster a Mentorship Culture: Encourage senior developers to mentor junior team members to ensure skills and knowledge are passed on within the team.

Common Misconceptions and Pitfalls

- Assuming One Expert is Enough: Relying on a single person for specialized knowledge without considering the risks of their absence can lead to critical bottlenecks.
- Overestimating Documentation as a Fix: While documentation is vital, it can't fully replace hands-on experience and collaboration, especially for complex systems or codebases.
- Assuming Bus Factor Doesn't Apply to Small Teams: Even in small teams, the loss of a key member can severely disrupt development, especially if that person holds essential, undocumented knowledge.
- Neglecting Non-Technical Roles: The Bus Factor is often thought of in technical terms, but key roles like project managers or product owners can also create vulnerabilities.
- Ignoring the Importance of Redundancy: Simply distributing knowledge across the team is not enough; cross-training and building redundancy in key roles are crucial to maintaining project continuity.

Related Concepts

1. Brooks' Law (The Mythical Man-Month)
2. "Adding manpower to a late software project makes it later."
3. This law underscores the importance of proper planning and knowledge distribution. It aligns with the Bus Factor by emphasizing that relying too much on a small group of experts can delay progress if those individuals are unavailable.
4. Conway's Law
5. "Organizations which design systems are constrained to produce designs which are copies of the communication structures of these organizations."
6. Conway's Law highlights the importance of how organizational structure and knowledge-sharing practices affect system architecture. A low Bus Factor often reflects poor communication and siloed knowledge within a team.
7. The Pareto Principle (80/20 Rule)
8. "80% of the effects come from 20% of the causes."

9. In the context of Bus Factor, this principle suggests that a small percentage of the team may hold a disproportionate amount of knowledge, making the project vulnerable if those individuals are unavailable. Balancing this distribution is critical.
10. The Law of Demeter (Principle of Least Knowledge)
11. "Only talk to your immediate friends."
12. This principle promotes reducing dependencies between modules or components, which can help mitigate Bus Factor risks. When teams follow this principle, individual knowledge is less likely to become a single point of failure.
13. The Principle of Redundancy
14. "Redundancy is the key to reliability."
15. In software, this principle emphasizes building redundant systems and processes to ensure continued operation in case of failure. A higher Bus Factor can be seen as a lack of redundancy in knowledge or expertise, increasing the risk of failure if key individuals are absent.

References

- Wikipedia, *Bus factor*, [pub: 3 Jan 2025, cited: 3 Jan 2025]

Conway's Law: Organizations design systems that mirror their communication structure

---

Definition and Origin

Conway's Law states, "Organizations which design systems are constrained to produce designs which are copies of the communication structures of these organizations.". In other words, the way teams are organized and communicate internally influences the design and architecture of the systems they create. If teams are siloed or fragmented, the resulting systems are likely to have similar fragmentation.

Conway's Law was coined by computer scientist Melvin Conway in 1968. He first introduced the idea in a paper titled "How Do Committees Invent?" where he observed that the structure of an organization often shapes the design of its software systems.

Context and Importance

Conway's Law holds significant relevance in the software and technology industries, where complex systems are often built by teams working in various specialized areas. The law highlights that the communication patterns and organizational structures within a company influence the design of its software. For example, if an organization is divided into multiple departments—such as front-end, back-end, and database teams—its software architecture is likely to reflect these silos, with distinct boundaries or interfaces between system components. This can lead to challenges in integration, maintenance, and scalability, as the system mirrors the disjointed communication and collaboration between teams.

The importance of Conway's Law in modern software development has only grown with the rise of agile methodologies, microservices, and distributed teams. As organizations adopt more flexible, decentralized structures to improve speed and innovation, the architecture of their software tends to evolve in ways that mirror these changes. For instance, an organization with a strong DevOps culture, where development and operations work closely together, is likely to produce systems that are more integrated, automated, and resilient. By understanding Conway's Law, companies can make more informed decisions about team structures and communication strategies to design systems that are both efficient and scalable, ultimately ensuring that organizational changes align with their technological goals.

Best Practices and Guidelines

Align Teams with System Components: Structure teams around key system components (e.g., front-end, back-end, database) to foster clearer ownership and efficient communication.

Promote Cross-Functional Collaboration: Encourage cross-functional teams (e.g., DevOps, product, and QA) to ensure cohesive, integrated system design and faster delivery.

Avoid Siloing: Minimize organizational silos that can lead to fragmented software architecture; encourage open communication across teams.

Iterate on Team Structures: Regularly reassess team structures and workflows to ensure alignment with evolving system architectures and business needs.

Leverage Microservices for Scalability: Use microservices or modular architectures to better align with decentralized, agile team structures and improve system flexibility.

Common Misconceptions and Pitfalls

- Misconception: Conway's Law is always deterministic: It's not inevitable that organizational structure directly dictates system architecture—other factors like technical constraints or leadership decisions also play a role.
- Pitfall: Overemphasizing team structure without cultural change: Simply reorganizing teams won't solve systemic issues unless communication practices and collaboration norms are also addressed.
- Misconception: Conway's Law only applies to large organizations: The law applies to all organizations, regardless of size, and can influence both small startups and large enterprises.
- Pitfall: Assuming that siloed teams are inherently bad: While silos can lead to fragmentation, they may be necessary for certain use cases (e.g., specialized expertise in critical areas), so context matters.
- Misconception: Microservices automatically solve Conway's Law: Adopting microservices architecture doesn't automatically lead to better communication or alignment; the organizational structure still needs to support decentralized collaboration.

Related Concepts

1. Brook's Law: "Adding manpower to a late software project makes it later."
2. This principle highlights how adding more resources (especially without proper organization) can lead to increased complexity and delays, aligning with Conway's Law by emphasizing the importance of effective team communication and structure.
3. Lehmans' Laws of Software Evolution: "A program that is used in a real-world environment must be continually adapted or it becomes progressively less useful."

4. This law underscores how the evolution of both software and its organizational context must be managed together, as organizational structures impact how easily software can evolve and adapt.
5. The Second System Effect (Brooks): "The second system is the most dangerous system a developer will ever design."
6. This concept points to the risk of overcomplicating software when attempting to improve upon the first system, often as a result of adding more layers of coordination or structure without understanding the consequences, which can mirror flaws in organizational design.
7. Putt's Law: "Software is like entropy: It tends to increase, unless acted upon by an outside force."
8. Like Conway's Law, this principle suggests that complexity in software naturally increases over time, often mirroring the structural complexities or inefficiencies within the organization responsible for it.
9. The Law of Leaky Abstractions (Joel Spolsky): "All non-trivial abstractions, to some degree, are leaky."
10. This law asserts that the higher-level abstractions in software often leak implementation details, which can be influenced by internal communication and organizational practices. Poor organizational design or siloed teams can exacerbate these leaks, leading to system architectures that are harder to manage and scale.

References

- Wikipedia, *Conway's law*, [pub: 12 Oct 2024, cited: 3 Jan 2025]

Dunbar's Number: cognitive limit to the number of people with whom one can maintain stable social relationships

---

Definition and Origin

Dunbar's Number is the theoretical limit to the number of stable social relationships an individual can maintain, typically around 150. This concept, proposed by anthropologist Robin Dunbar, suggests that humans can only comfortably interact with and maintain close ties to a group of this size, beyond which social cohesion and meaningful relationships may diminish.

Dunbar's Number was coined by British anthropologist Robin Dunbar. He proposed the concept in the early 1990s based on his research into primate brain size and social group dynamics, which suggested that humans can maintain stable social relationships with a maximum of around 150 people.

Context and Importance

In the context of software and technology, Dunbar's Number offers valuable insight into the dynamics of online communities, social networks, and organizational structures. As platforms like Facebook, Twitter, and LinkedIn facilitate vast networks of connections, the concept of Dunbar's Number suggests that while these platforms allow individuals to expand their reach to thousands or even millions of people, they may struggle to maintain the depth of relationship and meaningful engagement beyond a certain point. This limitation has led to the emergence of specialized platforms and tools designed to create smaller, more manageable social groups where genuine relationships can flourish—such as private messaging apps, niche communities, and professional networks focused on high-quality interaction.

For software developers and tech companies, understanding Dunbar's Number is crucial for fostering collaboration and innovation within teams. In large organizations, the number of people that can effectively communicate and work together without fracturing into silos is likely to be constrained by this cognitive limit. Tech companies often seek to design systems, platforms, and communication strategies that maximize the potential for effective, close-knit teamwork. This is why many organizations adopt "small team" models and encourage collaborative environments, often organizing groups into smaller units of 10-15 people. Ultimately, Dunbar's Number helps inform how digital and organizational structures can be designed to optimize both individual connections and collective productivity.

Best Practices and Guidelines

Limit team sizes: Organize development teams and departments to maintain smaller, cohesive groups (typically 5-15 people) to enhance communication, trust, and collaboration.

Foster meaningful engagement: In social platforms or networks, prioritize features that support deeper connections (e.g., messaging, groups) rather than merely expanding the number of contacts.

Leverage subgroups: For larger organizations or online communities, create smaller sub-teams or micro-communities within the broader network to maintain effective interaction and focus.

Design scalable communication tools: Build tools that facilitate seamless communication within smaller groups, while ensuring larger-scale communication can be managed effectively.

Encourage personal relationships: In remote or distributed teams, invest in tools and practices that help individuals connect on a personal level to strengthen social bonds within the limit of Dunbar's Number.

Common Misconceptions and Pitfalls

- More connections equal better networks: A common misconception is that expanding connections beyond 150 leads to stronger social networks. Maintaining meaningful relationships becomes harder as the group size increases.
- Dunbar's Number is rigid: Some believe the number 150 is a strict limit, but it can vary depending on the individual's social capacity, context, or the nature of the relationships (e.g., work vs. personal).
- Technology eliminates the limit: People often assume that digital tools and social platforms can bypass Dunbar's Number. While technology can extend reach, it doesn't necessarily increase the depth or quality of relationships.
- Larger teams are more productive: It's a pitfall to think that scaling teams indefinitely will lead to greater productivity. Larger teams can struggle with communication and coordination, diluting effectiveness.
- Dunbar's Number applies universally: The idea is often applied too broadly; the actual limit may differ depending on cultural, organizational, or personal factors. What works for one person or group may not apply to others.

Related Concepts

1. Brooks' Law (The Mythical Man-Month) "Adding manpower to a late software project makes it later." This law highlights the diminishing returns of scaling a team beyond an optimal size, similar to Dunbar's Number. As teams grow, communication complexity increases, reducing overall efficiency.
2. Conway's Law "Organizations which design systems are constrained to produce designs which are copies of the communication structures of these organizations." Just as Dunbar's Number limits the number of stable relationships an individual can maintain, Conway's Law suggests that the structure of a team or organization directly influences the structure of its software systems, often limiting scalability and flexibility.
3. The 2-Pizza Rule Coined by Amazon's Jeff Bezos, this rule states that a team should be small enough to be fed by two pizzas. This is in line with Dunbar's Number, emphasizing the value of smaller teams for effective communication and collaboration.
4. The Law of Diminishing Returns This principle suggests that as you increase the number of contributors to a project, the marginal benefit of each additional contributor decreases. As team sizes grow beyond an optimal threshold (such as the 150-person limit), the effectiveness of each new participant often decreases due to communication overhead.
5. The 10x Developer Principle While controversial, this principle posits that a small number of highly skilled developers can have an outsized impact on a project. This aligns with the idea that smaller, well-managed teams (in line with Dunbar's Number) can often outperform larger teams due to more effective communication and coordination.

References

- Wikipedia, *Dunbar's number*, [pub: 29 Dec 2024, cited: 3 Jan 2025]

Gustafson's Law: Suggests that for large problems, increasing the number of processors can yield near-linear speedup

---

Definition and Origin

Gustafson's Law is a principle in parallel computing that suggests the speedup of a program using multiple processors is limited more by the size of the problem being solved than by the number of processors. Specifically, as the problem size increases, the potential for parallelism also increases, allowing for better scalability. Unlike Amdahl's Law, which focuses on the fixed portion of the task, Gustafson's Law emphasizes that larger problems can benefit more from parallelization as resources (processors) grow.

Gustafson's Law was coined by John L. Gustafson in 1988. He proposed the law as an alternative to Amdahl's Law, offering a more optimistic perspective on the scalability of parallel computing systems. Gustafson's Law emphasizes that, as problem size increases, the potential for parallelism grows, allowing for better performance with more processors.

Context and Importance

Gustafson's Law emerged as a critical concept in parallel computing during a time when Amdahl's Law, which highlights the diminishing returns of parallelism for fixed problem sizes, was seen as a limiting factor in the adoption of multi-core and parallel processors. Amdahl's Law suggested that the speedup achieved by using multiple processors is constrained by the portion of the task that must be executed sequentially. However, Gustafson's Law presented a more optimistic outlook, arguing that by scaling the problem size proportionally with the number of processors, the overall performance could improve significantly. This shift in perspective has been particularly important as modern computing systems have evolved to include multi-core processors and large-scale distributed systems, which can leverage parallelism more effectively as tasks become more complex and data intensive.

In the context of software and technology, Gustafson's Law has provided valuable insights into the potential for scaling performance in real-world applications. As software developers increasingly face problems that require handling massive amounts of data—such as big data analytics, machine learning, and simulations—Gustafson's Law supports the idea that increasing the size of the problem can lead to better performance with parallel systems. This has implications for optimizing software architectures, cloud computing platforms, and high-performance computing systems. By recognizing that the ability to solve larger problems with parallelism can lead to exponential benefits, developers and engineers can design systems that are more efficient, scalable, and capable of meeting the growing computational demands of modern applications.

Best Practices and Guidelines

Scale problem size with resources: To maximize performance gains, increase the problem size proportionally with the number of processors or cores available, as larger tasks allow for more parallelism.

Optimize parallelism in large tasks: Design applications and algorithms with the assumption that problem size will grow, enabling better scalability and efficiency as computational resources expand.

Avoid bottlenecks in sequential portions: Minimize or eliminate parts of the task that must be executed sequentially to ensure that parallel portions dominate in large-scale problems.

Leverage distributed systems: In cloud or grid computing, take advantage of Gustafson's Law by distributing larger workloads across multiple machines, improving performance without hitting the limitations of sequential tasks.

Balance memory and compute demands: Ensure that both memory bandwidth and processing power scale effectively to handle the increased data size in parallel processing environments.

Common Misconceptions and Pitfalls

- Misunderstanding scalability limits: Believing that Gustafson's Law guarantees infinite scalability with more processors—while it provides better scaling than Amdahl's Law, it still faces practical limits due to hardware, communication overhead, and other system bottlenecks.
- Assuming linear performance gains: Mistaking the law's suggestion of increased scalability for a guarantee of linear speedup as more processors are added. Real-world performance improvements may be slower due to overhead, synchronization issues, and diminishing returns at higher processor counts.
- Ignoring sequential task overhead: Overlooking the impact of non-parallelizable portions of the code. Even though Gustafson's Law focuses on larger problems, the sequential tasks can still limit performance gains, especially in applications with significant serial dependencies.
- Underestimating resource contention: Failing to account for resource contention (e.g., memory bandwidth, cache, network) as the number of processors increases, which can reduce the expected performance improvements.
- Overfocusing on problem size: Misinterpreting Gustafson's Law to mean that simply increasing the problem size always leads to better performance, while neglecting the importance of efficient parallel algorithm design and optimization.

Related Concepts

1. Amdahl's Law: Amdahl's Law describes the theoretical speedup of a program as a function of the proportion of the program that can be parallelized. It suggests diminishing returns as the number of processors increases, emphasizing the importance of reducing the sequential portion of the task. Gustafson's Law provides an alternative by focusing on scaling problem size rather than parallelizing a fixed workload.
2. Amdahl's Law for Parallel Speedup: This variant of Amdahl's Law focuses specifically on how the overall speedup of a system is constrained by the non-parallelizable part of the computation. While Gustafson's Law asserts that larger problem sizes benefit more from parallelism, Amdahl's Law is critical for understanding limits in systems where the problem size is fixed.

3. Moore's Law: Moore's Law predicts that the number of transistors on a chip doubles approximately every two years, leading to exponential improvements in computing power. While not directly about parallelism, Moore's Law sets the stage for increasing computational resources, making it easier to apply Gustafson's Law and take advantage of scalable parallel systems.
4. Flynn's Taxonomy: Flynn's Taxonomy classifies computer architectures based on the number of instruction streams and data streams they can handle. It includes Single Instruction stream Multiple Data stream (SIMD) and Multiple Instruction stream Multiple Data stream (MIMD) systems, which are critical in understanding how different computing architectures scale, directly affecting the potential benefits outlined in Gustafson's Law.
5. Strong Scaling vs. Weak Scaling: These two concepts are crucial for understanding parallel performance. Strong scaling refers to improving execution time for a fixed problem size as processors increase, whereas weak scaling involves increasing both problem size and processors proportionally. Gustafson's Law aligns with weak scaling, suggesting that performance improves significantly when both problem size and parallel resources scale together.

References

- Wikipedia, *Gustafson's law*, [pub: 5 Dec 2024, cited: 3 Jan 2025]

Little's Law: Average items in queue equals arrival rate times waiting time

---

Definition and Origin

Little's Law is a fundamental theorem in queuing theory that relates the average number of items in a system (L), the average arrival rate of items (λ), and the average time an item spends in the system (W). It is expressed as:

$$L = \lambda * W$$

Where:

- L is the average number of items in the system.
- λ is the average arrival rate of items.
- W is the average time an item spends in the system.

Little's Law assumes a stable system and is used to understand and optimize processes like waiting lines, inventory management, and service systems.

Little's Law was formulated by John D. C. Little, an American mathematician and operations researcher, in the mid-1950s. Little published the law in 1961 in a paper titled "A Proof of the Queuing Formula L = λW", which formalized the relationship between the average number of items in a system, the arrival rate, and the average time spent in the system. This foundational result has since become widely used in fields such as operations management, manufacturing, and computer science.

Context and Importance

In the context of software and technology, Little's Law provides a powerful tool for managing and optimizing system performance, particularly in areas like software development, operations, and IT infrastructure. For instance, in software development, the law can be applied to measure and control workflow in Agile or DevOps environments. By understanding how the number of work items (features, tasks, bugs, etc.) in progress (L) relates to the rate at which work is completed (λ) and the time it takes to complete each work item (W), teams can better forecast project timelines, optimize their processes, and avoid bottlenecks. This insight can help engineers and managers make data-driven decisions on how to balance workload, prioritize tasks, and improve efficiency across the software lifecycle.

Moreover, Little’s Law is crucial in system performance analysis, particularly in managing traffic and load in software services, cloud systems, or web applications. For example, in a distributed computing environment, Little’s Law helps estimate the relationship between the number of requests in the system, the rate at which they are processed, and the time they take to be handled. Understanding this relationship allows software architects to optimize scalability, design for fault tolerance, and ensure minimal latency. In microservices architectures, where many independent services interact, Little's Law aids in anticipating and resolving performance issues by providing insights into capacity planning and resource allocation, thus improving overall user experience and system reliability.

Best Practices and Guidelines

Balance Work in Progress (WIP): Limit the number of tasks or requests in progress to optimize throughput and reduce bottlenecks, improving efficiency and reducing cycle times.

Measure and Optimize Flow: Regularly track the rate of work completion (λ) and average processing time (W) to identify opportunities for performance improvements.

Forecast and Prioritize: Use Little’s Law to predict project timelines and allocate resources effectively by understanding how task volume and completion rates affect delivery time.

Monitor System Capacity: Apply Little’s Law to manage system load and ensure servers, APIs, and microservices are scaled appropriately to handle traffic without causing delays.

Iterate and Improve: Continuously refine processes based on data from Little’s Law to streamline workflows, reduce wait times, and maintain high system reliability.

Common Misconceptions and Pitfalls

- Assumes Stable Systems: Little's Law assumes a stable, steady-state system, so it may not apply accurately during periods of high variability or system instability.

- Ignores System Complexity: It oversimplifies real-world systems by assuming linear relationships between variables, which may not account for complex dependencies or resource contention.
- Misinterpretation of Units: Failing to ensure consistent units (e.g., tasks per hour, minutes, etc.) for arrival rates, processing times, and queue lengths can lead to incorrect calculations.
- Overlooking External Factors: Little's Law doesn't account for external influences like sudden spikes in demand or resource limitations that can disrupt the flow and affect the relationship.
- Excessive Focus on Optimizing One Variable: Focusing too narrowly on reducing cycle time (W) or increasing throughput (λ) without considering system-wide trade-offs can lead to suboptimal results and overburdened resources.

Related Concepts

1. Amdahl's Law: Focuses on the potential speedup of a system when improving a specific part of the system. It emphasizes that improvements to a portion of a system with a fixed bottleneck can only provide limited overall performance gains, highlighting the importance of addressing system-wide constraints.
2. Brooks' Law: States that "adding manpower to a late software project makes it later." This principle parallels Little's Law by illustrating that simply increasing resources (throughput) in a system can often lead to inefficiencies and delays due to coordination overhead, emphasizing the importance of optimizing existing workflows.
3. Queuing Theory (General): Little's Law is a subset of queuing theory, which examines how queues (waiting lines) behave in systems. Applying general queuing principles can help understand and predict delays in software systems, particularly in environments like cloud computing or web services.
4. The Mythical Man-Month: Coined by Fred Brooks, this principle suggests that software projects don't scale linearly with the number of people working on them, similar to how Little's Law emphasizes the relationship between system capacity and performance. It underscores the complexity of increasing throughput (λ) in development environments.

5. Law of Conservation of Complexity: This principle suggests that complexity in a system tends to remain constant, regardless of how much effort is put into managing it. While Little's Law helps manage flow and performance, this law reminds us that increasing system efficiency may only shift the complexity elsewhere, rather than eliminate it entirely.

References

- Wikipedia, *Little's law*, [pub: 1 Sep 2024, cited: 3 Jan 2025]

Theory of Constraints

Definition and Origin

The Theory of Constraints (TOC) is a management philosophy that focuses on identifying and addressing the single most limiting factor (constraint) that prevents an organization from achieving its goals. By optimizing and systematically improving this constraint, the overall performance and efficiency of the system can be enhanced. TOC emphasizes continuous improvement and prioritizing efforts to remove bottlenecks in processes.

The Theory of Constraints (TOC) was developed by Dr. Eliyahu M. Goldratt, an Israeli business management expert. He introduced the concept in his 1984 book The Goal, which presented TOC through a fictional narrative about improving manufacturing processes. Goldratt's work revolutionized the way organizations approach problem-solving and process improvement.

Context and Importance

In the context of software development and technology, the Theory of Constraints (TOC) offers a valuable framework for improving operational efficiency by focusing on the bottlenecks that impede the flow of work. In software development, bottlenecks often emerge in areas such as code reviews, testing, deployment, or communication between cross-functional teams. Identifying and addressing these constraints helps teams optimize their processes, reduce delays, and deliver features or products faster without compromising quality. By continuously improving the constraint, development teams can enhance their throughput and reduce cycle times, aligning their processes with business goals more effectively. TOC encourages a shift from merely optimizing individual tasks to improving the overall system flow, ensuring smoother, more predictable delivery.

The importance of TOC in software and technology extends beyond just process improvement—it fosters a culture of continuous learning and adaptation. Technology organizations often deal with complex systems and fast-changing requirements, where new constraints can emerge as quickly as old ones are mitigated. By adopting the principles of TOC, teams can become more agile, responding to challenges in real-time. This approach also aligns with modern software methodologies, like Agile and DevOps, which emphasize iterative improvement and rapid feedback loops. Ultimately, TOC helps technology organizations focus on what matters most, ensuring that limited resources—whether human, technological, or financial—are directed toward the areas that will yield the greatest impact on overall performance.

Best Practices and Guidelines

Identify the Primary Constraint: Focus on the single most limiting factor in the software development process, such as bottlenecks in code review, testing, or deployment.

Optimize the Constraint: Prioritize improvements and resources to address the identified constraint, ensuring maximum throughput across the entire system.

Subordinate Everything Else: Align all other processes to support the optimization of the constraint, avoiding local optimizations that don't contribute to the overall flow.

Elevate the Constraint: If possible, increase the capacity of the constraint (e.g., adding resources or tools) to further enhance system performance.

Continuously Review and Improve: Regularly reassess and identify new constraints as the system evolves, fostering a culture of ongoing improvement.

Common Misconceptions and Pitfalls

- Focusing on Local Optimization: Trying to improve individual components or processes without considering the overall system can worsen performance, as it may shift bottlenecks elsewhere.
- Misidentifying the Constraint: Incorrectly diagnosing the real bottleneck can lead to wasted efforts on areas that do not significantly impact system throughput.
- Overlooking Human or Communication Constraints: Many organizations focus solely on technical constraints (e.g., servers, tools) and neglect human factors like team collaboration or communication bottlenecks.
- Assuming One-Time Fix: Treating the constraint as a one-off problem to be solved permanently rather than an ongoing challenge can hinder continuous improvement.
- Neglecting Systemic Impact: Changes to a constraint can introduce new bottlenecks or issues elsewhere, requiring a holistic view of the entire process rather than isolated improvements.

Related Concepts

1. Brook's Law (The Mythical Man-Month): "Adding manpower to a late software project makes it later." This principle emphasizes that simply adding resources to solve a bottleneck without addressing the underlying constraint can exacerbate inefficiencies, much like TOC highlights the need to focus on the actual constraint.
2. Little's Law: "Work-in-Progress (WIP) = Throughput × Cycle Time." This law emphasizes the relationship between the flow of work, its completion time, and the amount of work in progress. TOC encourages limiting WIP to ensure faster delivery and prevent bottlenecks from accumulating.

3. Conway's Law: "Organizations design systems that mirror their communication structure." This highlights that process bottlenecks in software development often stem from communication constraints between teams or departments, aligning with TOC's focus on removing organizational bottlenecks.
4. Pareto Principle (80/20 Rule): Often used in TOC, this principle asserts that roughly 80% of effects come from 20% of causes. In software, this means that a small number of constraints often limit system performance or productivity and focusing on those few can drive the greatest improvements.
5. The Law of Constraints in Agile: Agile methodologies often emphasize the flow of value through the system, which aligns with TOC's focus on identifying and managing the bottleneck. The principle of continuous improvement in Agile complements TOC by ensuring that constraints are systematically identified and addressed over time.

References

- Wikipedia, *Theory of constraints*, [pub: 7 Dec 2024, cited: 3 Jan 2025]

Two Pizza Rule: Team should be small enough that it can be fed with two pizzas

---

Definition and Origin

The Two Pizza Rule is a principle in team management that suggests a team should be small enough that it can be fed with two pizzas. The idea is that a team should consist of around 6-8 people, ensuring it's large enough for diverse skills but small enough to remain agile and communicate effectively.

The Two Pizza Rule was coined by Jeff Bezos, the founder of Amazon. He introduced the idea of promoting small, efficient teams that could remain agile and communicate easily, avoiding the inefficiencies of larger groups. The rule emphasizes the importance of keeping teams manageable and collaborative.

Context and Importance

The Two Pizza Rule is particularly important in the context of software development and technology teams, where agility, collaboration, and speed are crucial. In large-scale software projects, larger teams often face coordination issues, miscommunication, and delays due to the complexity of aligning many individuals across different roles. The rule advocates for smaller, more focused teams—ideally around 6 to 8 people—that can make decisions quickly, communicate effectively, and iterate faster. In software development, this is vital, as it allows for a more streamlined approach to problem-solving, faster prototyping, and a more efficient feedback loop. Smaller teams are also better positioned to adopt agile methodologies, which emphasize adaptability and rapid delivery, making the Two Pizza Rule an ideal fit for technology-driven environments.

Moreover, as technology teams grow, there's often a tendency for silos to form, creating barriers to effective communication and innovation. The Two Pizza Rule helps mitigate this by ensuring that team members are close enough to each other in both physical and conceptual space to maintain a high level of collaboration and alignment. It fosters a culture where each member's input is valued, and the team can move quickly to address challenges or pivot as necessary. In a rapidly evolving field like technology, this level of nimbleness is crucial, especially for companies that need to adapt quickly to changing market demands or customer needs. Therefore, by maintaining smaller, cross-functional teams, companies can stay more agile, reduce overhead, and foster an environment of continuous innovation.

Best Practices and Guidelines

Limit team size: Keep teams to 6-8 members to enhance communication, decision-making, and agility.

Promote cross-functional roles: Ensure team members have diverse skills to handle multiple aspects of development (coding, testing, design, etc.).

Foster direct communication: Avoid hierarchy and silos; prioritize open, face-to-face communication for faster problem-solving.

Encourage autonomy: Empower teams to make decisions independently without needing excessive approvals or coordination.

Adapt quickly: Maintain flexibility to pivot or iterate rapidly, leveraging small team structure to stay responsive to changes or feedback.

Common Misconceptions and Pitfalls

- Smaller teams are always more efficient: Not every team or project benefits from a small size; some tasks require more diverse expertise or resources than a small team can handle.
- Size alone guarantees success: The Two Pizza Rule emphasizes team size, but factors like leadership, team culture, and clarity of goals are equally important for success.
- All team members must be generalists: A small team doesn't mean everyone should wear every hat—specialized skills are still needed for complex tasks.
- Increased team size equals inefficiency: While large teams can create communication challenges, small teams can still suffer from lack of bandwidth or burnout if tasks are too complex or demanding.
- Avoiding larger teams leads to scalability issues: A small team may be effective in the short term, but scaling requires careful management of both team size and resources.

Related Concepts

1. Brook's Law (The Mythical Man-Month): Adding more people to a late software project makes it later. This law reinforces the idea that increasing team size can lead to inefficiencies, such as communication overhead and coordination complexity, which aligns with the Two Pizza Rule's emphasis on keeping teams small and manageable.
2. Conway's Law: Organizations design systems that mirror their communication structures. Smaller teams with simpler communication pathways tend to create more efficient, well-structured software. The Two Pizza Rule encourages such team structures to optimize collaboration and system design.
3. Law of the Instrument (Maslow's Hammer): If you only have a hammer, everything looks like a nail. In the context of small teams, this principle suggests that small, agile teams need to use the tools and methods best suited for their size—like lightweight frameworks and flexible architectures. Large teams may lack the speed and focus required for innovation in technology.

4. Pareto Principle (80/20 Rule): 80% of results come from 20% of the effort. Smaller teams are often more efficient at applying focused effort on high-impact tasks. By keeping teams small, you can ensure that resources are used optimally to achieve the majority of desired outcomes.
5. The 10x Engineer: Some engineers are far more productive than others, often by an order of magnitude. The Two Pizza Rule recognizes that high-performing individuals can achieve more with fewer resources. Smaller teams allow for more autonomy and faster decision-making, allowing "10x" engineers to shine and drive the project forward more efficiently.

References

- Amazon, *Two pizza teams*, [cited: 3 Jan 2025]

G. Management Principles

Cost of Delay: Quantifies the economic impact of delaying work, helping prioritize tasks based on their time-sensitive value.

Definition and Origin

Cost of Delay (CoD), as defined by Don Reinertsen, is the economic impact of delaying a project or decision. It quantifies the potential loss in value, revenue, or competitive advantage that results from not completing a task or initiative on time. CoD helps prioritize work by considering both the value of fast delivery and the cost incurred from postponing it, aiming to optimize decision-making and workflow efficiency.

The concept of Cost of Delay (CoD) is largely attributed to Don Reinertsen, who popularized it in his book "The Principles of Product Development Flow" (2009). Reinertsen applied it to product development and lean methodologies, arguing that the cost of delaying a decision, feature, or product launch is often higher than traditionally understood, and should be factored into prioritization and decision-making processes.

However, the broader idea of quantifying delays in terms of economic cost has roots in earlier work in economics, operations research, and production management, but it was Reinertsen who specifically framed it in the context of lean product development.

Context and Importance

In the context of software and technology, Cost of Delay (CoD), plays a critical role in decision-making and prioritization. In fast-paced environments like software development, where market conditions and customer demands can shift rapidly, delays in releasing features, updates, or products can lead to significant lost opportunities. CoD helps quantify these missed opportunities by illustrating the economic impact of postponing development efforts, such as delayed revenue, diminished customer satisfaction, or loss of competitive advantage. This makes CoD a powerful tool for aligning development teams with business goals, ensuring that the most valuable work is prioritized for the highest return on investment, and that features or initiatives that offer the greatest immediate value are not delayed unnecessarily.

The importance of CoD in software and technology is also tied to the nature of product iteration and time-to-market pressures. Unlike traditional manufacturing or static industries, technology products are subject to constant innovation cycles, and delays can directly affect user engagement, adoption, and retention. By considering the cost of delay, companies can shift from a mindset of "just-in-case" scheduling and resource allocation to one that values speed and responsiveness. This mindset fosters a more efficient workflow, encourages faster releases, and allows businesses to capitalize on opportunities quicker than competitors. Ultimately, embracing CoD enables software teams to make smarter trade-offs, balance risk, and focus on delivering the highest-value features without the costly consequences of delays.

Best Practices and Guidelines

Prioritize by Value, Not Effort: Use Cost of Delay to prioritize features or tasks based on their economic value, focusing on those that offer the highest return or customer impact if delivered sooner.

Quantify Delays: Estimate the tangible impact of delays, including lost revenue, market share, or customer satisfaction, to better understand the urgency and trade-offs.

Embrace Small Batches: Deliver smaller, more frequent releases to minimize delays and maximize feedback, reducing the Cost of Delay associated with large, slow releases.

Balance Flow and Risk: Manage work in progress (WIP) to reduce bottlenecks and delays while balancing the risk of feature overloading or focusing on too many parallel initiatives.

Decide Quickly: Accelerate decision-making to reduce the time spent in uncertainty, as delays in decisions can compound the Cost of Delay by prolonging critical development cycles.

Common Misconceptions and Pitfalls

- CoD is Only About Revenue: A common misconception is that Cost of Delay only applies to financial loss. It also includes factors like customer satisfaction, brand reputation, and competitive positioning.
- Focusing Solely on Urgency: Prioritizing tasks purely based on urgency can lead to suboptimal decisions. CoD should balance urgency with the potential value or impact of a task, not just speed.
- Assuming CoD Can Be Precisely Quantified: Some believe CoD can always be perfectly calculated, but it often involves estimates and approximations, especially in uncertain or rapidly changing environments.
- Overlooking the Hidden Costs of Delay: Many overlooks indirect delays, such as team morale, stakeholder frustration, or market shifts, which can amplify the true cost of waiting.
- Ignoring Long-Term Impact: Focusing too heavily on short-term costs can neglect the broader, long-term consequences of delays, such as lost strategic opportunities or innovation potential.

Related Concepts

1. Little's Law: Little's Law states that in any system with a stable flow, the average number of items in the system (Work in Progress, WIP) equals the average arrival rate of items multiplied by the average time an item spends in the system. In the context of CoD, it highlights the relationship between cycle time and the potential cost incurred due to delays—reducing WIP can decrease cycle time and, thus, the Cost of Delay.
2. The Iron Triangle (Scope, Time, Cost): This principle asserts that in project management, any change in one of the parameters (scope, time, or cost) will impact the other two. Cost of Delay can be used to measure the trade-offs between time and scope, helping teams decide whether reducing scope or extending time is more cost-effective in the face of delays.

3. The Law of Diminishing Returns: As more effort is invested into a feature or product, the incremental value of that additional effort decreases. This principle is crucial for understanding CoD, as it helps identify when further delays or efforts will produce less value or contribute more to overall cost than benefit, emphasizing the importance of timely delivery.
4. The 80/20 Rule (Pareto Principle): The Pareto Principle suggests that 80% of results come from 20% of the effort or features. When applying CoD, this principle helps prioritize the most valuable features or initiatives, allowing teams to focus on those that will deliver the most significant return in the shortest amount of time, reducing overall delay costs.
5. Flow Efficiency vs. Resource Efficiency: This principle distinguishes between optimizing the flow of work through the system and maximizing the utilization of individual resources. Cost of Delay encourages teams to focus on flow efficiency—reducing delays and bottlenecks—rather than overloading resources, which can increase delays and associated costs.

References

- Wikipedia, *Cost of delay*, [pub: 22 Nov 2023, cited: 3 Jan 2025]

The Dilbert Principle: Move incompetent employees to management positions

---

Definition and Origin

The Dilbert Principle is a satirical concept introduced by cartoonist Scott Adams in his Dilbert comic strip. It suggests that organizations tend to promote incompetent employees to management positions, where their inefficiency will not directly harm the company. The principle humorously highlights how organizations may reward mediocrity or avoid confronting inefficiencies by shifting underperforming workers into managerial roles.

Context and Importance

The Dilbert Principle is particularly relevant in the context of the software and technology industries, where rapid growth, innovation, and the complexity of managing large teams can sometimes lead to inefficiencies in organizational structures. In tech companies, skilled engineers or developers who excel at technical tasks are often promoted into management roles, despite lacking the leadership or management skills required. The result can be a mismatch of competencies, where technically gifted individuals struggle to oversee projects or teams effectively. This can lead to poor decision-making, slower development cycles, and increased frustration among developers who may feel their talents are being underutilized or misdirected.

Moreover, the Dilbert Principle highlights the challenges of hierarchical structures in tech companies, where individuals who are less capable at core tasks may find themselves advancing due to political maneuvering, seniority, or the inability to address performance issues directly. In software development, this can have serious consequences, as poor management can lead to inefficiencies like unclear project goals, scope creep, or ineffective communication across teams. The principle, therefore, serves as a reminder of the importance of aligning technical expertise with leadership roles and maintaining an organizational culture that prioritizes competency and performance over bureaucracy or hierarchy.

Best Practices and Guidelines

Promote based on leadership skills, not just technical expertise: Ensure that managers have the necessary soft skills, such as communication, team building, and decision-making, rather than promoting solely for technical ability.

Foster a merit-based culture: Reward performance and innovation at all levels, not just those in management, to prevent the rise of underperforming individuals into leadership roles.

Provide management training: Offer leadership development programs for technical staff to equip them with the skills required to manage teams effectively before promoting them to managerial positions.

Encourage peer feedback: Implement 360-degree reviews or regular team feedback to identify leadership strengths and weaknesses, reducing the likelihood of promoting ineffective managers.

Regularly reassess organizational structure: Continuously evaluate and adjust the management hierarchy to ensure it supports efficiency, accountability, and innovation rather than perpetuating ineffective leadership.

Common Misconceptions and Pitfalls

- Assuming all tech experts make good managers: Technical proficiency doesn't always translate to effective leadership; managerial roles require a different skill set, such as emotional intelligence and strategic thinking.
- Promoting to "solve" problems: Promoting underperforming employees to management in an attempt to move them out of critical roles can create more problems rather than solving them, leading to inefficiency and dissatisfaction.
- Overvaluing tenure: Promoting employees based on seniority rather than ability can lead to poor management, as long-term employees might not possess the skills needed to handle leadership responsibilities.
- Ignoring team dynamics: Promoting individuals without considering their ability to collaborate or manage diverse teams can harm morale and hinder performance.
- Perpetuating the cycle: Failing to address managerial incompetence can create a continuous cycle of ineffective leadership, which may result in high employee turnover and decreased productivity.

Related Concepts

1. Parkinson's Law: "Work expands to fill the time available for its completion." This law can be seen in many organizations, where inefficiencies in management or bureaucracy can lead to delays, as teams become bogged down by unnecessary tasks or poor decision-making by incompetent leaders.
2. The Peter Principle: "Employees tend to rise to their level of incompetence." Similar to the Dilbert Principle, the Peter Principle suggests that employees are often promoted until they are in a role where they can no longer perform effectively. In software development, this can result in technically skilled individuals being promoted to management without the necessary leadership skills.

3. Brooks' Law: "Adding manpower to a late software project makes it later." This principle highlights that increasing team size or management layers in an already struggling project can worsen the situation, especially when incompetence in leadership creates more confusion and inefficiencies.
4. The Law of the Instrument (Maslow's Hammer): "If all you have is a hammer, everything looks like a nail." In software, this can reflect how managers without a broad skill set may over-rely on a single method or tool, leading to poor decisions. Similarly, the Dilbert Principle suggests that promoting someone to management based on narrow expertise can limit their effectiveness in the role.
5. Conway's Law: "Organizations which design systems are constrained to produce designs which are copies of the communication structures of these organizations." This principle suggests that the inefficiencies or flaws in an organization's management structure (such as promoting incompetent employees into leadership) will often be reflected in the software systems they build, leading to poor-quality products or solutions.

References

- Wikipedia, *Dilbert principle*, [pub: 5 Aug 2023, cited: 3 Jan 2025]

Eisenhower Matrix: What is important is seldom urgent, and what is urgent is seldom important

---

Definition and Origin

The Eisenhower Matrix is a time management tool that helps prioritize tasks based on urgency and importance. It divides tasks into four quadrants:

- Quadrant I: Urgent and Important (Do it now) – Tasks to be done immediately.
- Quadrant II: Not Urgent but Important (Schedule it) – Tasks to schedule for later.
- Quadrant III: Urgent but Not Important (Delegate it) – Tasks to delegate if possible.

- Quadrant IV: Not Urgent and Not Important (Eliminate it) – Tasks to disregard or minimize.

This framework helps individuals focus on what truly matters while minimizing distractions.

The Eisenhower Matrix was popularized by Dwight D. Eisenhower, the 34th President of the United States, who used it to make decisions and prioritize tasks during his military career and presidency. While Eisenhower himself did not explicitly formalize the matrix, he is widely attributed with the concept because of his famous quote:

"What is important is seldom urgent, and what is urgent is seldom important."

Context and Importance

In the context of software development and technology management, the Eisenhower Matrix is an essential tool for managing the fast-paced, often chaotic nature of project tasks and deadlines. Developers and technology teams frequently juggle multiple priorities, ranging from urgent bug fixes to long-term feature development, infrastructure upgrades, and research. The Matrix helps software professionals focus on tasks that align with the project's core goals and broader organizational objectives. By using the matrix, teams can separate urgent issues (such as critical bugs) from important but non-urgent ones (like system optimizations or strategic features), ensuring that resources are allocated effectively to achieve the desired outcomes.

The importance of the Eisenhower Matrix in the tech field extends beyond individual task management; it also plays a key role in team productivity and project management. It aids in reducing burnout by preventing the overwhelming of developers with low-priority tasks and distractions that don't contribute to the long-term success of the product. With its clear delineation of tasks into four categories, teams can delegate less critical tasks to others or automate repetitive processes, allowing developers to focus on high-impact work. In fast-evolving technology environments, where adapting to change is key, the Eisenhower Matrix enables companies to make data-driven decisions, prioritize innovation, and avoid reactive firefighting—ultimately ensuring sustained productivity and alignment with strategic goals.

Best Practices and Guidelines

Prioritize critical bugs: Address urgent and important issues (e.g., system crashes or security vulnerabilities) immediately to prevent disruptions and maintain system integrity.

Schedule strategic improvements: Plan non-urgent but important tasks (e.g., refactoring code, adding new features) to ensure long-term product growth without neglecting core functionalities.

Delegate low-value tasks: Assign urgent, low-impact tasks (e.g., minor UI tweaks or routine maintenance) to other team members or automate where possible.

Eliminate distractions: Identify and avoid time-wasting activities that do not contribute to product goals or user experience (e.g., unnecessary meetings, redundant processes).

Regularly reassess priorities: Continuously evaluate and adjust tasks based on changing project needs, customer feedback, and emerging technologies to stay focused on high-value objectives.

Common Misconceptions and Pitfalls

- Equating urgency with importance: Many people assume urgent tasks are always important, leading to reactive work rather than strategic focus.
- Neglecting long-term planning: Focusing too heavily on urgent tasks can overshadow important but non-urgent work, like innovation or technical debt reduction, which impacts long-term success.
- Over-delegating: Delegating too many tasks, even those that are crucial, can result in loss of control or quality, especially in fast-moving tech projects.
- Lack of flexibility: Rigidly adhering to the matrix can lead to missed opportunities if priorities shift or new information arises.
- Misunderstanding "Eliminate" tasks: Not all tasks in the "Not Urgent, Not Important" quadrant should be eliminated; some might be useful for team morale or long-term experimentation.

Related Concepts

1. The Pareto Principle (80/20 Rule): Focus on the 20% of tasks (important and high impact) that will deliver 80% of the value. This complements the Eisenhower Matrix's emphasis on identifying high-priority, important tasks.
2. Law of the Instrument (Maslow's Hammer): The tendency to rely too heavily on a familiar tool or approach (e.g., solving every problem with code). The Eisenhower Matrix helps prevent this by encouraging teams to delegate or eliminate tasks that do not align with strategic goals, avoiding over-engineering or unnecessary complexity.
3. The Law of Leverage: In software, high-leverage tasks (such as building scalable infrastructure or automating testing) can have disproportionately large impacts on the project's success. The Eisenhower Matrix helps identify such high-leverage tasks and prioritize them accordingly.
4. YAGNI (You Aren't Gonna Need It): A principle that advises developers to avoid overbuilding features or solving problems that aren't immediate needs. The Matrix aids in focusing on what's urgent and important, helping prevent the trap of building unnecessary features that don't contribute to the current objectives.
5. The Principle of Least Astonishment: This principle advocates for minimizing surprises in both code and user experience. In the Eisenhower Matrix context, prioritizing important tasks helps ensure that the development process remains predictable and efficient, reducing the risk of unforeseen issues arising due to a lack of focus or planning.

References

- Wikipedia, *The Eisenhower Method*, [pub: 2 Jan 2025, cited: 3 Jan 2025]

Goodhart's Law: When measure becomes target, it ceases to be good measure

---

Definition and Origin

Goodhart's Law states: "When a measure becomes a target, it ceases to be a good measure." In other words, once a specific metric is used as the primary goal or incentive, people may manipulate or game the system in ways that make the metric less reliable or meaningful.

Goodhart's Law was coined by the British economist Charles Goodhart in 1975. He formulated the idea in the context of economic policy, particularly in relation to central banking and the use of monetary aggregates as targets for policy. Goodhart observed that once a policy target becomes the focus of decision-making, individuals and institutions would adjust their behavior in ways that undermine the reliability of the target itself.

Context and Importance

In the context of software and technology, Goodhart's Law highlights a critical challenge in metrics-driven development and performance evaluation. As companies rely on key performance indicators (KPIs), such as system uptime, user engagement, or code quality, these metrics can often become targets that development teams or automated systems optimize for, rather than actual outcomes. For example, if a development team is rewarded based on the number of features shipped, it might lead to rapid, shallow implementations rather than well-designed, sustainable solutions. Similarly, if user engagement is used as a measure of success, teams may resort to tactics like dark patterns or clickbait features that boost numbers temporarily but degrade user experience in the long term. In such cases, the very metrics intended to guide improvement can distort priorities and undermine overall objectives.

The importance of Goodhart's Law in the software and technology industries lies in its caution against over-reliance on narrow metrics without considering their broader impact. As software systems scale and complexity increases, focusing too much on specific targets can cause unintended consequences, such as technical debt, reduced quality, or unethical behavior. For instance, engineering teams might be optimized for speed or volume without adequately addressing maintainability or security. Understanding Goodhart's Law encourages companies to adopt more holistic and dynamic approaches to measuring success, incorporating a wider range of indicators that align with long-term value creation rather than short-term optimization. This perspective helps foster a balance between meeting immediate goals and sustaining ethical, sustainable growth in technology development.

Best Practices and Guidelines

Diversify Metrics: Use a combination of qualitative and quantitative metrics to avoid over-optimization of a single indicator.

Prioritize Long-Term Value: Focus on metrics that align with sustainable growth, such as system reliability and user satisfaction, rather than short-term gains.

Monitor Unintended Consequences: Regularly assess how metrics influence behavior and adjust them if they lead to counterproductive outcomes, like gaming the system.

Balance Speed and Quality: Ensure that targets like feature velocity don't undermine code quality, security, or maintainability.

Use Metrics as Guides, Not Targets: Treat metrics as indicators for improvement rather than rigid goals to hit, allowing for flexibility in achieving broader objectives.

Common Misconceptions and Pitfalls

- Over-Reliance on Quantitative Metrics: Believing that numerical targets alone can fully capture performance or success, without considering qualitative factors like user experience or team morale.
- Assuming Metrics Are Static: Treating metrics as fixed, without adapting them over time to reflect changing goals, technology, or business needs.
- Ignoring Context: Focusing on improving a single metric without understanding how changes might negatively impact other areas or the system as a whole.
- Short-Term Fixation: Prioritizing short-term improvements in metrics (e.g., speed, volume) at the expense of long-term value, innovation, or sustainability.
- Gamification of Metrics: Encouraging teams to "game" the system by optimizing for the metric itself, rather than addressing the underlying objectives the metric was meant to represent.

Related Concepts

1. Parkinson's Law: "Work expands to fill the time available for its completion." In the context of software, this suggests that if you set a target deadline for a project, the team may stretch the work to meet the deadline, potentially reducing efficiency or quality, similar to how Goodhart's Law highlights the distortion of targets.
2. Murphy's Law: "Anything that can go wrong will go wrong." In software development, this underscores the inevitability of failure or unexpected issues, highlighting the need for broad, adaptable metrics and planning rather than rigid targets that can be skewed or gamed, as seen in Goodhart's Law.
3. Hofstadter's Law: "It always takes longer than you expect, even when you take into account Hofstadter's Law." This reflects the unpredictability and complexity inherent in software projects, showing that focusing too narrowly on completion metrics without accounting for real-world complexity can lead to underperformance and misalignment with actual goals.
4. The Peter Principle: "Employees rise to the level of incompetence." In the context of software, this principle suggests that individuals may be promoted based on success in narrow, target-driven areas (e.g., hitting performance metrics) without having the necessary broader skills, leading to inefficiency or suboptimal results, as seen when Goodhart's Law distorts performance.
5. Conway's Law: "Organizations design systems that mirror their communication structure." In the context of Goodhart's Law, focusing too much on certain metrics can lead to organizational behavior that distorts product design or development processes, mirroring the priorities set by the metrics rather than the actual needs of the system or users.

References

- Wikipedia, *Goodhart's law*, [pub: 24 Dec 2024, cited: 3 Jan 2025]

Mythical Man-Month: You can't exchange time and people linearly

---

Definition and Origin

The Mythical Man-Month is a concept from software engineering, introduced by Fred Brooks in his book The Mythical Man-Month: Essays on Software Engineering (1975). It refers to the fallacy that adding more workers to a late software project will speed it up. In reality, increasing team size often leads to diminishing returns due to the added overhead in communication and coordination, making the project take longer or become more complicated. The term highlights the idea that "man-months" (a unit of work) are not interchangeable when it comes to complex tasks like software development.

Context and Importance

The concept of the Mythical Man-Month emerged from Fred Brooks' experiences managing the development of the IBM System/360 and its associated OS/360 software in the 1960s. During that time, Brooks and his team faced significant delays and challenges in delivering a complex system. In his book, he argued that software development is not like manufacturing, where additional labor can directly translate into faster output. Instead, software projects involve complex problem-solving, and the coordination overhead increases exponentially as the team size grows. Adding more developers to a project that is behind schedule leads to more communication, more management, and more integration work, which can further delay completion, rather than accelerate it. This insight has become a cornerstone of project management in the software and technology industries.

The importance of the Mythical Man-Month lies in its enduring relevance to modern software development and technology management. As software projects continue to grow in complexity, teams often face pressure to deliver quickly. The fallacy that adding more people can expedite delivery still persists, leading to overstaffed projects that struggle with inefficiency. Brooks' work emphasizes that quality and speed in software development are more closely tied to thoughtful design, clear communication, and well-managed teams rather than simply increasing headcount. His insights have influenced decades of software engineering practices, from agile methodologies to modern DevOps, encouraging more strategic approaches to team dynamics and project scope to avoid the pitfalls of the Mythical Man-Month.

Best Practices and Guidelines

Avoid Overstaffing: Adding more developers to a late project typically increases complexity and delays. Focus on efficient, well-coordinated teams instead.

Prioritize Communication: As team size grows, communication overhead skyrockets. Ensure clear, streamlined communication to maintain productivity.

Realistic Scheduling: Estimate timelines based on the complexity of the work, not just by scaling resources. More people do not guarantee faster delivery.

Small, Agile Teams: Opt for smaller, cross-functional teams that can work collaboratively and adapt quickly to changes.

Manage Expectations: Set realistic expectations for project timelines and scope, emphasizing quality and thoughtful design over speed or headcount.

Common Misconceptions and Pitfalls

- More People = Faster Delivery: The belief that increasing team size will speed up a project often leads to more coordination costs, not faster progress.
- Overloading Developers: Expecting a developer to complete more work in less time ("crunch mode") can reduce productivity and quality.
- Underestimating Complexity: Assuming that tasks are linear and can be split evenly among more people overlooks the inherent complexity of software development.
- Ignoring Knowledge Gaps: Adding new team members without considering onboarding or training can slow down the project as they need time to ramp up.
- Over-Reliance on Tools: Believing that better tools or technology alone will solve problems without addressing team dynamics and project management challenges.

Related Concepts

1. Brooks' Law: "Adding manpower to a late software project makes it later." This law, directly from Fred Brooks' book, captures the core idea that increasing team size on a delayed project often causes more problems than it solves.
2. Parkinson's Law: "Work expands to fill the time available for its completion." This principle suggests that projects often take longer than expected because tasks are overcomplicated or not managed well, reflecting the inefficiencies Brooks discusses in team expansion.
3. Conway's Law: "Organizations which design systems are constrained to produce designs which are copies of the communication structures of these organizations." This law highlights how team structure and communication influence software architecture, reinforcing the idea that more people can lead to more complexity.
4. The Law of Diminishing Returns: This principle states that, after a certain point, adding more resources (like people) to a project results in progressively smaller gains in output. It's closely related to Brooks' insights about increasing team size.
5. The Principle of Least Effort (Zipf's Law): While this law typically applies to language or behavior, in software development, it suggests that developers will naturally seek the simplest path to achieving a goal. If a project is over-staffed or mismanaged, it can lead to inefficiencies as developers focus on "easier" tasks instead of optimizing overall progress.

References

- Wikipedia, *The Mythical Man-Month*, [pub: 20 Aug 2024, cited: 3 Jan 2025]

The Pareto Principle: The 80/20 Rule

Definition and Origin

The Pareto Principle, also known as the 80/20 Rule, states that roughly 80% of effects come from 20% of causes. It suggests that a small proportion of inputs or efforts often leads to the majority of results or outcomes. This principle is widely applicable in areas like business, economics, and productivity.

The Pareto Principle was coined by Italian economist Vilfredo Pareto in the late 19th century. He originally observed that roughly 80% of Italy's land was owned by 20% of the population. Over time, the principle was generalized to suggest that this 80/20 distribution applies to many other areas, such as wealth distribution and business efficiency.

Context and Importance

In the context of software development and technology, the Pareto Principle is a valuable tool for prioritizing tasks, addressing issues, and optimizing resources. For example, in debugging, it is often found that 80% of software errors or bugs arise from just 20% of the code. Identifying and fixing this critical portion can lead to a significant improvement in the program's performance and stability. Similarly, in feature development, the principle suggests that 20% of the features will be used by 80% of the users, guiding product managers to focus on the most impactful and frequently used functionalities, rather than spreading resources thin across less popular features.

The Pareto Principle also plays a crucial role in streamlining technology teams and improving productivity. By analyzing code repositories, issue tracking systems, and user feedback, teams can identify the key areas that require attention and allocate resources more effectively. In a rapidly evolving tech environment, where time and attention are limited, applying the Pareto Principle helps companies and developers avoid wasted effort and focus on what will yield the most significant returns. Whether in software maintenance, user experience design, or project management, the principle empowers teams to maximize impact by focusing on the critical few factors that drive the majority of success.

Best Practices and Guidelines

Prioritize Bugs and Issues: Focus on fixing the 20% of bugs that cause 80% of the crashes or errors, improving software stability and user experience.

Optimize Core Features: Invest in the 20% of features that are most frequently used by 80% of users to maximize user satisfaction and adoption.

Efficient Resource Allocation: Allocate development resources to the 20% of tasks or modules that have the greatest impact on overall system performance or business goals.

Streamline Codebase: Identify and refactor the 20% of code that is responsible for 80% of maintenance problems, reducing technical debt and improving long-term code quality.

Data-Driven Decision Making: Use analytics to identify the 20% of user behavior or usage patterns that drive 80% of the value, guiding future development and innovation.

Common Misconceptions and Pitfalls

- Overgeneralization: Assuming the 80/20 distribution applies in all situations; not every scenario will follow this exact ratio, and outcomes may vary.
- Neglecting the Remaining 80%: Focusing too much on the "vital few" (20%) and ignoring the "trivial many" (80%) can lead to overlooking important but less visible issues or opportunities.
- Misinterpreting Proportions: The 80/20 rule doesn't always mean literal 80% vs. 20%; it highlights imbalances, but the actual proportions can vary significantly in different contexts.
- Short-Term Focus: Overemphasizing immediate results from the "critical few" and neglecting long-term strategy or holistic growth can create imbalances in development or business.
- Ineffective Implementation: Simply identifying the 20% of causes without clear action plans or continuous reassessment can lead to ineffective application of the principle.

Related Concepts

1. Murphy's Law: "Anything that can go wrong will go wrong." This law highlights the inevitability of issues arising in software development and is often used to justify the need to address the 20% of problems that cause 80% of the issues, as per the Pareto Principle.

2. Brook's Law: "Adding manpower to a late software project makes it later." This law suggests that more resources don't always solve problems efficiently. It aligns with the Pareto Principle by emphasizing the importance of focusing on the key tasks (the vital 20%) rather than overloading the process with too many resources or distractions.
3. Conway's Law: "Organizations design systems that mirror their communication structure." This principle reflects the impact that organizational focus has on software design. It suggests that if teams prioritize the right 20% of features or requirements, they can achieve better results, mirroring the Pareto rule in the realm of organizational productivity.
4. The Law of Leaky Abstractions: "All non-trivial abstractions are leaky." In software systems, simplifications often hide complexity. By applying the Pareto Principle, developers can focus on addressing the 20% of the abstraction layers that cause 80% of the complexity or performance issues, improving overall system reliability.
5. The 90/10 Rule (Hick's Law): "The time it takes to make a decision increases with the number and complexity of choices." While not strictly the same as Pareto's 80/20, this rule emphasizes that a small number of choices (or features) can significantly reduce cognitive load or complexity in both user interface design and software functionality—aligning with the idea of focusing on the most impactful elements.

References

- Wikipedia, *Pareto principle*, [pub: 24 Nov 2024, cited: 3 Jan 2025]

The Peter Principle: In a hierarchy, every employee tends to rise to their level of incompetence

---

Definition and Origin

The Peter Principle is a concept in management theory which states that in a hierarchical organization, people are often promoted based on their performance in their current role rather than their abilities in the new role. As a result, individuals tend to be promoted until they reach a position where they are no longer competent, leading to inefficiency.

The Peter Principle was coined by Dr. Laurence J. Peter, a Canadian educator and psychologist, in his 1969 book The Peter Principle: Why Things Always Go Wrong.

Context and Importance

The Peter Principle is particularly relevant in the software and technology industries, where rapid growth, complex hierarchies, and constant innovation often lead to individuals being promoted beyond their capabilities. In these fields, technical expertise is highly valued, so it's common for talented developers or engineers to be promoted into managerial or leadership roles. However, the skills required for technical work—such as coding, debugging, and system design—are vastly different from those required for managing teams, setting strategic direction, or overseeing large projects. As a result, individuals who were previously successful in their technical roles may struggle in managerial positions, leading to inefficiency, poor decision-making, or even team dissatisfaction.

Understanding the Peter Principle in technology helps companies recognize the need for specialized career tracks that allow technical experts to grow professionally without forcing them into roles for which they are not suited. Instead of promoting a talented developer to a managerial position, organizations can create pathways for senior technical roles, such as Lead Engineer, Technical Architect, or Principal Developer, where individuals continue to contribute at a high level without the burden of managing people. Recognizing the limitations of the Peter Principle can help reduce turnover, enhance team performance, and ensure that the right people are in the right positions, leading to better overall organizational success.

Best Practices and Guidelines

Create Dual Career Paths: Offer separate tracks for technical expertise and management to allow professionals to grow without being forced into roles that don't match their skills.

Evaluate Skills for Leadership: Promote based on leadership potential and managerial competencies, not just technical performance.

Provide Ongoing Training: Equip promoted individuals with leadership training to bridge the gap between technical and managerial roles.

Foster Cross-Functional Collaboration: Ensure that technical experts work closely with managers to align goals and expectations.

Monitor Performance Post-Promotion: Regularly assess how promoted employees are handling their new roles and offer support where needed.

Common Misconceptions and Pitfalls

- Assuming Expertise Equals Leadership: Promoting top performers in technical roles to management without considering their leadership skills can lead to inefficiency and dissatisfaction.
- Overlooking Role Fit: The Peter Principle assumes everyone thrives in higher positions; not all employees want or are suited for promotion.
- Promotion as Reward: Treating promotion as the only form of recognition can encourage employees to pursue roles they're not prepared for, leading to failure.
- Ignoring the Importance of Soft Skills: Relying solely on technical skills for promotion ignores the crucial importance of communication, empathy, and problem-solving in leadership.
- Underestimating Transition Challenges: Failing to provide adequate support or training during a role transition can exacerbate the mismatch between skills and responsibilities.

Related Concepts

1. Brooks' Law (The Mythical Man-Month): "Adding manpower to a late software project makes it later." This principle highlights that increasing team size or promoting individuals without the proper skills can result in inefficiencies, similar to the Peter Principle's assertion that promotion can lead to incompetence in new roles.
2. Conway's Law: "Organizations which design systems are constrained to produce designs which are copies of the communication structures of these organizations." When people are promoted beyond their competencies, communication breakdowns and inefficiencies can mirror the disorganization and poor results seen in software projects led by individuals who aren't suited for leadership.

3. Parkinson's Law: "Work expands to fill the time available for its completion." In software development, this law can be a pitfall when individuals are promoted without the necessary skills, causing inefficiency or over-complication in managing projects that could have been done more simply by a more competent individual.
4. The Law of Diminishing Returns: As individuals are promoted beyond their level of competence (as per the Peter Principle), their effectiveness in the role starts to decrease. In software, this can be seen when engineers or managers fail to deliver the expected results once they're placed in a position they cannot handle.
5. Shannon's Law (Information Theory): "The maximum amount of information that can be communicated through a channel is limited." As people move up the hierarchy in an organization, the complexity of their responsibilities and their ability to effectively communicate and process information may diminish, leading to inefficiencies and misunderstandings. This concept is related to the communication challenges faced by individuals promoted into roles they aren't equipped for.

References

- Wikipedia, *Peter principle*, [pub: 28 Nov 2024, cited: 3 Jan 2025]

Phoenix Project Principles: focus on collaboration, continuous improvement, automation, and optimizing workflows to deliver value faster.

Definition and Origin

The Phoenix Project Principles are core guidelines from The Phoenix Project, a book by Gene Kim, Kevin Behr, and George Spafford, that emphasize key practices for improving IT operations and organizational efficiency. They are based on Lean, Agile, and DevOps methodologies and focus on fostering collaboration, delivering value, and enhancing continuous improvement. The principles can be summarized as:

1. Focus on the flow of work: Minimize delays and bottlenecks to improve efficiency and delivery speed.

2. Ensure feedback loops: Implement regular feedback mechanisms to improve processes and outcomes.
3. Improve continually: Establish a culture of continuous improvement, learning, and adaptation.
4. Collaborate across silos: Break down departmental silos to enhance communication and teamwork.
5. Automate and standardize: Use automation and standardization to reduce manual effort and errors.
6. Work as a system: Treat the organization as an interconnected system, where changes in one part affect others.

These principles aim to enable organizations to better align IT and business goals, enhance productivity, and deliver value more effectively.

The Phoenix Project Principles were not directly "coined" by a single person but are largely based on the practices and philosophies outlined in the book The Phoenix Project: A Novel About IT, DevOps, and Helping Your Business Win (2013) by Gene Kim, Kevin Behr, and George Spafford.

The book, written in a novel format, illustrates the application of DevOps, Lean, and Agile principles within an IT organization. While the authors didn't explicitly label them as "Phoenix Project Principles," the key concepts outlined in the book have become widely recognized as foundational principles for improving IT operations, delivery, and collaboration.

Gene Kim, one of the authors, is particularly well-known for his advocacy of DevOps and Lean IT practices, and his work has heavily influenced the development of these principles within the context of organizational transformation and continuous improvement.

Context and Importance

The Phoenix Project Principles are crucial in the context of modern software development and IT operations because they provide a framework for overcoming the challenges that organizations face in delivering software quickly, reliably, and in alignment with business goals. As businesses increasingly depend on technology for competitive advantage, traditional approaches to IT often lead to slow, siloed, and inefficient workflows. The principles outlined in The Phoenix Project emphasize collaboration across departments, breaking down barriers between development, operations, and other business units. This is particularly important in today's environment, where faster delivery, higher quality, and the ability to respond quickly to market changes are imperative. By focusing on improving flow, establishing feedback loops, and fostering continuous improvement, organizations can streamline their software delivery pipeline, reduce risks, and meet customer expectations more effectively.

In the fast-evolving world of software and technology, the Phoenix Project Principles are important because they promote a shift toward DevOps and Agile methodologies—both of which emphasize iterative development, automation, and close collaboration between cross-functional teams. This helps organizations reduce inefficiencies and manual processes that lead to errors or delays in releasing new features or updates. The principles also prioritize automation, which not only speeds up repetitive tasks like testing and deployment but also ensures greater consistency and reliability in production environments. By adhering to these principles, companies can build a culture of continuous learning and improvement, fostering an environment that is more adaptive to change and better equipped to handle the complexities of modern software development. In essence, the Phoenix Project Principles are foundational for organizations striving to deliver high-quality software that can rapidly evolve with the demands of both the business and the market.

Best Practices and Guidelines

Optimize Workflow: Focus on reducing bottlenecks and delays in the software development and deployment pipeline to improve efficiency and speed.

Promote Cross-Functional Collaboration: Break down silos between development, operations, and other teams to enhance communication and alignment.

Implement Continuous Feedback: Establish regular feedback loops to quickly identify issues and improve processes, ensuring faster iteration and delivery.

Automate and Standardize Processes: Use automation for repetitive tasks (e.g., testing, deployment) to reduce errors and increase consistency.

Cultivate Continuous Improvement: Foster a culture of learning, experimentation, and adaptation to refine processes and respond to evolving business and technology needs.

Common Misconceptions and Pitfalls

- Overlooking Culture Change: Focusing solely on technical practices without addressing the need for a cultural shift in collaboration and communication can undermine the principles' effectiveness.
- Assuming Quick Results: Expecting immediate improvements after implementing the principles, without understanding that transformation requires sustained effort and iterative refinement.
- Neglecting the Bigger System: Focusing on optimizing individual parts of the process (e.g., development or operations) without considering how changes affect the entire system can create new bottlenecks.
- Misunderstanding Automation: Assuming automation alone will solve all problems, without recognizing that automation needs to be applied thoughtfully and in conjunction with process improvements.
- Focusing Too Much on Tools: Relying too heavily on specific tools or technologies, rather than emphasizing the underlying principles of collaboration, continuous improvement, and value delivery.

Related Concepts

1. The Agile Manifesto: Emphasizes individuals and interactions, working software, customer collaboration, and responding to change over rigid processes and tools. This aligns with the Phoenix Project's focus on collaboration and continuous feedback for adapting to changing needs.

2. The Law of Shitty Metrics (aka "Goodhart's Law"): "When a measure becomes a target, it ceases to be a good measure." This highlights the importance of using meaningful metrics that drive real value, rather than focusing on vanity metrics that don't support process improvement or customer value delivery, as advocated in the Phoenix Project's emphasis on continuous improvement and feedback.
3. DevOps Principles (The Three Ways):
    a. The First Way: Focus on creating fast and continuous flow of work.
    b. The Second Way: Implement feedback loops to detect issues early.
    c. The Third Way: Enable a culture of experimentation and continuous learning. These principles directly align with the Phoenix Project's focus on improving workflow, collaboration, and ongoing refinement.
4. The Toyota Production System (TPS) & Lean Principles: Emphasizes reducing waste, improving flow, and focusing on customer value. The Phoenix Project borrows heavily from these principles, especially in terms of eliminating bottlenecks and optimizing workflows for greater efficiency and value delivery.
5. Conway's Law: States that "organizations design systems that mirror their communication structure." The Phoenix Project highlights the importance of breaking down silos between teams, as this law suggests that aligning team structures with system goals results in more efficient, collaborative product development.

References

- Amazon, *The Phoenix Project*, [pub: 3 Sep 2024, cited: 3 Jan 2025]

Putt's Law: Technology is dominated by two types of people, those who understand what they do not manage and those who manage what they do not understand

---

Definition and Origin

Putt's Law states: "Technology is dominated by those who manage what they do not understand." It highlights the idea that people who are in charge of technological systems or innovations often lack a deep understanding of the technology itself, yet they have the power to shape its development and application.

Putt's Law was coined by Archibald Putt. The law humorously highlights the disconnect between management and the technical knowledge required to make effective decisions in technology, especially in large organizations.

Context and Importance

Putt's Law offers critical commentary on the dynamics of technology and software development, particularly highlighting the gap between decision-makers and technical expertise. In many organizations, especially large ones, senior management often holds significant influence over technological decisions without having a deep understanding of the underlying systems or complexities. This disconnect can result in poor decision-making, where priorities are set based on non-technical considerations, such as cost, time, or business trends, rather than on sound technical judgment. In the world of software and technology, such misalignments can lead to suboptimal product designs, inefficient workflows, and even failures in addressing real user needs.

The importance of Putt's Law lies in its reflection of the challenges faced by software engineers and technical teams when their expertise is not properly valued in strategic decision-making. In tech companies, the success of a product often depends on the nuanced understanding of developers, system architects, and engineers. When management dictates directions without grasping the technical realities, it can stifle innovation, hinder long-term sustainability, and create friction between those who understand the technology and those who control its application. By recognizing the limitations of decision-makers who lack technical expertise, organizations can strive for better collaboration between management and technical teams, ensuring that both sides contribute to shaping the technology in ways that are both feasible and effective.

Best Practices and Guidelines

Foster Collaboration: Ensure regular communication between management and technical teams to align business goals with technical feasibility.

Involve Experts Early: Include engineers and developers in the decision-making process from the outset to avoid costly missteps.

Promote Cross-Disciplinary Understanding: Encourage managers to gain a basic understanding of technology, while allowing technical teams to appreciate business priorities.

Value Long-Term Solutions: Avoid short-term fixes driven by non-technical considerations that may undermine the system's future scalability and stability.

Empower Technical Leaders: Give technical experts a seat at the table in strategic discussions to ensure informed decisions that consider the technical implications.

Common Misconceptions and Pitfalls

- Assuming Management Knows Best: Believing that managers, simply because they hold leadership roles, have the necessary technical knowledge to make effective decisions.
- Overlooking Technical Debt: Prioritizing speed or cost over thoughtful, sustainable architecture, leading to accumulating technical debt that hampers future development.
- Ignoring Engineer Input: Dismissing the insights of technical teams, assuming that non-technical managers can make better decisions without consulting experts.
- Focusing on Short-Term Results: Prioritizing immediate business goals without considering the long-term technical consequences, potentially undermining system performance or scalability.
- Misunderstanding the Complexity of Technology: Underestimating the complexity of software systems, leading to oversimplified or misguided expectations from both managers and customers.

Related Concepts

1. Conway's Law: "Organizations which design systems are constrained to produce designs which are copies of the communication structures of these organizations."
2. This law highlights how the structure of an organization directly impacts the architecture of the systems it builds, emphasizing the importance of organizational alignment for successful technical outcomes.
3. Brooks' Law: "Adding manpower to a late software project makes it later."
4. This principle, articulated by Fred Brooks, reflects the challenges of scaling teams to fix problems in delayed projects, emphasizing the inefficiency of adding people without understanding the existing technical complexities.
5. Lehman's Laws of Software Evolution: These laws describe how software systems tend to grow in complexity over time and require ongoing maintenance and adaptation. They stress the importance of long-term planning and adaptability, which can be undermined if management overlooks technical realities.
6. The Peter Principle: "In a hierarchy, every employee tends to rise to their level of incompetence."
7. In a tech context, this suggests that individuals may be promoted based on their technical skills but might not be competent in leadership roles that require understanding broader organizational or strategic challenges.
8. Parkinson's Law: "Work expands to fill the time available for its completion."
9. This principle often applies to software projects, where poorly defined deadlines and vague management directives can lead to unnecessary complexity or scope creep, exacerbating the disconnect between technical execution and business objectives.

References

- Wikipedia, *Putt's Law*, [pub: 16 Sep 2024, cited: 3 Jan 2025]

The RACI Matrix: Responsible, Accountable, Consulted, Informed

---

Definition and Origin

The RACI Matrix is a tool used in project management to clarify roles and responsibilities. It defines four key responsibilities for each task or deliverable:

- R (Responsible): The person who performs the work.
- A (Accountable): The person ultimately answerable for the task's completion and success.
- C (Consulted): Individuals whose input or expertise is needed.
- I (Informed): People who need to be kept updated on progress.

The matrix helps ensure clear communication and avoids confusion about roles within a project.

The RACI Matrix is commonly attributed to James R. Robinson, a management consultant who developed the framework in the 1970s to clarify roles and responsibilities in complex organizational structures. Robinson's goal was to improve clarity and communication in project management by explicitly defining the roles involved in each task or decision. Over time, the RACI Matrix has become a widely adopted tool for managing team responsibilities across various industries, including software and technology.

Context and Importance

In the context of Software and Technology projects, the RACI Matrix plays a critical role in managing complex workflows, ensuring that all team members understand their responsibilities across the various stages of development. Software projects often involve diverse teams with specialized skills, including developers, designers, testers, product managers, and other stakeholders. The RACI Matrix helps to delineate who is responsible for coding, testing, requirements gathering, design, deployment, and maintenance, thereby preventing overlapping duties or missed tasks. It also clarifies the chain of accountability, ensuring that every action or decision has a designated person who is ultimately answerable for its outcome.

The importance of the RACI Matrix in technology projects extends beyond simply organizing tasks; it fosters clear communication and transparency across cross-functional teams. By specifying who needs to be consulted or informed at each stage, it helps to streamline decision-making and avoid bottlenecks. For example, during a software release, the matrix can clearly show which developers are responsible for code implementation, who must approve the code, and who needs to be kept in the loop regarding release timelines. As technology projects often have tight deadlines and frequent iterations, using a RACI Matrix ensures that everyone is aligned, reduces the risk of errors or delays, and improves overall efficiency throughout the software lifecycle.

Best Practices and Guidelines

Define Roles Clearly: Ensure all roles (Responsible, Accountable, Consulted, Informed) are clearly assigned to avoid ambiguity in tasks like coding, testing, or deployment.

Limit Accountable to One: Only one person should be Accountable for each task to prevent confusion over decision-making authority.

Update Regularly: Revise the RACI Matrix as the project evolves to reflect changes in responsibilities, such as new team members or shifts in project scope.

Involve Key Stakeholders: Ensure the Consulted and Informed roles include relevant technical and business stakeholders, promoting communication and feedback loops.

Avoid Overloading: Limit the number of Consulted and Informed to prevent bottlenecks and keep workflows efficient.

Common Misconceptions and Pitfalls

- Overcomplicating Roles: Assigning too many Consulted or Informed roles can clutter the matrix and slow down decision-making, making it harder to focus on key tasks.
- Multiple Accountable Individuals: Having more than one person Accountable for a task can create confusion about ultimate responsibility and lead to lack of ownership.

- Static Document: Treating the RACI Matrix as a one-time document rather than a dynamic tool can result in outdated roles and missed responsibilities as the project progresses.
- Lack of Clarity in "Consulted": Misunderstanding the Consulted role as merely informational, rather than an active collaborator, can lead to key stakeholders not being fully engaged when their input is critical.
- Ignoring Team Feedback: Not involving team members in the creation or updating of the RACI Matrix may lead to misalignment and missed details, reducing its effectiveness.

Related Concepts

1. The Principle of Least Privilege (Security): This principle suggests that individuals should only be given the minimum level of access necessary to perform their tasks. In the context of a RACI Matrix, this supports the idea of clearly defining who is Responsible and Accountable for tasks, preventing unnecessary involvement from others and minimizing risk.
2. The Law of Demeter (Software Design): Often referred to as the "Principle of Least Knowledge," this law advises that objects should only communicate with their immediate collaborators. In relation to the RACI Matrix, it encourages a clear delineation of roles, ensuring that only relevant stakeholders are consulted or informed, rather than having an overload of cross-functional communication.
3. The Conway's Law: This law states that "organizations which design systems are constrained to produce designs which are copies of the communication structures of these organizations." The RACI Matrix directly supports this principle by clarifying communication flows and roles within a team, ensuring that the organizational structure is mirrored in the project's task distribution.
4. The Pareto Principle (80/20 Rule): The Pareto Principle, which suggests that 80% of effects come from 20% of causes, can be applied to the RACI Matrix by helping teams focus on the most critical roles and tasks. It highlights the need to prioritize the Responsible and Accountable roles, ensuring that effort is focused on high-impact areas rather than over-distributing responsibility.

5. The Principle of Separation of Concerns: This principle advocates for isolating different parts of a system to reduce complexity. The RACI Matrix helps implement this idea by clearly segmenting the responsibilities for each task or deliverable, ensuring that each team member focuses on their specialized role without overlapping with others' duties unnecessarily.

References

- Wikipedia, *Responsibility assignment matrix*, [pub: 9 Dec 2024, cited: 3 Jan 2025]

DARE Model: Deciders, Advisors, Recommenders, Execution

Definition and Origin

The DARE Model is a framework used to clarify roles in decision-making processes. It stands for:

- Deciders: Individuals who make the final decision.
- Advisors: Experts who provide insights and information to guide the decision.
- Recommenders: Those who suggest specific courses of action based on analysis or expertise.
- Execution: The individuals or teams responsible for implementing the decision.

This model helps to define responsibilities and streamline decision-making within organizations.

The DARE Model was developed by Chris Bradley, Martin K. S. Cohn, and Alison L. P. Knowles at McKinsey & Company. It was introduced in their 2018 book, "Strategy Beyond the Hockey Stick: People, Probabilities, and Big Moves to Beat the Odds," as a tool to improve strategic decision-making in organizations by clarifying roles and responsibilities.

The model helps leaders make better decisions by explicitly defining who is responsible for which part of the decision-making process, ensuring alignment and reducing confusion.

Context and Importance

In the context of software and technology, the DARE Model provides a clear framework for navigating complex decision-making processes, which are often pivotal in the fast-moving and highly collaborative environments of tech organizations. In software development, decisions related to architecture, design, resource allocation, and technology adoption can be fraught with uncertainty and require input from various stakeholders with differing expertise. By defining roles as Deciders, Advisors, Recommenders, and those responsible for Execution, the model ensures that the decision-making process is streamlined, and that individuals and teams understand their specific responsibilities. This reduces ambiguity and allows tech teams to move more efficiently from planning to implementation, while minimizing the risk of misalignment or bottlenecks.

The DARE Model is particularly valuable in the context of agile software development and DevOps, where fast-paced iterations and continuous integration require clear accountability and collaboration across cross-functional teams. In these environments, it's essential that the right people are empowered to make decisions, while others contribute through advice, recommendations, and execution. For example, a Decider in a tech organization might be a product manager or CTO who ultimately approves the use of a new technology stack, while Advisors could be technical architects providing insights into system architecture, and Recommenders could be engineers proposing solutions based on their day-to-day experience. This structure helps prevent decision paralysis, encourages ownership, and fosters a culture of informed decision-making that is crucial for the successful delivery of technology products.

Best Practices and Guidelines

Clarify Roles Early: Define and communicate the roles of Deciders, Advisors, Recommenders, and Execution teams from the outset to avoid confusion and ensure efficient collaboration.

Empower Deciders with Data: Ensure that Deciders have access to comprehensive, accurate information from Advisors and Recommenders to make informed choices.

Leverage Expertise: Engage Advisors and Recommenders early in the decision-making process to incorporate diverse technical perspectives and reduce blind spots.

Ensure Accountability: Hold Execution teams accountable for delivering decisions, ensuring that agreed-upon actions are implemented effectively and on time.

Iterate and Review: Regularly review decisions and outcomes to refine the process, identify areas for improvement, and adapt the model as needed in fast-changing tech environments.

Common Misconceptions and Pitfalls

- Confusing Roles: Misunderstanding or overlapping roles, such as Advisors acting like Deciders or Recommenders being mistaken for Execution, can create decision-making bottlenecks or lack of accountability.
- Overloading Deciders: Expecting Deciders to have deep expertise in every area can lead to delays or poor decisions. They should rely on Advisors and Recommenders for specialized insights.
- Ignoring Feedback Loops: Failing to regularly review decisions and outcomes can prevent necessary course corrections, leading to recurring mistakes or inefficiencies in Execution.
- Underutilizing Recommenders: Dismissing or overlooking Recommenders' input, even if they are not the final decision-makers, can result in missed opportunities for innovation or practical solutions.
- Lack of Clear Execution Ownership: Without clear execution responsibilities and follow-up, decisions can stall, leading to poor implementation or misalignment with the initial strategic goals.

Related Concepts

1. The Law of Leverage (Benedict's Law) "Leverage the expertise of others to make better decisions." This principle mirrors the DARE Model by emphasizing the value of Advisors and Recommenders in providing insights that empower Deciders to make informed, high-impact decisions without needing to be experts in every area.

2. The Principle of Least Surprise (Law of Least Astonishment) "Design systems to minimize unexpected behaviors or outcomes." This law relates to the need for clear and well-communicated roles in the DARE Model. Misunderstandings about roles or decisions can lead to unexpected and suboptimal outcomes, so clarity is key.
3. The 80/20 Rule (Pareto Principle) "80% of the results come from 20% of the effort." In decision-making, the Pareto Principle aligns with the DARE Model by showing how Deciders should focus on high-impact decisions while Advisors and Recommenders handle the detailed work, leading to more efficient use of resources.
4. Conway's Law "Organizations design systems that mirror their communication structures." This law highlights how the structure of decision-making roles in the DARE Model can directly influence the architecture and efficiency of the resulting software systems. Clear role definitions promote better collaboration and more effective system design.
5. The Principle of Simplicity (KISS: Keep It Simple, Stupid) "The simpler solution is often the better one." This principle emphasizes reducing complexity in both decision-making and execution. The DARE Model's clear delineation of roles helps avoid unnecessary complexity in the decision process, ensuring that decisions are straightforward and actionable.

References

- Wikipedia, *Responsibility assignment matrix*, [pub: 9 Dec 2024, cited: 3 Jan 2025]

H. Resource Allocation

Cost-Benefit Principle

Definition and Origin

The Cost-Benefit Principle is an economic concept stating that decisions should be made by comparing the costs of an action with its expected benefits. A decision is considered rational if the benefits outweigh or justify the costs. In essence, it suggests that resources should be allocated in a way that maximizes net benefits.

The Cost-Benefit Principle does not have a single inventor or founder, as it is a foundational idea in economics that has evolved over time.

Context and Importance

In the context of software and technology development, the Cost-Benefit Principle plays a crucial role in guiding decision-making throughout the project lifecycle. Software development often involves significant investment in terms of time, resources, and human capital. The principle helps developers, project managers, and stakeholders assess whether the benefits of a particular technology, feature, or approach outweigh the costs. For example, when choosing between different programming languages, frameworks, or third-party libraries, teams must evaluate the trade-offs in terms of development speed, maintainability, scalability, and potential long-term benefits. By using the Cost-Benefit Principle, companies can prioritize solutions that provide the highest value relative to their cost, ensuring more efficient use of resources.

The importance of the Cost-Benefit Principle extends beyond individual development decisions and impacts broader strategic choices in the technology sector. For tech companies and startups, adopting the principle is essential when evaluating potential investments in new technologies or products, especially in highly competitive and fast-evolving markets. A business may need to decide whether to invest in cutting-edge technologies like artificial intelligence, blockchain, or cloud infrastructure based on an analysis of the expected return on investment (ROI). By rigorously applying cost-benefit analysis, organizations can avoid overextending their budgets or pursuing high-risk ventures that do not align with their overall goals. This disciplined approach helps ensure sustainable growth and innovation while minimizing wasteful expenditures.

Best Practices and Guidelines

Quantify Costs and Benefits: Clearly define and measure both tangible and intangible costs (e.g., time, resources, risk) and benefits (e.g., user experience, scalability, revenue potential).

Prioritize High-Impact Decisions: Apply cost-benefit analysis to key strategic decisions, such as technology stack selection or major feature development, where the impact is significant.

Consider Long-Term Impacts: Account for future maintenance costs, scalability, and the long-term benefits of software solutions, not just immediate gains.

Iterate and Reassess: Continuously revisit cost-benefit assessments throughout the project lifecycle as new information and conditions evolve.

Involve Stakeholders: Collaborate with all relevant teams (e.g., engineering, marketing, finance) to ensure comprehensive evaluation of costs and benefits from multiple perspectives.

Common Misconceptions and Pitfalls

- Focusing Only on Short-Term Gains: Relying solely on immediate benefits and overlooking long-term costs or future scalability can lead to poor decision-making.

- Underestimating Hidden or Indirect Costs: Failing to account for hidden costs, such as maintenance, training, or downtime, can result in misleading assessments.
- Overlooking Non-Quantifiable Benefits: Discounting intangible benefits like user satisfaction, brand reputation, or innovation can skew the analysis.
- Assuming Perfect Information: Treating cost-benefit analysis as a one-time exercise rather than an iterative process can lead to decisions based on incomplete or outdated data.
- Ignoring Opportunity Costs: Failing to consider the potential value of alternative options or projects that are not pursued can result in suboptimal choices.

Related Concepts

1. Parkinson's Law: "Work expands to fill the time available for its completion." In software development, this suggests that the longer a project is allowed to take, the more resources (time and money) it will consume. Applying the Cost-Benefit Principle helps to avoid unnecessary expansion and ensures projects remain efficient and within budget.
2. The 80/20 Rule (Pareto Principle): "80% of the value comes from 20% of the effort." This principle emphasizes that a small portion of effort often yields the majority of benefits. In software development, focusing on the most impactful features or tasks (those with the highest benefit-to-cost ratio) can maximize efficiency and value.
3. Hofstadter's Law: "It always takes longer than you expect, even when you take into account Hofstadter's Law." This law highlights the common underestimation of project timelines and costs in software development. By applying cost-benefit analysis early on, teams can better anticipate these risks and plan accordingly.
4. The Law of Diminishing Returns: "After a certain point, adding more resources to a project will result in smaller increases in output." In software development, this suggests that investing excessively in refining or expanding features might not provide a proportional benefit. Cost-benefit analysis helps to identify when additional investments no longer justify the returns.

5. Moore's Law: "The number of transistors on a microchip doubles approximately every two years, leading to exponential increases in processing power." While primarily focused on hardware, Moore's Law influences software development decisions. The rapidly increasing computing power can shift cost-benefit calculations, making previously expensive or complex solutions more feasible and allowing developers to re-evaluate software architectures for better cost-efficiency.

References

- Wikipedia, *Cost–benefit analysis*, [pub: 6 Dec 2024, cited: 3 Jan 2025]
- Indeed, *A Definitive Guide To Cost-Benefit Principle*, [pub: 15 Aug 2024, cited: 3 Jan 2025]

Critical Mass Principle

Definition and Origin

The Critical Mass Principle refers to the minimum amount or level of resources, participants, or support required to initiate and sustain a process, movement, or system. Once this "critical mass" is reached, the process tends to gain momentum, grow, and become self-sustaining. It is commonly used in contexts like social movements, technology adoption, and organizational change.

Context and Importance

In the realm of software and technology, the Critical Mass Principle is crucial for the widespread adoption and success of a product or platform. When a software solution or technology reaches a critical mass of users, developers, or data, it often becomes self-sustaining and grows organically. For instance, social media platforms, collaborative tools, and open-source projects rely heavily on the principle of critical mass—once a certain threshold of active users or contributors is reached, network effects take over, leading to exponential growth. The increased user base attracts more developers, content creators, and third-party integrations, which in turn further boosts the platform's value, usability, and appeal. Without reaching this critical threshold, software may struggle to gain traction, and its growth could plateau or stagnate.

The importance of the Critical Mass Principle is particularly evident in the success of network-based technologies, such as cloud services, marketplaces, and communication platforms. In these cases, the product's utility often grows with the number of participants. For example, an online marketplace like eBay or a ride-sharing service like Uber depends on having enough users on both sides of the transaction—sellers and buyers, or drivers and passengers. Without a critical mass of participants, the platform cannot deliver the value that attracts new users, leading to a vicious cycle of low adoption. In software ecosystems, this principle also influences how developers prioritize features, scalability, and community engagement. A product's ability to scale effectively while maintaining network reliability is crucial once it crosses the critical mass threshold, making the principle a key consideration in the planning and development stages of software technology.

Best Practices and Guidelines

Focus on Early Adopters: Prioritize attracting and nurturing early adopters who can help demonstrate the value and build momentum for the technology.

Ensure Network Effects: Design products to become more valuable as more users or contributors join, leveraging feedback loops and community-driven growth.

Scale Gradually: Build infrastructure that can scale smoothly as user demand increases, ensuring reliability and performance once critical mass is reached.

Promote Viral Growth: Incorporate features that encourage users to invite others or share the platform, accelerating growth organically.

Iterate Based on User Feedback: Continuously improve the product based on user insights to enhance engagement and retention, critical to sustaining momentum.

Common Misconceptions and Pitfalls

- Assuming Growth Happens Automatically: Reaching critical mass doesn't guarantee automatic success; consistent effort in user engagement, marketing, and product refinement is still required.
- Neglecting Quality for Quantity: Focusing only on increasing user numbers without ensuring product quality or value can lead to churn, rather than sustained growth.
- Overestimating the Threshold: Underestimating the critical mass needed for network effects to kick in can result in premature scaling or failure to build necessary momentum.
- Ignoring Network Balance: Failing to maintain balance between different user groups (e.g., buyers and sellers, or creators and consumers) can hinder platform growth and viability.
- Relying Too Much on External Factors: Assuming external conditions, like market trends or media coverage, will drive critical mass without building a solid, self-sustaining ecosystem can backfire.

Related Concepts

1. Metcalfe's Law: This law states that the value of a network is proportional to the square of the number of connected users (n^2). As more users join a network, the value for each participant grows exponentially, making reaching critical mass crucial for the network's success.
2. Network Effects: This principle asserts that the value of a product or service increases as more people use it. A technology or platform gains more value as its user base grows, which, once critical mass is achieved, leads to self-perpetuating growth and adoption.
3. The Law of the Few (Tipping Point): Popularized by Malcolm Gladwell, this law suggests that a small number of people (Connectors, Mavens, and Salesmen) can create a tipping point that propels a product or idea into widespread adoption. These influential individuals help push the system toward critical mass.
4. The Butterfly Effect: In complex systems like software ecosystems, small initial changes can lead to significant, unpredictable outcomes. Once critical mass is reached, a small catalyst (like a viral feature or event) can trigger rapid, expansive growth.

5. Moore’s Law: While primarily focused on hardware, Moore's Law (the doubling of transistors on a chip every two years) has indirect implications for software. It highlights the importance of technological scalability and efficiency, which is vital for sustaining growth once a software platform reaches critical mass.

References

- Wikipedia, *Critical mass*, [pub: 6 Dec 2024, cited: 3 Jan 2025]

Margin of Safety

Definition and Origin

The Margin of Safety refers to the difference between the intrinsic value of an asset (such as a stock or investment) and its market price. It represents a buffer against potential errors in judgment or unexpected market fluctuations, offering protection to investors by ensuring they are purchasing the asset at a price significantly below its true value. A larger margin indicates lower risk.

The concept of Margin of Safety was popularized by Benjamin Graham, the father of value investing. He introduced it in his influential book, The Intelligent Investor (1949). Graham emphasized the importance of purchasing investments at a price below their intrinsic value to reduce the risk of loss. The idea was further refined and adopted by his student, Warren Buffett, who has often cited it as a key principle in his investment strategy.

Context and Importance

In the context of software and technology investments, the Margin of Safety concept plays a critical role due to the inherent volatility and uncertainty in the sector. Technology companies often face rapid innovation cycles, intense competition, regulatory challenges, and shifts in consumer behavior, which can make valuations highly speculative. A margin of safety in this domain might involve investing in tech companies that are undervalued relative to their long-term growth potential or having a robust moat (e.g., network effects, proprietary technology) that can safeguard their competitive advantage. In this way, the margin provides a buffer against the unpredictability of market conditions or unforeseen disruptions, such as technological obsolescence or regulatory changes.

For investors in software and tech stocks, a margin of safety also helps manage the risk of overpaying for high-growth companies whose valuations are often inflated by optimism about future earnings. With software and tech, future growth projections can be highly speculative, and even market leaders can face setbacks. A solid margin of safety ensures that an investor isn't relying solely on overly optimistic forecasts and provides room for error if those projections don't materialize. This protective strategy can be particularly valuable in tech, where shifts in consumer preferences or emerging competitors can quickly undermine the perceived value of even the most well-established companies.

Best Practices and Guidelines

Prioritize core competencies: Allocate resources to areas with the highest strategic value and competitive advantage, ensuring a stronger margin of safety in key areas.

Diversify investments: Spread resources across multiple projects or technologies to reduce the risk of relying on a single, potentially vulnerable initiative.

Build a buffer for R&D: Maintain a portion of the budget for research and development to future-proof the technology and adapt to emerging trends or disruptions.

Optimize operational efficiency: Ensure that resources are allocated to processes that maximize productivity and reduce waste, preserving financial stability and flexibility.

Monitor risk exposure: Regularly assess the risk profile of allocated resources, adjusting investments to maintain a margin of safety against market volatility and technological uncertainty.

Common Misconceptions and Pitfalls

- Overcommitting to a single project: Relying too heavily on one initiative can jeopardize the margin of safety, as unforeseen failures or shifts in the market can lead to significant losses.
- Ignoring long-term scalability: Focusing only on short-term resource allocation may neglect the long-term needs for scalability and adaptability in tech infrastructure, increasing vulnerability to disruptions.
- Underestimating technological obsolescence: Failing to allocate resources for updating or replacing outdated technologies can erode the margin of safety as new innovations make older systems obsolete.
- Overvaluing initial success: Assuming early success guarantees long-term sustainability without continued resource investment in innovation or maintenance can lead to complacency and eventual risk.
- Neglecting risk management: Not allocating enough resources to identify and mitigate risks (e.g., cybersecurity threats, regulatory compliance) leaves the company exposed to potential losses or legal challenges.

Related Concepts

1. The Law of Software Inertia. This principle states that software systems, once developed, tend to become more difficult and expensive to change over time. Companies that neglect ongoing maintenance or fail to innovate may face disruptions from newer technologies, reducing their margin of safety.
2. The Innovator's Dilemma (Clayton Christensen). This law highlights how established tech companies can be overtaken by disruptive innovations. The margin of safety is at risk if companies fail to anticipate or adapt to emerging technologies, even if they are currently dominant.

3. Network Effect Principle. A core principle in software and tech is that products become more valuable as more people use them. A strong network effect can create a significant margin of safety by defending market share, making it harder for competitors to disrupt the business.
4. The 10x Rule (Jason Fried, Basecamp). This rule suggests that software products or companies must aim for 10x improvements in performance, usability, or value to create lasting competitive advantages. A business with this mindset ensures a buffer against competitors and market shifts.
5. The Law of Continuous Improvement (Kaizen in Software). This principle stresses the importance of constant, incremental improvements in software products. By continually enhancing a product's quality, security, and features, companies can maintain a margin of safety against competitors and technological obsolescence.

References

- Wikipedia, *Margin of safety (financial)*, [pub: 15 Oct 2024, cited: 3 Jan 2025]

Opportunity Cost Principle

Definition and Origin

The Opportunity Cost Principle states that the cost of any decision is the value of the next best alternative that must be forgone. In other words, when you choose one option, the opportunity cost is the benefit you could have gained from choosing the second-best option instead.

The Opportunity Cost Principle was first introduced by the Austrian economist Friedrich von Wieser in the late 19th century. He articulated the concept in his book "The Natural Economics" (1889), where he emphasized that the true cost of any choice is the value of the next best alternative that is not chosen.

Although Wieser is credited with formalizing the concept, the underlying idea had been explored earlier by other economists, notably David Ricardo and Adam Smith, in more general terms related to the concept of cost. However, Wieser's work made the opportunity cost idea more explicit and central to economic theory.

Context and Importance

In the context of software and technology, the Opportunity Cost Principle plays a crucial role in resource allocation decisions. Companies must constantly choose between competing projects, whether it's investing in new software development, improving existing platforms, or exploring innovative technologies. The opportunity cost of these decisions can be substantial, as resources like time, talent, and capital are limited. For example, if a tech company chooses to allocate resources toward developing a new mobile app, the opportunity cost could be the potential revenue that might have been generated from enhancing its core software product, or the market share it could have captured by adopting a new emerging technology like AI. By understanding opportunity costs, companies can make more informed choices that align with long-term strategic goals rather than short-term gains.

The importance of the Opportunity Cost Principle in resource allocation within the software and tech industry cannot be overstated. In a rapidly evolving sector, misallocating resources can lead to missed opportunities, inefficiencies, or even technological obsolescence. Startups and large tech firms alike must constantly evaluate where to invest their scarce resources to maximize innovation, productivity, and competitive advantage. Failure to do so often results in a loss of potential value. By applying the opportunity cost framework, tech companies are better equipped to assess trade-offs, prioritize projects with the highest potential returns, and ensure that every resource is being used as effectively as possible to drive business success.

Best Practices and Guidelines

Prioritize high-impact projects: Allocate resources to initiatives that offer the greatest potential return, considering both short-term benefits and long-term strategic goals.

Evaluate trade-offs regularly: Continuously assess the opportunity costs of ongoing projects to ensure resources are not being tied up in lower-value activities.

Leverage data-driven decisions: Use analytics and metrics to measure potential outcomes and inform decisions about where resources will generate the most value.

Balance innovation with core development: Weigh the opportunity cost of pursuing new technologies against the need to maintain and improve existing software and infrastructure.

Involve cross-functional teams: Ensure diverse perspectives in resource allocation to identify overlooked alternatives and ensure a well-rounded evaluation of opportunity costs.

Common Misconceptions and Pitfalls

- Ignoring hidden costs: Focusing only on immediate costs without considering long-term implications or hidden costs (e.g., technical debt, maintenance) can lead to poor resource allocation decisions.
- Overestimating the value of new projects: Over-prioritizing trendy technologies or new projects without fully evaluating their potential opportunity costs can divert resources from higher-value initiatives.
- Underestimating the cost of delay: Delaying decisions or postponing projects can result in missed opportunities and lost market potential, which isn't always factored into the opportunity cost calculation.
- Focusing too narrowly on short-term gains: Prioritizing projects that offer immediate returns without accounting for their long-term strategic value can limit growth and innovation.
- Neglecting to reassess resource allocation: Failing to periodically reevaluate ongoing projects and resource distribution can result in stagnation or misallocation as market conditions and business needs evolve.

Related Concepts

1. Parkinson's Law: "Work expands to fill the time available for its completion." In the context of resource allocation, this law suggests that without proper prioritization and clear boundaries, projects may consume more resources (time, effort, etc.) than necessary, leading to inefficient use of valuable resources and potential missed opportunities.

2. The 80/20 Rule (Pareto Principle): "80% of effects come from 20% of causes." When applied to resource allocation, this principle encourages focusing on the small set of tasks or features that generate the most value. Understanding the opportunity cost of spreading resources too thin can help prioritize the most impactful initiatives.
3. Hofstadter's Law: "It always takes longer than you expect, even when you take into account Hofstadter's Law.": This principle underscores the importance of considering time and complexity when allocating resources to software projects. Opportunity costs can quickly accrue if the time and effort required for projects are underestimated.
4. The Iron Triangle (Project Management Triangle): "Scope, Time, and Cost are interdependent." This principle highlights the trade-offs between scope, time, and cost in resource allocation. Opportunity costs often arise when these three factors are not properly balanced, leading to delays or under-delivery on important projects.
5. Lehman's Laws of Software Engineering: "As software systems evolve, they tend to grow more complex and less efficient." This principle suggests that over time, software systems tend to accrue technical debt and become harder to maintain. Allocating resources to improve or refactor code can prevent the opportunity cost of future inefficiencies and balance the need for new features with ongoing system health.

References

- Wikipedia, *Opportunity cost*, [pub: 16 Dec 2024, cited: 3 Jan 2025]
- Wikipedia, *Friedrich von Wieser*, [pub: 19 Oct 2024, cited: 3 Jan 2025]

Principle of Scale

Definition and Origin

The Principle of Scale refers to the concept that as a system or application grows—whether in terms of users, data, or complexity—the resources and architecture required to maintain performance, reliability, and efficiency do not increase linearly. Instead, scaling often involves adapting the system's design, infrastructure, and resource allocation to accommodate exponential or non-linear growth, ensuring that the system can handle larger loads without significant degradation in performance or cost-effectiveness.

Context and Importance

In the context of software and technology, the Principle of Scale plays a crucial role in resource allocation, particularly when systems grow in size or complexity. As software applications or platforms scale—whether in terms of user base, data volume, or functionality—the resources needed to support them (such as computational power, memory, storage, and bandwidth) do not always scale linearly. For instance, a system designed for a small user base may require significantly different architecture, infrastructure, and optimization strategies when handling millions of users. Recognizing this principle allows engineers and developers to allocate resources effectively, ensuring that systems remain performant, reliable, and cost-efficient as they scale.

The importance of the Principle of Scale in resource allocation is underscored by the challenge of balancing performance with efficiency. As a system scales, the costs of adding new resources can increase disproportionately. Without proper understanding and application of scaling principles, organizations may over-provision resources (leading to waste and unnecessary expenses) or under-provision them (resulting in performance bottlenecks or service failures). For example, cloud-based platforms often rely on dynamic resource scaling mechanisms—such as auto-scaling services—where computing power and storage can be adjusted in real-time based on demand. Applying the Principle of Scale effectively in these scenarios ensures that resources are allocated in a way that supports both the system's growing needs and its overall sustainability. This balance is essential in maintaining competitive advantage, controlling operational costs, and delivering a seamless user experience.

Best Practices and Guidelines

Plan for Non-Linear Growth: Anticipate that resource needs may grow exponentially or at a faster rate than expected as systems scale; avoid linear assumptions in scaling strategies.

Optimize for Efficiency: Continuously monitor and optimize resource usage to avoid over-provisioning or under-provisioning, ensuring cost-effective allocation at every scale level.

Leverage Elastic Infrastructure: Use cloud-based solutions with auto-scaling capabilities to dynamically adjust resources based on real-time demand, minimizing waste while ensuring performance.

Decouple Components: Design systems with modular, decoupled architectures to enable more efficient scaling of individual components without impacting the entire system.

Measure and Monitor: Implement robust monitoring and performance tracking to identify scaling bottlenecks and adjust resource allocation proactively.

Common Misconceptions and Pitfalls

- Linear Scaling Assumption: Believing that resource needs will scale linearly with user growth or data volume, which often leads to inefficient or insufficient resource allocation.
- Ignoring Latency and Performance Bottlenecks: Focusing only on raw resource counts (e.g., CPUs or memory) without considering system architecture, which can lead to hidden performance issues as systems scale.
- Over-Provisioning Resources: Overestimating future demands and over-allocating resources upfront, leading to unnecessary costs and inefficient resource utilization.
- Neglecting Long-Term Maintenance: Failing to plan for the operational complexity that comes with scaling, such as monitoring, updating, and managing larger systems, which can create hidden maintenance burdens.
- Underestimating the Cost of Scaling Complexity: Not accounting for the increased complexity and overhead associated with scaling, such as the need for more sophisticated load balancing, failover mechanisms, and security measures.

Related Concepts

1. Moore's Law: The observation that computing power doubles approximately every two years, leading to increased resource availability at lower costs. This principle is key when considering how to allocate resources in a growing system, as it suggests that hardware scaling can provide rapid performance improvements over time.
2. Amdahl's Law: This law highlights the diminishing returns of scaling in parallel computing. It states that the overall speedup of a system is limited by the portion that cannot be parallelized. In resource allocation, it emphasizes the need for careful distribution of tasks and recognizing that some bottlenecks may not improve significantly with added resources.
3. Conway's Law: States that the design of a system is influenced by the organization that creates it. As systems scale, resource allocation decisions must also consider how the team and organizational structure evolve to manage larger, more complex systems.
4. Little's Law: In queuing theory, this law describes the relationship between the number of items in a system, the arrival rate, and the time they spend in the system. For resource allocation, it can guide the sizing of resource pools (like databases or queues) to ensure optimal throughput without overwhelming the system.
5. The CAP Theorem: In distributed systems, the CAP Theorem states that you can only achieve two out of three properties: Consistency, Availability, and Partition Tolerance. Understanding this trade-off is crucial for resource allocation in large-scale systems to ensure that performance, data integrity, and availability are balanced appropriately as the system grows.

References

- Wikipedia, *Economies of scale*, [pub: 19 Dec 2024, cited: 3 Jan 2025]

Resource Leveling Principle

Definition and Origin

The Resource Leveling Principle is a project management technique used to resolve resource over-allocation or conflicts by adjusting the project schedule. The goal is to ensure that resources are distributed evenly over time, minimizing periods of overwork or underutilization, while still meeting project deadlines and constraints. This often involves delaying non-critical tasks or redistributing tasks to optimize resource usage.

The Resource Leveling Principle is not attributed to a single individual as its inventor, but rather it evolved as part of the broader development of project management techniques. It is rooted in the concept of optimizing resource allocation, which became more formalized with the development of project management methodologies in the mid-20th century.

The principle is closely associated with the Critical Path Method (CPM) and Program Evaluation and Review Technique (PERT), which were developed in the 1950s and 1960s to improve project scheduling and management. The concept of leveling resources specifically emerged as a way to balance resource demand across project timelines.

While there isn't one person credited with coining "Resource Leveling," it became widely recognized and formalized as project management practices and tools (like Microsoft Project) evolved in the 1980s and beyond.

Context and Importance

In the context of Software and Technology projects, resource leveling plays a critical role in managing the complex, dynamic nature of these projects, which often involve highly specialized skills and tight timelines. Software development is typically resource-intensive, requiring a balance between developers, designers, testers, and other roles. As such, project managers need to carefully allocate resources to ensure that no team member is overloaded while also avoiding underutilization of skilled resources. The rapid pace of technological change and the increasing complexity of projects, such as developing new software products or maintaining legacy systems, make resource leveling especially important. Proper leveling ensures that critical tasks are completed on time without overwhelming resources, and it helps to prevent delays caused by bottlenecks or resource shortages.

The importance of resource leveling in Software and Technology projects is also tied to the nature of these projects, where shifts in scope, unanticipated technical challenges, or changes in team composition can disrupt the project schedule. By evenly distributing resource demand, project managers can adapt to these changes without sacrificing quality or timelines. Resource leveling also helps in optimizing team productivity, as overworked employees are prone to burnout and mistakes, while underused resources may lead to inefficiencies. In a competitive technology environment, the ability to balance resource allocation effectively can be the difference between meeting client expectations, delivering on time, or facing costly delays. Therefore, resource leveling is an essential technique for maintaining project stability, ensuring high-quality outcomes, and supporting team well-being.

Best Practices and Guidelines

Prioritize Critical Tasks: Focus on leveling resources around critical tasks to avoid project delays while ensuring key milestones are met.

Monitor Resource Utilization: Regularly track resource allocation and workload to prevent over- or under-utilization, adjusting as needed.

Use Buffer Time Wisely: Incorporate buffer time in non-critical tasks to absorb delays without affecting overall project timelines.

Leverage Automation Tools: Utilize project management software to automate resource leveling and track resource availability in real time.

Ensure Cross-Training: Promote skill diversification within teams to improve flexibility in resource allocation and reduce dependency on specific roles.

Common Misconceptions and Pitfalls

- Over-Emphasizing Schedule Over Resources: Focusing too much on meeting deadlines without considering the impact on resource workload can lead to burnout and inefficiency.
- Assuming Static Resource Availability: Underestimating the variability in resource availability (e.g., vacations, illness, other projects) can result in unanticipated delays.

- Neglecting Non-Critical Tasks: Over-leveling critical tasks while ignoring non-critical ones can lead to resource imbalances later in the project.
- Over-Leveraging Buffer Time: Relying too heavily on buffer time to absorb delays can create a false sense of security, leading to potential schedule creep.
- Ignoring Skill Diversification: Assuming all resources can easily switch between tasks without considering skill gaps can result in delays and lower quality output.

Related Concepts

1. Brooks' Law: "Adding manpower to a late software project makes it later.". This principle highlights the complexity of resource management in software projects. Simply adding more resources to a delayed project can worsen the situation if resource leveling isn't carefully managed, as it can introduce additional coordination challenges.
2. The Iron Triangle (Project Management Triangle): Time, Cost, and Scope are the three constraints of any project. The Resource Leveling Principle must balance these three constraints by managing resource allocation in a way that doesn't compromise the project's schedule, budget, or scope, ensuring no one constraint is overburdened.
3. Little's Law: "The average number of items in a system is equal to the arrival rate multiplied by the average time an item spends in the system." In the context of software projects, this law underscores the importance of managing the flow of tasks through the system. Leveling resources can prevent task congestion by ensuring an optimal flow of work through the system, reducing delays and bottlenecks.
4. Conway's Law: "Organizations design systems that mirror their communication structure.". This principle highlights that resource distribution and management (such as in leveling) are deeply influenced by organizational structure. Misalignment between resource allocation and the structure of teams can create inefficiencies, making resource leveling more critical.

5. Parkinson's Law: "Work expands to fill the time available for its completion.". In software projects, this law implies that tasks may take longer if the available resources and time aren't effectively leveled. Proper resource leveling can help prevent tasks from expanding beyond what's necessary by ensuring realistic timelines and manageable workloads.

References

- Wikipedia, *Resource leveling*, [pub: 9 Aug 2022, cited: 3 Jan 2025]

Technology & Innovation

I. Technological Evolution

Amara's Law: We overestimate short-term and underestimate long-term effects

Definition and Origin

Amara's Law is a principle named after Roy Amara, a futurist and researcher who suggested that "We tend to overestimate the effect of a technology in the short run and underestimate the effect in the long run". This law reflects a common cognitive bias, particularly in the context of technological advancements, where initial hype or excitement often leads to inflated expectations about the immediate impact of a technology. Over time, however, the true consequences of technology often unfold more slowly and are often more profound than anticipated.

In software and technology, this principle highlights how new innovations or tools may not yield immediate transformative results but might lead to more profound and far-reaching impacts over time.

Context and Importance

Amara's Law is especially relevant in the field of software and technology, where rapid innovation and disruptive changes are commonplace. In the short term, new technologies often generate inflated expectations. This is evident in the initial excitement that surrounds emerging technologies such as artificial intelligence, blockchain, or quantum computing. Developers, investors, and the public often anticipate rapid transformations, expecting these technologies to quickly solve major problems or revolutionize industries. However, in reality, the practical challenges, limitations, and unforeseen consequences of these technologies tend to slow their progress, leading to a period of disillusionment. Amara's Law helps to explain why early hype surrounding new software technologies often fails to meet expectations in the short term.

In the long term, however, Amara's Law highlights the deeper, often more profound effects that these technologies have on society. While early optimism may fade, the true impact of software innovations often takes years or even decades to fully materialize. Over time, these technologies can reshape industries, redefine work processes, and create entirely new fields. For example, the internet, which was once seen as a niche tool for researchers, has now transformed every aspect of communication, business, and culture. Amara's Law serves as a reminder for both developers and users of technology to balance short-term hype with a more patient and strategic outlook, acknowledging that the full potential of innovations often becomes clearer only over time.

Best Practices and Guidelines

Manage Expectations: Avoid overhyping new technologies in the short term; recognize that initial limitations often lead to slower-than-expected adoption.

Focus on Long-Term Vision: Be patient and track the evolution of technology over time, understanding that its full impact often emerges gradually.

Assess Feasibility Realistically: Prioritize realistic milestones and achievable outcomes during the early stages of technology development.

Monitor Shifts in Impact: Regularly evaluate how emerging technologies evolve and adapt as their true potential becomes clearer.

Foster Incremental Innovation: Focus on building and iterating gradually rather than aiming for immediate, disruptive breakthroughs.

Common Misconceptions and Pitfalls

- Overestimating Immediate Results: Believing new technologies will instantly deliver transformative outcomes, leading to disappointment when progress is slower than anticipated.
- Underestimating Long-Term Impact: Dismissing emerging technologies as unimportant in the short term, failing to recognize their potential for significant long-term disruption.

- Ignoring the Complexity of Scaling: Assuming that initial success in a lab or prototype phase will easily translate into widespread adoption or practical use.
- Focusing on Hype Over Substance: Prioritizing flashy features or trends without considering real-world feasibility, sustainability, and societal readiness.
- Neglecting Adaptation and Evolution: Overlooking the ongoing evolution of technologies, which can mature in unexpected ways and outgrow early limitations.

Related Concepts

1. Moore's Law: The observation that the number of transistors on a microchip doubles approximately every two years, leading to exponential growth in computing power and driving technological advancement. While Amara's Law cautions about overestimating short-term impact, Moore's Law highlights the rapid pace of hardware improvement that fuels long-term technological shifts.
2. Hype Cycle (Gartner): This model illustrates the stages of technological innovation, from the "Innovation Trigger" to the "Peak of Inflated Expectations," followed by a "Trough of Disillusionment," and eventually the "Slope of Enlightenment." Similar to Amara's Law, the Hype Cycle underscores the over-optimism of early expectations and the eventual realization of a technology's true value.
3. Parkinson's Law: "Work expands to fill the time available for its completion." While not strictly about technology, this principle relates to software development timelines, where projects often overrun initial expectations. It aligns with Amara's Law by suggesting that, like technological impact, project timelines are often inaccurately estimated.
4. The Law of Accelerating Returns (Ray Kurzweil): This law asserts that technological progress accelerates over time due to self-reinforcing feedback loops. It complements Amara's Law by explaining how long-term technological effects often surpass initial predictions, driving exponential advancements beyond the early phases.

5. The Peter Principle: "In a hierarchy, every employee tends to rise to their level of incompetence." This principle can relate to technology teams or software development projects, where early success and innovation can lead to overconfidence and eventual mismanagement. Like Amara's Law, it points to the risks of overestimating capabilities before maturity or proper scaling.

References

- Wikipedia, *Amara's law*, [pub: 1 Jan 2025, cited: 3 Jan 2025]

Andy and Bill's Law: The likelihood of a project succeeding is inversely proportional to the number of people who are already convinced it will fail.

Definition and Origin

Andy and Bill's Law is an informal concept that states: "The likelihood of a project succeeding is inversely proportional to the number of people who are already convinced it will fail."

In essence, it suggests that the more people that are pessimistic about a project, the more likely it is to succeed, often because the naysayers' objections can spark innovation, problem-solving, and resilience in those who are committed to its success.

"Andy and Bill's Law" is attributed to Andy Grove (former CEO of Intel) and Bill Gates (co-founder of Microsoft). The idea is based on their experiences in the tech industry, where they observed that many successful projects faced strong initial skepticism, but ultimately succeeded due to the perseverance and innovation of those involved.

While there is no formal record of them explicitly coining the term "Andy and Bill's Law," the concept draws from their views on leadership and overcoming doubt. Grove and Gates both frequently discussed how being underestimated or facing resistance could fuel innovation and drive success.

Context and Importance

In the context of software and technology, Andy and Bill's Law emphasize a crucial dynamic: innovation often thrives under adversity. Both Andy Grove and Bill Gates experienced firsthand how new ideas and technologies were frequently met with skepticism, resistance, and criticism from various stakeholders, including investors, competitors, and even internal teams. In an industry that evolves rapidly, those who initially believe in a groundbreaking idea despite external doubt tend to push through the challenges, refine their solutions, and eventually prove the critics wrong. This law underscores the importance of persistence and conviction in the face of doubt—traits that are essential in the high-risk, high-reward world of software and technology development.

The law also speaks to the idea that early opposition can fuel critical thinking and problem-solving. In software development, where new technologies often disrupt established norms and business models, having the courage to challenge conventional wisdom and pursue untested ideas can lead to breakthroughs. Whether it's creating a new programming language, developing innovative software architecture, or launching a disruptive product, the resistance faced early on can serve as a test of the project's viability. If those who believe in the project's potential can overcome these challenges, they often end up creating something that reshapes the industry, just as both Intel and Microsoft did. Andy and Bill's Law, in this way, serves as both a strategic and philosophical reminder to embrace the inevitable skepticism that accompanies ambitious innovation.

Best Practices and Guidelines

Embrace Early Skepticism: View doubt as a signal to refine your ideas, not as a barrier.

Focus on Conviction: Stay committed to your vision, even when faced with widespread criticism.

Use Resistance to Drive Innovation: Let opposition inspire creative problem-solving and improvements.

Challenge Conventional Wisdom: Push boundaries in technology and development, even if it disrupts established norms.

Test Ideas Relentlessly: Overcome initial setbacks through continuous iteration and testing to prove skeptics wrong.

Common Misconceptions and Pitfalls

- Ignoring Feedback: Believing that skepticism is always wrong, leading to dismissing valid concerns that could improve the idea.
- Overconfidence in Resistance: Assuming that opposition automatically means success, without considering the actual viability of the idea.
- Underestimating the Need for Adaptation: Focusing too much on proving skeptics wrong instead of adjusting the approach based on real-world feedback.
- Overvaluing Perceived Resistance: Conflating initial skepticism with long-term market rejection, leading to premature decisions to double down on a flawed idea.
- Burnout from Conflict: Failing to recognize that consistent opposition without strategic adjustment can drain resources and morale.

Related Concepts

1. The Law of Leaky Abstractions (Joel Spolsky): This principle states that all abstractions leak, meaning that the higher-level models or technologies we use in software will inevitably hide certain complexities that may become apparent later. Similar to Andy and Bill's Law, it highlights how initial assumptions, or optimism can be undermined by unforeseen challenges, requiring adaptation and innovation to succeed.
2. The 90-90 Rule (Fred Brooks): This rule observes that "The first 90% of the work takes 90% of the time, and the remaining 10% takes the other 90%." It aligns with the spirit of Andy and Bill's Law, as it reflects how initial progress on software projects may look promising, but real challenges often emerge as the project matures, requiring persistence and overcoming skepticism.

3. Brooks' Law ("Adding manpower to a late software project makes it later"): Brooks' Law emphasizes the counterintuitive nature of software development, where adding resources to solve problems too late in the game can actually exacerbate delays. This resonates with Andy and Bill's Law in that overcoming skepticism about timelines or resource constraints may be crucial to the success of a project, but rushing to "fix" things may only worsen outcomes.
4. The Law of the Instrument (Abraham Maslow): Often summarized as "If all you have is a hammer, everything looks like a nail," this law highlights the dangers of over-relying on a single tool or method. In the context of software, it underscores the importance of remaining open to alternatives and adapting in the face of early doubts, rather than sticking rigidly to one solution.
5. The Pareto Principle (80/20 Rule): The Pareto Principle states that roughly 80% of the effects come from 20% of the causes. In software development, this can reflect how a small portion of the effort or innovation can yield disproportionate results, similar to how overcoming early skepticism with targeted innovation often drives the majority of a project's success.

References

- Wikipedia, *Andy and Bill's law*, [pub: 8 Jan 2024, cited: 3 Jan 2025]

Bell's Law: new classes of computers are created approximately every decade, resulting in new industries, new opportunities, and new ways of thinking

---

Definition and Origin

Bell's Law states that a new class of computing systems—defined by significant changes in hardware architecture—emerges approximately every 10 to 15 years, leading to a new generation of applications, systems, and industries. This law highlights how technological advancements in hardware, such as processing power or memory, drive the creation of new computing paradigms and capabilities.

Bell's Law was coined by Gordon Bell, an American computer scientist and engineer, in 1972. He is also known for his work at Digital Equipment Corporation (DEC) and his contributions to the development of computer systems and architecture. Bell's Law describes the emergence of new classes of computers and systems driven by advances in hardware.

Context and Importance

Bell's Law, formulated by Gordon Bell in 1972, has had a profound impact on how we understand the evolution of computing technology and its relationship to software development. At its core, the law posits that every 10 to 15 years, a new class of computing systems emerges, which reshapes the technological landscape and drives the creation of new software ecosystems. During the early 1970s, computing was largely dominated by mainframe computers, and software applications were tailored to that specific hardware architecture. However, Bell's Law predicted that advancements in hardware would lead to the development of smaller, more powerful, and specialized systems, such as minicomputers, personal computers, and mobile devices, each fostering unique software environments. This shift significantly influenced how software is designed, leading to a more diverse range of applications optimized for new hardware platforms, from desktop applications to mobile apps and cloud computing solutions.

The importance of Bell's Law extends beyond just hardware and software development; it emphasizes the dynamic interaction between hardware innovations and the corresponding software that utilizes those capabilities. As new computing paradigms emerge, software must evolve to leverage the increased processing power, memory capacity, and new input/output interfaces. For instance, the rise of personal computers in the 1980s gave birth to an entirely new software industry, with graphical user interfaces (GUIs) and productivity tools becoming mainstream. Similarly, the advent of smartphones and cloud computing has spurred the development of mobile apps, web services, and complex data analytics platforms. Bell's Law highlights how the cycle of innovation in hardware creates opportunities for new software industries and how those industries, in turn, drive further technological advancements, creating a continual feedback loop that accelerates progress in both domains.

Best Practices and Guidelines

Anticipate Emerging Platforms: Regularly monitor hardware innovations to predict new computing classes that will require specialized software solutions.

Design for Scalability: Build software with flexibility to adapt to rapidly evolving hardware, ensuring long-term viability across different generations of systems.

Embrace Modularity: Use modular architectures in software design to easily integrate with new hardware platforms as they emerge.

Foster Cross-Disciplinary Collaboration: Encourage collaboration between hardware engineers and software developers to ensure that software fully leverages the capabilities of new hardware.

Plan for Disruption: Stay agile and open to rethinking core software designs as new technologies emerge, aligning with shifts in computing paradigms dictated by Bell's Law.

Common Misconceptions and Pitfalls

- Overlooking Long-Term Trends: Believing that existing computing models will remain dominant indefinitely, ignoring the inevitable disruptions Bell's Law predicts.
- Underestimating Software Overhaul Requirements: Assuming that software will seamlessly transition to new hardware without significant redesign or optimization.
- Focusing Only on Current Technology: Failing to anticipate the next computing class and its specific needs, which can lead to missed opportunities or obsolete software.
- Assuming Hardware Improvements Are Linear: Misjudging the pace and impact of hardware advancements, which often occur in breakthroughs rather than steady progress.
- Ignoring User Experience Evolution: Neglecting how new hardware capabilities change user expectations, leading to software that doesn't fully leverage the potential of emerging platforms.

Related Concepts

1. Moore’s Law: States that the number of transistors on a microchip doubles approximately every two years, leading to exponential increases in computing power. This law drives the hardware advancements that Bell's Law hinges on, directly impacting software development as new capabilities become available.
2. Metcalfe’s Law: Suggests that the value of a network is proportional to the square of the number of connected users. As new computing platforms emerge (e.g., mobile or cloud), software must adapt to leverage the growing interconnectedness, driving the creation of network-dependent applications.
3. Wirth’s Law: Posits that software tends to become more complex over time as hardware improves, often leading to slower performance despite greater hardware capabilities. This principle underscores the need for software to optimize for new hardware architectures to avoid inefficiency.
4. The Law of Accelerating Returns: Coined by Ray Kurzweil, it states that the rate of progress in technology accelerates over time, compounding itself. In the context of Bell’s Law, this law highlights the exponential growth of new computing classes and the accelerating demand for software that keeps pace.
5. The Principle of Least Astonishment: A software design principle stating that systems should behave in a way that users expect. As new computing systems emerge under Bell’s Law, developers must ensure that software remains intuitive and responsive to the evolving user interface and interaction paradigms introduced by new hardware.

References

- Wikipedia, *Bell's law of computer classes*, [pub: 16 Apr 2024, cited: 3 Jan 2025]

Dennard Scaling

Definition and Origin

Dennard Scaling refers to the observation, made by Robert Dennard in 1974, that as transistors on a microchip become smaller, their power density stays constant, meaning that both their power consumption and heat generation per unit of area remain the same. This scaling allowed for increased performance (more transistors) without a proportional increase in power consumption, leading to faster and more efficient processors. However, Dennard scaling began to break down in the mid-2000s as transistors reached physical limits, resulting in challenges in continuing performance improvements.

Context and Importance

Dennard Scaling was a foundational principle in the development of modern computing and technology. During the late 20th and early 21st centuries, it enabled the exponential growth in processor performance that fueled advancements in software, hardware, and consumer electronics. As transistors became smaller and more densely packed on integrated circuits, processors could execute more instructions per second while maintaining manageable power consumption and heat dissipation. This allowed software developers to write increasingly complex and resource-intensive applications, as hardware improvements kept pace with growing demands for processing power. Key innovations in fields like gaming, scientific computing, machine learning, and cloud computing were made possible because Dennard Scaling made higher computational performance accessible at lower costs.

As the limits of Dennard Scaling became apparent in the mid-2000s, particularly as transistors reached sizes of just a few nanometers, the promise of continuous performance improvements from smaller transistors began to wane. This shift forced both hardware and software industries to adapt. In hardware, companies began focusing on multi-core architectures, parallel processing, and specialized accelerators like GPUs to boost performance without relying on clock speed improvements. In software, developers faced challenges in optimizing applications to take advantage of multi-core processors, leading to the rise of parallel computing frameworks and more efficient algorithms. The end of Dennard Scaling signified a pivotal shift in how computing progress was pursued, emphasizing more specialized hardware designs and rethinking software to exploit these new hardware architectures.

Best Practices and Guidelines

Optimize for Parallelism: Leverage multi-core and multi-threaded architectures to maximize performance, as single-core clock speeds no longer scale significantly.

Use Specialized Hardware: Utilize accelerators (e.g., GPUs, TPUs) and custom processors to offload specific tasks and improve efficiency in computationally intensive applications.

Focus on Energy Efficiency: Optimize software to minimize power consumption, as raw performance gains are increasingly limited by power and thermal constraints.

Embrace Software-Hardware Co-Design: Develop software that is tightly coupled with hardware capabilities, ensuring better resource utilization and performance.

Adapt to Heterogeneous Architectures: Design applications to run efficiently across diverse hardware platforms (e.g., CPUs, GPUs, FPGAs) by exploiting their unique strengths.

Common Misconceptions and Pitfalls

- Performance Will Always Increase with Smaller Transistors: As Dennard Scaling slows down, performance gains from shrinking transistors have plateaued, requiring new approaches like multi-core or specialized processors.
- Moore's Law and Dennard Scaling Are the Same: While both describe trends in semiconductor progress, Moore's Law refers to transistor density, while Dennard Scaling focuses on power consumption relative to transistor size.
- More Cores = Linear Performance Gains: Simply adding more cores doesn't guarantee linear performance improvement; software must be optimized for parallelism to take full advantage of multi-core processors.
- Smaller Transistors Are Always More Efficient: At extremely small transistor sizes, leakage current and other non-ideal factors become more prominent, leading to inefficiencies despite the reduced size.

- CPU Performance Gains Will Continue Without Major Changes: Relying on traditional CPU performance improvements under Dennard Scaling can result in stagnation, as the limitations of clock speed and power scaling force shifts toward alternative architectures.

Related Concepts

1. Amdahl's Law – This principle highlights the limits of parallelism in software. It states that the speedup of a program from parallelization is constrained by the serial portion of the code. As Dennard Scaling has slowed, Amdahl's Law underscores the need for optimizing the parts of software that remain sequential, despite the availability of more cores.
2. Gustafson's Law – In contrast to Amdahl's Law, Gustafson's Law argues that the potential for speedup with parallelization grows as the problem size increases, making it more relevant in the context of modern applications where larger datasets and more parallel tasks are increasingly common.
3. Koomey's Law – This principle states that the energy efficiency of computers doubles approximately every 1.5 years, similar to Moore's Law. As Dennard Scaling wanes, Koomey's Law becomes increasingly important, driving software development to optimize power usage, particularly in the context of mobile devices and cloud computing.
4. Law of Diminishing Returns – In software performance, this law reflects the reality that as systems become more complex and hardware scaling slows (due to Dennard Scaling limitations), further improvements in performance require exponentially more effort, often leading to diminishing returns for performance optimization.
5. The Free Lunch is Over (multi-core programming) – Coined by Herb Sutter, this principle reflects the shift from single-threaded performance gains to the need for parallel programming. With the end of Dennard Scaling, software must adapt to increasingly parallel hardware, highlighting the importance of multi-core and GPU-accelerated architectures.

References

- Wikipedia, *Dennard scaling*, [pub: 26 Dec 2024, cited: 3 Jan 2025]

Gilder's Law

Definition and Origin

Gilder's Law states that the bandwidth of communication systems (such as the internet) will increase at an exponential rate, roughly doubling every 12 to 18 months, leading to a rapid expansion in the capacity for transmitting information. This law emphasizes the growth of bandwidth in comparison to the speed of processing power, suggesting that increased bandwidth will drive advancements in technologies and services that require high-speed communication.

Gilder's Law was coined by George Gilder, an American author, economist, and technology analyst. He introduced the concept in his 1994 book, Telecosm: How Infinite Bandwidth Will Revolutionize Our World. Gilder's Law focuses on the rapid expansion of communication bandwidth, predicting that its growth will outpace other technological developments, especially processing power.

Context and Importance

Gilder's Law holds significant relevance to the software and technology sectors, particularly in the context of data transmission and communication systems. As internet bandwidth has exponentially increased over the past few decades, the capacity to transfer massive amounts of data in real time has fundamentally reshaped how software operates. The law predicted a future where communication systems could handle far more data than traditional processing power could ever manage alone. This shift paved the way for innovations in cloud computing, video streaming, real-time collaboration tools, and the proliferation of the Internet of Things (IoT), all of which rely on high-bandwidth networks. Software developers, in turn, have been able to create increasingly sophisticated applications that leverage these advances in bandwidth, from advanced AI systems to high-definition content delivery.

Moreover, Gilder's Law underscores the role of bandwidth in driving the next wave of technological evolution, highlighting that progress is not solely dependent on the performance of individual devices or processors. As networks have become faster and more reliable, software architectures have adapted to harness these improvements. For instance, the rise of edge computing and content delivery networks (CDNs) directly stems from the availability of vast bandwidth, allowing for the efficient distribution of heavy workloads across networks. The interplay between bandwidth and software innovation is evident in areas like 5G technology, which promises to accelerate the deployment of new applications like autonomous vehicles and smart cities. As such, Gilder's Law continues to be a critical framework for understanding the dynamic relationship between infrastructure and software evolution in an increasingly connected world.

Best Practices and Guidelines

Design for Scalability: Build software that can take advantage of rapidly increasing bandwidth by ensuring it can scale to handle higher data throughput and real-time communication.

Embrace Distributed Architectures: Leverage cloud computing, edge computing, and decentralized networks to optimize performance and reduce latency, capitalizing on vast bandwidth.

Prioritize Data Efficiency: While bandwidth increases, optimizing how data is compressed and transmitted can still reduce costs and improve the overall user experience.

Future-Proof Applications: Anticipate continuous improvements in bandwidth and develop software with flexible architectures that can adapt to new network capabilities without significant rewrites.

Innovate with Real-Time Features: Utilize the growing bandwidth to integrate more real-time, data-heavy features (e.g., live video, virtual reality, AI applications) into software solutions.

Common Misconceptions and Pitfalls

- Assuming Bandwidth Alone Drives Innovation: Gilder's Law focuses on bandwidth growth, but other factors like software optimization, hardware capabilities, and latency also play crucial roles in shaping technological progress.
- Overestimating Immediate Impact: While bandwidth is growing, the full potential of increased capacity may take time to materialize in consumer-facing applications, especially in regions with infrastructure limitations.
- Neglecting Network Congestion: More bandwidth doesn't automatically solve issues like network congestion or latency; managing traffic and optimizing network protocols are still essential.
- Ignoring Security Challenges: With higher bandwidth comes greater vulnerability; faster data transmission increases the potential for cyberattacks, requiring stronger security measures.
- Underestimating Dependency on Local Infrastructure: While global bandwidth improves, the actual performance still depends heavily on local network infrastructure, which may not scale at the same rate as global bandwidth increases.

Related Concepts

1. Moore's Law: This principle states that the number of transistors on a microchip doubles approximately every two years, leading to an exponential increase in processing power. While Gilder's Law focuses on bandwidth growth, Moore's Law addresses the parallel increase in computational capacity, which together enable more complex and bandwidth-heavy applications.
2. Metcalfe's Law: Metcalfe's Law posits that the value of a network is proportional to the square of the number of connected users. As bandwidth increases, the potential value of networks grows exponentially, fostering the development of more robust, interconnected systems and applications, much like Gilder's Law anticipates.
3. Kryder's Law: Similar to Moore's Law, Kryder's Law describes the exponential increase in storage capacity and density over time. As both storage and bandwidth expand rapidly, software applications are able to handle larger datasets and more complex tasks, enabling new types of data-driven services and cloud applications.

4. Shannon-Hartley Theorem: This principle outlines the theoretical maximum data transfer rate for a communication channel, given its bandwidth and noise level. Gilder's Law aligns with this by suggesting that as bandwidth grows, the practical capacity for transmitting information increases, unlocking more possibilities for data-heavy software.
5. Law of Software Convergence: This principle asserts that as technology evolves, distinct technologies (like hardware, software, and networks) tend to converge into more integrated, unified systems. Gilder's Law highlights the importance of network bandwidth in this convergence, as high-bandwidth networks are essential to support the increasingly interconnected and sophisticated software environments.

References

- CIO Wiki, *Gilder's Law*, [pub: 8 Mar 2024, cited: 3 Jan 2025]

Grosch's Law

Definition and Origin

Grosch's Law is a principle in computer science that states that the performance of a computer improves roughly in proportion to the square of its cost. In other words, doubling the cost of a computer typically results in roughly quadrupling its processing power. The law is often used to illustrate the relationship between cost and performance in computing hardware.

Grosch's Law was coined by Herbert A. Grosch, an American computer scientist, in the 1960s. Grosch observed that, for many computers, the performance (processing power) increased approximately with the square of their cost. He introduced this rule to highlight the relationship between the price of a computer and its performance, noting that higher-cost machines generally offered a disproportionately greater increase in performance.

Context and Importance

Grosch's Law, formulated in the 1960s, initially reflected the hardware-centric view of computing, where the performance of machines was closely tied to their cost. At the time, computers were expensive, and software development was often limited by the hardware's computational power. Grosch's Law illustrated that investing more money in higher-end systems would yield disproportionately higher performance, which was a key consideration for organizations making purchasing decisions. The principle helped highlight the limitations of less expensive machines for complex tasks and led to an understanding that for certain workloads, high-cost systems could offer significant returns in terms of processing capability and efficiency.

In the context of modern software and technology, Grosch's Law is less directly relevant, as advances in software optimization, distributed computing, and cloud services have shifted the focus away from purely hardware-bound performance. However, it remains significant as a historical lens to understand how early computing environments shaped software development and system design. Today, while hardware has become much more affordable and powerful, the law's core idea still influences the way technology companies think about scaling systems—particularly in areas like cloud computing, where cost/performance trade-offs in terms of computational resources continue to be a key consideration for infrastructure choices. Additionally, it highlights the diminishing returns of simply upgrading hardware in the face of increasingly complex software, which often requires more nuanced approaches to performance optimization.

Best Practices and Guidelines

Balance cost and performance: When selecting hardware or cloud services, ensure that the performance improvement justifies the additional cost, especially for non-critical applications.

Optimize software first: Prioritize software optimization before scaling hardware, as improvements in algorithms or code efficiency can often yield greater gains than hardware upgrades.

Consider diminishing returns: Be mindful that beyond a certain point, increasing hardware investment (e.g., doubling server capacity) may not proportionally improve performance.

Leverage cloud scalability: Use cloud services that allow flexible scaling to match actual demand, avoiding over-investment in hardware that may not deliver proportional benefits.

Plan for long-term growth: When upgrading infrastructure, plan for future needs and potential software advancements rather than focusing solely on immediate performance boosts.

Common Misconceptions and Pitfalls

- Assuming linear cost-performance relationship: Grosch's Law suggests a squared relationship, so expecting a linear improvement with cost increases can lead to underestimating the diminishing returns on higher-end hardware.
- Overemphasis on hardware upgrades: Relying too much on expensive hardware to solve performance issues may overlook the importance of optimizing software and algorithms.
- Ignoring software-hardware mismatch: Grosch's Law focuses on hardware performance, but in modern systems, software inefficiencies or mismatches with hardware can negate any performance gains from upgrading the hardware.
- Overlooking the impact of cloud scalability: In a cloud-first world, the law's relevance may be overstated, as cloud services offer more flexible and granular performance scaling, often making hardware-based thinking less relevant.
- Neglecting non-performance costs: Grosch's Law mainly addresses performance relative to cost, but it doesn't consider other costs such as maintenance, power consumption, and operational complexity, which can diminish the overall value of higher-cost systems.

Related Concepts

1. Moore's Law Principle: The number of transistors on a microchip doubles approximately every two years, leading to an exponential increase in computing power and a decrease in cost per transistor. Relation to Grosch's Law: Both highlight the relationship between cost and performance, though Moore's Law emphasizes technological advancements and miniaturization in hardware, whereas Grosch's Law focuses on the square of performance relative to cost.

2. Amdahl's Law Principle: The speedup of a system from parallelization is limited by the portion of the system that cannot be parallelized. Relation to Grosch's Law: While Grosch's Law assumes scaling performance with cost, Amdahl's Law points out that real-world performance gains are often constrained by non-parallelizable tasks, emphasizing that simply increasing resources doesn't guarantee linear performance improvements.
3. Wirth's Law Principle: Software is getting slower more rapidly than hardware is getting faster. Relation to Grosch's Law: While Grosch's Law addresses hardware performance, Wirth's Law highlights the paradox that software complexity often outpaces hardware improvements, undermining the idea that simply investing more in hardware will yield proportional gains in performance.
4. Brooks' Law Principle: Adding more developers to a late software project makes it later. Relation to Grosch's Law: While Grosch's Law focuses on cost vs. performance in hardware, Brooks' Law emphasizes that scaling human resources doesn't always scale productivity in software development, highlighting inefficiencies in "over-scaling" solutions.
5. Conway's Law Principle: Organizations are constrained to produce systems that mirror their communication structure. Relation to Grosch's Law: Both laws deal with scaling and system design, but Conway's Law shifts focus to organizational and communication structures, suggesting that the design of a system (software or hardware) often reflects the organizational structure rather than simply scaling resources for better performance.

References

- Wikipedia, *Grosch's law*, [pub: 6 May 2024, cited: 3 Jan 2025]

Kryder's Law: Magnetic disk storage density doubles annually

Definition and Origin

Kryder's Law is the observation that the storage density of hard drives (and other magnetic storage media) increases at an exponential rate, typically doubling approximately every 18 months to two years, leading to a rapid reduction in the cost per gigabyte of storage. It is named after Mark Kryder, a former executive at Seagate Technology.

Kryder's Law was coined by Mark Kryder, who was a former executive and Chief Technology Officer at Seagate Technology. He observed the exponential increase in storage density of hard drives and the corresponding reduction in the cost per gigabyte over time.

Context and Importance

Kryder's Law has significant implications for both software development and technological innovation, particularly in the realm of data storage. As storage capacities increased exponentially, driven by advancements in hard drive technology, software developers were able to build applications that could handle vastly larger datasets without running into storage limitations. This trend has been crucial for industries ranging from data analytics to artificial intelligence, where vast amounts of data are critical for training algorithms and making informed decisions. As storage became cheaper and more abundant, software could evolve to handle more complex tasks, enabling innovations such as cloud computing, big data platforms, and the rapid growth of digital media.

The law also had an important influence on the economics of technology. With storage costs decreasing rapidly, businesses and consumers could afford to store vast quantities of data at lower costs, which in turn fueled the expansion of the digital economy. It supported the shift toward data-centric services, such as streaming platforms, social media, and SaaS applications, where large-scale data storage was a foundational requirement. Kryder's Law played a role in reducing barriers to entry for startups and small companies, allowing them to leverage affordable storage solutions to compete with larger firms. This democratization of data storage helped accelerate innovation and the growth of the technology industry overall.

Best Practices and Guidelines

Plan for Data Growth: Anticipate rapid increases in storage requirements as data volumes expand, leveraging Kryder's Law to design scalable systems.

Optimize Storage Efficiency: While storage costs decrease, focus on optimizing data storage and retrieval to avoid unnecessary bloat or inefficiencies.

Leverage Cloud Solutions: Take advantage of the decreasing cost of storage to utilize cloud-based services, offering flexibility and scalability.

Invest in Data Security: As data storage grows, prioritize robust security measures to protect increasingly large datasets from breaches or loss.

Adapt Software Architectures: Build applications that can dynamically handle larger datasets, incorporating distributed and cloud-native architectures to ensure future scalability.

Common Misconceptions and Pitfalls

- Storage Growth Doesn't Equal Performance Growth: Kryder's Law refers to storage density and cost, but it doesn't guarantee improvements in storage speed or overall system performance.
- Endless Cheap Storage: The law suggests lower costs over time, but it doesn't mean storage will remain unlimited or free costs can still rise due to factors like materials, energy, and market demands.
- Assuming Unlimited Data Handling: Relying solely on cheap storage can lead to inefficiencies if data management and retrieval strategies are not optimized for scalability.
- Overlooking Non-Storage Bottlenecks: While storage may become cheaper, other bottlenecks such as network bandwidth or processor power may still limit performance and efficiency.
- Neglecting Environmental Impact: The exponential growth of data storage can lead to increased energy consumption and electronic waste, which may be overlooked in the drive for cheaper, more abundant storage.

Related Concepts

1. Moore's Law: This principle states that the number of transistors on a microchip doubles approximately every two years, leading to exponential increases in computing power. Like Kryder's Law, Moore's Law drives rapid advancements in technology, enabling more powerful software applications to handle growing data storage and processing demands.
2. Metcalfe's Law: This law posits that the value of a network is proportional to the square of the number of connected users. As storage becomes cheaper and more abundant, the growth of connected devices and platforms (such as IoT and social media) accelerates, increasing the value and potential of data-driven applications and networks.
3. Harrison's Law of Software Engineering: This law suggests that the complexity of software systems increases over time. With the exponential growth of data storage, managing and scaling software to handle larger datasets becomes more complex, requiring more sophisticated design and architecture.
4. Wirth's Law: This principle states that software tends to become slower faster than hardware becomes faster. Despite cheaper and more abundant storage, software may not keep up with hardware improvements unless developers focus on optimizing performance alongside increasing storage capacity.
5. Parkinson's Law: "Work expands to fill the time available for its completion." In the context of storage, this principle suggests that as storage becomes more affordable and abundant, the tendency might be to store more data than necessary, leading to inefficiencies and bloat in software systems unless storage practices are carefully managed.

References

- Wikipedia, *Mark Kryder*, [pub: 1 May 2024, cited: 3 Jan 2025]

Metcalfe's Law: Network value grows with square of users

Definition and Origin

Metcalfe's Law states that the value of a network is proportional to the square of the number of connected users or devices. In other words, as more participants join a network, its overall value increases exponentially due to the growing number of potential connections.

Metcalfe's Law was coined by Robert Metcalfe, the co-inventor of Ethernet and founder of 3Com. He formulated the law in the 1980s to describe the value of a telecommunications network, asserting that the value of a network increases roughly with the square of the number of connected users.

Context and Importance

Metcalfe's Law has profound implications in the software and technology sectors, especially in the context of network-based platforms, social media, and digital ecosystems. As technologies like the internet, mobile networks, and cloud computing continue to interconnect millions, the value of these platforms grows exponentially as more users and devices join. In software development, platforms that facilitate user interaction—such as social media networks, online marketplaces, or communication tools—become significantly more valuable as their user base expands. The increasing number of connections enables new services, features, and innovations that are not possible in smaller, less-connected systems, driving the network effect and creating a competitive advantage for large platforms like Facebook, Twitter, and WhatsApp.

The importance of Metcalfe's Law in technology also extends to the economic models of companies and investors. Companies leveraging network effects can experience rapid growth in user acquisition, retention, and monetization, making them highly attractive in the market. For instance, firms like Uber and Airbnb benefit from the growing number of users that enhance the overall utility of their platforms, reducing transaction costs and increasing overall platform activity. Understanding Metcalfe's Law is critical for predicting the success of network-dependent technologies and identifying investment opportunities. It underscores the notion that in the digital age, network size can be as valuable—if not more so—than traditional metrics like product features or service quality, emphasizing the strategic importance of growing a robust user base.

Best Practices and Guidelines

Focus on Network Growth: Prioritize user acquisition and engagement to expand the network, as its value increases exponentially with more users and connections.

Leverage Network Effects: Build features that enhance interactions between users, creating additional value as the network grows (e.g., social sharing, user-generated content).

Optimize Scalability: Ensure the platform can handle increased user activity and data flow, maintaining performance as the network size expands.

Encourage Ecosystem Development: Support third-party integrations and partnerships to further enhance the network's value and create a broader ecosystem.

Monetize the Network: Identify sustainable revenue models that benefit from the growing user base, such as targeted advertising, premium subscriptions, or data-driven services.

Common Misconceptions and Pitfalls

- Assuming Linear Growth: Many mistakenly expect network value to grow linearly with users, when in reality, it grows exponentially, making early growth more critical than later stages.
- Neglecting Network Quality: Simply having more users doesn't guarantee value—network effects require meaningful interactions and quality connections, not just sheer volume.
- Overlooking Infrastructure Needs: As networks grow, scaling infrastructure and maintaining performance can become a significant challenge, often underestimated in early stages.
- Ignoring Negative Network Effects: Larger networks can suffer from congestion, reduced user experience, or decreased privacy, which can diminish value if not properly managed.
- Focusing Solely on User Acquisition: Prioritizing user growth without considering retention, engagement, and the creation of a robust, active user community can limit the full potential of the network.

Related Concepts

1. Reed's Law: This law suggests that the value of a network grows exponentially not just with the number of users, but with the number of groups or sub-networks formed within the larger network. It asserts that the value increases with the ability to form meaningful groups and communities, often growing faster than Metcalfe's Law predicts.
2. Sarnoff's Law: While Metcalfe's Law focuses on the network of users, Sarnoff's Law applies to one-to-many broadcasting networks, where the value is proportional to the number of viewers or listeners. It emphasizes the value of broadcast-style networks, like TV or radio, as linear with the audience size rather than exponential.
3. Moore's Law: Although it pertains to the hardware side, Moore's Law (the doubling of transistors on a chip every two years) indirectly supports Metcalfe's Law by enabling better, more scalable infrastructure. The increase in computing power allows networks to handle more users and data efficiently, facilitating the growth of network-based value.
4. The Network Effect: This principle describes how a product or service becomes more valuable as more people use it, much like Metcalfe's Law, but it encompasses a broader range of products and platforms beyond just telecommunications. The more users interact with a platform, the more value it generates for everyone, driving innovation and creating positive feedback loops.
5. The Law of Diminishing Returns: In the context of Metcalfe's Law, this law warns that as a network grows extremely large, the additional value generated by each new user may decrease, especially if the network becomes too saturated or inefficient. It's important to balance growth with the quality and manageability of the network to avoid this phenomenon.

References

- Wikipedia, *Metcalfe's law*, [pub: 10 Sep 2024, cited: 3 Jan 2025]

Moore's Law: Computing power doubles approximately every two years

---

Definition and Origin

Moore's Law is the observation that the number of transistors on a microchip—and thereby computing power—tends to double approximately every two years, leading to the continuous improvement in performance and reduction in cost of electronic devices.

Moore's Law was coined by Gordon Moore, co-founder of Intel, in 1965. He observed that the number of transistors on a microchip was doubling approximately every two years, leading to exponential increases in computing power and decreases in cost. This observation became a key driver of the semiconductor industry's progress.

Context and Importance

Moore's Law has been a foundational principle driving the rapid advancement of both hardware and software in the tech industry. By predicting that computing power would double roughly every two years, it set the pace for innovations in microelectronics, leading to the miniaturization and performance gains seen in modern computing devices. For software development, this exponential increase in hardware capability has allowed programs to become more complex, data-rich, and sophisticated. Software developers could rely on the continuous improvement of hardware to push the boundaries of what was possible, leading to innovations in fields such as artificial intelligence, data science, and graphics rendering. Essentially, as hardware became faster and more powerful, software could evolve to leverage these advancements, enabling the creation of more feature-rich applications and systems.

The importance of Moore's Law goes beyond just hardware; it has shaped the overall trajectory of technology, influencing not only how software is written but also how it is used. As processing power increased, it facilitated the rise of cloud computing, big data analytics, and real-time applications that rely on massive amounts of computational resources. For businesses and consumers, this created new possibilities—from more immersive user experiences in gaming and virtual reality to advancements in medical technology, scientific research, and communication tools. In a broader sense, Moore's Law has spurred continuous innovation, providing the technological foundation for the digital transformation that has become central to modern economies and daily life. However, as transistor sizes approach physical limits, the future of Moore's Law has become uncertain, driving the exploration of new paradigms like quantum computing and specialized processors.

Best Practices and Guidelines

Leverage increasing hardware capabilities: Optimize software to take advantage of faster processors and larger memory, improving performance and efficiency.

Plan for scalability: Design applications with the assumption that computing power will continue to grow, enabling scalability for future demand.

Stay adaptable: Keep software architectures flexible to integrate emerging technologies and take advantage of future hardware advancements.

Optimize for parallelism: As processors evolve with more cores, optimize software for parallel processing to maximize performance.

Monitor hardware trends: Stay informed about the physical limits of Moore's Law and explore alternative technologies, like specialized chips or quantum computing, for future growth.

Common Misconceptions and Pitfalls

- Moore's Law guarantees continuous growth: It's often misunderstood as a guarantee of perpetual performance improvements, but it's slowing down as physical limits of silicon-based technology are approached.
- Only hardware is affected: Many believe Moore's Law only applies to hardware, but software must evolve to fully leverage increased processing power.
- Cheaper hardware automatically improves software: More powerful hardware doesn't always result in better software—developers must optimize code and design for evolving technology.
- Moore's Law applies equally to all sectors: The impact of Moore's Law varies across industries; some may see limited benefits in certain domains, especially with the rise of specialized processors.

- Exponential growth in performance means linear software improvements: Assuming that increased hardware performance directly leads to linear software improvements can overlook the complexities of software optimization and architectural constraints.

Related Concepts

1. Graham's Law of Software Efficiency: This principle suggests that software performance often improves at a rate slower than hardware advancements. While hardware capabilities may double, the efficiency of software typically increases at a much slower pace, emphasizing the need for careful software optimization.
2. Wirth's Law: Coined by Niklaus Wirth, this law states that software is getting slower more rapidly than hardware becomes faster. It highlights the tendency for software to consume increasing amounts of computational resources, often outpacing the gains in hardware performance.
3. Amdahl's Law: This law provides insight into the limitations of parallel computing, stating that the maximum speedup of a system is limited by the sequential portion of a task. As hardware advances with more cores, software must be designed to fully utilize these capabilities, or the gains will be marginal.
4. Conway's Law: It suggests that software systems often mirror the organizational structures of the teams that build them. In the context of Moore's Law, as hardware evolves rapidly, software development teams must adapt their structure and processes to efficiently handle the complexities of scaling software with increasing computing power.
5. Brooks' Law: Proposed by Fred Brooks, this law states that adding manpower to a late software project makes it later. As hardware improves, the temptation to add features or increase the scope of software projects can lead to delays if not properly managed, highlighting the importance of optimizing software processes rather than simply relying on faster hardware.

References

- Wikipedia, *Moore's law*, [pub: 30 Dec 2024, cited: 3 Jan 2025]

Rose's Law

Definition and Origin

Rose's Law is the observation that the number of qubits on quantum computing chips doubles approximately every 18 months, similar to Moore's Law in classical computing. The term was coined by Steve Jurvetson to highlight the rapid pace of quantum computing advancements in terms of qubit scaling.

Rose's Law was coined by Steve Jurvetson, a venture capitalist and early investor in quantum computing. He introduced the term to describe the rapid growth in the number of qubits on quantum chips, observing that the number of qubits doubles approximately every 18 months, mirroring the exponential progress seen in Moore's Law for classical computing.

Context and Importance

Rose's Law, coined by venture capitalist Steve Jurvetson, holds significant implications for the future of quantum computing, which is poised to revolutionize software and technology. As quantum processors grow in power, with qubits doubling approximately every 18 months, the increasing availability of qubits enhances the potential for quantum algorithms to solve complex problems that are intractable for classical computers. This rapid scaling mirrors Moore's Law, which has driven exponential growth in classical computing for decades. In the realm of software development, the rise of quantum computing offers exciting possibilities, including breakthroughs in cryptography, drug discovery, material science, optimization problems, and machine learning. The scaling of quantum hardware, as predicted by Rose's Law, is vital for creating the computational resources necessary for quantum software to mature and perform in real-world applications.

From a technology standpoint, the implications of Rose's Law are immense. As quantum chips advance in capability, software developers and researchers can look forward to increasingly powerful quantum algorithms capable of tackling some of the world's most pressing problems, from improving artificial intelligence to accelerating simulations in various fields like physics and chemistry. Additionally, the pace of quantum hardware development could drive competition, fostering innovation and pushing the boundaries of what is possible in both hardware and software. The rapid progression of qubit capacity also brings new challenges, such as developing error correction techniques and scalable quantum programming languages, but the pace of growth outlined by Rose's Law suggests that the technology is advancing quickly enough to meet these hurdles. The law underscores the accelerating nature of quantum computing and emphasizes the need for parallel advancements in quantum software to fully leverage the potential of future quantum processors.

Best Practices and Guidelines

Prepare for Rapid Change: Anticipate that quantum hardware will evolve quickly, with qubits doubling approximately every 18 months, and adapt software development strategies accordingly.

Focus on Scalability: Design quantum algorithms with scalability in mind, ensuring they can efficiently handle increasing qubit numbers as hardware improves.

Collaborate Across Disciplines: Work closely with hardware engineers and quantum physicists to bridge the gap between quantum software development and advancing hardware capabilities.

Prioritize Quantum Error Correction: As qubit count grows, prioritize developing robust error correction techniques to maintain reliability and stability in quantum computations.

Invest in Cross-Platform Compatibility: Develop quantum software with flexibility, ensuring it can run across multiple quantum computing platforms as the ecosystem matures and diversifies.

Common Misconceptions and Pitfalls

- Assuming Linear Progress: A common misconception is that the growth of qubits will always be linear or predictable. While Rose's Law suggests exponential growth, technological hurdles can slow progress at times.
- Overestimating Immediate Impact: Many assume that the rapid increase in qubits will lead to immediate breakthroughs in quantum computing applications, overlooking the need for corresponding advancements in error correction and algorithm development.
- Neglecting Hardware Limitations: The focus on qubit count can overshadow critical hardware challenges such as qubit coherence, gate fidelity, and scalability, which are essential for practical quantum computing.
- Underestimating Software Challenges: Some assume quantum software will automatically scale with increased qubit numbers, ignoring the complexity of developing algorithms that can effectively leverage large quantum systems.
- Overlooking Ecosystem Development: As hardware improves, there's a misconception that software and infrastructure will naturally keep pace, while in reality, creating a robust quantum ecosystem (tools, languages, platforms) requires substantial parallel development.

Related Concepts

1. Moore's Law: The most directly related principle, Moore's Law observes that the number of transistors on a microchip doubles approximately every two years, driving the exponential growth of classical computing power. This mirrors Rose's Law, which predicts the rapid scaling of qubits in quantum computing hardware.
2. Wirth's Law: This principle states that software tends to become slower faster than hardware becomes faster. While hardware improvements like qubit scaling in quantum computing follow rapid growth, the development of software to utilize that power often lags behind, emphasizing the importance of matching software development pace with hardware advances.

3. Brook's Law: "Adding manpower to a late software project makes it later." This law highlights the difficulty of scaling up software development teams and resources, which may apply to quantum software projects that require specialized expertise to match the rapid scaling of quantum hardware.
4. Lehman's Laws of Software Evolution: These laws describe how software tends to evolve over time, often becoming more complex and less maintainable. In the context of quantum computing, as qubits increase, the complexity of quantum algorithms and the software needed to support them will also grow, requiring careful attention to maintainable and adaptable software design.
5. Metcalfe's Law: This principle states that the value of a network is proportional to the square of the number of connected users. Applied to software and quantum computing, as quantum processors grow in power, the value of quantum systems and algorithms increases exponentially, driving the interconnectedness of quantum networks, collaborations, and cross-platform development.

References

- Wikipedia, *Rose's law*, [pub: 25 Apr 2024, cited: 3 Jan 2025]

Swanson's Law

Definition and Origin

Swanson's Law, proposed by Richard Swanson, states that the cost of solar photovoltaic (PV) cells tends to decrease by approximately 20% for every doubling of cumulative global solar PV production. This mirrors the learning curve phenomenon, where technological advancements and economies of scale drive down costs over time as more units are produced and experience is gained.

Swanson's Law was coined by Richard Swanson, the founder of SunPower Corporation. He observed the relationship between the growth in solar photovoltaic (PV) production and the declining costs of solar cells and formulated the law to capture this trend. Swanson introduced it in 2008 to describe the consistent reduction in the price of solar cells as global production increased.

Context and Importance

Swanson's Law, although originally applied to the solar energy industry, offers valuable insights that extend beyond photovoltaics, particularly to the realm of software and technology. In the context of software development, the law reflects the broader principle of how scaling production, improving engineering processes, and accumulating knowledge lead to cost reductions and performance improvements. As more software is developed and released, the tools, frameworks, and development processes mature, making it easier and cheaper to build, deploy, and maintain new technologies. Similar to Swanson's observation with solar panels, the efficiency and affordability of software products tend to improve as the industry grows, learns, and develops better practices.

The importance of Swanson's Law in the technology sector lies in its ability to highlight the potential for rapid innovation driven by economies of scale. For example, in software, as more companies adopt cloud computing, artificial intelligence, or open-source technologies, the associated costs of developing, deploying, and scaling such technologies drop over time. The growth in data and computational power, as seen in advancements like Moore's Law, complements this trend, leading to the development of increasingly sophisticated software at a lower cost. This creates a virtuous cycle where innovation accelerates because technologies become both cheaper and more accessible. Swanson's Law, in this broader context, emphasizes the symbiotic relationship between production growth, cost reduction, and technological progress, which is crucial for the continued evolution of the software industry.

Best Practices and Guidelines

Scale Drives Efficiency: As usage of software and technology increases, processes improve, leading to lower development and operational costs.

Leverage Open Source: Embrace open-source tools and libraries, which benefit from community-driven improvements, reducing costs and enhancing performance over time.

Focus on Automation: Invest in automation to streamline repetitive tasks, which decreases long-term operational expenses as systems scale.

Iterate and Learn: Continuously improve software products by learning from user feedback and internal data to drive down development costs and enhance functionality.

Invest in Ecosystem Growth: Encourage collaboration and ecosystem-building (e.g., through APIs, integrations) to expand the reach of technology, which accelerates innovation and cost reduction.

Common Misconceptions and Pitfalls

- Overestimating Immediate Cost Reductions: Assuming rapid cost drops in the short term; Swanson's Law operates over longer timeframes and requires significant cumulative production or adoption.
- Ignoring Quality in Scaling: Focusing solely on scaling without maintaining product quality can lead to inefficiencies or failures despite cost reductions.
- Neglecting Innovation: Relying too heavily on cost reductions through scale may lead to stagnation if innovation isn't prioritized alongside growth.
- Assuming Linear Cost Decreases: Misunderstanding that cost reductions follow a strict 20% decrease for each doubling of production; actual reductions may vary based on external factors like market conditions or technological breakthroughs.
- Underestimating the Role of External Factors: Overlooking external factors (e.g., regulatory changes, resource availability) that can disrupt cost trends and technological progress.

Related Concepts

1. Moore's Law: As the number of transistors on a microchip doubles approximately every two years, computing power increases, leading to greater efficiency and reduced costs in software development and technology infrastructure.
2. The Law of Software Entropy: This principle suggests that software systems naturally degrade or become more complex over time unless actively managed and refactored. Unlike Swanson's Law, which predicts cost reductions through scale, this law emphasizes the need for continuous maintenance to avoid rising technical debt.

3. Brooks' Law: The principle that "adding manpower to a late software project makes it later." It highlights that scaling a software team inefficiently can lead to diminishing returns, underscoring the importance of managing growth carefully, which parallels Swanson's focus on scaling production processes effectively.
4. Conway's Law: "Organizations design systems that mirror their own communication structure." This principle emphasizes that scaling organizations and improving development processes often leads to more efficient and robust software systems, much like Swanson's Law suggests for physical technology.
5. The Law of Diminishing Returns in Software: As software projects increase in size or complexity, the cost of adding additional features or solving new problems increases disproportionately. While Swanson's Law implies cost reduction over time through scaling, this principle warns against unchecked growth that leads to inefficiencies or complexity.

References

- Wikipedia, *Swanson's law*, [pub: 19 Jul 2024, cited: 3 Jan 2025]

Wright's Law: Experience Curve

Definition and Origin

Wright's Law, also known as the Experience Curve, posits that as the cumulative production of a product increases, the cost of producing each unit decreases at a predictable rate. This is typically attributed to improvements in efficiency, learning, and economies of scale. In general, for each doubling of production, costs tend to decrease by a fixed percentage, often around 20-30%.

Wright's Law was coined by Theodore Paul Wright, an American engineer, in 1936. He formulated the law based on his analysis of the aviation industry, particularly the costs associated with aircraft production. Wright observed that as the cumulative production of aircraft increased, the cost of producing each subsequent aircraft decreased, leading him to propose the relationship between cumulative production and cost reduction.

Context and Importance

Wright's Law, originally formulated in the context of manufacturing, has been increasingly applied to software and technology industries, where rapid innovation and scaling are common. In software, the law can be seen in the way development costs decrease over time as companies gain experience, streamline processes, and leverage reusable code and libraries. As more software is developed, tools and platforms improve, and the learning curve for developers shortens. This results in more efficient software production, faster development cycles, and reduced costs for scaling up applications or systems. Much like in manufacturing, each iteration of software development benefits from accumulated knowledge, resulting in improvements in speed, performance, and cost efficiency.

In the tech industry, Wright's Law also underscores the importance of network effects and economies of scale. As companies expand their user base and infrastructure, their ability to deliver services or products at lower costs improves. For example, cloud computing platforms like AWS, Google Cloud, and Azure have reduced the cost of infrastructure over time due to their increasing scale and accumulated expertise. Similarly, software companies like Microsoft and Adobe benefit from decades of experience, enabling them to offer more advanced products at competitive prices. Understanding Wright's Law in this context helps companies in the technology sector make better predictions about cost reductions and efficiency gains as they scale, guiding strategic decisions around pricing, product development, and investment in innovation.

Best Practices and Guidelines

Leverage experience and iteration: Focus on continuous improvement and learning within development teams to reduce costs and increase efficiency over time.

Invest in automation and reusable code: Build reusable components, libraries, and automated testing to streamline development and accelerate production.

Scale strategically: As your user base or product offerings grow, take advantage of economies of scale to reduce per-unit costs and increase system efficiency.

Emphasize long-term vision: Understand that cost reductions and performance improvements will accelerate as cumulative development and deployment experience builds.

Foster innovation and tool improvement: Prioritize enhancing development tools, platforms, and workflows to continually improve the speed and quality of software production.

Common Misconceptions and Pitfalls

- Assuming linear cost reduction: Wright's Law suggests a consistent percentage cost reduction, but real-world reductions may vary depending on factors like technology shifts, market dynamics, and unexpected challenges.
- Neglecting external factors: Focusing only on cumulative production without accounting for changes in technology, market demand, or external disruptions can lead to overly optimistic cost predictions.
- Overestimating scalability: The law assumes efficiency improvements with scale, but sometimes the complexity of software, user needs, or infrastructure limitations can slow down cost reductions.
- Ignoring diminishing returns: In some cases, after a certain point, the rate of cost reduction may slow or plateau, especially when most "easy wins" have already been achieved.
- Underestimating upfront investment: Early stages of development may involve significant upfront costs and learning curves before the benefits of Wright's Law materialize, leading to unrealistic expectations about early-stage profitability.

Related Concepts

1. Moore's Law: This principle states that the number of transistors on a microchip doubles approximately every two years, leading to exponential increases in computing power and reductions in hardware costs. Like Wright's Law, it emphasizes the impact of scale and innovation over time in driving down costs and improving performance in technology.

2. Parkinson's Law: "Work expands to fill the time available for its completion." While not directly about cost reduction, this law is often cited in software development to highlight inefficiencies and unnecessary complexity that can arise over time, potentially counteracting the benefits predicted by Wright's Law if not managed properly.
3. The Law of Leaky Abstractions: In software design, this principle suggests that higher-level abstractions (such as libraries or frameworks) often leak details of lower-level systems, leading to inefficiencies and unexpected costs. This can create a counterbalance to the anticipated efficiency gains from Wright's Law if abstractions introduce complexity rather than simplifying development.
4. Conway's Law: "Organizations which design systems are constrained to produce designs which are copies of the communication structures of these organizations." This law highlights how organizational structure influences software design and development, impacting the efficiency gains that might otherwise align with Wright's Law in terms of reducing costs over time.
5. The 90/10 Rule (Pareto Principle): This principle suggests that 90% of software development effort often goes into solving just 10% of the most complex problems. While Wright's Law focuses on the efficiency of scaling, the Pareto Principle can help highlight areas where focus on the most impactful problems can drive substantial cost reduction and performance improvement.

References

- Wikipedia, *Experience curve effects*, [pub: 9 Nov 2024, cited: 3 Jan 2025]

J. AI & Robotics

The AI Effect: Once AI solves a problem, it's no longer considered AI

Definition and Origin

The AI Effect refers to the phenomenon where tasks once considered to require human-like intelligence are reclassified as mere automation once machines are able to perform them. As AI systems become capable of handling increasingly complex tasks, the definition of what constitutes "artificial intelligence" continually shifts, making previously difficult tasks seem routine and diminishing the perceived complexity of AI.

Context and Importance

The AI Effect in the context of software and technology highlights the shifting perceptions of artificial intelligence as it increasingly automates tasks once thought to require human intelligence. As AI systems evolve and successfully handle tasks like language translation, image recognition, and decision-making, what was previously considered "intelligent" behavior becomes redefined. This effect can lead to the continuous expansion of the definition of what qualifies as AI, as more mundane or routine activities are delegated to machines. The result is a blurred line between traditional automation, machine learning, and true artificial intelligence, influencing how we perceive the potential of AI and its place in various industries. This phenomenon not only challenges our understanding of intelligence but also leads to the normalization of AI in everyday applications, from customer service chatbots to autonomous vehicles.

Understanding the AI Effect is crucial for developers, policymakers, and society at large, as it impacts how AI technologies are designed, implemented, and governed. It serves as a reminder that AI's capabilities should not be overestimated or misunderstood, especially when integrating AI into software products. By continually redefining what is considered intelligent behavior, the AI Effect can influence public expectations, regulatory frameworks, and ethical considerations. Properly managing this shifting perception ensures that the limitations and risks of AI are clearly communicated, preventing overhyped claims and mitigating biases in AI systems. In software and technology development, recognizing the AI Effect helps create realistic roadmaps for AI's integration into society while promoting responsible innovation.

Best Practices and Guidelines

Clarify Definitions and Scope: Clearly differentiate between narrow AI (task-specific) and general AI (human-like cognition) to avoid overhyping or underestimating AI's capabilities.

Avoid Over-automation: Recognize that while AI can automate tasks, human oversight is often necessary for tasks requiring judgment, creativity, and ethical decision-making.

Ensure Transparency and Accountability: Maintain transparency in AI development, ensuring that algorithms and decisions made by AI systems are explainable and accountable to users and stakeholders.

Regularly Reassess AI Capabilities: Continuously evaluate the evolving capabilities of AI systems and reassess their scope, so expectations stay aligned with their actual limitations and advancements.

Mitigate Bias and Unintended Consequences: Implement robust data management and testing processes to identify and address biases in AI models, ensuring fair and ethical outcomes.

Common Misconceptions and Pitfalls

- AI is Becoming "Truly Intelligent": Misconception: As AI systems perform more tasks previously thought to require human intelligence, there's a tendency to assume that AI is getting closer to true human-like cognition or consciousness. In reality, most AI is highly specialized and lacks general intelligence.
- AI Can Replace Humans in All Tasks: Misconception: The AI Effect often leads to the assumption that AI can take over any job or cognitive task. However, AI excels in narrow, well-defined tasks but struggles with creativity, intuition, and complex human emotions.
- AI Can Understand Context Like Humans: Misconception: AI systems often appear to understand context or perform sophisticated tasks, but they do so based on patterns and data rather than true comprehension. This can lead to errors or biases when situations deviate from the training data.
- "If It Can Do This, It Must Be AI": Pitfall: The AI Effect leads people to classify any advanced automation or machine learning system as "AI." This can cloud discussions about the real potential, limits, and risks of AI by conflating it with general automation or data processing.
- AI is Inherently Objective: Misconception: Many believe that AI, being a machine, is purely objective and free from human bias. In reality, AI systems inherit biases from the data they're trained on, leading to flawed or unfair outcomes when applied in real-world scenarios.

Related Concepts

1. Moravec's Paradox
2. The Turing Test
3. Asimov's Laws of Robotics
4. The Law of Accelerating Returns (Kurzweil's Law)
5. The Principle of Computationalism

References

- Wikipedia, *AI effect*, [pub: 3 Nov 2024, cited: 3 Jan 2025]

Asimov's Laws of Robotics (1st, 2nd, 3rd)

Definition and Origin

Isaac Asimov's Laws of Robotics are three ethical principles designed to govern the behavior of robots and ensure their safe interaction with humans. They are:

1. First Law: A robot may not injure a human being or, through inaction, allow a human being to come to harm.
2. Second Law: A robot must obey the orders given it by human beings, except where such orders would conflict with the First Law.
3. Third Law: A robot must protect its own existence as long as such protection does not conflict with the First or Second Laws.

These laws were introduced in Asimov's science fiction stories and explore the complex ethical dilemmas and unintended consequences of artificial intelligence.

Asimov's Laws of Robotics were coined by Isaac Asimov, a renowned science fiction author and biochemist. He introduced these laws in his short stories and novels, beginning with the 1942 story "Runaround," which is part of his I, Robot collection. Asimov created the laws to explore the ethical dilemmas and potential consequences of artificial intelligence and robotics, making them central to many of his works.

Context and Importance

Isaac Asimov's Laws of Robotics, though originally conceived for science fiction, have become a significant touchstone in the ongoing discourse around artificial intelligence (AI) and robotics in the real world. In an era of rapidly advancing technology, Asimov's laws are often referenced as a conceptual framework to explore the ethical and moral challenges of building autonomous machines. The laws address fundamental concerns about how AI systems and robots should behave in relation to human beings, ensuring that safety, obedience, and self-preservation are prioritized in a way that prevents harm. As software becomes more integrated into everyday life, from self-driving cars to AI-based healthcare tools, these principles prompt important questions about how we program and regulate AI to act in ways that align with human values and prevent unintended consequences, such as AI systems making harmful decisions based on faulty programming or misinterpreting their directives.

In the broader context of software and technology, Asimov's Laws are not just a theoretical framework but serve as a starting point for discussions on AI governance, ethics, and regulation. As robots and AI systems are entrusted with increasingly complex tasks—such as medical diagnosis, decision-making in finance, or surveillance—ensuring that these systems are safe and align with societal values becomes crucial. Asimov's Laws emphasize that technological autonomy should not come at the expense of human welfare, highlighting the importance of designing systems that can adapt to ethical dilemmas and prioritize human safety. While these laws are far from a complete solution to the ethical issues raised by AI, they have influenced the development of modern AI safety protocols and regulations, acting as a cultural touchstone that encourages deeper reflection on the responsibilities of those creating and deploying powerful technologies.

Best Practices and Guidelines

Prioritize Human Safety: Ensure AI systems and robots are designed to avoid causing harm to humans, both through direct action and by preventing inaction that could lead to harm.

Clear Ethical Instructions: Program AI to follow human instructions, but with built-in safeguards that prevent harmful outcomes if commands conflict with safety protocols.

Autonomy with Accountability: Allow AI systems to protect their functionality and existence, but only if such actions do not interfere with human safety or ethical guidelines.

Continuous Monitoring: Regularly audit and test AI systems to ensure they comply with safety standards, are free from biases, and behave ethically in real-world scenarios.

Transparent Decision-Making: Design AI systems with explainable decision-making processes, ensuring their actions can be understood, evaluated, and corrected by humans when necessary.

Common Misconceptions and Pitfalls

- Over-Simplification of Ethics: Asimov's Laws may give the false impression that ethical decision-making in AI can be reduced to simple rules, while real-world scenarios often involve complex, nuanced dilemmas that are difficult to codify.
- Assumption of Infallibility: The laws suggest that robots will always act in predictable ways, but in practice, AI systems may malfunction, misinterpret commands, or encounter ambiguous situations that lead to unintended consequences.
- Neglect of External Factors: The Laws focus on direct interactions with humans but often overlook external influences like societal impacts, environmental consequences, or the behavior of other systems that may complicate ethical considerations.
- False Sense of Security: Relying on the Laws as a comprehensive solution can create a false sense of security, leading to insufficient scrutiny of AI's potential for harm, bias, or ethical lapses in more complex, real-world applications.
- Conflicting Priorities: The Laws assume a clear hierarchy of priorities (safety first, obedience second, self-preservation third), but in real-world systems, these priorities might conflict in unpredictable ways, requiring more sophisticated ethical frameworks.

Related Concepts

1. The Principle of Least Astonishment (also known as the Principle of Least Surprise): AI and software should behave in a way that users can easily predict and understand. This principle ensures that systems do not take unexpected actions that could harm users or cause confusion, much like Asimov's first law of not causing harm through action or inaction.
2. The Fail-Safe Principle: Software and AI systems should be designed to handle failures gracefully and prevent catastrophic consequences. This aligns with Asimov's focus on ensuring robots do not harm humans, even if an unforeseen error occurs in their operation.
3. The Responsibility Principle: Developers and operators of AI systems are responsible for ensuring that the technology adheres to ethical guidelines and does not cause harm. This mirrors Asimov's emphasis on human safety and accountability in the operation of robots.

4. The Transparency Principle: AI systems should be transparent in their decision-making, allowing humans to understand how they reach conclusions. This relates to Asimov's second law, where robots must obey humans, but it also emphasizes that those instructions should be clear, understandable, and justifiable.
5. The Alignment Principle: AI systems should align with human values and goals to ensure that their actions and outcomes are beneficial. This is akin to Asimov's laws of ensuring that robots act in the best interest of humans, obey instructions without conflict, and prioritize safety and wellbeing.

References

- Wikipedia, *Three Laws of Robotics*, [pub: 2 Jan 2025, cited: 3 Jan 2025]

The Chinese Room Argument

Definition and Origin

The Chinese Room Argument is a thought experiment by philosopher John Searle that challenges the notion of "strong AI," which claims that a machine could have a mind and consciousness merely by processing information in the right way. In the argument, a person who does not understand Chinese is inside a room with a set of instructions for manipulating Chinese symbols. The person can produce correct responses to Chinese input by following the instructions, but without understanding the language. This suggests that syntactic manipulation of symbols (as done by computers) does not equate to understanding or consciousness.

The Chinese Room Argument was coined by philosopher John Searle in 1980. It was introduced as part of his critique of the concept of "strong AI" — the idea that a machine could truly understand and have consciousness simply by processing information in the right way.

Context and Importance

The Chinese Room Argument was introduced by John Searle as a philosophical challenge to the claims of "strong AI," which posits that machines could achieve true understanding and consciousness if they process information in ways that mimic human cognitive processes. In the context of software and technology, the argument directly addresses the limitations of current artificial intelligence systems. These systems, while capable of processing vast amounts of data and performing tasks that appear intelligent (such as natural language processing or machine learning), do so through syntactic manipulation of symbols without any actual comprehension of their meaning. For example, an AI like a chatbot can generate human-like text but does not understand the content in the way a human does. The Chinese Room demonstrates that even if a machine appears to "understand" a language or solve problems, it does so in a purely mechanical way, without any awareness or true understanding.

The importance of the Chinese Room Argument lies in its challenge to the assumptions underlying many AI systems and their development. While modern software technologies, such as deep learning and neural networks, have made remarkable strides in areas like image recognition, translation, and decision-making, Searle's thought experiment raises important questions about whether these systems are truly intelligent or merely sophisticated mimicry. It forces us to reconsider the nature of consciousness, understanding, and whether it is possible for machines to ever have experiences in the way humans do. This has profound implications for the ethical development of AI, particularly in fields like autonomous decision-making, human-computer interaction, and the potential for machines to replace human workers. Ultimately, the Chinese Room Argument challenges the notion that advanced computational abilities equate to real understanding or consciousness in machines, urging a more cautious and critical approach to AI development.

Best Practices and Guidelines

Distinguish between simulation and understanding: Recognize that AI can simulate intelligent behavior without truly understanding the underlying concepts.

Question AI's cognitive capabilities: Avoid equating complex algorithms or data processing with human-like comprehension or consciousness.

Prioritize transparency in AI systems: Ensure that AI processes are interpretable, clarifying that performance doesn't imply true awareness or reasoning.

Consider ethical implications: Be mindful of the consequences of deploying AI systems that might appear "aware" but lack genuine understanding or empathy.

Focus on human-centered AI: Design AI to assist and augment human decision-making, acknowledging the limits of machine cognition.

Common Misconceptions and Pitfalls

- Assuming AI can "think" like humans: The Chinese Room Argument highlights that machines may mimic human behavior but don't truly understand or experience consciousness.
- Equating advanced computation with understanding: Just because an AI performs complex tasks doesn't mean it possesses awareness or genuine comprehension.
- Confusing syntactic processing with semantics: AI can manipulate symbols (syntax) without grasping their meaning (semantics), which is a key distinction in the argument.
- Overlooking the role of context: AI's "responses" might seem intelligent but often lack the depth and adaptability human understanding brings, especially in new or ambiguous situations.
- Underestimating the ethical implications of AI: Misunderstanding the Chinese Room can lead to overestimating AI's capabilities and mistakenly attributing moral or decision-making authority to machines.

Related Concepts

1. Turing Test (Alan Turing): The Turing Test is a measure of a machine's ability to exhibit intelligent behavior indistinguishable from that of a human. The Chinese Room Argument critiques this, highlighting that passing the Turing Test doesn't prove genuine understanding or consciousness, only successful imitation.

2. Goodhart's Law: "When a measure becomes a target, it ceases to be a good measure." Applied to AI, this principle suggests that optimizing for specific outputs (like correct responses in natural language) can lead to systems that appear intelligent without understanding, akin to the Chinese Room's symbol manipulation.
3. Chinese Remainder Theorem: While not directly tied to the Chinese Room Argument, this theorem relates to modular arithmetic in computing, where different processes handle separate parts of a task. The Chinese Room Argument is similar, illustrating that AI can piece together information without understanding its holistic meaning or context.
4. Shannon's Information Theory: Claude Shannon's theory distinguishes between the transmission of information (syntax) and the meaning of that information (semantics). The Chinese Room Argument emphasizes that AI can handle syntax well but cannot grasp semantics, reflecting Shannon's distinction.
5. Moravec's Paradox: This principle suggests that high-level tasks, like solving mathematical problems, are easier for AI than low-level tasks, like recognizing faces. The Chinese Room Argument underscores this, showing that AI can appear intelligent in specific tasks without possessing true understanding or awareness.

References

- Wikipedia, *Chinese room*, [pub: 3 Jan 2025, cited: 3 Jan 2025]

ELIZA Effect

Definition and Origin

The ELIZA Effect refers to the tendency of people to anthropomorphize or attribute human-like qualities to machines or computer programs, especially when these systems appear to engage in conversation or exhibit behaviors that mimic human interactions. The term originates from the early computer program ELIZA, developed in the 1960s, which simulated conversation by using pattern matching and substitution techniques. Despite its simplicity, users often believed ELIZA was capable of understanding or having emotional depth.

The term ELIZA Effect was coined by cognitive scientist and AI researcher Joseph Weizenbaum, the creator of the ELIZA program. He introduced the concept in the 1970s to describe the phenomenon where people attribute more understanding or intelligence to a simple computer program than it actually possesses, simply because it mimicked human-like conversation. Weizenbaum was both fascinated and concerned by how easily users were willing to treat ELIZA as if it were truly intelligent, which led him to explore deeper questions about human-computer interaction and the nature of artificial intelligence.

Context and Importance

The ELIZA Effect is significant in the context of software and technology because it highlights the psychological and emotional responses that users can have toward computer systems, especially those designed to simulate human interaction. As technology evolves, users are increasingly exposed to AI-driven systems, chatbots, virtual assistants, and other forms of automation that mimic human behaviors. Despite the underlying simplicity or lack of genuine understanding in these systems, users often attribute human-like qualities to them. This phenomenon underscores a crucial challenge in human-computer interaction: the risk of overestimating the capabilities of technology. The ELIZA Effect serves as a cautionary reminder of the importance of designing transparent systems that make clear the limitations of AI, preventing misunderstandings and over-reliance on tools that can appear deceptively intelligent but are fundamentally limited in their capabilities.

The ELIZA Effect also holds importance in shaping how AI systems are integrated into various domains such as customer service, healthcare, and mental health. In these contexts, human-like interactions may foster trust and engagement, but they can also lead to unintended consequences if users mistakenly believe they are interacting with systems that possess true emotional intelligence or decision-making abilities. This can affect critical areas like patient care or the accuracy of advice provided by automated systems. As technology continues to advance, understanding the ELIZA Effect can help developers create more ethical, responsible, and user-aware AI systems, ensuring that users maintain realistic expectations and do not place undue reliance on tools that are not fully capable of providing nuanced or context-sensitive responses.

Best Practices and Guidelines

Clarify Limitations: Ensure AI systems clearly communicate their capabilities and limitations to users, preventing misconceptions about their intelligence or emotional understanding.

Maintain Transparency: Design systems that make it obvious when users are interacting with automated tools, avoiding any misleading impressions of human-like behavior.

Avoid Over-Personalization: Limit over-personalized responses in AI interactions to prevent users from attributing human traits or emotions to the system.

User Education: Educate users about the underlying technology, ensuring they understand that AI systems are not sentient and operate based on algorithms, not understanding.

Ethical Design: Implement ethical guidelines in AI development to ensure that systems do not exploit users' emotional responses or mislead them into over-relying on automation.

Common Misconceptions and Pitfalls

- Overestimating Intelligence: Users may assume AI systems have true understanding or reasoning capabilities, mistaking pattern-matching responses for genuine intelligence.
- Emotional Misattribution: Users might attribute emotions or empathy to AI, believing it can understand or feel, when it is simply generating scripted responses.
- Reliance on Automation: People may depend on AI for decisions or advice, assuming it has human-level judgment or wisdom, which can lead to poor outcomes.
- Trust in Inaccurate Responses: The appearance of coherent conversation can lead users to trust AI-generated information, even if it's incorrect or incomplete.
- Perceived Authenticity: Users might perceive AI interactions as more human-like than they are, leading to a false sense of connection or miscommunication.

Related Concepts

1. The "Automation Bias" (or "Computerization Bias"): This principle describes the tendency of users to over-rely on automated systems, even when they are flawed or incorrect, because of the perceived authority or infallibility of technology. This is directly related to the ELIZA Effect, where users might trust AI outputs as more intelligent or accurate than they actually are.
2. Weizenbaum's Law: Derived from Joseph Weizenbaum, the creator of ELIZA, this informal law warns that users will often treat machines as though they understand and possess human-like qualities, even if they are fundamentally simple programs. This reflects the core idea behind the ELIZA Effect—the misattribution of human-like intelligence to non-human systems.
3. Shannon's Maxim ("The Map is Not the Territory"): This principle, rooted in information theory, suggests that models (including AI systems) are simplifications of the real world. The ELIZA Effect can occur when users fail to distinguish between a simplistic model (like a chatbot) and true human understanding or cognition, confusing the "map" with the "territory."
4. Goodhart's Law: This law posits that when a metric becomes a target, it ceases to be a good metric. In the context of AI, this can manifest when developers optimize for superficial aspects of human interaction (e.g., conversational coherence) that encourage users to attribute real intelligence to the system, which can lead to misguided expectations and trust in flawed systems.
5. The "Turing Test" Paradox: While the Turing Test aims to evaluate whether a machine can exhibit behavior indistinguishable from a human, it highlights the potential danger of users attributing more intelligence to a system based solely on its ability to mimic human conversation. This paradox relates to the ELIZA Effect, as users may believe the machine "understands" when it is merely simulating understanding.

References

- Wikipedia, *ELIZA effect*, [pub: 17 Dec 2024, cited: 3 Jan 2025]

Moravec's Paradox: Easy human tasks are hard for AI, and vice versa

Definition and Origin

Moravec's Paradox is the observation that tasks requiring high-level reasoning, which are difficult for humans, are relatively easy for computers, while tasks humans find effortless, like perception and sensorimotor skills, are extremely difficult to program and automate. This paradox highlights that those evolutionarily ancient abilities, like vision and movement, are more complex computationally than abstract reasoning.

Moravec's Paradox was articulated by Hans Moravec, a robotics researcher, in the 1980s. It was further elaborated and popularized by cognitive scientists like Rodney Brooks and Marvin Minsky. Moravec's insights were based on his work in artificial intelligence and robotics, where he observed the stark contrast between the capabilities of machines and humans in different domains.

Context and Importance

Moravec's Paradox underscores the surprising difficulty of replicating tasks that humans perform effortlessly, such as perception, motor skills, and intuitive decision-making, in software and technology. While early AI research focused on emulating human reasoning through logic and symbolic processing, researchers discovered that tasks like playing chess or solving mathematical problems were easier for computers than basic sensorimotor functions like recognizing faces or walking. This paradox arises because such "simple" human abilities are the result of millions of years of evolutionary refinement, embedding highly complex processes into our neural systems. In contrast, reasoning and abstract thought are relatively recent developments, requiring less "computational effort" when translated into algorithms.

Moravec's Paradox has profound implications for fields like robotics, AI, and human-computer interaction. It explains why technologies that mimic human reasoning, such as expert systems or decision-making tools, often outpace those requiring perceptual or physical skills, like autonomous vehicles or humanoid robots. Recognizing this paradox helps developers prioritize the development of specialized algorithms and hybrid systems that combine human strength with machine efficiency. It also sheds light on the importance of leveraging machine learning and sensor-based technologies to tackle perception and motor challenges, ensuring more robust and reliable AI solutions in domains ranging from healthcare to autonomous navigation. Understanding this paradox equips the software and technology industry to set realistic expectations and strategic goals for automation and AI development.

Best Practices and Guidelines

Leverage Machine Learning for Perceptual Tasks: Use data-driven approaches like neural networks to address challenges in perception and motor skills rather than relying solely on rule-based systems.

Combine Human and Machine Strengths: Focus on creating hybrid systems where machines handle structured reasoning while humans manage tasks requiring intuition or adaptability.

Set Realistic Expectations: Acknowledge the complexity of "simple" tasks like vision or movement when designing AI and robotics solutions to avoid underestimating development efforts.

Prioritize Incremental Improvements: Break down complex sensorimotor challenges into smaller, manageable components to achieve steady progress in automation.

Optimize for Specific Contexts: Design AI solutions tailored to the environment and task requirements, minimizing unnecessary complexity while maximizing efficiency.

Common Misconceptions and Pitfalls

- Assuming Easy Tasks for Humans Are Easy for Machines: Misjudging the complexity of sensorimotor and perceptual tasks, leading to underestimated development timelines and costs.

- Overvaluing High-Level Reasoning: Believing AI's strength in abstract reasoning translates to proficiency in tasks like vision or physical interaction.
- Ignoring the Role of Evolutionary Development: Overlooking that tasks humans perform effortlessly are backed by millions of years of neural optimization, making them computationally demanding to replicate.
- Relying Solely on Rule-Based Systems: Attempting to address perception and motor challenges with deterministic algorithms rather than adaptive machine learning techniques.
- Expecting Generalized AI Solutions: Assuming a single AI system can seamlessly handle both high-level reasoning and sensorimotor skills without specialized design.

Related Concepts

1. Polanyi's Paradox: "We know more than we can tell." This principle highlights the difficulty of programming implicit knowledge, such as intuition or motor skills, which aligns with the challenges of Moravec's Paradox.
2. Brooks' Subsumption Architecture: Emphasizes that intelligence emerges from layering simple behaviors (e.g., walking or obstacle avoidance) rather than top-down reasoning, a key strategy for addressing Moravec's Paradox in robotics.
3. Hebert Simon's Bounded Rationality: Suggests that decision-making is limited by the information available and cognitive capacity, paralleling the need for pragmatic, task-specific AI solutions.
4. Moore's Law: The exponential growth of computing power supports tackling computationally intensive tasks like perception and motor skills over time, indirectly addressing challenges posed by Moravec's Paradox.
5. The AI Effect: The tendency to undervalue achievements in AI once they are solved, illustrating the ongoing underappreciation of "simple" tasks like perception, central to Moravec's Paradox.

References

- Wikipedia, *Moravec's paradox*, [pub: 27 Dec 2024, cited: 3 Jan 2025]

The Turing Test Principle

Definition and Origin

The Turing Test Principle, proposed by Alan Turing in 1950, evaluates a machine's ability to exhibit intelligent behavior indistinguishable from that of a human. If a human evaluator cannot reliably differentiate between the responses of the machine and a human in a natural language conversation, the machine is said to pass the test.

The Turing Test Principle was coined and proposed by Alan Turing, a British mathematician and computer scientist, in his seminal 1950 paper titled "Computing Machinery and Intelligence". In this paper, Turing introduced the test as an operational measure of a machine's ability to demonstrate human-like intelligence.

Context and Importance

The Turing Test Principle, introduced by Alan Turing in 1950, emerged as a foundational concept in artificial intelligence (AI) during the early days of computing. It was designed as a practical framework to assess whether a machine could mimic human intelligence convincingly enough to deceive a human judge in a conversation. This principle challenged the traditional view of intelligence, shifting the focus from whether machines could "think" in a human sense to whether they could act in a way indistinguishable from humans. By framing intelligence in terms of observable behavior rather than intrinsic qualities, the Turing Test laid the groundwork for empirical evaluation in AI development, paving the way for fields like natural language processing, conversational agents, and machine learning.

The Turing Test remains a vital benchmark for understanding human-like behavior in AI systems, even in today's advanced technological landscape. While no longer the definitive measure of intelligence, it has inspired countless innovations in AI software, such as chatbots, virtual assistants, and generative AI models. It emphasizes the importance of human-centered design in technology, as passing the test requires machines to understand, interpret, and respond to human input effectively. Moreover, the Turing Test continues to provoke philosophical and ethical discussions about the nature of intelligence and consciousness in machines, guiding modern debates about the implications of AI in society. Its legacy persists as a reminder of the intricate interplay between technology and humanity in the pursuit of artificial intelligence.

Best Practices and Guidelines

Focus on Natural Language Understanding: Develop AI systems with advanced natural language processing to handle diverse and nuanced human interactions effectively.

Emphasize Contextual Awareness: Ensure AI can understand and adapt to context, maintaining coherence and relevance in conversations.

Incorporate Ethical Design: Prioritize transparency and avoid deceptive practices that could mislead users about the AI's capabilities or identity.

Balance Human-Like Behavior and Utility: Strive for AI that mimics human interaction while maintaining its functional purpose and efficiency.

Continuously Test and Evaluate: Use iterative testing with diverse user groups to refine AI behavior and ensure it aligns with the Turing Test's principles and user expectations.

Common Misconceptions and Pitfalls

- Passing the Test Equals True Intelligence: Successfully mimicking human conversation does not equate to true understanding or consciousness; it only demonstrates functional mimicry.

- Focus on Deception: The goal is not to deceive users but to create meaningful interactions. Emphasizing trickery can lead to unethical AI applications.
- Only Language Matters: The Turing Test focuses on language but doesn't account for broader aspects of intelligence, such as perception, creativity, or problem-solving.
- One-Time Success: Passing the test in a single interaction does not guarantee long-term or consistent performance in diverse, real-world scenarios.
- Simplicity Equals Success: A machine passing the Turing Test doesn't mean it has comprehensive intelligence; it could be using simple patterns or pre-programmed responses.

Related Concepts

1. The Laws of Robotics (Asimov's Laws): While not directly related to the Turing Test, Isaac Asimov's famous three laws for AI and robots influence the ethical development of AI systems, ensuring they interact safely and responsibly with humans.
2. Goodhart's Law: "When a measure becomes a target, it ceases to be a good measure." This relates to the Turing Test, where AI may optimize for passing the test rather than demonstrating true intelligence or usefulness.
3. The Principle of Transparency: This principle emphasizes that AI systems should be transparent in their decision-making processes. In relation to the Turing Test, it suggests that systems should not attempt to hide their artificial nature, promoting ethical and clear interactions.
4. The Chinese Room Argument (John Searle): This thought experiment questions whether passing the Turing Test proves true understanding or merely the appearance of it, highlighting the difference between simulating behavior and actual comprehension.
5. Moravec's Paradox: Suggests that tasks humans find easy (like visual recognition) are often difficult for AI, while tasks that are difficult for humans (like mathematical calculations) are relatively easy for machines. This highlights the limitations of using the Turing Test to measure overall intelligence.

References

- Wikipedia, *Turing test*, [pub: 3 Jan 2025, cited: 3 Jan 2025]

Uncanny Valley

Definition and Origin

The Uncanny Valley refers to the unsettling or eerie feeling people experience when something that looks and behaves almost like a human being, but not quite perfectly, evokes discomfort or revulsion. This phenomenon typically occurs with robots, avatars, or artificial figures that closely resemble humans but still display subtle imperfections or unnatural characteristics.

The term "Uncanny Valley" was coined by Japanese roboticist Masahiro Mori in 1970. In his original paper, Mori described how humanoid robots or figures that appear almost human, but not quite, can create a feeling of discomfort or eeriness in people. He proposed that as robots become more humanlike, our emotional response to them becomes increasingly positive—up to a certain point—after which, small imperfections cause a dramatic drop in comfort, creating the "valley" in the emotional response curve.

Context and Importance

The Uncanny Valley concept has significant implications for the development of AI software and technology, particularly in fields like robotics, virtual assistants, and avatars. As artificial intelligence systems become more sophisticated in mimicking human appearance, behavior, and speech, developers face the challenge of creating lifelike experiences without triggering discomfort or unease in users. In AI-driven applications such as virtual reality (VR), video games, and digital assistants, designers must strike a delicate balance between realism and artificiality. If an avatar or robot looks too much like a human but lacks subtle cues such as fluid facial expressions or natural body movements, it can fall into the uncanny valley, where its almost-human appearance creates an unsettling feeling for the user.

Understanding the Uncanny Valley is crucial for the future of human-computer interaction (HCI). As AI technology continues to evolve, there is increasing interest in creating human-like robots and digital interfaces that can better serve in healthcare, customer service, and entertainment, among other industries. By studying and addressing the uncanny valley, developers can design AI systems that feel more engaging and comfortable, avoiding alienation or fear. For example, subtle adjustments to voice tone, facial expressions, or even the way a robot moves can help ease the discomfort users might feel when interacting with a humanoid AI, thus making the technology more effective and socially acceptable.

Best Practices and Guidelines

Aim for Subtle Realism: Avoid over-ambitious human-like appearances; opt for designs that are clearly non-human but still relatable.

Focus on Fluidity: Ensure smooth, natural movements and expressions to prevent robotic or stiff behavior that can trigger discomfort.

Perfect Imperfections: Small, intentional imperfections (like slight asymmetries) can make AI appear more approachable and less unnerving.

Consider Context: Tailor the level of human resemblance to the task—simple, functional interfaces can work better than overly lifelike ones for certain applications.

Test User Reactions: Continuously gather user feedback to identify and address moments of discomfort or unease in AI interactions.

Common Misconceptions and Pitfalls

- More Realism Equals Better Experience: Overly human-like designs can backfire, creating discomfort rather than enhancing user engagement.
- Humans Want Perfect Mimicry: Users don't necessarily want robots or AI to perfectly resemble humans; authenticity often matters more than perfection.

- The Uncanny Valley Is Only About Appearance: It also includes behavior—awkward or unnatural movements, speech, or interactions can trigger discomfort even if the appearance is fine.
- The Valley Is Always Deep: Not all near-human representations cause the uncanny effect; it depends on context and individual perception.
- Avoiding the Uncanny Valley Means Avoiding Realism: A non-human design can still be relatable and effective without falling into the uncanny valley, as long as it's engaging and functional.

Related Concepts

1. The Media Equation (Reeves & Nass): This principle suggests that people tend to treat computers, robots, and other media as if they were human, which is crucial in understanding how AI can either evoke empathy or discomfort based on its human-like qualities.
2. The Eliza Effect: Refers to the tendency of users to attribute human-like qualities to AI or machines, even when their responses are simplistic or scripted. This principle highlights the potential for a mismatch between user expectations and AI behavior, especially when attempting to humanize technology.
3. Mori's Law of Human-Like Robots: A principle stemming directly from the Uncanny Valley hypothesis, this law states that as robots become more human-like, people's emotional responses improve, until a point where near-human realism creates a sharp emotional dip due to imperfections, leading to discomfort or unease.
4. Fitts's Law (in Human-Computer Interaction): This law suggests that as the interface (including AI avatars or robots) becomes more human-like and complex, the potential for errors or awkward interactions increases. It's important to balance realism with usability to avoid the uncanny valley effect.
5. HCI's Principle of Affordances: This principle states that AI should communicate its purpose clearly through design. If an AI's behavior or appearance misleads users into expecting more human-like interaction, it can create an uncomfortable tension if the AI falls short, exacerbating the uncanny valley effect.

References

- Wikipedia, *Uncanny valley*, [pub: 2 Jan 2025, cited: 3 Jan 2025]

Winograd Schema Challenge

Definition and Origin

The Winograd Schema Challenge is a test designed to evaluate a machine's ability to understand and resolve ambiguous sentences using common sense reasoning. It consists of pairs of sentences that differ by a single word, where the meaning of the sentence hinges on correctly resolving an ambiguous pronoun or reference. To answer correctly, the machine must demonstrate an understanding of context and subtle linguistic cues, something that is challenging for traditional AI systems.

The Winograd Schema Challenge was coined by Terry Winograd, a prominent computer scientist and artificial intelligence researcher. He introduced the challenge in 2010 as a way to address limitations in current AI systems' ability to understand and reason with natural language. The challenge was designed as a more difficult alternative to the Turing Test, focusing on testing common-sense reasoning and linguistic ambiguity resolution.

Context and Importance

The Winograd Schema Challenge emerged as a critical benchmark in the field of artificial intelligence (AI) due to its focus on assessing machines' ability to perform common-sense reasoning and resolve linguistic ambiguities. Traditional AI systems, even those with advanced natural language processing (NLP) capabilities, struggle with tasks that require understanding context, interpreting pronouns, and making judgments based on everyday knowledge. The Winograd Schema Challenge highlights this gap by presenting carefully crafted sentences where a machine must correctly disambiguate pronouns or references based on real-world knowledge and logic. Unlike simpler sentence completion tasks, the challenge requires an AI to apply deep reasoning skills and interpret subtle language cues in a way that mimics human understanding. This makes the challenge a valuable test for pushing the boundaries of AI and examining its limitations.

The importance of the Winograd Schema Challenge in AI development lies in its focus on evaluating true comprehension rather than just pattern recognition. Many state-of-the-art AI systems excel at parsing large amounts of text and generating responses based on statistical associations or machine learning models trained on vast datasets. However, these systems often fail when asked to resolve nuanced, context-dependent scenarios that involve reasoning beyond simple correlations. By emphasizing the need for common-sense reasoning and contextual awareness, the Winograd Schema Challenge encourages the development of more sophisticated AI systems that can better mimic human cognitive abilities. It also serves as a critical tool for researchers to identify areas where current AI systems still fall short and where improvements are necessary for achieving true artificial general intelligence (AGI).

Best Practices and Guidelines

Focus on Common-Sense Reasoning: Ensure AI systems can disambiguate pronouns and references using contextual knowledge, not just pattern recognition.

Context Awareness: Design tests that require understanding the broader context of a sentence, beyond simple syntax or surface-level patterns.

Human-Like Interpretation: Aim to create systems that demonstrate reasoning similar to human cognitive abilities, such as understanding subtle linguistic cues and real-world logic.

Avoid Overfitting: Prevent AI models from relying solely on training data correlations; emphasize reasoning that applies to unseen examples or novel situations.

Encourage Robust Evaluation: Use the Winograd Schema Challenge as a benchmark to identify gaps in AI comprehension, particularly in tasks requiring nuanced understanding.

Common Misconceptions and Pitfalls

- Assuming Surface-Level Understanding: Many AI systems excel at pattern recognition but fail to grasp the deeper meaning of a sentence, leading to incorrect disambiguation of pronouns.
- Overfitting to Specific Datasets: Training models on fixed Winograd schema examples can lead to overfitting, where the system memorizes answers rather than generalizing to new contexts.
- Neglecting Real-World Context: AI models may struggle when they lack external knowledge or common-sense reasoning, making it difficult for them to handle real-world ambiguity.
- Misunderstanding Ambiguity: Some systems may misinterpret or ignore the subtle linguistic cues necessary to resolve ambiguity, assuming that a single answer is always correct.
- Overreliance on Statistical Patterns: AI models may prioritize statistical associations from large datasets rather than understanding the underlying logic and reasoning required to solve the challenge.

Related Concepts

1. Moravec's Paradox: This principle highlights that tasks which are easy for humans (like common-sense reasoning and interpreting ambiguous language) are often difficult for machines. The Winograd Schema Challenge directly tests this paradox, as it requires AI to handle tasks that humans find effortless but are complex for current AI systems.
2. The Frame Problem: This law in AI refers to the difficulty of representing and reasoning about the context in which actions or events occur, especially when there are many irrelevant details. The Winograd Schema Challenge tests an AI's ability to distinguish relevant context and resolve ambiguities, which directly engages the frame problem.
3. Shannon's Maxim (Shannon's Law of Communication): "The enemy of communication is ambiguity." In the context of the Winograd Schema Challenge, this principle underscores the importance of clarity and understanding in AI's communication abilities, emphasizing that AI must resolve ambiguity accurately to communicate effectively.

4. Occam's Razor: This principle suggests that, when faced with multiple explanations, the simplest one is often the best. In the Winograd Schema Challenge, an AI must apply common-sense reasoning to determine the most logical, contextually appropriate interpretation, often seeking the simplest and most plausible explanation of a sentence's meaning.
5. AI Alignment Problem: This refers to the challenge of aligning AI systems' behavior with human values and understanding. The Winograd Schema Challenge serves as a benchmark to measure how well AI aligns with human-like reasoning, as it requires systems to use human-like interpretation of ambiguous language to resolve sentences in a way that would match human intuition.

References

- Wikipedia, *Winograd schema challenge*, [pub: 31 Jul 2024, cited: 3 Jan 2025]

K. Technology & Society

Carr's Law

Definition and Origin

Carr's Law, articulated by Nicholas Carr, suggests that as technology becomes more advanced and integrated into daily life, its complexity and impact on society tend to become less visible and more invisible. Specifically, the law posits that as technological systems evolve, they shift from being specialized tools requiring expertise to ubiquitous, almost invisible utilities that are taken for granted, similar to electricity. This transition alters the way people interact with and understand technology, often reducing awareness of its influence and implications.

Carr's Law was coined by Nicholas Carr, a well-known technology writer and author, particularly recognized for his books such as The Shallows and Does IT Matter? The law is a concept he introduced in his writings, particularly in the context of how technology evolves and integrates into society. It is not a formal scientific law but rather an idea that reflects his observations about the increasing ubiquity and invisibility of technology as it becomes more embedded in everyday life.

Context and Importance

Nicholas Carr's Law offers a thought-provoking lens through which to understand the evolution of software and technology. Initially, technology, whether hardware or software, often required specialized expertise and was closely tied to specific business functions or industrial needs. In its early stages, such as with mainframe computing or early enterprise software, it was a domain managed by IT specialists and required considerable investment and knowledge to operate. However, as technology advances, Carr's Law suggests that it becomes increasingly standardized and embedded in everyday operations, transitioning from specialized tools to utility-like services. This shift is evident in the way software platforms, from cloud computing to SaaS applications, have become widely accessible and standardized. The complexity of these technologies is often hidden from end-users, as they now interact with intuitive, user-friendly interfaces that abstract away the underlying complexities.

The importance of Carr's Law in the context of software and technology is multifaceted. First, it challenges businesses to rethink how they perceive technological value. As software becomes a ubiquitous utility, it can be difficult to differentiate between products and services based purely on their technological innovation. This democratization of technology means that competitive advantage often comes not from owning advanced technology but from how companies leverage it creatively or integrate it into their business models. Moreover, Carr's Law also highlights potential risks in over-relying on "invisible" technology: as we become more dependent on these systems, we risk losing sight of their underlying vulnerabilities, ethical considerations, or societal impacts. Understanding this transition encourages companies, policymakers, and users to think critically about the evolving role of technology in society and the broader implications of its pervasive presence.

Best Practices and Guidelines

Embrace Standardization: As technology becomes a utility, focus on integrating standardized, scalable solutions (e.g., cloud platforms, SaaS) that streamline operations and reduce complexity.

Differentiate Through Innovation: In a world where technology is ubiquitous, competitive advantage often comes from creative use and integration of technology, not just owning advanced tools.

Prioritize Usability: Aim for simplicity and user-friendly interfaces that abstract technical complexity, ensuring broad accessibility and seamless adoption.

Monitor Dependencies: While technology becomes invisible, remain vigilant about potential risks, vulnerabilities, and ethical considerations hidden in complex systems.

Adapt to Technological Shifts: Recognize the trend of technology becoming a commodity and continuously reassess strategies to stay ahead as new tools evolve into invisible utilities.

Common Misconceptions and Pitfalls

- Overestimating Technological Uniqueness: Believing that owning or developing cutting-edge technology provides a sustainable competitive advantage, when in fact, technology quickly becomes standardized and widely accessible.
- Ignoring Hidden Complexities: Assuming that as technology becomes more invisible, it is free of complexity or risk—leading to neglect of underlying issues like security, maintenance, and ethical concerns.
- Underestimating the Importance of Adaptation: Focusing too heavily on current technologies without recognizing that tomorrow's tools will become invisible utilities, making it harder to differentiate based on technology alone.
- Overreliance on External Providers: Assuming cloud-based or third-party software providers can handle everything, ignoring the importance of retaining control over critical data, security, and long-term strategic direction.
- Neglecting Human Skills: Overlooking the need for human expertise in leveraging technology effectively, as the shift toward invisible systems may lead to a false belief that no specialized knowledge is necessary.

Related Concepts

1. Moore's Law: The observation that the number of transistors on a microchip doubles approximately every two years, leading to exponential increases in computing power. Like Carr's Law, Moore's Law highlights the rapid pace of technological advancement, but Moore's focuses on hardware, while Carr's emphasizes the shift of technology into ubiquitous utility.
2. Metcalfe's Law: The value of a network grows exponentially as the number of users increases. This is related to Carr's Law in that as technology becomes more widespread and invisible, its utility increases, transforming from a specialized tool to a broader, essential service.
3. The Law of Increasing Returns: This principle posits that as technology becomes more widely adopted, its benefits and efficiencies grow, often leading to dominant platforms or standards. Carr's Law aligns with this in showing how as software becomes standardized, its value grows across industries and users, creating a network effect.

4. ** Conway's Law**: "Organizations which design systems are constrained to produce designs which are copies of the communication structures of these organizations." As software becomes more embedded and invisible, this law suggests that the organizational structures that develop software can influence the way that invisible, utility-like systems are structured and integrated across industries.
5. The Network Effect: This principle states that the value of a product or service increases as more people use it. Carr's Law relates to this idea by demonstrating how the invisibility and ubiquity of technology enhances its value in a broader context, turning software into a utility that everyone uses and depends upon.

References

- Wikipedia, *Nicholas G. Carr*, [pub: 17 Nov 2024, cited: 3 Jan 2025]

Clarke's Laws (1st, 2nd, 3rd)

Definition and Origin

Clarke's Laws, proposed by science fiction writer Arthur C. Clarke, consist of three adages that outline key ideas about the relationship between science, technology, and human understanding:

1. First Law: "When a distinguished but elderly scientist states that something is possible, he is almost certainly right. When he states that something is impossible, he is very probably wrong."
2. Second Law: "The only way of discovering the limits of the possible is to venture a little way past them into the impossible."
3. Third Law: "Any sufficiently advanced technology is indistinguishable from magic."

These laws highlight the evolving nature of scientific knowledge and the often-blurred line between the possible and the impossible as technology advances.

Context and Importance

Clarke's Laws are particularly relevant in the context of software and technology, where rapid innovation continuously challenges conventional boundaries. The first law, which emphasizes the probability of new discoveries being initially dismissed as impossible, resonates strongly in the tech world. Historically, many groundbreaking ideas—like the personal computer, the internet, or artificial intelligence—were considered unfeasible or far-fetched until technological advancements proved otherwise. In software development, this mindset encourages risk-taking and thinking beyond current limitations, prompting engineers and developers to push boundaries and explore new paradigms. As technology evolves, ideas once deemed "impossible" are gradually realized, further accelerating progress in ways that were once unimaginable.

The third law, which states that "any sufficiently advanced technology is indistinguishable from magic," is particularly poignant in modern software and technology. As technologies like machine learning, quantum computing, and blockchain become more sophisticated, their operations often appear mysterious or even magical to those without specialized knowledge. This gap between understanding and application highlights the transformative potential of technology; innovations can become so advanced that they fundamentally alter the way we interact with the world, yet their inner workings may remain opaque to most. Clarke's laws serve as a reminder that, in the world of software and technology, the line between what is possible and impossible is constantly shifting, encouraging both innovation and a rethinking of what might be achievable in the future.

Best Practices and Guidelines

Embrace the impossible: Challenge assumptions and explore ideas that seem unfeasible; today's "impossible" may become tomorrow's breakthrough.

Innovate beyond limits: Use emerging technologies as a springboard to push the boundaries of what's currently possible in software development.

Expect skepticism: Understand that pioneering ideas will often face resistance, but perseverance can lead to revolutionary advancements.

Simplify complexity: Recognize that advanced technologies may seem like magic to users, so focus on making them intuitive and accessible.

Encourage risk-taking: Foster a culture of experimentation, where failures are viewed as learning opportunities and steppingstones to success.

Common Misconceptions and Pitfalls

- Assuming limits are fixed: Believing that current technological boundaries are permanent can stifle innovation; what seems impossible today may be achievable tomorrow.
- Underestimating progress: Overlooking the pace of technological advancement can lead to missed opportunities; innovation often outpaces our expectations.
- Over-reliance on current expertise: Relying too heavily on existing knowledge or experience can limit creative thinking and hinder breakthroughs.
- Confusing complexity with magic: Assuming that sophisticated technologies are too advanced to understand or integrate can lead to resistance and underuse of powerful tools.
- Ignoring skepticism: Dismissing the value of challenging conventional wisdom can result in missed opportunities for growth or transformative change.

Related Concepts

1. Moore's Law: "The number of transistors on a microchip doubles approximately every two years, leading to exponential growth in computing power.": Like Clarke's First Law, Moore's Law highlights the rapid pace of technological progress and the idea that what seems impossible today can become commonplace tomorrow.
2. Brooks' Law: "Adding manpower to a late software project makes it later.": This principle suggests that technological progress isn't always linear or predictable, echoing Clarke's Second Law about venturing beyond current limits to discover new solutions.
3. The Law of Leaky Abstractions: "All non-trivial abstractions, to some degree, are leaky.": In the context of Clarke's Third Law, this suggests that even highly advanced technologies (which may seem magical) have underlying complexities that can eventually reveal themselves, challenging the "magic-like" simplicity of high-level interfaces.

4. Conway's Law: "Organizations which design systems are constrained to produce designs which are copies of the communication structures of these organizations.": Similar to Clarke's Laws, Conway's Law reflects how organizational thinking influences technological progress and how innovation can often be stymied by rigid, conventional structures.
5. The Pareto Principle (80/20 Rule): "80% of the effects come from 20% of the causes.": In software development, this law suggests that focusing on the most impactful features or technologies can yield significant results, paralleling Clarke's idea that venturing past conventional limits (often involving a small amount of breakthrough work) can result in major advancements.

References

- Wikipedia, *Clarke's three laws*, [pub: 27 Dec 2024, cited: 3 Jan 2025]

Doctorow's Law

Definition and Origin

Doctorow's Law states that when someone places a lock on something you own, without providing you with the key, their intent is not to protect your interests, but to control or restrict your use of it. Essentially, it's a warning about the misuse of control or restrictions, often for profit or power, rather than for your benefit.

Cory Doctorow himself coined the law. It is a concept he frequently discusses in his writings and public speaking, particularly around issues of digital rights, copyright, and consumer freedoms. The law reflects his concerns about the increasing trend of digital restrictions (like DRM) and the ways in which companies limit users' control over their own property for commercial or strategic reasons.

Context and Importance

Cory Doctorow's Law is particularly relevant in the context of software and technology, where digital restrictions and proprietary control have become increasingly common. As technology has advanced, many software and hardware products have incorporated "locks," such as digital rights management (DRM), encryption, and other forms of restriction, that limit users' ability to fully control or modify the devices and services they purchase. For instance, software companies often use DRM to prevent unauthorized copying or modification of their products, while hardware manufacturers may lock down devices (such as smartphones or gaming consoles) to prevent users from installing third-party software or performing repairs. In these cases, the "lock" is intended to enforce the company's business model rather than to benefit the user, restricting freedom and flexibility in ways that may not align with the original consumer's intentions.

The importance of Doctorow's Law in this context is its challenge to the growing trend of control over users by corporations. It serves as a critique of the practice where companies impose these digital locks, often under the guise of protecting users from security risks or ensuring product integrity, but in reality, they are limiting the autonomy of consumers and stifling competition. Doctorow's Law emphasizes that when users are unable to freely modify, repair, or use their devices as they see fit, it creates an imbalance of power, where users become dependent on corporations for even the most basic functions. This undermines the principles of ownership and the open nature of technology, encouraging the development of "walled gardens" and creating barriers to innovation. As such, the law serves as a call for greater consumer rights, transparency, and accountability in the tech industry.

Best Practices and Guidelines

Prioritize User Control: Ensure that users retain full control over the software and hardware they own, including the ability to modify, repair, or replace components without artificial restrictions.

Avoid Proprietary Lock-ins: Avoid implementing DRM, encryption, or other proprietary systems that limit a user's ability to freely use or share purchased products.

Transparent Licensing: Use clear, open, and fair licensing terms that allow users to understand the boundaries of their rights and freedoms with the product.

Support Open Standards: Promote the use of open standards and interoperable systems to prevent vendor lock-in and encourage user choice and flexibility.

Respect Consumer Ownership: Design technology with the understanding that ownership should grant users full access, control, and responsibility over their devices and software.

Common Misconceptions and Pitfalls

- Misconception: Locks are for user protection: Companies often argue that restrictions (like DRM or encryption) are for user security, but they may be more focused on protecting their own interests (e.g., preventing piracy) rather than ensuring the user's safety or freedom.
- Pitfall: Assuming "ownership" means control: Many consumers assume that purchasing a product means full ownership and control, but restrictive software or hardware locks can limit their ability to use, modify, or repair their own property.
- Misconception: Restrictions are harmless: While a lock may seem minor, it can lead to long-term issues, such as reduced device functionality, increased costs for repairs, or forced obsolescence, ultimately harming the user experience.
- Pitfall: Believing you can trust the vendor to act in your best interest: Companies may claim that restrictions are in place for your benefit (e.g., to prevent malicious use), but in reality, these measures often prioritize their business model over your actual needs and freedom.
- Misconception: Restrictions only affect "pirates" or "hackers": In reality, even well-meaning consumers who want to personalize or repair their devices can be negatively impacted by unnecessary digital locks, which can limit their rights and usability.

Related Concepts

1. The Right to Repair: This principle asserts that consumers should have the right to repair and modify the products they own, including electronics and software. Digital locks or restrictions that prevent repairs or modifications contradict this right and limit consumer freedom.

2. The Digital Millennium Copyright Act (DMCA): The DMCA criminalizes the circumvention of digital locks (DRM), even when those locks hinder the user's ability to fully control or use their property. This law has been criticized for protecting corporate interests over consumer rights and limiting the ability to repair or modify devices.
3. The Open-Source Movement: Open-source principles emphasize user control, transparency, and the freedom to modify software. It stands in contrast to proprietary software practices that lock users into specific ecosystems or restrict access to source code, aligning with the idea that ownership should come with freedom.
4. The Fair Use Doctrine: This principle in copyright law allows users to use copyrighted material for purposes such as criticism, education, or research without permission. Restrictions like DRM that block fair use effectively undermine users' rights to make legitimate use of the content they own.
5. The Consumer Privacy Bill of Rights: While focused on data privacy, this principle advocates for greater user control over personal information. Similarly, Cory Doctorow's Law extends to the concept of ownership and control over technology—users should have the right to control their devices and the data they generate without undue restrictions imposed by manufacturers.

References

- Wikipedia, Cory Doctorow, [pub: 16 Dec 2024, cited: 3 Jan 2025]

Gartner Hype Cycle

Definition and Origin

The Gartner Hype Cycle is a graphical representation that shows the maturity, adoption, and social application of specific technologies over time. It consists of five key phases:

1. Innovation Trigger: The emergence of a new technology or concept.
2. Peak of Inflated Expectations: Over-enthusiasm and unrealistic expectations lead to hype.

3. Trough of Disillusionment: Interest wanes as technology fails to meet expectations.
4. Slope of Enlightenment: Gradual understanding of the technology's potential and limitations.
5. Plateau of Productivity: The technology reaches mainstream adoption and becomes widely used.

The Hype Cycle helps businesses understand the likely trajectory of emerging technologies and make more informed decisions about investments and innovation.

Context and Importance

The Gartner Hype Cycle serves as a crucial framework in the software and technology industry by helping organizations understand the often unpredictable and volatile journey of new technologies. Emerging technologies tend to go through an exaggerated period of hype and inflated expectations, followed by a sharp decline in interest as the reality of their limitations becomes apparent. By plotting these technologies on the Hype Cycle, businesses can better anticipate the challenges and opportunities associated with adopting or investing in new innovations. The cycle provides a structured lens through which to assess where a technology stands in its evolution, helping companies avoid premature adoption during the "Peak of Inflated Expectations" or the pitfalls of disillusionment during the "Trough of Disillusionment."

In the fast-paced world of software and technology, where new developments can quickly reshape industries, the Hype Cycle is especially important for guiding strategic decision-making. It encourages a more cautious, informed approach to innovation, balancing the excitement around cutting-edge advancements with a realistic understanding of their maturity and practical use. For companies, the ability to recognize where a technology is in the Hype Cycle can help prioritize research and development investments, manage risks, and align technological advancements with long-term goals. By leveraging the Hype Cycle, businesses are better positioned to make decisions that align with both current capabilities and future potential, ensuring they adopt technologies that can deliver genuine value rather than succumbing to fleeting trends.

Best Practices and Guidelines

Monitor Emerging Technologies: Regularly track new technologies on the Hype Cycle to assess their maturity and relevance to your business strategy.

Avoid Early Overcommitment: Resist the temptation to adopt technologies during the "Peak of Inflated Expectations" unless they align with clear business needs.

Plan for the Trough of Disillusionment: Prepare for a period of setbacks and challenges after initial excitement wanes, ensuring realistic expectations are set.

Focus on the Slope of Enlightenment: Invest in technologies when early adopters demonstrate practical use cases and the technology's value is becoming clearer.

Align with Long-Term Goals: Evaluate how technologies will support your company's strategic vision, emphasizing those that reach the "Plateau of Productivity" for stable, sustainable growth.

Common Misconceptions and Pitfalls

- Assuming All Hype is Valid: Not every emerging technology on the rise will reach mainstream adoption; hype doesn't guarantee long-term value.
- Premature Adoption: Jumping into technologies too early, during the "Peak of Inflated Expectations," can lead to wasted resources and unmet ROI.
- Ignoring the Trough of Disillusionment: Failing to anticipate the inevitable setbacks and challenges after initial hype can result in unrealistic expectations and poor planning.
- Overlooking the Plateau of Productivity: Focusing too much on flashy innovations and neglecting technologies that have matured and are proven can lead to missed, stable opportunities.
- Overemphasis on Short-Term Trends: Mistaking short-lived hype for long-term relevance can lead businesses to chase fleeting trends rather than sustainable innovations.

Related Concepts

1. Moore's Law (Performance and Adoption)

2. Amara's Law (Overestimating Short-Term Impact)
3. Hick's Law (Choice and Decision-Making)
4. The Law of Diffusion of Innovations (Adoption Curve)
5. Shannon's Law (Information and Communication Limits)

References

- Wikipedia, *Gartner hype cycle*, [pub: 1 Jan 2025, cited: 3 Jan 2025]

Jevons Paradox

Definition and Origin

Jevons Paradox refers to the phenomenon where improvements in the efficiency of resource use lead to an overall increase in the consumption of that resource, rather than a decrease. This occurs because increased efficiency lowers the cost of using the resource, which can lead to higher demand and greater total consumption. The paradox is named after the British economist William Stanley Jevons, who observed this effect in the context of coal use during the Industrial Revolution.

Jevons Paradox was coined by the British economist William Stanley Jevons in 1865. He observed this paradox in his work The Coal Question, where he noted that improvements in the efficiency of coal use led to an increase in overall coal consumption, rather than a reduction. Jevons argued that as technologies make the use of a resource more efficient, they tend to reduce the cost of using that resource, which can stimulate demand and increase its total consumption.

Context and Importance

Jevons Paradox has gained increasing relevance in the context of software and technology, particularly as innovations lead to more efficient use of resources like computing power, energy, and data. As software systems become more optimized, cloud infrastructure improves, and algorithms become more efficient, the cost of performing tasks or processing data typically decreases. This can stimulate greater demand for the same resources, as businesses and consumers seek to use technology more extensively. For instance, the more efficient data centers become in terms of energy consumption, the lower the operational cost per transaction or service. However, this reduction in cost can incentivize greater use of services like cloud computing, leading to a paradoxical increase in overall energy consumption across the technology sector.

The importance of Jevons Paradox in technology is especially pronounced in discussions around sustainability. As companies continue to develop more energy-efficient software, hardware, and infrastructure, there is a risk that the gains made through efficiency improvements could be offset by rising demand for digital services and data storage. This raises concerns about the long-term environmental impact of the tech industry. Understanding and addressing Jevons Paradox can help guide the development of policies and technologies that not only improve efficiency but also ensure that such improvements contribute to actual reductions in resource consumption, rather than merely enabling higher consumption levels. This paradox challenges the idea that technological advancements alone will solve environmental problems, highlighting the need for broader systemic approaches to sustainability.

Best Practices and Guidelines

Efficiency Gains May Increase Overall Usage: As software or technology becomes more efficient (e.g., faster, cheaper), it can lead to greater overall demand, offsetting the environmental or resource-saving benefits.

Avoid Over-Optimization: Excessive focus on optimizing for efficiency could inadvertently encourage increased consumption, creating a rebound effect that neutralizes sustainability goals.

Holistic Impact Assessment: Evaluate the broader impact of technological improvements, considering both direct efficiency gains and indirect effects like market expansion or new use cases.

Sustainability by Design: Prioritize not only performance optimization but also sustainable design principles to minimize resource consumption and environmental impact throughout the product lifecycle.

Behavioral Considerations: Address the potential for increased demand due to efficiency by incorporating usage limits or promoting responsible consumption practices within technology solutions.

Common Misconceptions and Pitfalls

- Efficiency Always Leads to Resource Savings: A common misconception is that making technology more efficient will always reduce total resource consumption, ignoring the potential for increased demand and usage.
- Short-Term Gains are Sustainable: People often believe that immediate reductions in resource use from efficiency improvements will result in long-term environmental benefits, without considering the rebound effect over time.
- One-Time Efficiency Gains Solve the Problem: Assuming that a single round of efficiency improvements will solve sustainability issues, without recognizing the need for ongoing, systemic changes to consumption patterns.
- Technology Can Fix Sustainability Alone: Believing that technological advances alone will reduce resource use, without acknowledging the necessity of behavioral or policy shifts to curb overall consumption.
- Assuming Linear Relationships: Underestimating the non-linear nature of Jevons Paradox, where improvements in efficiency can disproportionately drive higher demand, leading to unintended environmental consequences.

Related Concepts

1. Moore's Law (Technology Efficiency and Demand): As computing power doubles roughly every two years, the increased efficiency can lead to greater software usage and new applications, amplifying overall resource consumption rather than reducing it.

2. Brook's Law (Software Complexity): The addition of more resources (e.g., developers) to a software project often increases its complexity, potentially leading to inefficiency, which mirrors the rebound effect seen in Jevons Paradox where more efficiency can drive greater demand and complexity.
3. Le Chatelier's Principle (System Reactions to Changes): In software systems, small improvements in performance or resource efficiency may lead to unexpected system-wide demands or changes, similar to how increased efficiency can cause a rise in consumption.
4. The Law of Diminishing Returns: In software and technology, continuing to optimize performance after a certain point may result in progressively smaller gains, while the increased efficiency might lead to greater usage, amplifying the paradox.
5. The Principle of Least Astonishment (Unexpected Outcomes): While improving software efficiency to satisfy user needs, developers may overlook how these gains could unintentionally increase user demand or shift behavior in ways that expand overall resource consumption, akin to Jevons Paradox.

References

- Wikipedia, *Jevons paradox*, [pub: 10 Sep 2024, cited: 3 Jan 2025]

Melvin Kranzberg's Laws (1st through 6th)

Definition and Origin

Melvin Kranzberg's Laws are six principles that describe the relationship between technology and society. They highlight the complex and often unpredictable nature of technological development and its social impacts. The six laws are:

1. Technology is neither good nor bad; nor is it neutral – Technology's effects depend on how it is used and the context in which it is applied.
2. Invention is the mother of necessity – New technologies create needs and demands that were previously unrecognized.

3. Things don't happen by themselves – Technological change often requires social, economic, and political conditions to facilitate its development.
4. Although technology might be a prime element in many public issues, nontechnical factors take precedence in technology-policy decisions – Social, cultural, and political factors often influence the direction and regulation of technological innovation.
5. All technology is other technology – New technologies are shaped by and often evolve from existing ones, creating a continuum of technological development.
6. Technology is a very human activity – Technological development is driven by human needs, desires, and limitations.

These laws emphasize the interconnectedness of technology with human behavior, society, and the environment.

Melvin Kranzberg, a historian of technology, coined the six laws. He formulated them as a way to express his insights on the complex relationship between technology and society. Kranzberg was a pioneer in the field of the history of technology, and his laws were designed to provoke thought about how technological developments shape, and are shaped by, social, political, and cultural contexts. These laws were first articulated in the 1980s and became foundational in discussions of the social impact of technology.

Context and Importance

Melvin Kranzberg's Laws offer a valuable framework for understanding the evolving relationship between technology, society, and culture, especially when applied to software and digital technologies. The rapid and transformative nature of software development means that technologies often advance much faster than society's ability to fully grasp, regulate, or adapt to them. For example, the first law, "Technology is neither good nor bad; nor is it neutral," resonates strongly in the software world, where programs can be used for both beneficial purposes (such as improving healthcare) and harmful ones (such as enabling surveillance or spreading misinformation). The ethical implications of software development, particularly in areas like artificial intelligence and data privacy, hinge on the choices made by developers and the broader societal context in which these technologies are deployed.

Kranzberg's laws also highlight the unpredictable and often unintended consequences of technological innovation. The second law, "Invention is the mother of necessity," is particularly relevant to software and technology industries, where new inventions frequently create entirely new demands. The smartphone, for example, introduced apps that transformed everything from communication to commerce, creating new industries and needs in the process. At the same time, the fourth law, "Although technology might be a prime element in many public issues, nontechnical factors take precedence in technology-policy decisions," underscores the importance of considering social, legal, and political factors when addressing the regulatory challenges of software. From issues like algorithmic accountability to cybersecurity policies, Kranzberg's insights remind us that technological innovation cannot be divorced from the societal and political structures that shape it. In this way, his laws remain a crucial lens for understanding the role of software in shaping our modern world.

Best Practices and Guidelines

Evaluate technology contextually – Recognize that software is neither inherently good nor bad; its impact depends on how it is used and the societal context in which it operates.

Anticipate unintended consequences – Acknowledge that new software innovations often create unforeseen needs, challenges, or ethical dilemmas that require ongoing attention and adaptation.

Incorporate diverse perspectives – Understand that social, cultural, and political factors must shape software development, influencing both design and policy decisions.

Foster responsible innovation – Prioritize ethical considerations in software development, ensuring that technology serves the broader good and avoids harm.

Recognize interconnectedness – Appreciate that all software builds on previous technologies and evolves within an ecosystem of interrelated systems and ideas.

Common Misconceptions and Pitfalls

- Technology is neutral – A common misconception is that technology itself is impartial, when in reality, its effects depend heavily on how and by whom it is used.
- Invention creates immediate necessity – People often assume that new technologies automatically solve problems, overlooking the complex social, economic, and ethical challenges they may introduce.
- Technological change happens independently – It's a pitfall to believe that technological advancements occur in isolation; they are shaped by broader social, political, and historical factors.
- Focus on technical solutions alone – A misconception is that solving technical problems can fix societal issues; non-technical factors (e.g., policies, culture) often play a more decisive role.
- New technologies are entirely distinct – The idea that each new software or technology is completely revolutionary ignores how most innovations are built upon existing technologies and systems.

Related Concepts

1. The Law of Leaky Abstractions (Joel Spolsky)
2. Brooks' Law (Fred Brooks)
3. The Principle of Least Astonishment
4. The Iron Law of Oligarchy (Robert Michels, applied to software development)
5. The Pareto Principle (80/20 Rule)

References

- Wikipedia, *Melvin Kranzberg*, [pub: 3 Jan 2024, cited: 3 Jan 2025]

The Shirky Principle

Definition and Origin

The Shirky Principle is the idea that "institutions will try to preserve the problem to which they are the solution." In other words, organizations or systems often work to maintain or even exacerbate the issues they are designed to address, because doing so helps preserve their own existence and relevance. The principle highlights how institutional inertia can prevent innovation or the resolution of problems, as organizations may prioritize their survival over finding the most efficient solution.

The Shirky Principle was coined by Clay Shirky, a prominent writer and thinker on the impact of the internet and digital technologies on society. He introduced this concept in the context of his discussions about the internet, social media, and organizational behavior, emphasizing how institutions often prioritize self-preservation over solving the problems they were created to address. The principle reflects Shirky's broader ideas about the dynamics of technology, social change, and the evolution of institutions in the digital age.

Context and Importance

The Shirky Principle is highly relevant in the context of software and technology because it sheds light on the tendency of established tech companies and platforms to resist or delay changes that would disrupt their business models or user experiences, even when those changes might ultimately benefit the broader ecosystem. In the world of software development, large institutions—such as software vendors, social media platforms, and even tech giants like Google or Microsoft—often continue to support outdated systems or practices because they have a vested interest in maintaining their current infrastructure and user base. This inertia can delay innovation, making it harder for newer, more efficient technologies or open-source alternatives to gain traction. For example, the slow adoption of newer, more secure, or privacy-conscious technologies can sometimes be attributed to the vested interests of legacy players who are unwilling to adapt for fear of losing market share or disrupting their revenue streams.

The Shirky Principle also plays a key role in how software ecosystems evolve over time. In many cases, the problems that institutions like software vendors or tech corporations were originally created to solve become less relevant or are addressed by more nimble, decentralized alternatives. However, these institutions can be reluctant to abandon the solutions they provide, even when those solutions are no longer optimal. In the world of technology, this principle helps explain the rise of open-source software, decentralized applications, and new collaborative models like those found in the blockchain space. As smaller, more flexible projects emerge, they challenge the old guard, often offering more user-centric, transparent, or innovative solutions. The Shirky Principle underscores the friction between these two forces: the inertia of large institutions trying to maintain relevance versus the disruptive potential of new technologies that can solve problems more effectively or efficiently.

Best Practices and Guidelines

Embrace Disruption: Recognize that established software solutions may resist change and actively seek opportunities to innovate with new technologies or approaches.

Challenge Legacy Systems: Evaluate existing platforms and tools critically, even if they are entrenched, and be willing to abandon or overhaul them when more efficient alternatives emerge.

Promote Open-Source Alternatives: Support and contribute to open-source projects that can offer decentralized, transparent, and more adaptable solutions, bypassing institutional inertia.

Focus on User-Centric Design: Prioritize solutions that solve real user problems over institutional convenience or preservation of outdated models.

Encourage Agile Development: Adopt agile methodologies that allow for flexibility, quick iteration, and responsiveness to new technologies, rather than clinging to legacy systems.

Common Misconceptions and Pitfalls

- Underestimating Institutional Inertia: Believing that organizations will easily embrace change, when in reality, they often resist because it threatens their stability or existing revenue models.
- Assuming Technological Progress is Inevitable: Overestimating the speed at which outdated systems will be replaced, as institutions may slow or block innovation to preserve their relevance.
- Misidentifying the Root Problem: Confusing the symptoms of a problem with its cause, leading to solutions that merely sustain the institution rather than address the actual issue.
- Overlooking the Role of Culture: Ignoring how organizational culture and internal politics can hinder technological evolution, even when external factors seem to demand change.
- Misjudging Disruptive Potential: Underestimating how quickly new, smaller competitors or decentralized technologies can outmaneuver larger institutions by addressing problems more effectively.

Related Concepts

1. Conway's Law: "Organizations design systems that mirror their communication structures."
2. The Law of Leaky Abstractions: "All non-trivial abstractions, to some degree, are leaky."
3. Parkinson's Law: "Work expands to fill the time available for its completion."
4. The Peter Principle : "In a hierarchy, every employee tends to rise to their level of incompetence."
5. The Innovator's Dilemma: "Companies that are leaders in their industries often fail because they focus on sustaining innovations and ignore disruptive technologies."

References

- Wikipedia, *Clay Shirky*, [pub: 20 Aug 2024, cited: 3 Jan 2025]

Thiel's Law

Definition and Origin

Thiel's Law states that a startup that is not expanding its market to a monopolistic position is likely to be overtaken by competition. In other words, a company must aim to dominate a niche or unique segment of the market to avoid being outpaced by rivals. It emphasizes the importance of creating a product or service that is so unique or superior that competition becomes irrelevant.

Thiel's Law was coined by Peter Thiel, a prominent entrepreneur, investor, and co-founder of PayPal. He introduced the concept in his book Zero to One (2014), where he discusses the importance of creating monopoly-like businesses by developing unique and innovative products or services.

Context and Importance

Thiel's Law is particularly relevant in the context of software and technology industries, where competition is intense, and rapid innovation can quickly render a product or service obsolete. In these sectors, companies that fail to establish a dominant position in a unique niche or provide a breakthrough innovation risk being overshadowed by faster-moving competitors. Unlike traditional industries where competition might be more gradual, the technology landscape tends to favor businesses that can scale quickly, often leveraging network effects, proprietary algorithms, or unique user bases. Thiel's Law stresses the critical need for companies in these fields to think in terms of monopoly—creating products or platforms that are so differentiated, efficient, or indispensable that they are not easily replaced or replicated by others.

In the software and tech world, Thiel's Law serves as a reminder that true value comes not from simply competing in crowded markets but from owning a distinct space where competition becomes irrelevant. For instance, companies like Google, Facebook, and Apple dominate their respective niches because they've created platforms that have massive network effects or unique technological advantages that are hard for new entrants to replicate. By focusing on monopoly-building rather than incremental competition, these companies benefit from economies of scale, brand loyalty, and reduced pressure from new competitors. Thiel's Law thus highlights a strategic mindset for technology entrepreneurs: to innovate in ways that go beyond improvement and aim for technological leaps that can reshape entire industries.

Best Practices and Guidelines

Focus on Unique Innovation: Develop a product or service that solves a problem in a novel way, making it hard for competitors to replicate.

Own a Niche: Target a small, specific market first, and dominate it before expanding, ensuring you become the go-to solution in that space.

Leverage Network Effects: Build platforms or services that become more valuable as more users join, creating a self-reinforcing cycle of growth.

Prioritize Scalability: Design your technology to scale rapidly and efficiently, enabling exponential growth without proportionate increases in cost.

Avoid Incrementalism: Strive for breakthrough innovations that can leapfrog existing solutions, rather than just competing on marginal improvements.

Common Misconceptions and Pitfalls

- Focusing Too Broadly: Trying to serve a large, generalized market early on can spread resources too thin and invite overwhelming competition.
- Relying on Incremental Improvements: Thinking small, incremental changes will outpace competition rather than aiming for transformative innovation that disrupts the market.
- Ignoring the Power of Differentiation: Believing that competition can be beaten through better execution alone, rather than developing a truly unique and hard-to-replicate product or technology.
- Underestimating the Importance of Timing: Entering a market too early or too late without considering market readiness can undermine the chance to build a monopoly.
- Overlooking Network Effects: Failing to build or integrate network effects, which are often essential for achieving dominance and scaling rapidly, can limit long-term success.

Related Concepts

1. The Network Effect (Metcalfe's Law): The value of a network increases exponentially as more users join it. This principle is crucial in software and tech, where companies that build platforms (e.g., social media, marketplaces, or SaaS tools) benefit from a growing user base that makes the service more valuable over time, creating a self-reinforcing competitive advantage.
2. The Innovator's Dilemma (Clayton Christensen): This principle explains how established companies often fail to adopt disruptive innovations because they focus too heavily on improving existing products for their current customers. Like Thiel's Law, it underscores the importance of breakthrough innovation over incremental changes, especially for companies in the tech industry that need to stay ahead of disruptive competitors.
3. The Pareto Principle (80/20 Rule): In software and technology, the 80/20 Rule suggests that 80% of value often comes from 20% of users, features, or efforts. Companies that focus on the most valuable aspects of their product, aligning with a niche market, are more likely to dominate that niche and avoid being diluted by competition.
4. Saturation Point (Network Saturation): This concept in software refers to the point at which a platform or product has acquired a critical mass of users and is essentially "saturated." Once reached, growth becomes exponential, and competition becomes less of a threat, similar to the monopolistic position Thiel advocates for. This is particularly true in tech, where dominating a specific market segment first can create a barrier to entry for competitors.
5. The Law of Increasing Returns: This principle, often applied to software and technology platforms, suggests that as a company's product improves, gains momentum, and attracts more users, it becomes more valuable and harder to disrupt. It emphasizes that software companies benefiting from network effects, economies of scale, and user lock-in can achieve monopolistic advantages, aligning with Thiel's perspective on dominance.

References

- Wikipedia, *Peter Thiel*, [pub: 21 Dec 2024, cited: 3 Jan 2025]

Varian's Rule

Definition and Origin

Varian's Rule is a principle in economics that suggests when consumers are uncertain about their future income, they will adjust their current consumption and savings behavior based on their expectations of future income changes. Essentially, it posits that people tend to consume more if they expect future income to rise and save more if they expect future income to fall.

Varian's Rule is named after Hal R. Varian, an American economist and professor at the University of California, Berkeley. He introduced the rules in his work related to consumer behavior, particularly in the context of intertemporal choice and the effect of income expectations on consumption and saving decisions. Varian's contributions are influential in the field of microeconomics, especially regarding how individuals make decisions about consumption over time under uncertainty.

Context and Importance

Varian's Rule, when applied to software and technology, provides valuable insights into consumer behavior and decision-making in markets where future expectations play a crucial role. In technology, especially in areas like software adoption, product upgrades, and cloud services, users often make decisions based on anticipated improvements or changes to products. For example, if consumers expect that a software company will release major updates or a new version in the near future, they might delay their current purchase or subscription, preferring to save resources for the upgraded product. Conversely, if users expect future prices to rise or availability to decrease, they may choose to buy or subscribe to software sooner, aligning their behavior with Varian's Rule, which suggests that expectations about the future drive consumption and investment decisions.

The rule also holds importance in pricing strategies for technology companies. Understanding how future expectations shape user behavior can help firms optimize their pricing and release schedules. For instance, subscription-based models, prevalent in cloud computing and software-as-a-service (SaaS), can be designed with future pricing changes in mind. If users expect that the cost of a service will increase, they may be incentivized to commit to longer-term contracts or sign up early. Varian's Rule also applies in markets where new technologies (e.g., artificial intelligence, virtual reality) are emerging, with consumers often waiting for greater functionality or stability in new products. By recognizing the role of future income and expectations in shaping current demand, software and technology firms can align their product development, pricing strategies, and marketing to better anticipate and respond to consumer behaviors.

Best Practices and Guidelines

Anticipate Consumer Timing: Understand that users may delay purchases or upgrades based on expectations of future product improvements or price changes.

Price Sensitivity: Adjust pricing strategies to reflect expected future trends, offering incentives for early adoption or long-term subscriptions if users expect future price increases.

Leverage Future Expectations: Use communication about upcoming features or updates to influence consumer behavior, encouraging early investment based on perceived future value.

Monitor Market Signals: Keep track of competitor advancements and market trends, as consumers may adjust their purchasing decisions based on anticipated changes in the broader tech landscape.

Flexible Models: Offer adaptable pricing or subscription models (e.g., tiered plans) that allow consumers to align their spending with their expectations of future income or product enhancements.

Common Misconceptions and Pitfalls

- Overestimating Consumer Rationality: Assuming that consumers always make optimal decisions based on future expectations, when in reality, many are influenced by biases, short-term emotions, or imperfect information.
- Ignoring External Factors: Believing that future income expectations alone drive decisions, while neglecting other variables like technological disruption, market competition, or sudden economic changes.
- Underestimating Discounting: Failing to account for how consumers heavily discount future benefits, meaning they may not always act as predicted by Varian's Rule, especially when future income changes are uncertain or distant.
- Misjudging Consumer Patience: Assuming that all consumers will delay purchases for future benefits, when in fact many prioritize immediate consumption or gratification, even if they expect future changes.
- Overcomplicating Pricing Strategies: Trying to over-engineer pricing or discount models based on expected future income behavior, when simpler models might be more effective in appealing to a broader range of consumers.

Related Concepts

1. Metcalfe's Law: The value of a software product or network increases exponentially with the number of users. As consumers anticipate the growing utility of software over time with more users, they may adjust their behavior to adopt early and participate in expanding networks, similar to Varian's Rule about future expectations influencing consumption.
2. Parkinson's Law of Data: "Data expands to fill the space available for storage." In the context of software, this can be linked to Varian's Rule as users might delay their adoption of data-intensive applications or storage solutions, expecting future innovations in data management or lower storage costs.
3. The Law of Software Efficiency: Over time, software products tend to improve in efficiency as developers refine the code and fix bugs. Consumers may delay purchasing or upgrading their software based on the expectation that future versions will perform more efficiently, similar to Varian's Rule about future expectations driving consumption.

4. Shannon's Law (Information Theory): In the context of technology, this law suggests that the capacity of a communication channel is limited by bandwidth and noise. Software companies might apply this by expecting that as technology and data transmission capabilities improve, consumers will gravitate toward products that promise better speed and quality in the future.
5. Goodhart's Law: "When a measure becomes a target, it ceases to be a good measure." This principle can be applied to software development and pricing strategies, where an overemphasis on future consumer behavior predictions (such as income expectations) can lead to misalignment of product offerings, causing them to lose relevance or effectiveness in the long run.

References

- Wikipedia, *Varian Rule*, [pub: 24 Sep 2024, cited: 3 Jan 2025]

Zuboff's Laws

Definition and Origin

Zuboff's Laws, formulated by Shoshana Zuboff, describe the dynamics of surveillance capitalism in the digital age. They explain how companies collect, commodify, and exploit personal data for profit. The laws are often summarized as:

1. The Law of the Platform: Digital platforms act as intermediaries that capture data about individuals' behavior to shape and influence their actions.
2. The Law of Extraction: Personal data is extracted from individuals, often without their full knowledge or consent, and then monetized by companies.
3. The Law of Invisibility: The processes of data extraction and surveillance are often hidden or obscured from users, preventing awareness or informed consent.

These laws reflect Zuboff's central critique of how surveillance capitalism manipulates personal information for corporate gain.

Shoshana Zuboff is credited with formulating the concept of "Zuboff's Laws," which describe the practices of surveillance capitalism. She introduced these ideas in her influential 2019 book, The Age of Surveillance Capitalism: The Fight for a Human Future at the New Frontier of Power. Zuboff is a scholar and professor emerita at Harvard Business School, and she coined these laws to explain how tech companies extract and monetize personal data. While the term "Zuboff's Laws" is not a formal designation, it is a way to refer to her key insights regarding the mechanisms of surveillance capitalism.

Context and Importance

Zuboff's Laws are highly significant in the context of software and technology because they expose the underlying mechanisms through which tech companies monetize personal data. In an era dominated by platforms like Google, Facebook, Amazon, and others, software systems are designed not just to deliver services but also to capture, analyze, and leverage user behavior to generate profit. These platforms are not just intermediaries, but powerful tools of data extraction, where users unknowingly become the product. By transforming personal data into a commodity, companies can target individuals with precision, manipulating behavior through personalized advertising and algorithmic recommendations. The result is a technology ecosystem that prioritizes data accumulation over user autonomy and privacy, creating a feedback loop where software is designed to maximize engagement, often at the expense of transparency and consent.

The importance of Zuboff's Laws lies in their critique of how technology, particularly through the business models of large platforms, has reshaped the relationship between individuals and their digital environments. Zuboff's insights challenge the conventional view of technology as neutral or purely service-oriented, urging society to reconsider the ethical implications of data-driven practices. By highlighting the hidden nature of data extraction (the Law of Invisibility), the commodification of personal experiences (the Law of Extraction), and the manipulation of user behavior (the Law of the Platform), Zuboff draws attention to the vast, unregulated power that technology companies wield. In the context of software development and technology policy, these laws serve as a call for greater transparency, accountability, and regulation to ensure that the digital world operates in ways that respect user privacy, autonomy, and human dignity.

Best Practices and Guidelines

Prioritize User Consent: Ensure clear, transparent consent mechanisms for data collection, giving users control over their personal information.

Limit Data Collection: Only gather essential data needed for functionality, avoiding excessive or intrusive data extraction.

Ensure Data Transparency: Provide users with accessible, understandable explanations of how their data is used and monetized.

Design for User Autonomy: Create systems that empower users to manage their data, opt out of tracking, and control algorithmic influences.

Promote Ethical Accountability: Build technology with ethical frameworks that protect privacy and prevent manipulative practices, ensuring companies are held accountable for their data practices.

Common Misconceptions and Pitfalls

- Assuming Consent is Sufficient: Simply obtaining user consent (often in fine print) does not guarantee informed consent or ethical data use; transparency and understanding are key.
- Overlooking Data Ownership: Many believe that users "own" their data, but in reality, tech companies often retain control and exploit it for profit, leading to a power imbalance.
- Underestimating Behavioral Manipulation: Not recognizing how deeply algorithms can influence decision-making, from purchasing habits to political views, often results in unexamined harm.
- Ignoring Long-term Impacts: Focusing only on immediate benefits of data collection (like personalization) without considering the long-term consequences of surveillance capitalism.
- Believing Privacy Settings are Enough: Relying solely on privacy settings does not address the underlying issue of how user data is commodified and used beyond individual control.

Related Concepts

1. The Law of Privacy by Design (Ann Cavoukian): This principle emphasizes integrating privacy features into the design and architecture of software from the outset, rather than as an afterthought. It aligns with Zuboff's call for transparent and ethical data practices, ensuring users' privacy is safeguarded throughout the entire development lifecycle.
2. The Principle of Least Privilege: This principle suggests that software should collect and access the minimum amount of data necessary for functionality. It directly supports Zuboff's Law of Extraction by advocating for limiting data collection to what is absolutely essential, reducing unnecessary surveillance.
3. The Right to Be Forgotten (GDPR): A cornerstone of the European Union's General Data Protection Regulation (GDPR), this principle allows individuals to request that their personal data be erased from company databases. It challenges the notion that data should be continuously extracted and commodified, reflecting Zuboff's call for user autonomy and control.
4. The Transparency Principle: This principle dictates that users should have clear, understandable insights into what data is being collected, how it's being used, and who is accessing it. It directly complements Zuboff's Law of Invisibility by advocating for transparency in data practices, fostering informed consent and user awareness.
5. The Ethics of AI and Algorithmic Accountability: This set of guidelines encourages software developers and organizations to ensure that AI systems are transparent, fair, and accountable. It aligns with Zuboff's critique of how algorithms manipulate user behavior, calling for ethical oversight and the mitigation of harm caused by AI-driven data exploitation.

References

- Wikipedia, *Surveillance capitalism*, [pub: 12 Aug 2024, cited: 3 Jan 2025]

Human Factors & UX

L. User Experience

Aesthetic-Usability Effect: Users perceive aesthetically pleasing designs as more user-friendly, even if they are not functionally superior

Definition and Origin

The Aesthetic-Usability Effect refers to the phenomenon where users perceive aesthetically pleasing products as easier to use, even if they are not functionally superior. In other words, visually attractive designs can lead to more positive user experiences and a greater sense of ease or satisfaction, even if the usability is objectively the same as less visually appealing designs.

The Aesthetic-Usability Effect was introduced by Japanese researcher Kurosu and Kashimura in a 1995 study. They found that users often perceive aesthetically pleasing designs as more user-friendly, even when the functionality of the design remains unchanged. This concept has since become an important consideration in user experience (UX) and product design.

Context and Importance

In the context of software and technology, the Aesthetic-Usability Effect emphasizes the powerful role of design aesthetics in shaping user perceptions and interactions. When users encounter a visually appealing interface or application, they are more likely to approach it with a positive attitude, assuming that it is also user-friendly, even if its functionality is identical to a less attractive design. This effect is particularly relevant in today's competitive digital landscape, where users are not only looking for efficient and functional tools but also for engaging, intuitive, and enjoyable experiences. A clean, aesthetically pleasing design can set a product apart in crowded markets, fostering a sense of trust, comfort, and satisfaction that can significantly influence user retention and adoption.

The importance of the Aesthetic-Usability Effect in software and technology cannot be overstated, as it directly impacts user engagement, satisfaction, and overall success. Attractive designs are often perceived as more polished, reliable, and easy to use, which can help reduce cognitive load and increase user confidence. This is especially true in consumer-facing applications, where first impressions are critical. A good visual design can create an emotional connection with users, making them more likely to engage with the product longer and recommend it to others. For developers and designers, understanding this effect underscores the need to balance functionality with aesthetics, ensuring that both usability and visual appeal are prioritized in the design process to create products that resonate with users and stand the test of time.

Best Practices and Guidelines

Prioritize Simplicity and Clarity: Clean, minimalistic designs improve usability by reducing cognitive load and making interactions intuitive.

Ensure Visual Consistency: Consistent color schemes, typography, and iconography create a cohesive user experience, enhancing both aesthetics and usability.

Align Functionality with Design: Make sure that visual elements support, rather than hinder, the software's core functionality to avoid frustrating users.

Use Feedback and Affordances: Incorporate visual cues (e.g., buttons that look clickable) to guide users and make interfaces feel responsive and easy to navigate.

Test with Real Users: Regularly evaluate both the visual appeal and usability of designs through user testing to ensure they meet user expectations and needs.

Common Misconceptions and Pitfalls

- Aesthetics Alone Improve Usability: A visually appealing design doesn't automatically make the product easier to use if the underlying functionality is poor or unintuitive.

- Complex Designs Are Always Better: Overly intricate or decorative designs can overwhelm users, creating confusion and making interfaces harder to navigate.
- User Preferences Are Universal: Different users have varied tastes and cultural backgrounds, so a design that appeals to one group may not be effective for another.
- Aesthetic Design = Fancy Graphics: Aesthetic appeal doesn't always mean flashy or detailed graphics; simplicity, whitespace, and intuitive layout can be just as powerful.
- Initial Visual Appeal Guarantees Long-Term Success: A product that looks good at first may still fail if it doesn't provide consistent, meaningful functionality or performance over time.

Related Concepts

1. Jakob's Law of Usability: Users spend most of their time on other sites or apps, so they prefer designs that feel familiar. Aesthetic consistency with widely recognized design patterns makes an interface both visually appealing and easier to use.
2. Fitts's Law: The time required to move to a target (e.g., a button or link) is a function of the distance to the target and its size. Aesthetically pleasing designs that prioritize user-friendly layout and size can enhance usability by improving navigation efficiency.
3. Hick's Law: The more choices a user has, the longer it will take them to make a decision. A clean, minimalistic design with fewer, well-organized options (a key aesthetic principle) helps reduce decision fatigue and speeds up user interaction.
4. Tesler's Law (Law of Conservation of Complexity): Every system has an inherent complexity, and it cannot be reduced below a certain level. Aesthetic design should aim to simplify the presentation of complex functions without sacrificing their necessary complexity, leading to an intuitive and pleasing user experience.
5. The Aesthetic-Usability Effect: As already discussed, this principle directly links visual appeal with perceived usability. Well-designed, attractive interfaces often lead users to believe the system is easier to use, even if it isn't objectively more efficient or functional.

References

- Wikipedia, *Aesthetic–usability effect*, [pub: 12 Sep 2024, cited: 3 Jan 2025]

Fitts's Law: Time to target depends on distance and size

Definition and Origin

Fitts's Law is a principle in human-computer interaction and motor control that predicts the time required to move to a target is influenced by two factors: the distance to the target and the size of the target. Specifically, the farther the target and the smaller the target, the longer it will take to reach it. Mathematically, it is expressed as:

Time = a + b * log2(2D/W)

Where:

- D = distance to the target,
- W = width of the target,
- a and b are constants that depend on the specific task.

In essence, it describes the trade-off between accuracy and speed in tasks requiring precise movement.

Fitts's Law was coined by psychologist Paul Fitts in 1954. He developed the law as part of his research on human motor behavior and how individuals interact with targets in tasks involving precision and movement. His original work, published in the Journal of Experimental Psychology, aimed to quantify the relationship between the speed of movement, target distance, and target size in manual tasks.

Context and Importance

Fitts's Law has become a foundational principle in the field of human-computer interaction (HCI) and software design. In the context of user interface (UI) design, the law helps inform how interactive elements—such as buttons, icons, and other clickable objects—are placed on screens. By understanding Fitts's Law, designers can optimize the size and placement of these elements to enhance user efficiency and satisfaction. For example, larger targets that are closer to the user's point of interaction (such as the edges of the screen) are easier and quicker to reach, improving overall usability. In contrast, smaller or more distant targets tend to slow down user actions, increasing frustration and reducing effectiveness, especially in tasks requiring precision.

The law also plays a critical role in the design of mobile and touch-based interfaces, where screen size and physical interaction constraints are more pronounced. Fitts's Law has practical implications for everything from the design of on-screen buttons and sliders to the placement of navigational elements like menus or toolbars. As the demand for more intuitive and user-friendly applications continues to grow, Fitts's Law provides valuable guidance on how to strike the right balance between accessibility, speed, and accuracy in interface design. By leveraging this principle, software developers and UX designers can ensure that users can complete tasks with minimal effort and maximum efficiency, which is essential in a world increasingly reliant on technology for both professional and personal activities.

Best Practices and Guidelines

Increase target size for frequent actions: Make buttons, icons, and clickable elements larger to reduce the time required for users to interact with them, especially for common or critical actions.

Place important controls near the edges: Position frequently used controls or targets closer to the screen edges, where they are easier to reach, particularly on touch devices.

Group related elements together: Cluster similar items to reduce the distance between them, allowing users to navigate and select faster.

Minimize unnecessary precision: Avoid requiring excessive precision for interactions; ensure controls are appropriately sized and spaced to accommodate typical user movements.

Design for ergonomic reach: On mobile or desktop interfaces, place primary controls within comfortable reach to prevent user fatigue and reduce interaction time.

Common Misconceptions and Pitfalls

- Larger targets always improve usability: Simply increasing the size of targets may not always be effective; too large or cluttered elements can overwhelm the interface and reduce overall usability.
- Distance is the only factor that matters: While distance plays a role, target size is equally important. Both factors must be balanced for optimal design—focusing only on one can lead to suboptimal user experience.
- Fitts's Law applies only to physical interfaces: Fitts's Law is often thought to apply only to physical movements, but it's also relevant to digital interactions, such as clicking and tapping in software and apps.
- Smaller screens always make tasks harder: While screen size can affect interaction time, the design and arrangement of UI elements (like button placement) can mitigate the challenges posed by smaller screens.
- Users will always adapt to poor design: Overestimating users' ability to adapt to inefficient layouts can lead to frustration and slower task completion, violating core principles of user experience.

Related Concepts

1. Hick's Law: The time it takes to make a decision increases with the number of options available. In software design, reducing cognitive load by limiting choices or grouping similar options together complements Fitts's Law by making it easier for users to interact quickly with UI elements.
2. Jakob's Law of Internet User Experience: Users spend most of their time on other websites, so they prefer designs that are familiar. By applying this principle, designers can reduce the distance and time needed to find targets by adhering to common UI patterns that users are accustomed to.

3. Law of Proximity (Gestalt Principles): Elements that are close to each other are perceived as related. In UI design, grouping related buttons or features together reduces the cognitive and physical effort required to interact with them, supporting faster task completion in line with Fitts's Law.
4. The 80/20 Rule (Pareto Principle): 80% of user actions typically come from 20% of features. By making these core features easily accessible (e.g., larger, well-placed targets), you can significantly enhance interaction speed, in alignment with Fitts's Law.
5. Fowler's Law of Minimal User Input: The fewer the number of actions required to complete a task, the better the user experience. This principle works hand-in-hand with Fitts's Law by promoting designs where users spend less time navigating between or reaching for small, distant targets, making tasks quicker and easier.

References

- Wikipedia, *Fitts's law*, [pub: 23 Aug 2024, cited: 3 Jan 2025]

Hick's Law: Decision time increases with number of choices

Definition and Origin

Hick's Law, also known as the Hick-Hyman Law, describes the relationship between the number of choices presented to a person and the time it takes them to make a decision. Specifically, it states that as the number of options increases, the time required to make a decision also increases, but at a logarithmic rate. This means that while decision time does increase with more choices, the rate of increase slows down as the number of options becomes very large.

The law is based on experiments conducted by psychologists William Edmund Hick and Ray Hyman in the 1950s, which showed that the more choices a person has, the more cognitive processing is required to evaluate and select from those choices. In practical terms, Hick's Law implies that user interfaces with fewer, more focused options generally lead to faster, more efficient decision-making, improving user experience and reducing cognitive load. It is often applied in fields like user experience (UX) design, web design, and software development to create simpler, more intuitive systems that help users achieve their goals quickly.

Context and Importance

Hick's Law is highly relevant in software and technology design, especially in user interface (UI) and user experience (UX) design. In digital environments, users are often presented with multiple options—menus, buttons, links, and choices—that they must navigate to complete tasks. The principle of Hick's Law suggests that as the number of available options increases, users will take longer to make a decision, which can lead to frustration, reduced efficiency, and a suboptimal user experience. For example, if a website or app presents too many menu items or overly complex choices, it can overwhelm the user, slowing down their decision-making process. Designers must balance the amount of information and options presented to ensure users can find what they need quickly and intuitively.

The importance of Hick's Law in technology also extends to reducing cognitive load, which is essential for maintaining engagement and usability. By understanding this principle, developers can streamline interfaces, prioritize simplicity, and avoid unnecessary complexity. It encourages designers to limit the number of choices presented at any given moment, thereby enhancing usability and improving user satisfaction. In practical terms, this could mean breaking down tasks into smaller steps, using clear categorization, or offering progressive disclosure of options. By applying Hick's Law, software products and websites become more efficient, intuitive, and user-friendly, ensuring that users can achieve their goals with minimal frustration.

Best Practices and Guidelines

Limit choices: Present a manageable number of options to avoid overwhelming users and reduce decision-making time.

Use progressive disclosure: Reveal more options gradually as needed, keeping the interface clean and simple initially.

Prioritize key actions: Highlight the most important tasks or features, ensuring users can quickly identify what matters most.

Group similar options: Organize choices into logical categories to help users process information faster.

Simplify decision paths: Minimize steps and streamline workflows, reducing cognitive load for a smoother user experience.

Common Misconceptions and Pitfalls

- More options = better: Offering more choices does not necessarily enhance user experience; it can lead to decision fatigue and delays.
- Users can handle unlimited options: Even tech-savvy users are impacted by cognitive overload; too many options can confuse and frustrate everyone.
- Hick's Law applies equally to all contexts: The effect of increasing choices varies depending on the task complexity; not all situations are equally impacted.
- Only visible options matter: Hidden or indirect choices (e.g., secondary menus) can still contribute to decision time if users need to navigate to find them.
- Users always make decisions rationally: Emotional factors, prior knowledge, and expectations also play a role in decision speed, not just the number of options.

Related Concepts

1. Fitts' Law: The time to acquire a target (e.g., click a button or link) is a function of the distance to the target and its size. This principle emphasizes the ease of selecting elements based on their proximity and size, which, when combined with Hick's Law, can help optimize user interactions.
2. Miller's Law: The average person can hold 7 (plus or minus 2) pieces of information in their short-term memory. This principle underscores the need to limit the amount of information and choices presented at any one time, aligning with Hick's Law to avoid cognitive overload.

3. Law of Proximity: Items that are close together are perceived as related. In UI design, this principle helps guide how information is grouped, supporting the idea that clear categorization of options reduces decision time, in line with Hick's Law.
4. Jakob's Law: Users spend most of their time on other websites, so they expect your site to work the same way. By following familiar design patterns and minimizing unnecessary choices, this principle complements Hick's Law by making decisions faster due to users' prior experiences.
5. The Paradox of Choice: While not a formal "law," this principle, popularized by psychologist Barry Schwartz, suggests that too many choices can lead to anxiety, paralysis, and dissatisfaction. This supports Hick's Law, reinforcing that offering fewer, well-curated choices leads to better user outcomes.

References

- Wikipedia, *Hick's law*, [pub: 29 Apr 2024, cited: 3 Jan 2025]

Jakob's Law: Users spend most time on other sites

Definition and Origin

Jakob's Law states that users spend most of their time on other websites and digital platforms, and as a result, they become accustomed to the design patterns, conventions, and behaviors they encounter there. This principle suggests that when users visit a new website or application, they bring with them expectations shaped by their prior experiences. They expect the interface, navigation, and interactions to follow familiar, established patterns they've seen elsewhere, such as in other websites, apps, or software they frequently use.

The law highlights the idea that users' mental models—how they expect things to work—are largely based on their experiences with other platforms. This means that when designing a new website or software, it is important to align with these common conventions, as deviation from them can lead to confusion, increased cognitive load, and friction in user interaction. Jakob's Law encourages designers to prioritize usability and intuitiveness by leveraging the patterns users already know, helping them to quickly understand and navigate new interfaces without unnecessary effort. By doing so, products become easier to use and more likely to meet user expectations, improving both user satisfaction and engagement.

Jakob's Law was coined by Jakob Nielsen, a prominent usability expert and co-founder of the Nielsen Norman Group. Nielsen introduced the concept in the late 1990s, emphasizing the idea that users' expectations and behavior are shaped by their experiences with other websites, leading to the need for designers to follow familiar patterns for a more intuitive and efficient user experience.

Context and Importance

Jakob's Law is particularly relevant in the context of software and technology because it underscores the importance of consistency and familiarity in user interface (UI) design. As users interact with a variety of websites, apps, and digital platforms, they develop mental models based on the patterns, layouts, and interactions they encounter. Whether it's navigation menus, button placements, or overall design structure, users expect similar conventions across different platforms. This expectation is critical in software design: if a new app or website deviates too much from these learned behaviors, users may find it unintuitive, frustrating, or difficult to use. Jakob's Law encourages designers to align their digital products with existing patterns, ensuring a smoother and more predictable user experience.

The importance of Jakob's Law in software and technology extends beyond simple usability—it's about reducing cognitive load and enhancing efficiency. When a user visits a website or opens an app, they don't want to spend time figuring out how to interact with it; they expect to quickly recognize patterns that they've encountered on other platforms. For software developers and UI designers, this means prioritizing simplicity, consistency, and convention. By doing so, they can create products that users can navigate with ease, leading to higher satisfaction, faster adoption, and ultimately greater success in the competitive digital landscape. Adhering to Jakob's Law isn't just about making things look familiar, but about meeting user expectations in a way that fosters engagement and loyalty.

Best Practices and Guidelines

Adopt Familiar UI Patterns: Use established design conventions (e.g., navigation bars, buttons, icons) to align with users' previous experiences across other platforms.

Simplify Interactions: Avoid introducing overly complex or unique workflows; ensure users can quickly understand how to interact with your software.

Consistency is Key: Maintain uniformity in design elements, terminology, and interactions to reduce confusion and improve usability.

Prioritize Common Features: Include widely recognized features, such as search bars and dropdown menus, where users expect them to be.

Test for User Expectations: Conduct usability testing to ensure your design meets user expectations based on their prior experiences with other digital products.

Common Misconceptions and Pitfalls

- Over-relying on Imitation: Simply copying design patterns from other sites without considering your users' unique needs can lead to a generic or ineffective user experience.
- Ignoring Context: Assuming that all users share the same expectations as those from mainstream websites may overlook specific audience preferences or cultural differences.

- Neglecting Innovation: Focusing too much on familiarity can stifle innovation, preventing you from creating unique solutions or differentiating your product.
- Underestimating Accessibility: Following common design patterns without considering accessibility needs (e.g., for users with disabilities) can make your product exclusionary.
- Assuming All Users Are the Same: Not all users have the same level of digital literacy or familiarity with certain platforms, so relying too heavily on general patterns may not meet every user's needs.

Related Concepts

1. Hick's Law: The time it takes to make a decision increases with the number and complexity of choices. By using familiar design patterns, you reduce cognitive load, allowing users to make decisions more quickly and easily.
2. Fitts's Law: The time to move to a target is a function of the target size and distance. This law emphasizes the importance of placing clickable elements (like buttons) in easily accessible, predictable locations, which aligns with the concept of familiarity in Jakob's Law.
3. Law of Proximity (Gestalt Principle): Objects that are close to each other are perceived as related. In software design, grouping related elements together in predictable ways improves the clarity and ease of use, supporting user expectations shaped by other sites.
4. Postel's Law (Robustness Principle): Be conservative in what you do, and liberal in what you accept from others. This principle encourages flexibility in user inputs and interactions, creating a forgiving environment that aligns with user behavior expectations shaped by their prior experiences.
5. The Principle of Least Astonishment: A system should behave in a way that least surprises the user. By adhering to familiar design patterns, you minimize unexpected behaviors that could confuse users, creating a smoother experience in line with Jakob's Law.

References

- Wikipedia, *Jakob Nielsen*, [pub: 12 Nov 2024, cited: 3 Jan 2025]

Miller's Law: To effectively understand someone, you should first assume they are being truthful

Definition and Origin

Miller's Law, in the context of communication, suggests that to effectively understand someone, you should first assume they are being truthful. Then, you should mentally explore what could be true based on their statements, allowing for a clearer understanding of their perspective or message.

Miller's Law was coined by cognitive psychologist George A. Miller. He is best known for his work on cognitive psychology and information processing, particularly his research on memory. However, the specific "Miller's Law" you're referring to—concerning the assumption of truthfulness in communication—is often linked to the work of George A. Miller in his broader exploration of cognitive processes, though it may be more accurately understood as a principle drawn from his theories rather than a single formal law.

Miller's most famous contribution is his work on the "magic number seven," which refers to the limit of items people can hold in their short-term memory. But when it comes to communication, the law you're referring to may stem from his exploration of how we process and interpret information from others.

Context and Importance

Miller's Law plays an important role in the design of software and technology, particularly in the realm of user experience (UX) and interface design. In a world where users interact with complex systems, understanding how to effectively communicate and process information is crucial. The law suggests that, in order for users to fully grasp and engage with a system, they must first be able to trust and believe the information presented to them. This means that software must be intuitive, provide clear instructions, and offer consistent feedback. When users feel confident that the system is reliable, they can focus on processing the information being given rather than questioning its validity. In practical terms, this translates to designing interfaces that anticipate user needs and present information in a way that feels seamless, transparent, and trustworthy.

Miller's Law also underpins the broader field of human-computer interaction (HCI), where understanding cognitive limitations—such as the "magic number seven" (the limit of items most people can hold in working memory)—is vital. Effective software and technology design takes into account these cognitive constraints by simplifying complex information into manageable chunks. For example, when building software systems, developers may organize information hierarchically, break down tasks into smaller steps, and minimize cognitive overload. These strategies, based on the idea that users are more likely to engage with and understand content when they trust it and can process it in digestible portions, enhance usability and foster user satisfaction. Ultimately, Miller's Law is foundational in creating digital experiences that prioritize clarity, usability, and user trust, all of which are essential for successful software adoption and engagement.

Best Practices and Guidelines

Assume User Trust: Design interfaces and systems with the assumption that users trust the information provided, fostering a seamless, non-distracting experience.

Simplify Information: Break down complex data or tasks into smaller, digestible chunks to match cognitive processing limits (e.g., "7 ± 2" rule).

Prioritize Clarity: Ensure clear, intuitive navigation and communication, making it easy for users to understand without confusion or second-guessing.

Maintain Consistency: Provide consistent design patterns and feedback, so users can build trust and familiarity with the system over time.

Minimize Cognitive Load: Avoid overwhelming users with excessive information or choices, focusing on essential tasks and reducing decision fatigue.

Common Misconceptions and Pitfalls

- Assuming Universal Trust: Believing that all users will inherently trust the system, when in reality, user trust often depends on transparency and past experiences.

- Overloading with Information: Ignoring cognitive limits by presenting too much information at once, leading to confusion or decision paralysis.
- Underestimating User Skepticism: Assuming users will immediately believe the system is truthful without validating or cross-checking information.
- Neglecting User Context: Failing to account for varying user knowledge or expertise, leading to overly simplistic or overly complex interfaces.
- Ignoring User Feedback: Not incorporating consistent, clear feedback mechanisms, which can erode trust if users feel uncertain about system responses.

Related Concepts

1. Hick's Law: This law states that the time it takes for a user to make a decision increases with the number of choices available. This relates to Miller's Law in that both emphasize the importance of limiting cognitive load to improve user experience.
2. Fitts's Law: Fitts's Law suggests that the time required to move to a target area is a function of the distance to the target and the size of the target. It relates to Miller's Law by supporting the idea that simplifying interactions (e.g., reducing distance or increasing target size) can improve usability and user trust.
3. The Principle of Least Surprise: This principle posits that users should not be surprised by unexpected behaviors in software. It aligns with Miller's Law by ensuring that users can predict and trust the system's responses, which aids in understanding and reduces cognitive strain.
4. Gestalt Principles of Perception: These principles describe how humans organize visual elements into groups or patterns. In line with Miller's Law, these principles suggest that grouping information in a way that fits cognitive limitations can enhance understanding and reduce mental effort.
5. Jakob Nielsen's Usability Heuristics: Particularly, the heuristics around Consistency and Standards and Error Prevention resonate with Miller's Law. Consistency helps users trust the system, while minimizing errors aids in reducing the cognitive load necessary for processing and decision-making.

References

- Wikipedia, *Miller's law*, [pub: 16 Nov 2024, cited: 3 Jan 2025]

Norman Strange Attractor: Chaotic systems, driven by strange attractors, exhibit sensitive dependence on initial conditions

---

Definition and Origin

A strange attractor, as defined by Norman Packard in the context of chaos theory, is a complex, non-periodic structure within a dynamical system that draws the system's trajectories toward it over time. Unlike a simple attractor, which might be a point, circle, or limit cycle, a strange attractor exhibits a fractal, irregular shape and shows sensitivity to initial conditions. This sensitivity leads to chaotic behavior, where small changes in initial conditions result in vastly different outcomes, making long-term prediction impossible, though the system remains deterministic. Strange attractors are typically found in systems that exhibit chaos, such as weather patterns or certain fluid dynamics.

The concept of the strange attractor was introduced by mathematician and physicist David Ruelle and Florence Takens in 1971, as part of their work on the study of chaotic systems. They showed that even deterministic systems could exhibit chaotic behavior due to the existence of strange attractors, which are neither periodic nor predictable.

Did you know that strange attractors are closely related to fractals, which are mathematical structures that exhibit self-similarity at various scales? This connection between chaos and fractals helps explain the unpredictable yet structured nature of many natural phenomena.

Context and Importance

In the context of software and technology, strange attractors and the chaotic behavior they represent have profound implications, particularly in fields like machine learning, artificial intelligence, and algorithm design. Chaotic systems, driven by strange attractors, exhibit sensitive dependence on initial conditions, where small changes can lead to dramatically different outcomes. This characteristic has inspired approaches to problem-solving in complex, non-linear systems where traditional linear methods fail. For example, in neural networks and optimization problems, strange attractors provide a framework to understand how systems might converge (or fail to converge) to stable solutions, even in the face of seemingly small perturbations. Understanding the behavior of strange attractors can help engineers design more robust algorithms that are less sensitive to noise and minor disturbances, leading to more reliable and adaptive systems.

Furthermore, the concept of strange attractors is crucial in simulating nonlinear dynamics in software tools, particularly for applications that deal with complex, unpredictable real-world systems, such as weather forecasting, stock market prediction, or cryptography. In these domains, systems are inherently chaotic, and the role of strange attractors is to offer a way of modeling and predicting the long-term behavior of the system, even if it cannot be precisely determined. Technologies such as genetic algorithms and swarm intelligence, which rely on iterative, feedback-driven processes, also draw inspiration from chaotic dynamics. By acknowledging the presence of strange attractors, software developers can better account for unpredictability and design systems that simulate or navigate complex, real-world phenomena, enhancing both their capability and flexibility in uncertain environments.

Best Practices and Guidelines

Account for Sensitivity to Initial Conditions: Design systems with robustness to small variations in input, as chaotic behavior may arise from even slight differences in initial states.

Implement Nonlinear Models: Use chaotic and nonlinear models where applicable, especially in fields like machine learning, optimization, and forecasting, to capture complex, unpredictable patterns.

Monitor for Long-term Stability: In dynamic systems, be aware that chaotic behavior may stabilize over time into patterns governed by strange attractors, which could influence system performance and predictability.

Avoid Overfitting: In chaotic systems, avoid overly rigid models that assume predictable behavior; instead, focus on flexible, adaptive algorithms that can cope with inherent unpredictability.

Leverage Chaos for Innovation: Explore chaotic dynamics in creative problem-solving, such as in generative design, cryptography, or AI, where non-linear complexity can enhance innovation and resilience.

Common Misconceptions and Pitfalls

- Misunderstanding Predictability: Assuming chaotic systems governed by strange attractors are entirely unpredictable; while long-term predictions are difficult, short-term behavior can still be modeled or approximated.
- Overlooking Sensitivity to Initial Conditions: Ignoring the dramatic impact of small changes in input, which can lead to vastly different outcomes and undermine system stability or performance.
- Assuming Stability from Complex Patterns: Mistaking the intricate patterns of a strange attractor for stability—chaotic systems may appear stable in the short term but can still exhibit unpredictable long-term behavior.
- Neglecting Computational Cost: Failing to recognize the high computational complexity in simulating or modeling chaotic systems, which can lead to inefficient or resource-heavy algorithms.
- Misapplying Chaos to All Systems: Incorrectly applying chaotic models to all types of problems, even when linear or simpler models might be more appropriate and efficient for specific use cases.

Related Concepts

1. Law of Sensitive Dependence on Initial Conditions (Butterfly Effect): In chaotic systems, small variations in initial inputs can lead to vastly different outcomes, a core feature of strange attractors. This law is critical when designing systems where minute changes can significantly impact results (e.g., machine learning, simulations).
2. Complexity Theory (Emergent Behavior): This principle suggests that complex behavior can emerge from simple rules or interactions, much like how strange attractors emerge in chaotic systems. Software systems should be designed to recognize and handle emergent properties, especially when modeling dynamic or nonlinear environments.
3. Law of Unpredictability (Chaos Theory): Chaos theory asserts that deterministic systems can behave unpredictably. When designing algorithms for chaotic systems, it's essential to acknowledge that complete predictability is often impossible, and systems should be built to adapt and handle uncertainty.
4. The Principle of Nonlinearity: Chaotic systems governed by strange attractors are inherently nonlinear. In software design, understanding nonlinearity is crucial when developing models, such as in neural networks or genetic algorithms, where small changes in inputs can lead to disproportionate changes in output.
5. The Law of Increasing Computational Complexity: As systems become more complex and chaotic (e.g., when simulating strange attractors), the computational requirements for accurate modeling and prediction increase. Software must be optimized to balance the need for precision with resource constraints, ensuring scalability in complex systems.

References

- Wikipedia, *Attractor*, [pub: 24 Dec 2024, cited: 3 Jan 2025]
- Wikipedia, *Chaos theory*, [pub: 17 Nov 2024, cited: 3 Jan 2025]
- Wikipedia, *Norman Packard*, [pub: 3 Jul 2024, cited: 3 Jan 2025]

Peak-End Rule: People remember experiences based on their most intense moments

---

Definition and Origin

The Peak-End Rule is a psychological principle stating that people judge experiences based largely on their most intense (peak) moments and how they end, rather than the overall experience. This means that the emotional highs and lows, along with the final moments, disproportionately influence how the entire experience is remembered.

The Peak-End Rule was proposed by psychologists Barbara Fredrickson and Daniel Kahneman. Their research suggests that people evaluate experiences based on the most intense (peak) moments and the final moments, rather than the entire duration of the experience. This principle is central to understanding how we remember and assess past events.

Context and Importance

In the context of software and technology, the Peak-End Rule has significant implications for user experience (UX) design and customer satisfaction. When users interact with software applications, websites, or digital products, their overall perception of the experience is heavily influenced by the most emotionally intense moments during their use (such as encountering a particularly frustrating bug or experiencing a delightful feature) and how the interaction ends. For example, if a user has a seamless experience using an app but encounters a frustrating bug at the end of the session, their overall assessment of the app may be negatively skewed, despite the majority of their experience being positive. By focusing on optimizing both peak moments (such as error-free performance or engaging features) and ensuring a smooth, satisfying ending (like quick task completion or an intuitive sign-off), developers can create a more memorable and positive user experience.

The Peak-End Rule is crucial for customer retention and brand loyalty in the competitive software and technology industry. Since users often evaluate software based on how they feel during key moments and their final impression, businesses that prioritize resolving pain points and enhancing positive peaks in user interactions are more likely to foster long-term relationships. For instance, if users encounter a delightful surprise, such as a personalized recommendation or a simple but thoughtful interaction, coupled with a quick and easy exit or log-off, they are more likely to return to the product and recommend it to others. In a market where attention spans are short and users are quick to abandon subpar experiences, the Peak-End Rule highlights the importance of managing both critical moments and overall user satisfaction to ensure long-term engagement.

Best Practices and Guidelines

Optimize Key Moments: Focus on enhancing high-impact moments, such as user onboarding, feature interactions, and error resolutions, to create memorable peaks.

Ensure a Positive End: Ensure that the user's final interaction (e.g., logging off, completing a task) is smooth, satisfying, and free of frustration.

Minimize Frustrations: Address and reduce negative experiences or interruptions that could become intense low points, especially toward the end of a session.

Personalize Experiences: Tailor interactions to individual users, making moments of delight feel personal and meaningful.

Streamline Onboarding & Exit: Design intuitive, quick onboarding and clear, efficient exits to shape positive first and last impressions.

Common Misconceptions and Pitfalls

- Focusing Only on the Peak: Overemphasizing a single high point without considering the entire user journey can lead to a skewed or incomplete experience.
- Ignoring Endings: Neglecting the final moments of an experience, assuming they're less important, can result in a negative lasting impression.

- Assuming Users Remember Peaks: Believing users always recall peak moments accurately can lead to misinterpreting user feedback or prioritizing the wrong features.
- Underestimating Negative Peaks: A small but intense negative experience, like a frustrating bug, can outweigh an overall positive experience if not properly addressed.
- Treating All Users Similarly: Failing to recognize that different users may have different emotional triggers and experiences can lead to one-size-fits-all solutions that don't leverage the Peak-End Rule effectively.

Related Concepts

1. Hick's Law: The time it takes for a user to make a decision increases with the number of choices available. This principle emphasizes the importance of reducing cognitive load at critical moments, which can influence both the "peak" and "end" experiences by making decisions simpler and more intuitive.
2. Fitts's Law: The time to acquire a target is a function of the distance to and size of the target. This principle highlights the importance of designing interactive elements that are easy to click or tap, reducing frustration and creating smoother user interactions—critical for positive peak and end experiences.
3. The Law of Peak-End Neglect: A user's memory of a system or interface will often be biased by the best and worst parts of their experience. This directly complements the Peak-End Rule by emphasizing that software should focus on both delivering delightful high points and avoiding major pitfalls.
4. Tesler's Law (Law of Conservation of Complexity): Every application has an inherent level of complexity, but it's the developer's job to manage this complexity, hiding unnecessary complexity from the user. By simplifying tasks at key moments (especially at the peak and end), developers ensure a more positive overall experience.
5. Aesthetic-Usability Effect: Users often perceive aesthetically pleasing design as easier to use. Positive emotional reactions triggered by good design can enhance the "peak" moments of an experience, reinforcing the Peak-End Rule's emphasis on emotional highs and positive closures.

References

- Wikipedia, *Peak–end rule*, [pub: 8 Jul 2024, cited: 3 Jan 2025]

Progressive Enhancement Principle: ensures core functionality is accessible to all users on all devices

---

Definition and Origin

The Progressive Enhancement Principle is a web design strategy that prioritizes providing a basic, functional experience to all users, regardless of their browser or device capabilities. It then progressively adds more advanced features for users with modern browsers or devices that support them, ensuring accessibility and usability at all levels.

The Progressive Enhancement principle was coined by Steve Champeon in 2003.

Context and Importance

The Progressive Enhancement Principle emerged in response to the increasing complexity of web technologies and the diversity of devices and browsers used to access the internet. In the early 2000s, web developers faced a fragmented ecosystem where users interacted with websites on various browsers, each with different levels of support for emerging web standards. Rather than focusing solely on creating an experience that worked for the most advanced browsers, Progressive Enhancement emphasized building a solid, functional base experience first, ensuring that even users on older browsers or low-bandwidth connections could access the core content of a website. This approach was particularly crucial as it aligned with the goal of creating an inclusive web where accessibility was a priority, and everyone could engage with digital content.

In the context of software and technology, the importance of Progressive Enhancement extends beyond just web design. It embodies the principle of adaptability, ensuring that software and web applications remain functional across different environments, user needs, and hardware capabilities. By following this principle, developers can create applications that work on a wide range of devices—from low-end smartphones to high-performance computers—while still taking advantage of advanced features and capabilities in more capable environments. This approach not only helps to maintain broad user accessibility but also allows for continuous improvement and evolution of digital experiences, ensuring that technology can evolve without leaving users behind.

Best Practices and Guidelines

Start with a solid foundation: Ensure core functionality is available and accessible on all devices and browsers, even those with limited capabilities.

Layer enhancements progressively: Add advanced features and functionality based on the capabilities of the user's device or browser, ensuring a graceful experience on more powerful systems.

Prioritize accessibility: Focus on making content and functionality available to as many users as possible, including those with disabilities or using assistive technologies.

Use feature detection: Instead of relying on browser detection, implement techniques to check for specific capabilities and adapt the user experience accordingly.

Ensure backward compatibility: Design with older devices and browsers in mind, while still taking advantage of modern technologies for users with up-to-date systems.

Common Misconceptions and Pitfalls

- It's only for web design: Progressive Enhancement is not limited to web development; it applies to all software and technology systems that need to accommodate varying levels of device and browser capabilities.

- It requires building separate versions: You don't need separate versions of a site or app; instead, use responsive design and feature detection to create a single experience that adapts to different environments.
- It's only about visual design: Progressive Enhancement also focuses on functionality and accessibility, ensuring that content is accessible and usable even without advanced styling or JavaScript.
- It's a fallback, not a primary design approach: Progressive Enhancement is a proactive design strategy, not just an afterthought to "fix" unsupported features—core functionality should always be designed first.
- It's always slower or less efficient: When done correctly, Progressive Enhancement can optimize performance by serving lightweight experiences to devices that don't need heavy features, leading to faster load times for all users.

Related Concepts

1. Graceful Degradation: Often contrasted with Progressive Enhancement, this principle focuses on ensuring that software remains functional even if advanced features are not supported. While Progressive Enhancement builds from a baseline up, Graceful Degradation starts with a full-featured experience and ensures it still works without those features for less capable environments.
2. Responsive Web Design (RWD): This principle emphasizes designing software that adapts to various screen sizes and devices, ensuring a functional experience across platforms. Like Progressive Enhancement, RWD prioritizes a baseline usable experience while progressively improving design and layout as device capabilities increase.
3. The Principle of Least Power: This principle suggests using the simplest and least powerful technologies that can achieve the desired result. By focusing on core functionality and avoiding unnecessary complexity, it aligns with Progressive Enhancement's goal of building scalable, lightweight experiences for a broad range of users.

4. Universal Accessibility: This principle advocates for designing technology that is usable by all people, regardless of their abilities or disabilities. Progressive Enhancement aligns closely with Universal Accessibility by ensuring that web content and applications are usable on a variety of devices and are accessible to individuals with diverse needs.
5. Fail-Safe Design: This principle ensures that if an error occurs, the system will fail in a way that doesn't disrupt the user experience. Progressive Enhancement supports this by ensuring that, even when advanced features like JavaScript or CSS aren't supported, the basic functionality and content are still available to the user.

References

- Wikipedia, *Progressive enhancement*, [pub: 12 Dec 2024, cited: 3 Jan 2025]

Serial Position Effect: Tendency to remember items at the beginning and end of a list

---

Definition and Origin

The Serial Position Effect refers to the tendency for people to more easily remember items at the beginning (primacy effect) and the end (recency effect) of a list, while forgetting those in the middle. This cognitive phenomenon occurs because items at the start are rehearsed more, and those at the end are still fresh in memory.

The Serial Position Effect was first described by the American psychologist Hermann Ebbinghaus in the late 19th century. Ebbinghaus is best known for his pioneering work on memory and forgetting. His research on the serial position effect showed that people tend to remember the first and last items in a list better than those in the middle. This finding was later expanded upon by other psychologists, such as Murdock in the 1960s.

Context and Importance

The Serial Position Effect is an important consideration in the design of user interfaces, software applications, and website layouts, as it can directly influence how users interact with and retain information. When presenting a list of items or options, such as in menus, dashboards, or settings, designers must account for the tendency of users to remember the first and last items more easily. This effect can be strategically leveraged to prioritize important features, notifications, or calls to action, ensuring that critical items are either placed at the beginning or end of a list. For example, in an e-commerce application, placing the most popular products at the top or bottom of a list can improve user experience and increase conversions, as these items are more likely to be noticed and remembered by users.

In the realm of software development, understanding the Serial Position Effect can also enhance the design of tutorials, onboarding processes, and information presentation. By structuring information so that essential content appears at the beginning or end of a sequence, developers can improve user comprehension and retention. Additionally, considering this effect can help prevent cognitive overload by reducing the amount of information placed in the middle, where users may struggle to retain details. In the context of notifications or alerts, placing the most important or urgent information at the start or end of the message can ensure that it captures attention effectively, leading to better user engagement and response times. This understanding of human memory and perception can ultimately lead to more intuitive and effective software experiences.

Best Practices and Guidelines

Prioritize key items: Place important features or actions at the beginning or end of lists or menus to leverage the primacy and recency effects.

Simplify middle content: Avoid overloading the middle of a list or screen with crucial information, as users may struggle to retain it.

Optimize notifications: Position urgent or critical alerts at the beginning or end of messages to ensure they grab attention.

Strategic onboarding: Place essential instructions or guidance at the start or end of onboarding processes for better user retention and comprehension.

Test user flows: Conduct usability testing to confirm that users naturally prioritize the first and last items in different contexts.

Common Misconceptions and Pitfalls

- Assuming it applies equally to all contexts: The Serial Position Effect may not be as strong in certain situations, such as when users have prior knowledge or expectations about the content.
- Overusing the effect: Relying too heavily on placing important items only at the beginning or end can make the middle feel neglected, leading to a less balanced user experience.
- Ignoring cognitive load: Focusing only on primacy and recency without considering the user's overall cognitive load can overwhelm users and reduce their ability to retain information.
- Assuming a uniform attention span: Not all users have the same attention span, so the effect might not always work as expected across diverse audiences.
- Underestimating the role of design: The Serial Position Effect interacts with visual hierarchy and design layout, so relying solely on position without considering design can lessen its impact.

Related Concepts

1. Hick's Law: The time it takes to make a decision increases with the number of options available. This law relates to the Serial Position Effect, as users may struggle more with remembering and choosing from a large list, especially when critical items are buried in the middle.
2. Fitts's Law: This principle states that the time to acquire a target is a function of the distance to and size of the target. It aligns with the Serial Position Effect by highlighting that users are more likely to interact with items that are easily accessible or placed at the start or end of a list.
3. Miller's Law: Humans can typically hold 7 (plus or minus 2) items in their short-term memory. The Serial Position Effect plays into this by suggesting that users are better at recalling the first and last items in a list, which aligns with the limits of human memory.

4. Gestalt Principles (Proximity & Similarity): These principles explain how users group information visually. In relation to the Serial Position Effect, grouping important items at the beginning or end can make them easier to recall and prioritize, influencing the way users mentally organize information.
5. Law of Prägnanz (Simplicity): This principle asserts that users tend to perceive the simplest possible interpretation of complex images or information. When applying the Serial Position Effect, simplifying the content at the beginning and end of a sequence can improve retention and understanding.

References

- Wikipedia, *Serial-position effect*, [pub: 30 May 2024, cited: 3 Jan 2025]

Tesler's Law: Every application has an inherent amount of complexity that cannot be removed or hidden

---

Definition and Origin

Tesler's Law, also known as the "Law of Conservation of Complexity," states that "every application has an inherent amount of complexity that cannot be removed or hidden. Instead, it must be addressed either through product development or user interaction." In other words, complexity is unavoidable in any system, and it must be managed in a way that makes it understandable or accessible to the user, either by simplifying the interface or making the development process more transparent.

Tesler's Law was coined by Larry Tesler, a computer scientist known for his work in human-computer interaction. Tesler is particularly recognized for his contributions to the development of user-friendly software interfaces, and the law reflects his belief that complexity in software or systems is inevitable and must be managed effectively either through design or user interaction.

Context and Importance

Tesler's Law is deeply significant in the context of software and technology because it emphasizes the inescapable nature of complexity in systems. As software and technology continue to evolve, the underlying processes and functionality often grow more sophisticated. No matter how intuitive the user interface may be, the complexity inherent in the system—whether from the underlying code, data structures, or processes—remains. Tesler's Law highlights that rather than attempting to eliminate or hide this complexity, developers must either streamline it or present it in a way that users can understand and interact with effectively. This recognition is crucial for creating products that are both powerful and usable.

The importance of Tesler's Law in software development is reflected in the way user interfaces and experiences are designed. For example, a complex operation in a piece of software can be made more accessible through careful interface design, allowing users to perform intricate tasks without needing to understand every detail of how the system works. Similarly, for developers, the law reinforces the need to address complexity early in the product design phase. By acknowledging that complexity cannot be completely eliminated, companies can focus on making it manageable and transparent, thus enhancing usability, user satisfaction, and overall product success.

Best Practices and Guidelines

Acknowledge inherent complexity: Understand that every system has unavoidable complexity that must be managed, not eliminated.

Simplify user interactions: Design interfaces that make complex tasks as intuitive as possible without oversimplifying essential functions.

Optimize for transparency: When complexity can't be hidden, make it clear and understandable for the user through guidance or support.

Balance between power and usability: Ensure users can perform advanced tasks without overwhelming them with technical details.

Iterate based on user feedback: Continuously refine the system by considering how users interact with and navigate its complexity.

Common Misconceptions and Pitfalls

- Underestimating complexity: Believing that all complexity can be hidden or eliminated, which can lead to oversimplified designs that lack necessary functionality.
- Assuming users will adapt: Expecting users to naturally understand and handle complex systems without adequate guidance or design support.
- Overloading interfaces: Trying to hide complexity by cramming too many features into a single interface, which can overwhelm users.
- Focusing only on simplicity: Prioritizing minimalism at the cost of excluding important features or advanced functionalities that users may need.
- Neglecting user testing: Failing to test how users interact with complex elements, assuming they will figure it out without feedback on usability.

Related Concepts

1. The Law of Leaky Abstractions (Joel Spolsky) – This law suggests that abstractions, such as APIs or user interfaces, often "leak" complexity to the user or developer. No matter how simplified the abstraction is, underlying complexities can still surface.
2. Shannon's Law (Claude Shannon) – A fundamental principle of information theory, it posits that there is a limit to how much information can be transmitted efficiently, relating to how much complexity can be effectively communicated or handled by a system or user.
3. Hick's Law – This law states that the time it takes for a user to make a decision increases with the number of available options. It ties into Tesler's Law in that as complexity increases, user experience can suffer unless carefully managed.
4. The 80/20 Rule (Pareto Principle) – Often applied in software development, this rule states that 80% of a system's usage typically comes from 20% of its features. It suggests that managing complexity means focusing on the most used parts of a system while simplifying or hiding less critical areas.
5. Fitts's Law – This law predicts that the time required to move to a target area is a function of the distance to the target and the size of the target. It is relevant to user interface design, where managing complexity through effective design reduces the time users spend interacting with complex elements.

References

- Wikipedia, *Law of conservation of complexity*, [pub: 6 Dec 2024, cited: 3 Jan 2025]

Von Restorff Effect: Items that is noticeably different from a group are more likely to be remembered

---

Definition and Origin

The Von Restorff effect, also known as the "isolation effect," refers to the phenomenon where an item that is noticeably different from the surrounding items is more likely to be remembered. In other words, unique or distinctive stimuli stand out and are more easily recalled compared to other, more typical items.

The Von Restorff effect was coined by the German psychiatrist and pediatrician Hedwig von Restorff in 1933. She discovered that items that are distinctive or stand out from a group are more likely to be remembered than those that are similar to others.

Context and Importance

In the context of software and technology, the Von Restorff effect plays a significant role in user interface (UI) and user experience (UX) design. By leveraging the isolation effect, designers can strategically highlight key elements such as buttons, notifications, or call-to-action prompts to attract the user's attention. For instance, a unique color or shape applied to an important feature, like a "Submit" button or an error message, ensures that it stands out among other less crucial elements on the screen. This helps in guiding users through interfaces more efficiently, improving usability and the overall user experience. In crowded screens with abundant data or options, utilizing the Von Restorff effect enables designers to prioritize critical information without overwhelming the user.

The Von Restorff effect is also crucial in technology marketing and product design. When companies release new software or hardware, using distinctive branding or visual cues can make certain features or aspects of the product more memorable. For instance, Apple often uses contrasting colors and bold visual elements in their products and marketing, making specific features more attention-grabbing and memorable to consumers. This can enhance recall and decision-making, increasing user engagement and product retention. By applying the Von Restorff effect, businesses can increase visibility for particular elements, ultimately improving the effectiveness of marketing campaigns, product interfaces, and user retention strategies.

Best Practices and Guidelines

Highlight Key Actions: Use distinctive colors, shapes, or animations to make important buttons (e.g., "Submit") or calls to action stand out.

Create Visual Hierarchy: Employ contrast to ensure critical information (e.g., error messages or notifications) grabs attention without overwhelming the interface.

Avoid Overuse: Limit the use of isolation to a few elements to prevent clutter and ensure only the most crucial features stand out.

Enhance User Flow: Apply the effect to guide users through complex tasks or processes by emphasizing next steps or critical choices.

Consistency in Design: Use unique visual cues sparingly, maintaining a balance between standout elements and overall design cohesiveness.

Common Misconceptions and Pitfalls

- Overusing Contrast: Applying distinctive design elements to too many items can lead to confusion and reduce the effectiveness of the Von Restorff effect.
- Ignoring Context: Using isolation without considering the user's cognitive load may make interfaces feel disjointed or overwhelming.
- Prioritizing Style Over Function: Focusing too much on making elements stand out visually can detract from usability and clarity.

- Assuming All Attention Is Positive: Drawing attention to negative elements (e.g., errors) too aggressively can cause frustration instead of guiding users.
- Overloading with Unique Features: Relying on the Von Restorff effect for every key element can make the design feel inconsistent or chaotic.

Related Concepts

1. Hick's Law: The time it takes to make a decision increases with the number of options presented. The Von Restorff effect can simplify decision-making by drawing attention to important choices in a sea of options.
2. Fitts' Law: The time to move to a target is based on its size and distance. The Von Restorff effect can be used to make important buttons or actions more prominent, improving the speed and ease of interaction.
3. Miller's Law: The average number of objects an individual can hold in their working memory is 7 (±2). The Von Restorff effect can help reduce cognitive overload by making key elements stand out and easier to remember.
4. Jakob's Law: Users spend most of their time on other websites and expect your site to work the same way. Utilizing familiar and distinctive visual cues in line with the Von Restorff effect can enhance usability and ensure a smoother user experience.
5. The Aesthetic-Usability Effect: Users often perceive aesthetically pleasing design as more usable. The Von Restorff effect can help make critical UI elements both visually distinct and aesthetically appealing, boosting user engagement and satisfaction.

References

- Wikipedia, *Von Restorff effect*, [pub: 20 Dec 2024, cited: 3 Jan 2025]

Yerkes–Dodson Law

Definition and Origin

The Yerkes–Dodson Law is a psychological principle that describes the relationship between arousal (or stress) and performance. It suggests that performance improves with moderate levels of arousal, but when arousal becomes too high or too low, performance declines. Essentially, there is an optimal level of arousal for peak performance, with too little leading to underperformance and too much leading to anxiety or overexertion.

The Yerkes–Dodson Law was coined by psychologists Robert M. Yerkes and John D. Dodson in 1908. They conducted research on the relationship between arousal and performance in animals, and their findings were later applied to human behavior.

Context and Importance

In the context of software and technology, the Yerkes-Dodson Law offers valuable insight into how developers and teams perform under different levels of stress or pressure. In high-tech environments, developers often face tight deadlines, complex problem-solving, and constant changes in requirements, all of which can lead to varying levels of arousal. At moderate levels of stress, individuals may feel motivated and focused, improving creativity and productivity. However, excessive stress, such as working under intense pressure or burnout, can significantly hinder cognitive functions, leading to mistakes, decreased efficiency, and poor decision-making. Conversely, too little stress or lack of challenges may lead to boredom or a lack of initiative, resulting in subpar performance. Balancing these factors is crucial for optimal performance in technology-related roles.

The Yerkes-Dodson Law also has practical implications for designing technology systems, managing teams, and ensuring the well-being of individuals working in the field. For software companies, understanding this principle can help in designing work environments that foster just the right amount of challenge and support. For example, providing clear goals, reasonable deadlines, and regular breaks can help maintain a moderate level of stress that encourages high productivity without leading to burnout. Similarly, it can inform strategies for user interface (UI) design or game development, where user engagement thrives at an optimal level of challenge. In both cases, understanding and applying the Yerkes-Dodson Law can lead to better outcomes, whether in employee performance or product development.

Best Practices and Guidelines

Manage Workload and Deadlines: Set realistic, achievable deadlines to maintain moderate stress levels that promote focus and productivity without causing burnout.

Encourage Breaks and Downtime: Regular breaks help lower stress and prevent cognitive overload, allowing for sustained high performance.

Foster a Challenging but Supportive Environment: Provide tasks that challenge skills but are not overwhelming, ensuring employees stay engaged without feeling excessively stressed.

Monitor Work Intensity: Be mindful of workload spikes, as prolonged high-stress situations can lead to errors and decreased quality in work.

Prioritize Mental Health: Offer resources for stress management and promote a work-life balance to avoid long-term negative effects of high arousal.

Common Misconceptions and Pitfalls

- Assuming More Stress Equals Better Performance: High stress does not always lead to better performance; it can cause anxiety and reduce cognitive function beyond an optimal level.
- Ignoring Individual Differences: The optimal stress level varies among individuals; what works for one person may not work for another, leading to ineffective approaches.
- Equating Low Stress with Low Effort: Low stress doesn't mean low effort; it can signal disengagement, boredom, or lack of challenge, all of which can reduce performance.
- Underestimating the Impact of Long-Term Stress: Chronic high stress can accumulate over time, leading to burnout, decreased performance, and mental health issues, even if short-term effects seem manageable.
- Misapplying the Law to All Situations: The Yerkes-Dodson Law primarily applies to tasks of moderate complexity; it doesn't necessarily hold for highly complex or routine tasks.

Related Concepts

1. Pareto Principle (80/20 Rule): This principle suggests that 80% of results come from 20% of efforts. In software development, it highlights the importance of focusing on key tasks that drive the most value, similar to how moderate levels of stress can lead to peak performance.
2. Law of Diminishing Returns: This law states that after a certain point, additional effort or resources yield progressively smaller benefits. It aligns with the Yerkes-Dodson Law in that excessive effort (or stress) beyond an optimal point can reduce overall performance.
3. Brooks' Law: It states that adding more developers to a late software project only makes it later. This highlights the negative impact of overloading a team with too much pressure or complexity, paralleling the adverse effects of excessive stress in the Yerkes-Dodson Law.
4. Fitts' Law: This law describes the relationship between the distance to a target and the time it takes to reach it, emphasizing that more complex or difficult tasks take more time. It is related to the idea that optimal challenge levels can improve performance but only when within manageable limits.
5. Cognitive Load Theory: This principle suggests that learners or workers can only process a certain amount of information at a time. It ties to the Yerkes-Dodson Law by showing that cognitive overload (too much stress or complexity) can negatively affect performance, while a moderate challenge supports better outcomes.

References

- Wikipedia, *Yerkes–Dodson law*, [pub: 22 Mar 2024, cited: 3 Jan 2025]

M. Human Behavior

1-9-90 Rule

Definition and Origin

The 1-9-90 Rule is a concept often applied in social media, marketing, or content creation, which suggests that:

- 1% of users create content or initiate actions (e.g., posts, contributions).
- 9% engage with and interact with the content (e.g., likes, shares, comments).
- 90% are passive consumers, simply viewing or consuming content without actively participating.

It emphasizes the disparity in participation levels among users in online platforms.

The 1-9-90 Rule is often attributed to Jakob Nielsen, a prominent usability expert and founder of the Nielsen Norman Group. He introduced the concept in the context of online communities and participation, emphasizing that in any given online community or platform, only a small percentage of users actively contribute, while the majority either engage passively or not at all.

Though the rule is widely recognized and applied, Nielsen's work on the concept was part of broader research on user behavior, particularly in relation to online communities and content creation.

Context and Importance

The 1-9-90 Rule, when applied to software and technology, highlights the distribution of user engagement and behavior within digital platforms, online communities, and social networks. In these environments, the rule suggests that a small group of users (about 1%) are responsible for creating the bulk of content, such as software features, bug reports, or user-generated posts. A slightly larger group (9%) participates by interacting with this content—commenting, providing feedback, or using features actively. The remaining 90% primarily consume the content without contributing. This rule serves as a crucial insight for software developers, digital marketers, and platform designers, as it underscores the need for tools and strategies that encourage wider participation and support the small, yet vital group of contributors who drive innovation and activity within the ecosystem.

Understanding the 1-9-90 Rule is important in software and technology development because it emphasizes the value of community engagement in product evolution and user adoption. Recognizing that the majority of users are passive consumers means that developers should design systems that make it easy for the active 1% and 9% to contribute valuable content and feedback. Furthermore, this rule aids in prioritizing resources, as platforms can focus on fostering relationships with power users and incentivizing engagement from the larger community. By effectively managing these dynamics, tech companies can enhance user experience, increase platform engagement, and drive continuous improvements to the software or service.

Best Practices and Guidelines

Encourage Contribution: Design tools that make it easy for the 1% (content creators) and 9% (engagers) to share feedback, contribute features, and interact.

Reward Engagement: Offer incentives like badges, recognition, or exclusive access to encourage active participation from the 9% group.

Simplify Consumption: Make it easy for the 90% to consume content without overwhelming them, ensuring they have a seamless user experience.

Foster Community: Build support networks and communities where users can connect, share knowledge, and collaborate, driving more interaction.

Monitor Behavior: Analyze user activity to identify power users and tailor strategies to retain and support them while increasing engagement across the platform.

Common Misconceptions and Pitfalls

- Overestimating User Engagement: Believing that most users will actively contribute, leading to unrealistic expectations for content creation or feedback.
- Neglecting Passive Users: Focusing only on the 1% and 9% can overlook the value of the 90%, who can still influence the platform through consumption patterns.
- Assuming Content Will Go Viral: Expecting that a small amount of content will automatically reach a large audience without factoring in the passive majority.
- Underestimating the Need for Encouragement: Not providing enough incentives or ease for users to engage, leading to low interaction rates despite available opportunities.
- Ignoring the Power of the 9%: Failing to recognize that the 9% of active users often have significant influence in spreading content or shaping discussions.

Related Concepts

1. Pareto Principle (80/20 Rule): This principle suggests that 80% of outcomes come from 20% of causes. Similar to the 1-9-90 Rule, it emphasizes the imbalance in effort and results, where a small percentage of users drive the majority of content and engagement.
2. Network Effects: The value of a software or platform increases as more people use it. This law relates to the 1-9-90 Rule because while the majority may consume content passively, their participation grows the platform's overall value, attracting more users.
3. The Long Tail Theory: In digital platforms, a small number of items or users (the "head") account for the majority of traffic, while a large number of items or users (the "tail") collectively add up to a significant portion. It relates to the 1-9-90 Rule by highlighting the disproportionate contribution of a few users versus many passive ones.

4. Brooks' Law (Adding manpower to a late software project makes it later): This principle is relevant because focusing too much on engaging only the highly active users (1%) may distract from managing a broader user base effectively, thus slowing down overall development and adoption.
5. Law of Participation Inequality: Also known as the "1% Rule," this law states that in most online communities, a small fraction of users will contribute the majority of the content, closely mirroring the 1-9-90 Rule and reinforcing the idea that engagement is highly skewed.

References

- Wikipedia, *1% rule*, [pub: 20 Dec 2024, cited: 3 Jan 2025]

Confirmation Bias

Definition and Origin

Confirmation bias is the tendency to search for, interpret, and remember information in a way that confirms one's preexisting beliefs or opinions, while giving less consideration to information that contradicts them.

Confirmation bias was first coined by British psychologist Peter Wason in the 1960s. He introduced the concept while studying reasoning and decision-making processes, particularly in his "selection task" experiments. His work highlighted how people tend to seek out evidence that supports their hypotheses rather than testing them in a way that could potentially disprove them.

Context and Importance

In the context of software development and technology, confirmation bias can significantly impact decision-making and problem-solving. Developers, designers, or engineers may become fixated on a particular solution or approach due to their prior experiences or preferences, leading them to overlook better alternatives. For instance, when debugging a software issue, a developer may focus on a solution they've successfully used in the past, even if it's not the most appropriate for the current problem. This bias may cause them to disregard new methods, tools, or insights that could lead to a more efficient or effective resolution. In technology companies, confirmation bias can also affect team collaboration, as individuals may favor ideas or suggestions that align with their own views, which stifles innovation and progress.

The importance of recognizing and mitigating confirmation bias in the tech industry lies in its potential to limit growth and hinder optimization. When confirmation bias takes hold in product design, development, or testing, it can lead to flawed products, poor user experiences, and missed opportunities for improvement. For instance, a tech company may dismiss user feedback that challenges the current design or functionality of a product, leading to features that do not meet user needs. In a rapidly evolving industry, where innovation and adaptability are key, awareness of confirmation bias enables more objective decision-making and encourages openness to new perspectives, ultimately driving better products, services, and technological advancements.

Best Practices and Guidelines

Encourage diverse perspectives: Actively seek input from different team members to challenge assumptions and uncover blind spots.

Test all hypotheses: Regularly test solutions that could disprove your initial assumptions, not just those that confirm them.

Review user feedback objectively: Analyze user feedback and data without bias, focusing on issues rather than supporting preconceived solutions.

Use data-driven decision-making: Rely on analytics and empirical evidence rather than personal experience or opinions when making key tech decisions.

Foster a culture of openness: Promote a mindset where questioning and re-evaluating assumptions is seen as a strength, not a weakness.

Common Misconceptions and Pitfalls

- Only affects individuals with strong opinions: Confirmation bias can impact anyone, regardless of how open-minded they consider themselves.
- Only occurs consciously: People may not be aware that they are prioritizing confirming information and ignoring contradictory evidence.
- Is limited to belief-based situations: Confirmation bias can also occur in problem-solving, technical decisions, and data interpretation, not just in personal beliefs.
- Is always harmful: While it can lead to poor decision-making, confirmation bias can sometimes reinforce productive behaviors or validate accurate insights.
- Can be easily overcome with awareness alone: Overcoming confirmation bias often requires systematic practices, such as structured decision-making and critical thinking techniques, not just awareness.

Related Concepts

1. Hick's Law: This principle states that the time it takes to make a decision increases with the number of options available. Confirmation bias can exacerbate this by leading individuals to focus on fewer, familiar options that confirm their existing preferences, rather than considering all possibilities.
2. Parkinson's Law: "Work expands to fill the time available for its completion." This law can interact with confirmation bias when teams focus on familiar approaches or assumptions, stretching out development cycles because they resist questioning the methods that feel most comfortable or validated by previous success.
3. Occam's Razor: The principle suggests that the simplest solution is often the best. In the context of confirmation bias, developers may overlook the simplest, most straightforward solution in favor of complex ones that confirm their previous approaches or preconceived notions.

4. The Law of Leaky Abstractions (Joel Spolsky's Law): This law suggests that higher-level abstractions often hide important details, which can result in poor decisions. Confirmation bias might cause developers to avoid considering the "leaky" details in lower layers, reinforcing inefficient or incorrect abstractions.
5. The Principle of Least Astonishment: This principle emphasizes that a system should behave in a way that least surprises the user. Confirmation bias can lead developers to create interfaces or functionality that align with their own expectations, rather than taking a user-centric approach that tests assumptions and incorporates diverse feedback.

References

- Wikipedia, *Confirmation bias*, [pub: 6 Dec 2024, cited: 3 Jan 2025]

Cognitive Load Theory

Definition and Origin

Cognitive load refers to the mental effort required to process and understand information. It involves the capacity of working memory to handle tasks or information, with a high cognitive load potentially overwhelming the brain's ability to effectively learn or solve problems. Cognitive load can be categorized into three types: intrinsic (inherent to the task), extraneous (unnecessary distractions), and germane (effort to integrate and understand).

Cognitive load theory was developed by Dr. John Sweller, an Australian educational psychologist, in the 1980s. Sweller's research focused on how the design of instructional materials can affect learning, particularly in terms of the limitations of working memory. His theory emphasizes the importance of managing cognitive load to optimize learning and avoid overloading the learner's cognitive resources.

Context and Importance

In the context of software and technology, cognitive load plays a critical role in the design of user interfaces (UIs) and user experiences (UX). As software becomes more complex, users are required to process increasing amounts of information and make decisions quickly. If an interface demands too much mental effort from users—due to overwhelming features, poor organization, or unclear navigation—it can result in confusion, frustration, and mistakes. Software designers and developers need to minimize unnecessary cognitive load by simplifying workflows, making the design intuitive, and ensuring that key information is readily accessible without requiring excessive mental processing. By doing so, they can improve the usability and effectiveness of applications, leading to a more seamless and productive user experience.

Cognitive load is also important in technology development for tasks such as coding, debugging, and learning new programming languages or tools. Developers often face high cognitive load when juggling multiple complex tasks or trying to learn new systems, leading to reduced efficiency, increased errors, and slower problem-solving. To alleviate this, technology tools and development environments can be designed to support developers by offering features like syntax highlighting, auto-completion, and contextual suggestions that reduce the cognitive burden. Additionally, breaking down complex tasks into smaller, manageable components helps developers focus on one thing at a time, improving their productivity and overall performance. In both UI/UX design and software development, understanding and managing cognitive load is essential for creating effective and user-friendly technologies.

Best Practices and Guidelines

Simplify User Interfaces: Design intuitive, minimalistic interfaces that present only essential information to avoid overwhelming users.

Chunk Information: Break down complex tasks or content into smaller, manageable units to reduce mental strain.

Provide Clear Feedback: Offer immediate, clear feedback for user actions to reduce uncertainty and support decision-making.

Use Consistent Layouts: Ensure consistency in design elements (e.g., buttons, navigation) to reduce cognitive effort in learning the interface.

Minimize Distractions: Limit unnecessary visual clutter, pop-ups, or non-essential information to keep users focused on their task.

Common Misconceptions and Pitfalls

- More Information Equals Better Understanding: Overloading users with excessive information or options can increase cognitive load and hinder learning or decision-making.
- Cognitive Load Only Applies to Beginners: Even experienced users can experience high cognitive load if interfaces or tasks are poorly designed or overly complex.
- Minimalism Means Simplicity: Too much simplicity can result in insufficient context or functionality, leading to confusion or frustration.
- One Size Fits All: Different users have varying cognitive capacities, so a design that works for one group may not be effective for another.
- Reducing Cognitive Load Means Reducing Content: It's about finding a balance—too little content can be just as problematic as too much. The goal is to streamline without losing essential information.

Related Concepts

1. Fitts' Law: This law states that the time required to move to a target is a function of the distance to the target and its size. In terms of cognitive load, this principle emphasizes the importance of placing interactive elements (like buttons or menus) within easy reach to reduce the effort needed to interact with an interface.
2. Miller's Law: It suggests that the average number of objects an individual can hold in working memory is about seven. In software design, this highlights the importance of limiting the number of options or choices presented at once to avoid overwhelming the user.
3. Hick's Law: This principle states that the more choices a user has, the longer it takes them to make a decision. To reduce cognitive load, interfaces should aim to limit the number of options presented to users, streamlining their decision-making process.

4. The Principle of Least Effort: This principle suggests that users tend to follow the path of least resistance when interacting with systems. Software should be designed to minimize the mental effort needed to accomplish tasks, providing shortcuts or automating repetitive actions where possible.
5. Tesler's Law (Law of Conservation of Complexity): This law posits that every system has an inherent level of complexity that must be handled by either the user or the system. It encourages designers to offload as much cognitive burden as possible to the system (e.g., through automation or intelligent interfaces) to minimize the cognitive load on users.

References

- Wikipedia, *Cognitive load*, [pub: 29 Dec 2024, cited: 3 Jan 2025]

Choice Paralysis

Definition and Origin

Choice paralysis, also known as decision paralysis, is a psychological condition where an individual becomes overwhelmed or unable to make a decision due to the presence of too many options. This overabundance of choices can lead to anxiety, stress, or indecision, often resulting in avoiding making any choice at all.

The concept of "choice paralysis" or "decision paralysis" was popularized by psychologists Barry Schwartz in his 2004 book The Paradox of Choice. Schwartz argues that while having more choices can be seen as beneficial, it can actually lead to negative outcomes such as anxiety, dissatisfaction, and the inability to make decisions. Although the phenomenon had been observed earlier, Schwartz's work brought significant attention to it in the context of consumer behavior and decision-making.

Context and Importance

In the context of software and technology, choice paralysis is increasingly relevant as consumers and users are confronted with an overwhelming array of tools, applications, and features. With the rapid advancement of technology, there is a constant surge in new software options, each claiming to offer unique benefits, which can overwhelm users trying to select the best fit for their needs. For example, in areas like productivity apps, project management tools, or even social media platforms, users may face a plethora of choices, each with complex features and customization options. This abundance can cause significant indecision, delaying action and reducing overall satisfaction with the selected tool, even if it is effective.

The importance of understanding and addressing choice paralysis in software and technology lies in its impact on user experience and adoption. When users are unable to make a clear decision due to too many options, they may delay or avoid using new technology altogether, which can hinder the success of software products. Designers and developers can mitigate this by simplifying user interfaces, offering curated recommendations, and focusing on key features that meet the majority of user needs. By reducing cognitive load and offering guidance, companies can help users feel more confident in their choices, leading to higher satisfaction, increased engagement, and improved long-term retention.

Best Practices and Guidelines

Simplify Options: Limit choices to a manageable number, focusing on the most essential features or products to avoid overwhelming users.

Curated Recommendations: Offer personalized suggestions or defaults based on user preferences or past behavior to guide decision-making.

Clear Value Proposition: Highlight the key benefits and differentiators of each option to help users easily compare and understand their choices.

Progressive Disclosure: Present information in stages, revealing more details as needed rather than overwhelming users with everything at once.

User Education: Provide tutorials or onboarding processes that help users quickly understand how to make the most of their chosen tool or software.

Common Misconceptions and Pitfalls

- More Choices Lead to Better Satisfaction: Offering too many options can overwhelm users and decrease satisfaction, contrary to the belief that more choices always result in better outcomes.
- Assuming Users Prefer Full Control: Not all users want complete customization or control; many prefer simplified, guided choices to reduce decision-making stress.
- Decision Fatigue Doesn't Happen: Continuous exposure to too many decisions, even small ones, can lead to decision fatigue, affecting overall satisfaction and productivity.
- All Users Have the Same Needs: Assuming that every user will have identical preferences can result in overly complex systems that don’t cater to diverse needs effectively.
- Choice Paralysis Only Affects New Users: Even experienced users can suffer from choice paralysis, particularly when facing unfamiliar or overly complicated features in software or tools.

Related Concepts

1. Hick's Law: The time it takes to make a decision increases with the number and complexity of options. This principle suggests that limiting choices can speed up decision-making and reduce cognitive load.
2. Paradox of Choice: Popularized by Barry Schwartz, this principle states that while more options seem desirable, too many can lead to anxiety, dissatisfaction, and ultimately indecision, hindering decision-making.
3. Fitts's Law: This law suggests that the time required to select an option is affected by its size and distance. When applied to choice paralysis, it means that choices should be clearly presented and easily accessible to minimize decision-making effort.
4. The Law of Least Effort: This principle states that users tend to choose the option that requires the least cognitive and physical effort. Simplifying choices and providing defaults can help mitigate choice paralysis.

5. Miller's Law: This principle suggests that humans can typically process only 7 (+/- 2) items at a time. Applying this to software design means that limiting the number of visible options can reduce cognitive overload and help users make quicker decisions.

References

- Wikipedia, *Analysis paralysis*, [pub: 10 Sep 2024, cited: 3 Jan 2025]

The Dunning-Kruger Effect

Definition and Origin

The Dunning-Kruger Effect is a cognitive bias where individuals with low ability or knowledge in a particular area overestimate their competence, while those with higher ability tend to underestimate their skills. This phenomenon occurs because the less skilled individuals lack the expertise to accurately assess their own performance.

The Dunning-Kruger Effect was coined by social psychologists David Dunning and Justin Kruger in 1999. They published their findings in a study that demonstrated how individuals with low ability in certain tasks tend to overestimate their competence.

Context and Importance

The Dunning-Kruger Effect has significant relevance in the fields of software development and technology, where rapidly changing landscapes and the complexity of tasks can make it difficult for individuals to accurately assess their skills. In these environments, novice developers or individuals with limited experience may overestimate their understanding of programming languages, algorithms, or system architecture. This overconfidence can lead to poor decision-making, suboptimal coding practices, and the development of flawed solutions. For example, a beginner might believe they fully understand how a software system works, which can result in inefficient code or incomplete testing, affecting the overall quality of a product.

On the other hand, highly skilled professionals in software and technology may experience the opposite effect, underestimating their expertise due to the broad scope of their knowledge. They may be more critical of their own work or assume others possess the same level of understanding, leading to difficulties in communication or collaboration. Recognizing the Dunning-Kruger Effect can improve team dynamics and decision-making within the tech industry. By encouraging a culture of continuous learning, feedback, and humility, organizations can foster environments where individuals are better able to assess their abilities accurately and seek the help or resources, they need for improvement. This ultimately promotes better problem-solving, innovation, and the delivery of high-quality products.

Best Practices and Guidelines

Encourage self-reflection: Foster a culture where developers regularly assess their skills and knowledge to identify areas for growth.

Promote continuous learning: Support ongoing education and training to bridge gaps in knowledge and prevent overconfidence.

Seek peer feedback: Create an environment where team members provide constructive feedback to help each other recognize strengths and weaknesses.

Cultivate humility: Emphasize the value of learning from mistakes and the importance of asking for help when needed.

Balance confidence with caution: Ensure that both beginners and experts recognize the limits of their knowledge and avoid making unsupported assumptions.

Common Misconceptions and Pitfalls

- Overestimating expertise: Believing you have mastery over a topic or task when you have limited knowledge, leading to errors or missed details.
- Underestimating the complexity of tasks: Simplifying problems and overconfidence in handling challenges that require deeper understanding or experience.

- Ignoring feedback: Dismissing constructive criticism because you feel your abilities are already sufficient, hindering personal growth.
- Assuming others know less: Believing that everyone else has the same level of knowledge, which can lead to communication breakdowns and inefficiency.
- Confusing confidence with competence: Assuming that high confidence in one's abilities always correlates with actual skill or expertise.

Related Concepts

1. The Peter Principle: This principle states that people are often promoted based on their performance in their current role until they reach a position where they are no longer competent. It aligns with the Dunning-Kruger Effect by highlighting how individuals may overestimate their abilities until they are placed in roles that require a higher skill level.
2. Brooks' Law: This law states that "adding manpower to a late software project makes it later." It relates to the Dunning-Kruger Effect by demonstrating that individuals with limited understanding of project management or software development may overestimate their capacity to handle complex tasks, leading to delays and inefficiencies when more people are added without proper expertise.
3. Conway's Law: This law suggests that the structure of a software system mirrors the communication structure of the organization that designs it. It ties into the Dunning-Kruger Effect by implying that inexperienced or less-skilled individuals may fail to recognize how their limited understanding of system design can result in suboptimal architecture or poor software development practices.
4. The 10x Rule: The idea that highly skilled developers are significantly more productive than average developers. The Dunning-Kruger Effect is related to this principle, as novice developers may not recognize the value of experience, leading them to overestimate their own productivity and efficiency compared to highly skilled peers.

5. The Law of Triviality (Parkinson's Law of Triviality): This principle suggests that people tend to focus on less important tasks that they can easily understand and overlook more complex, critical issues. In the context of the Dunning-Kruger Effect, it explains how individuals with limited knowledge may overfocus on simpler tasks, overestimating their ability to solve complex problems that require deeper expertise.

References

- Wikipedia, *Dunning–Kruger effect*, [pub: 28 Dec 2024, cited: 3 Jan 2025]

Flow Theory

Definition and Origin

Flow Theory, developed by Mihaly Csikszentmihalyi, describes a mental state of complete immersion and focused engagement in an activity. In this state, individuals experience deep enjoyment, intrinsic motivation, and heightened performance. Flow occurs when the challenge of a task closely matches the individual's skills, leading to a sense of control, timelessness, and optimal experience. This theory highlights the importance of balance between skill level and challenge to achieve peak performance and personal fulfillment.

Flow Theory was coined and developed by Hungarian psychologist Mihaly Csikszentmihalyi. He introduced the concept in the 1970s and further expanded on it in his book Flow: The Psychology of Optimal Experience (1990).

Context and Importance

Flow Theory has become increasingly relevant in the context of software development and technology, as it offers valuable insights into optimizing user experience and productivity. In software design, particularly in gaming, apps, and other interactive technologies, creating environments that foster flow can significantly enhance user engagement and satisfaction. By ensuring that the difficulty level of tasks or challenges is well-matched to the user's skill set, designers can encourage users to enter a state of flow, where they are fully immersed and focused on the activity. This results in a seamless experience that feels rewarding, motivating users to continue interacting with the product or system. In game design, for example, the balance between challenge and skill is key to keeping players engaged and invested in the game.

For software developers and technology professionals, Flow Theory also has significant implications for productivity and performance. When developers experience flow while coding, they enter a state of heightened concentration, where distractions fade and creative problem-solving flourishes. In this state, developers are more likely to produce high-quality work efficiently, as they are deeply absorbed in the task at hand. Flow encourages intrinsic motivation, leading to a sense of accomplishment and satisfaction. Understanding and implementing Flow Theory in both the design of software and the workflows of development teams can foster an environment where both users and creators experience greater satisfaction, leading to more successful and sustainable technological products.

Best Practices and Guidelines

Match Skill and Challenge: Design tasks or experiences that align users' skills with an appropriately challenging level of difficulty to maintain engagement without causing frustration.

Provide Clear Goals: Ensure users or developers have clear objectives, offering direction and focus for their tasks.

Offer Immediate Feedback: Implement real-time feedback to help users or developers adjust their actions and stay in the flow state.

Minimize Distractions: Design interfaces and work environments that reduce interruptions and distractions to maintain deep focus.

Encourage Autonomy: Provide users or developers with a sense of control over their actions, fostering intrinsic motivation and engagement.

Common Misconceptions and Pitfalls

- Flow is only for "fun" activities: Flow can occur in any task, whether it's work-related, creative, or leisure, as long as the challenge matches the individual's skill level.
- Flow happens automatically: Flow requires intentional design of tasks or environments to create the right conditions; it doesn't happen by chance.
- Flow is the same as being busy: Flow involves deep focus and productivity, while being busy can often mean superficial or scattered activity without meaningful engagement.
- Flow is easy to achieve: Achieving flow requires a balance between challenge and skill, which can be difficult to maintain consistently.
- Flow is only about individual experience: Group activities and collaborative work can also foster flow, as long as the collective experience is well-aligned with the group's skills and goals.

Related Concepts

1. The Law of the Instrument (Maslow's Hammer): This principle suggests that if a person has a tool (e.g., a specific technology or skill), they may over-rely on it, potentially hindering the flow experience. In software development, this is a caution against sticking to one tool or framework that doesn't suit the task at hand, which can disrupt optimal engagement.
2. Hick's Law: This principle posits that the more choices a user has, the longer it will take them to make a decision. To facilitate flow, interfaces should minimize unnecessary options and streamline choices, helping users stay focused and avoid decision paralysis.
3. Fitts's Law: This law suggests that the time required to move to a target is a function of the target size and distance. For software interfaces, it emphasizes the importance of designing intuitive, easily navigable environments that allow users to interact with the system quickly and smoothly, supporting uninterrupted flow.

4. The Pareto Principle (80/20 Rule): This principle states that 80% of results often come from 20% of the effort. In the context of Flow Theory, it suggests focusing on key tasks that provide the most value or satisfaction, allowing users or developers to concentrate on meaningful work that enhances engagement.
5. The Law of Proximity: In design, this law states that elements that are close to each other are perceived as related. For Flow, it means designing interfaces with logically grouped, accessible features to reduce cognitive load, helping users maintain focus and flow.

References

- Wikipedia, *Flow (psychology)*, [pub: 19 Dec 2024, cited: 3 Jan 2025]

Fundamental Attribution Error

Definition and Origin

The Fundamental Attribution Error refers to the tendency to overestimate the influence of internal, personal factors (such as a person's character or disposition) when explaining others' behaviors, while underestimating the impact of external, situational factors. It leads to a biased judgment, often assuming that others' actions are driven by their personality rather than by their circumstances.

The concept of the Fundamental Attribution Error was coined by social psychologist Lee Ross in 1977. Ross and his colleagues conducted experiments that highlighted how people tend to attribute others' behaviors to their personal characteristics while overlooking the influence of situational factors. This error is a key concept in social psychology.

Context and Importance

In the context of Software & Technology, the Fundamental Attribution Error (FAE) can significantly influence how developers, project managers, and users interpret issues or failures. For instance, when a software bug or a system crash occurs, teams may be quick to attribute the problem to an individual developer's lack of skill or carelessness, rather than considering external factors such as tight deadlines, inadequate resources, or complex system interactions. This type of error can lead to misjudgments that affect team dynamics, productivity, and even the design and testing of software, as it may prompt unnecessary blame and reduce opportunities for constructive problem-solving.

Understanding and mitigating The Fundamental Attribution Error is crucial in fostering a more collaborative and effective technology environment. By recognizing that behaviors and outcomes in software development are often shaped by a mix of internal and external factors, teams can create a culture of empathy and shared responsibility. This encourages better communication, accountability, and ultimately, more innovative solutions. It also helps in designing systems with better error handling and debugging processes, acknowledging that mistakes often arise from complex factors, not just individual faults. This mindset can improve the overall efficiency and adaptability of technology organizations.

Best Practices and Guidelines

Acknowledge external factors: Consider environmental influences like time constraints, resource limitations, or system complexities when evaluating performance or failures.

Promote a culture of collaboration: Encourage open communication and team problem-solving rather than assigning blame to individuals.

Use data-driven analysis: Base decisions on objective metrics and testing, rather than jumping to conclusions based on perceived personal shortcomings.

Encourage empathy: Foster understanding among team members that mistakes often result from a mix of internal and external factors.

Create a feedback-oriented environment: Focus on constructive feedback and process improvements instead of attributing errors solely to personal negligence.

Common Misconceptions and Pitfalls

- Blaming individuals for team failures: Assuming that poor performance is solely due to personal shortcomings, ignoring external factors like workload or lack of resources.
- Overlooking systemic issues: Focusing on individual mistakes instead of considering flaws in the process, tools, or environment that may contribute to errors.
- Ignoring context in decision-making: Making quick judgments about others' behaviors without understanding the situation or circumstances they were facing.
- Fostering a culture of blame: Encouraging a blame-oriented work environment rather than promoting learning, growth, and shared responsibility.
- Assuming consistency across situations: Believing that someone's behavior in one scenario reflects their overall character, without considering that circumstances may differ in other contexts.

Related Concepts

1. The Pareto Principle (80/20 Rule): In software development, 80% of issues often arise from 20% of causes (like system complexity or design flaws), not just from individual errors. Focusing on the "personal" factor without considering system-level issues can lead to misattributions.
2. Law of Leaky Abstractions: In technology, abstractions (like libraries or frameworks) often leak, meaning underlying issues in the system become visible at higher levels. This principle reminds us that problems may not always be caused by the individual but by deeper, more complex factors within the technology stack.
3. The Principle of Least Astonishment: This principle suggests that a system should behave in a way that users expect, given their understanding. Misattributions of behavior, such as blaming users for errors, may stem from poor design or unexpected system behavior rather than user fault.

4. Brooks' Law (Adding manpower to a late software project makes it later): Overestimating the capability of individual developers or teams in addressing complex issues, without acknowledging external constraints like tight deadlines or limited resources, mirrors the Fundamental Attribution Error by neglecting broader situational factors.
5. Conway's Law: This law states that the design of a system mirrors the communication structure of the organization that develops it. Misattributions of errors to individuals can ignore the systemic influence of organizational structures or communication flaws within development teams.

References

- Wikipedia, *Fundamental attribution error*, [pub: 12 Dec 2024, cited: 3 Jan 2025]

The Pygmalion Effect

Definition and Origin

The Pygmalion Effect is a psychological phenomenon where higher expectations placed on individuals lead to improved performance, while lower expectations result in worse outcomes. It highlights the power of belief and how the attitudes and perceptions of others can influence someone's abilities and success.

The Pygmalion Effect was coined by psychologists Robert Rosenthal and Lenore Jacobson in the 1960s. Their research demonstrated that teachers' expectations of students' potential could significantly influence their academic performance. This concept was inspired by the Greek myth of Pygmalion, where a sculptor's belief in the beauty of his creation led it to come to life.

Context and Importance

In the context of software development and technology, the Pygmalion Effect highlights the significant influence of leadership, management, and team dynamics on individual and group performance. In tech teams, when managers or senior developers believe in the capabilities of their team members and set high expectations, these individuals are more likely to rise to the challenge, fostering a culture of innovation and productivity. For example, when software engineers are encouraged to take on complex tasks or are trusted with high-impact projects, they may develop the confidence and motivation to meet those expectations, thus improving both their personal and collective output.

The importance of the Pygmalion Effect in technology also extends to user experience (UX) design and product development. If developers and designers are expected to create innovative, user-centered designs, their confidence in meeting these goals can translate into higher-quality, user-friendly products. Similarly, if tech leaders maintain high standards for innovation, research, and adaptability, these expectations can inspire greater creativity and problem-solving within their teams. However, the opposite is also true: if expectations are low, the team's potential may be stifled, leading to subpar work and missed opportunities for growth. Thus, the Pygmalion Effect underscores the power of belief in shaping a tech organization's culture, efficiency, and overall success.

Best Practices and Guidelines

Set High, Clear Expectations: Encourage team members with challenging yet achievable goals to inspire growth and innovation.

Provide Positive Reinforcement: Recognize and celebrate accomplishments, reinforcing belief in team members' abilities.

Foster a Growth Mindset: Cultivate an environment where mistakes are seen as learning opportunities, boosting confidence and performance.

Encourage Autonomy: Empower developers and engineers to take ownership of projects, increasing their investment and motivation.

Lead by Example: Demonstrate confidence in your team's abilities, setting the tone for high standards and commitment to success.

Common Misconceptions and Pitfalls

- Overemphasis on Unreasonable Expectations: Setting unrealistically high goals can lead to stress and burnout rather than fostering growth.
- Assuming Performance Will Improve Without Support: Expectations alone aren't enough; adequate resources, guidance, and training are essential for success.
- Neglecting Individual Differences: Not all team members respond to high expectations the same way; personalized approaches are often necessary.
- Ignoring the Impact of Negative Expectations: Low or negative expectations can have a significant, often overlooked, detrimental effect on performance and morale.
- Overlooking the Importance of Feedback: Without regular constructive feedback, high expectations can feel disconnected from practical outcomes and hinder progress.

Related Concepts

1. Brooks' Law (The Mythical Man-Month): This principle states that adding more people to a late software project only makes it later. It aligns with the Pygmalion Effect in that expectations of productivity can be influenced by how a team is managed. Unrealistic expectations or improper allocation can worsen performance rather than improve it.
2. Hawthorne Effect: Similar to the Pygmalion Effect, this principle suggests that individuals will change their behavior when they are aware of being observed or when expectations are placed on them. In a software development context, team members may perform better if they feel their work is being noticed and valued.
3. The Peter Principle: This principle asserts that individuals are often promoted to the level of their incompetence. It connects to the Pygmalion Effect by showing that expectations can be set too high, leading to poor performance if individuals are placed in roles beyond their current capabilities without proper support.

4. Law of Software Entropy: The idea that software systems naturally deteriorate over time without continuous improvement or maintenance. While not directly tied to the Pygmalion Effect, it highlights the need for consistent nurturing of software projects and teams, where high expectations alone are insufficient without ongoing investment and care.
5. Conway's Law: This law suggests that the design of a system reflects the communication structure of the organization that creates it. In the context of the Pygmalion Effect, this law illustrates how high expectations in communication and collaboration can lead to more efficient and innovative software designs, while low expectations may hinder team performance.

References

- Wikipedia, *Pygmalion effect*, [pub: 10 Oct 2024, cited: 3 Jan 2025]

Theory of Planned Behavior

Definition and Origin

The Theory of Planned Behavior (TPB) is a psychological framework that predicts and explains human behavior based on three key factors:

1. Attitude: The individual's positive or negative evaluation of the behavior.
2. Subjective Norms: The perceived social pressure to perform or not perform the behavior.
3. Perceived Behavioral Control: The individual's belief in their ability to perform the behavior, influenced by external factors or resources.

These factors together shape behavioral intentions, which are the best predictors of actual behavior.

The Theory of Planned Behavior (TPB) was developed by Icek Ajzen in 1985. It expanded on his earlier work, the Theory of Reasoned Action (TRA), by incorporating the concept of perceived behavioral control to account for behaviors that individuals may not have complete control over. This addition made TPB more applicable to a wider range of behaviors.

Context and Importance

The Theory of Planned Behavior (TPB) plays a crucial role in understanding and predicting user adoption and behavior within the realm of software and technology. In the rapidly evolving tech industry, user acceptance of new software, tools, or technological innovations is often influenced by more than just technical features. TPB helps explain how individual attitudes, social pressures, and perceived control over technology adoption impact decision-making. For example, when designing a new software product, developers and marketers can use TPB to assess whether potential users perceive the technology as useful and easy to integrate into their daily activities. Understanding the factors that drive technology adoption, such as user attitudes toward the software or the influence of social networks, helps guide the design and marketing strategies to increase user engagement.

The importance of TPB in technology and software extends beyond initial adoption to include ongoing use and long-term engagement with technology. Perceived behavioral control, a core component of TPB, is particularly significant when users face barriers like lack of skills, resources, or technical support. In software development, addressing these barriers through user-friendly interfaces, training programs, or technical support can enhance the user's sense of control and increase the likelihood of sustained use. Additionally, TPB can be instrumental in understanding resistance to new technologies, as negative attitudes or societal pressures may hinder adoption. By integrating the insights from TPB, companies can create more effective strategies for both introducing and maintaining technology products in the market.

Best Practices and Guidelines

Focus on User Perceptions: Design software with user-friendly interfaces and features that align with users' positive attitudes toward ease of use and usefulness.

Leverage Social Influence: Incorporate social proof, such as testimonials or community engagement, to enhance subjective norms and encourage adoption.

Ensure Accessibility: Address perceived behavioral control by minimizing technical barriers and providing resources like tutorials or support to boost user confidence.

Highlight Benefits: Clearly communicate the practical advantages of the software to strengthen users' attitudes and intentions to use it.

Monitor and Adapt: Regularly gather feedback to refine software based on evolving user attitudes, societal trends, and external constraints.

Common Misconceptions and Pitfalls

- Overemphasis on Attitudes: Assuming that positive attitudes alone are sufficient for behavior change, without considering the influence of subjective norms or perceived control.
- Ignoring External Barriers: Underestimating the impact of external factors (e.g., resources, environment) that can affect perceived behavioral control, hindering actual behavior.
- Assuming Uniform Intentions: Believing that strong intentions automatically lead to behavior, without considering the role of unforeseen circumstances or practical limitations.
- Neglecting Social Influences: Failing to account for the power of peer pressure or societal expectations, which can significantly shape behavior and decisions.
- Overlooking Dynamic Change: Treating intentions and behaviors as static, rather than acknowledging that they can evolve over time based on new experiences or external influences.

Related Concepts

1. Technology Acceptance Model (TAM): A widely used framework that builds on TPB, focusing on perceived ease of use and perceived usefulness as key predictors of user adoption and behavior in technology environments.

2. Unified Theory of Acceptance and Use of Technology (UTAUT): Integrates elements of TPB and other models, emphasizing performance expectancy, effort expectancy, social influence, and facilitating conditions as factors influencing technology use.
3. Diffusion of Innovations Theory: While not a direct extension of TPB, it explores how new technologies spread across populations, considering how user attitudes, social influences, and perceived ease of adoption contribute to the adoption process.
4. Fogg Behavior Model (FBM): Focuses on three factors—motivation, ability, and triggers—as key components in determining user behavior, aligning with TPB's emphasis on attitudes, perceived control, and social influence.
5. Cognitive Load Theory (CLT): Though primarily focused on cognitive processes, CLT intersects with TPB by highlighting how perceived complexity (part of perceived behavioral control) can impact technology adoption and user experience.

References

- Wikipedia, *Theory of planned behavior*, [pub: 30 Dec 2024, cited: 3 Jan 2025]

Systems & Security

N. System Design

ACID Properties

Definition and Origin

ACID properties refer to a set of four key principles that ensure reliable processing of database transactions. These principles are:

1. Atomicity: Guarantees that a transaction is either fully completed or not carried out at all—it's an all-or-nothing principle.
2. Consistency: Ensures that a transaction transitions the database from one valid state to another, preserving all predefined rules, including constraints and data integrity.
3. Isolation: Ensures that transactions are carried out independently, without interference, so that the intermediate states of one transaction remain hidden from others.
4. Durability: Guarantees that once a transaction is committed, its changes are permanent, even in the case of system failures.

Together, these properties maintain the reliability and integrity of a database.

The concept of ACID properties was introduced by Jim Gray, a renowned computer scientist, in the late 1970s. Jim Gray is often credited with developing the foundational concepts for transaction management in databases. He formalized these properties to describe the key aspects of database transaction systems, aiming to ensure data consistency, reliability, and integrity in multi-user environments.

Context and Importance

ACID properties are essential in the context of software and technology, particularly in the design and operation of relational database management systems (RDBMS). In software applications, databases often serve as the central repository for critical business data, and transactions are the operations that modify this data. ACID properties ensure that these transactions are handled in a way that guarantees the database remains in a consistent state, even under challenging conditions such as system failures, concurrency issues, or unexpected errors. The principles of Atomicity, Consistency, Isolation, and Durability form a foundation that protects against partial updates, data corruption, or conflicting data when multiple users or systems access the database concurrently.

The importance of ACID properties extends to maintaining data integrity, reliability, and predictability in modern software systems. For businesses, this means that critical operations such as financial transactions, inventory management, or user authentication are carried out with the certainty that data remains accurate and secure. For example, if a banking system performs a money transfer between two accounts, ACID properties ensure that either the entire transaction succeeds (money is deducted from one account and added to the other) or fails completely (no partial changes). The implementation of ACID properties builds trust in software solutions, as users and businesses can depend on the accuracy and resilience of the data handling, even in the face of hardware failures, crashes, or high concurrency environments.

Best Practices and Guidelines

Ensure Transaction Atomicity: Design transactions to be atomic, so they either complete entirely or have no effect, avoiding partial updates to the database.

Maintain Consistency: Define clear database constraints, rules, and validation logic to ensure that transactions leave the database in a valid and consistent state.

Use Isolation Levels Appropriately: Choose the right isolation level (e.g., Read Committed, Serializable) to balance data consistency and performance based on application needs.

Implement Durable Storage: Ensure that once a transaction is committed, changes are permanently stored, even in the event of system crashes or power failures.

Optimize Concurrency Handling: Design systems to handle concurrent transactions efficiently without violating isolation, using techniques like locking, versioning, or optimistic concurrency control.

Common Misconceptions and Pitfalls

- Assuming ACID Guarantees Performance: ACID properties can impact performance, especially with high transaction volumes, due to the overhead of maintaining consistency, isolation, and durability.
- Misunderstanding Isolation Levels: Higher isolation levels (e.g., Serializable) can prevent data anomalies but may lead to increased locking, reduced concurrency, and slower performance.
- Overlooking the Impact of Durability: Durability may require significant I/O operations (like writing to disk), leading to delays if not properly optimized, especially in large-scale systems.
- Atomicity Doesn't Guarantee Correctness: Atomicity ensures that a transaction is completed fully or not at all, but it does not ensure that the transaction is logically correct or valid.
- ACID Doesn't Solve All Data Issues: While ACID properties ensure integrity during transactions, they do not address issues like eventual consistency in distributed systems or data availability in case of network partitioning (which might require a different approach like BASE).

Related Concepts

1. CAP Theorem (Brewer's Theorem): This principle states that in a distributed system, it is impossible to guarantee all three of the following simultaneously: Consistency, Availability, and Partition Tolerance. This relates to ACID because, in distributed systems, maintaining ACID properties (especially consistency) can conflict with achieving high availability or tolerance to network partitions.

2. BASE (Basically Available, Soft state, Eventual consistency): BASE is an alternative to ACID for systems that prioritize availability and scalability over strict consistency. It suggests that systems may tolerate temporary inconsistencies, focusing on availability and eventual consistency rather than enforcing immediate consistency like ACID.
3. Sharding: This technique involves distributing database data across multiple machines (shards). While sharding can improve scalability and performance, it introduces challenges in maintaining ACID properties, particularly consistency and atomicity, across multiple shards.
4. Eventual Consistency: This concept, common in distributed databases (like NoSQL systems), emphasizes that while data may not be immediately consistent across all nodes, it will eventually reach consistency. This contrasts with ACID's strict consistency and highlights the trade-offs in distributed systems.
5. Two-Phase Commit Protocol (2PC): This protocol is used to ensure atomicity and consistency in distributed transactions. It ensures that a transaction is either fully committed or fully rolled back across all participating systems, which aligns with the principles of ACID, particularly atomicity and consistency, in distributed environments.

References

- Wikipedia, *ACID*, [pub: 11 Oct 2024, cited: 3 Jan 2025]

BASE Properties

Definition and Origin

BASE properties refer to the key attributes of an idealized database system, which emphasize flexibility and scalability in distributed environments. BASE stands for:

1. Basically Available: The system guarantees availability, meaning it will always respond to requests, though it might not be consistent at all times.
2. Soft state: The state of the system can change over time, even without input, due to eventual consistency.

3. Eventual consistency: The system will eventually reach consistency, but this might not be immediate, allowing for temporary inconsistency.

BASE properties are often associated with NoSQL databases that prioritize scalability and availability over strict consistency, as opposed to the ACID properties used in traditional relational databases.

Context and Importance

BASE properties play a significant role in the context of modern software and technology, especially as distributed systems and NoSQL databases have become more prevalent. Traditional relational databases, following the ACID properties (Atomicity, Consistency, Isolation, Durability), are ideal for applications requiring strong consistency and data integrity. However, the rise of large-scale, distributed systems that support big data, real-time applications, and cloud-based services often necessitates a shift in focus. BASE properties address the challenges of maintaining availability and scalability in such environments, where ensuring perfect consistency at all times is often impractical due to latency, network partitions, and system failures.

The importance of BASE properties lies in their ability to strike a balance between performance, availability, and consistency, making them crucial for applications that prioritize uptime and responsiveness. For example, in large-scale web applications like e-commerce platforms, social media, or cloud services, users expect quick responses even when some parts of the system are temporarily unavailable or inconsistent. BASE allows these systems to remain operational and handle massive volumes of data while tolerating temporary inconsistencies. By embracing eventual consistency and soft states, software developers can design systems that are more resilient, flexible, and scalable, which is vital for meeting the growing demands of modern technology landscapes.

Best Practices and Guidelines

Prioritize Availability: Design systems to ensure high availability, even if some nodes or components experience failures, by using replication and fault-tolerant architectures.

Embrace Eventual Consistency: Accept that data consistency may not be immediate, but will converge over time, and implement strategies to handle temporary inconsistencies (e.g., conflict resolution).

Use Soft State: Allow system states to evolve dynamically, enabling scalability and responsiveness without requiring constant synchronization.

Implement Data Partitioning: Distribute data across multiple nodes to scale horizontally, improving performance and reducing single points of failure.

Optimize for Latency and Throughput: Focus on minimizing response times and maximizing throughput by tolerating temporary inconsistencies in exchange for faster data access and system resilience.

Common Misconceptions and Pitfalls

- Assuming Immediate Consistency: A common misconception is expecting data to be fully consistent across all nodes at all times, which can lead to unrealistic expectations and performance bottlenecks in distributed systems.
- Overlooking Conflict Resolution: Ignoring the need for conflict resolution strategies can result in data inconsistencies and errors, especially when updates occur simultaneously in different system nodes.
- Neglecting System Behavior Under Partitioning: Misunderstanding the impact of network partitions, leading to challenges in balancing availability and consistency, can create significant downtime or incorrect data in systems.
- Confusing BASE with ACID: Believing BASE is simply a weaker version of ACID can cause confusion; BASE prioritizes availability and partition tolerance at the expense of immediate consistency, which is a fundamental difference.
- Inadequate Monitoring for Soft States: Failing to implement sufficient monitoring tools for tracking system state evolution can lead to unanticipated errors or performance issues as data changes over time.

Related Concepts

1. CAP Theorem (Brewer's Theorem): This principle states that a distributed system can only guarantee two of the following three properties: Consistency, Availability, and Partition Tolerance (CAP). BASE properties are often a response to the trade-offs made in CAP, particularly emphasizing Availability and Partition Tolerance over immediate Consistency.
2. Eventual Consistency: A key concept in BASE, eventual consistency asserts that in distributed systems, all replicas of data will eventually converge to the same value, but not necessarily immediately. This is important for systems prioritizing availability over consistency.
3. BASE vs. ACID: While ACID properties (Atomicity, Consistency, Isolation, Durability) are foundational to traditional databases, BASE properties serve as an alternative for distributed systems that prioritize availability and scalability over strict consistency.
4. Sharding: This principle involves distributing data across multiple machines (shards) to improve scalability and performance. BASE properties align well with sharding as it allows data to be partitioned, enabling systems to remain available even during network partitions.
5. Event-Driven Architecture: Systems designed with event-driven principles often align with BASE properties by decoupling components and allowing for eventual consistency between them. This architecture helps achieve high availability and responsiveness without needing to wait for full consistency across all parts of the system.

References

- Wikipedia, *Eventual consistency*, [pub: 12 Dec 2024, cited: 3 Jan 2025]

CAP Theorem

Definition and Origin

The CAP Theorem (Consistency, Availability, Partition Tolerance) states that in a distributed data system, it is impossible to guarantee all three of the following simultaneously:

1. Consistency: Ensures that every read operation returns the most up-to-date write, even in the event of system failures, maintaining data accuracy and integrity across all transactions.
2. Availability: Guarantees that every request, whether read or written, will receive a response, even if some nodes are unavailable or experiencing issues.
3. Partition Tolerance: Tolerance ensures that the system remains functional even in the presence of network partitions or communication failures between nodes.

A distributed system can satisfy at most two of these properties at the same time, but not all three.

The CAP Theorem was coined by Eric Brewer, a computer scientist and professor at the University of California, Berkeley. He introduced the concept in 2000 during a keynote address at the Symposium on Principles of Distributed Computing (PODC). The theorem was formally proved by Seth Gilbert and Nancy Lynch in 2002. Brewer's insights laid the foundation for understanding trade-offs in distributed systems.

Context and Importance

The CAP Theorem plays a crucial role in understanding the limitations and trade-offs in distributed systems, particularly in the context of cloud computing, databases, and microservices architectures. As modern software systems increasingly scale across multiple nodes and geographic locations, the challenges of maintaining data consistency, availability, and partition tolerance become significant. The CAP Theorem provides a framework for developers and architects to make informed decisions about which trade-offs to prioritize based on the specific needs of their applications. For example, in systems like NoSQL databases (e.g., Cassandra, MongoDB), architects might choose availability and partition tolerance over consistency in scenarios where uptime is critical and eventual consistency is acceptable. Understanding these trade-offs is vital when designing systems that need to handle large volumes of data and provide uninterrupted service despite network or hardware failures.

The importance of the CAP Theorem also extends to fault tolerance and resilience in distributed applications. It highlights the inherent tension between trying to maintain a perfect balance of all three properties (Consistency, Availability, and Partition Tolerance) and forces developers to make strategic compromises based on their application's requirements. In real-world scenarios, a network partition can occur at any time, which may lead a system to either reject requests or provide outdated data, depending on its configuration. By embracing the CAP Theorem, technology teams can better plan for failure modes, ensuring that their systems are robust, scalable, and capable of handling various real-world scenarios without sacrificing critical performance characteristics.

Best Practices and Guidelines

Assess Application Requirements: Prioritize Consistency, Availability, or Partition Tolerance based on your system's specific needs (e.g., banking apps may prioritize consistency, while social media apps may prioritize availability).

Plan for Network Partitions: Design systems with the assumption that network partitions can occur, and ensure they can continue functioning, even if consistency must be temporarily sacrificed.

Choose the Right Database: Select a database or storage solution that aligns with your system's CAP trade-offs (e.g., Cassandra focuses on AP, MongoDB can be configured for CP or AP).

Implement Eventual Consistency Where Necessary: For systems where availability is crucial, embrace eventual consistency and ensure users are informed about potential data inconsistencies during transient failures.

Monitor and Adjust: Continuously monitor system performance and make adjustments as usage patterns evolve, ensuring that the chosen CAP trade-offs still meet business and user needs.

Common Misconceptions and Pitfalls

- All Three Properties Are Achievable: A common misconception is that it's possible to achieve Consistency, Availability, and Partition Tolerance simultaneously at all times. The CAP Theorem clearly states that only two of these can be guaranteed at once, not all three.
- Choosing Between CAP Is Binary: People often think that choosing a CAP trade-off means a strict, permanent decision. In reality, many systems allow dynamic configurations or tunable consistency, so trade-offs can evolve depending on the use case or network conditions.
- Partition Tolerance Is Optional: Some assume partition tolerance isn't always necessary, but in distributed systems, network failures are inevitable. Without Partition Tolerance, a system can fail completely if a partition occurs, making it a critical property in any real-world distributed system.
- CAP Applies Only to Databases: While CAP is often discussed in the context of databases, it applies to any distributed system. This includes messaging queues, microservices architectures, and even cloud-based storage solutions, where similar trade-offs must be considered.
- Consistency Means Instant Consistency: Many confuse Consistency with Immediate Consistency (strong consistency), but in distributed systems, consistency can mean eventual consistency. Systems like AP configurations may guarantee consistency over time, not immediately after every write.

Related Concepts

1. Brewer's Conjecture (CAP Theorem): As mentioned, Eric Brewer's original principle asserts that in a distributed system, you can only achieve at most two out of three guarantees: Consistency, Availability, and Partition Tolerance. This foundational law guides system architects in making trade-offs based on business and technical requirements.
2. BASE (Basically Available, Soft state, Eventually consistent): BASE is an alternative to ACID for distributed systems, particularly in NoSQL databases. It embraces eventual consistency and prioritizes Availability and Partition Tolerance, often seen in AP systems, where data consistency might not be immediate but will eventually stabilize.

3. Amdahl's Law: This law applies to the scalability of parallel computing and distributed systems. It highlights that the potential performance improvement of a system is limited by the non-parallelizable portion of the system. In the context of CAP, this reinforces the challenge of scaling while maintaining consistency across distributed nodes.
4. The Brewer-Lynch Theorem: This is a formal proof that supports the CAP Theorem. It mathematically proves that no distributed system can simultaneously guarantee Consistency, Availability, and Partition Tolerance during a network partition, providing a rigorous foundation for the trade-offs discussed in CAP.
5. PACELC Theorem: An extension of CAP, PACELC stands for Partition Tolerance, Availability, Consistency, Else, and Latency/Consistency. It refines the CAP model by stating that even if there's no network partition, systems still have to balance between Latency and Consistency. This helps address trade-offs in more complex, real-world distributed systems.

References

- Wikipedia, *CAP theorem*, [pub: 5 Dec 2024, cited: 3 Jan 2025]

Emergence

Definition and Origin

Emergence in system design refers to the phenomenon where complex behaviors, patterns, or properties arise from the interaction of simpler components within a system, without being explicitly programmed or planned. These emergent properties are not directly predictable from the individual parts but instead emerge from their relationships and interactions over time.

The concept of emergence in system design does not have a single inventor or coiner, but it has roots in multiple fields, including philosophy, biology, and physics. The term "emergence" was first introduced in the 19th century by the British philosopher George Henry Lewes in his work Problems of Life and Mind (1875), where he used it to describe phenomena that arise from simpler interactions but are not reducible to the sum of those parts.

Context and Importance

In software and technology, emergence plays a crucial role in understanding how complex systems and applications behave when multiple components interact in unforeseen ways. As software systems grow in size and complexity, they often exhibit behaviors or properties that are not explicitly designed, but arise from the interactions between various modules, users, and subsystems. For example, in distributed systems, issues like network congestion or failure handling can lead to emergent behaviors like self-healing or load balancing, even though these outcomes were not directly programmed. Similarly, in machine learning, algorithms can exhibit emergent patterns that weren't anticipated in the original design, such as new insights derived from data correlations or the unexpected development of certain behaviors in artificial agents.

The importance of emergence in software and technology lies in its ability to offer robust, adaptive, and scalable solutions. When designed with an understanding of emergent behavior, software can become more resilient and capable of adapting to changing environments without requiring constant intervention or redesign. For instance, in web services or microservices architectures, emergent behaviors like fault tolerance and dynamic scaling are not manually programmed but arise naturally as components work together. Embracing emergence allows developers to focus on creating flexible, modular systems where high-level behaviors can evolve and adapt, ensuring that systems can grow, evolve, and maintain functionality even as new requirements or conditions emerge. This approach is especially vital in environments that require high reliability, such as cloud computing, AI-driven systems, or real-time analytics platforms.

Best Practices and Guidelines

Design for Flexibility: Build modular, loosely coupled components that can evolve independently, allowing emergent behaviors to develop naturally without disrupting the entire system.

Embrace Decentralization: Distribute decision-making and processing across the system to foster self-organization and adaptation, key aspects of emergent behavior.

Enable Feedback Loops: Implement continuous feedback mechanisms to allow the system to learn, adapt, and optimize dynamically in response to changing conditions.

Test for Unintended Outcomes: Anticipate and test for potential emergent behaviors through simulations and stress testing to understand how components interact under various conditions.

Monitor and Iterate: Continuously observe system performance and refine designs based on emerging patterns, ensuring that the system adapts efficiently over time.

Common Misconceptions and Pitfalls

- Emergence Equals Unpredictability: Emergent behavior doesn't mean complete unpredictability; it can often be understood and managed through patterns and feedback loops, though it may be hard to fully predict in advance.
- Assuming Emergence is Always Positive: Not all emergent behaviors are desirable; some can lead to inefficiencies, security vulnerabilities, or system failures if not carefully managed.
- Overlooking Complexity: Emergence doesn't eliminate complexity; it often introduces new, unforeseen layers of complexity that need to be addressed through robust monitoring and system design.
- Ignoring the Role of Context: Emergent behaviors can be highly context-dependent, and what works in one system or environment may not translate to others, leading to false expectations.
- Thinking Emergence Happens Automatically: Emergent properties don't simply occur by themselves; intentional design choices, like modularity and feedback mechanisms, are crucial to guiding beneficial emergent behaviors.

Related Concepts

1. Law of Large Numbers (or Emergent Complexity): As a system grows in size or complexity, simple rules and interactions between components can lead to emergent behaviors that are more complex than what would be expected from the individual parts. This principle emphasizes that larger systems often produce behaviors or properties that are not directly tied to their individual components.
2. Conway's Law: This law states that "organizations which design systems are constrained to produce designs which are copies of the communication structures of these organizations." In terms of emergence, Conway's Law suggests that emergent behaviors in software systems often mirror the structure and communication patterns of the teams that build them. Complex, decentralized communication structures in a team can lead to emergent, decentralized behaviors in the software.
3. Brooks' Law (Adding more people to a late project makes it later): Although originally a critique of human resource management in software development, this law indirectly relates to emergence by highlighting how complexity and emergent inefficiencies grow in systems as more components (or developers) are added. The more complex the system, the more difficult it becomes to predict emergent behaviors and maintain control.
4. The Principle of Least Astonishment: In system design, this principle suggests that the system should behave in a way that users or developers expect, minimizing surprises. While emergence can bring unforeseen benefits, it can also lead to emergent behaviors that are confusing or undesirable, so designers must anticipate and mitigate unexpected outcomes that violate this principle.
5. Lehman's Laws of Software Evolution: One of the key laws in Lehman's set of principles is the idea that "a system that is used in the real world evolves." Emergent behavior is a result of the continual evolution of software systems, as they adapt to new requirements and external factors over time. The law highlights the inevitability of emergence as software grows and interacts with real-world conditions.

References

- Wikipedia, *Emergence*, [pub: 28 Dec 2024, cited: 3 Jan 2025]

Feedback Loops

Definition and Origin

A feedback loop is a process in which the output of a system is fed back into the system as an input, influencing its subsequent behavior. There are two main types:

- Positive feedback loop: Amplifies changes or outputs, driving the system further from its original state.
- Negative feedback loop: Reduces or dampens changes, helping the system maintain stability or return to equilibrium.

Feedback loops are common in natural, biological, and engineered systems, helping them adapt or maintain balance.

Context and Importance

In software and technology, feedback loops play a crucial role in improving system performance, user experience, and continuous development. In software development, feedback loops are often embedded within the processes of testing, deployment, and iteration. For example, in Agile development, feedback from users, stakeholders, and automated testing helps guide the next iteration of a product, ensuring that features evolve to meet user needs and quality standards. Similarly, in DevOps practices, continuous integration and continuous deployment (CI/CD) rely on feedback loops to ensure that code changes are consistently tested and deployed, allowing teams to detect issues early, improve system stability, and accelerate the release cycle. The rapid response to feedback within these loops helps software adapt quickly to changing requirements, user demands, and environmental factors.

In the broader landscape of technology, feedback loops are central to the development of machine learning (ML) and artificial intelligence (AI) systems, where the algorithm's output is continuously evaluated and refined based on feedback from its performance. For example, in reinforcement learning, an agent learns by interacting with its environment, receiving feedback in the form of rewards or penalties, and adjusting its behavior accordingly. This type of feedback loop enables AI systems to improve over time, making them more effective at decision-making, prediction, and problem-solving. Additionally, user interactions with technology, whether in web apps, mobile devices, or IoT systems, generate feedback that can be used to fine-tune algorithms and interfaces, optimizing performance, personalization, and overall user satisfaction. In all of these cases, feedback loops are foundational to creating more adaptive, responsive, and efficient technologies.

Best Practices and Guidelines

Ensure Continuous Monitoring: Implement real-time tracking and automated testing to gather consistent feedback on system performance, bugs, and user behavior.

Prioritize User-Centric Feedback: Regularly collect feedback from users through surveys, usage data, and usability tests to guide feature development and improve user experience.

Iterate Rapidly: Use short development cycles (e.g., Agile sprints) to incorporate feedback quickly and continuously refine the product or system.

Automate Feedback Integration: Leverage CI/CD pipelines and automated testing tools to streamline feedback integration and accelerate response times to issues.

Balance Positive and Negative Feedback: Address both amplifying (positive) and stabilizing (negative) feedback within systems to optimize performance and ensure stability.

Common Misconceptions and Pitfalls

- Assuming Feedback is Always Positive: Not all feedback leads to improvement. Positive feedback can lead to system instability, while negative feedback may limit innovation or growth.
- Ignoring the Speed of Feedback: Delayed feedback can hinder timely adjustments, leading to wasted resources or missed opportunities. Quick, real-time feedback is essential for effective decision-making.
- Over-reliance on Automated Feedback: Solely depending on automated feedback (e.g., from tools or algorithms) can overlook critical human insights, leading to decisions that miss the mark with users.
- Focusing Only on Short-Term Feedback: Relying too heavily on immediate feedback may cause you to overlook long-term trends or deeper systemic issues that need attention.
- Underestimating Feedback Complexity: Feedback loops can be non-linear and interact in unexpected ways. Failing to account for complex interdependencies may result in unintended consequences or inefficiencies.

Related Concepts

1. Law of Continuous Improvement (Kaizen): Rooted in Agile development, this principle emphasizes that software should be continuously improved through iterative cycles, with feedback from users, testing, and performance metrics driving constant refinement.
2. Pareto Principle (80/20 Rule): Often applied in software development, this principle suggests that 80% of the impact comes from 20% of the features or issues. Feedback loops can help identify and prioritize those key areas for optimization, leading to more focused improvements.
3. Hick's Law: In the context of user experience and feedback loops, Hick's Law states that the time it takes for users to make a decision increases with the number of available choices. By gathering user feedback, software can be refined to simplify choices and enhance decision-making efficiency.

4. The Law of Leaky Abstractions: This law, coined by Joel Spolsky, suggests that abstractions in software (like APIs or frameworks) inevitably leak details of their underlying complexity. Feedback loops, especially in debugging and testing, help identify when abstractions break down, ensuring better design and performance.
5. Conway's Law: This principle asserts that the structure of a system mirrors the communication structures of the organization that builds it. In the context of feedback loops, it highlights the importance of effective communication within teams to ensure that feedback is shared quickly and accurately, influencing system design and improvements.

References

- Wikipedia, *Feedback*, [pub: 30 Dec 2024, cited: 3 Jan 2025]

Gall's Law: Complex systems that work evolved from simple systems

---

Definition and Origin

Gall's Law states that a successful complex system typically evolves from a simple, functional system, rather than being designed from scratch. A complex system built from the ground up usually fails, and attempts to fix it are ineffective; instead, it must be restructured from a working, simpler foundation.

Gall's Law was coined by John Gall, an American physician and systems theorist, in his book Systemantics: How Systems Work and Especially How They Fail (1975). In this book, Gall explores the behavior of systems, particularly how they evolve and fail, and formulates the law as a principle regarding the development of complex systems.

Context and Importance

Gall's Law holds significant relevance in the context of software development and technology, particularly when it comes to designing and maintaining complex systems. In the tech world, many software systems, especially large-scale ones, tend to evolve over time. Early versions of these systems are often simple, with a focus on solving a specific problem. As new features and functionalities are added, the system grows more complex. Gall's Law underscores the idea that this organic evolution, building upon working and functional components, is more likely to result in a successful, adaptable system than attempting to design a fully-fledged, complex system from scratch. This is especially important in the rapidly evolving fields of software and technology, where requirements frequently shift, and systems need to remain flexible and scalable.

In software development, Gall's Law also highlights the pitfalls of overengineering. Many technology projects fail when they try to anticipate every possible requirement upfront, leading to a bloated, unmanageable system that is difficult to adjust to real-world needs. By starting with a simple, functional prototype or minimum viable product (MVP) and iterating based on feedback, developers can create systems that evolve in response to actual use cases and real-world challenges. This approach is crucial for innovation, as it allows for continuous improvement and adaptation, reducing the risks of failure and ensuring that the system remains aligned with user needs. Gall's Law encourages a pragmatic, adaptive mindset, emphasizing that even in complex environments, simplicity and incremental development are key to long-term success.

Best Practices and Guidelines

Start Simple: Begin with a small, functional prototype or MVP, focusing on core features and user needs.

Iterate Gradually: Evolve the system over time based on real-world feedback and requirements, rather than trying to predict everything upfront.

Avoid Overengineering: Resist the temptation to design overly complex systems at the outset; complexity should emerge organically.

Embrace Flexibility: Build systems with modularity and adaptability in mind to accommodate future changes and growth.

Learn from Failures: If a complex system isn't working, refactor or rebuild from a simpler, functioning foundation instead of trying to patch up the original.

Common Misconceptions and Pitfalls

- Complexity Equals Capability: Believing that more complex systems are inherently better or more powerful, when in reality, they are harder to maintain and more prone to failure.
- Designing for Perfection Upfront: Assuming you can anticipate all future needs and requirements in the initial design, which often leads to overengineering and wasted resources.
- Ignoring Evolution: Thinking that once a complex system is built, it can be simply patched or fixed without needing to rethink its foundation or approach.
- Underestimating the Value of Simplicity: Overlooking the importance of starting simple and gradually scaling, instead rushing to build something large and complicated from the beginning.
- Assuming Linear Growth: Believing that a complex system will smoothly evolve from a small one, without accounting for unforeseen challenges, changes in requirements, or new technologies.

Related Concepts

1. The Law of Leaky Abstractions (Joel Spolsky): This law states that "all non-trivial abstractions, to some degree, are leaky." It highlights how complex systems often hide low-level details that eventually surface, emphasizing the importance of understanding and managing complexity in software design. Like Gall's Law, it suggests that complexity often emerges from simpler foundations over time.
2. The Pareto Principle (80/20 Rule): This principle suggests that 80% of the effects come from 20% of the causes. In software development, this translates to focusing on a small set of key features or components that deliver the most value, rather than overcomplicating the system with unnecessary features from the start.

3. KISS (Keep It Simple, Stupid): This principle stresses that systems should be designed as simply as possible to meet the needs of users. Starting with a simple system, as Gall's Law suggests, avoids the pitfalls of unnecessary complexity and helps ensure the system remains manageable and adaptable.
4. YAGNI (You Aren't Gonna Need It): This software development principle advises against adding functionality that is not currently needed. It emphasizes starting with a simple system and evolving it only based on real requirements, aligning with Gall's Law's advocacy for iterative, organic growth of systems.
5. The Boy Scout Rule: This rule encourages developers to always leave the codebase cleaner than they found it. Similar to Gall's Law, it emphasizes the importance of continuous improvement and evolution, where systems should be refactored and simplified as they grow, rather than patched together in increasingly complex ways.

References

- Principles Wiki, *Gall's Law*, [pub: 20 Oct 2021, cited: 3 Jan 2025]
- Wikipedia, *John Gall (author)*, [pub: 22 Nov 2024, cited: 3 Jan 2025]

Principle of Least Privilege: Restricts user access to the minimum necessary permissions to perform required tasks

---

Definition and Origin

The Principle of Least Privilege (PoLP) is a security concept that suggests giving users, processes, or systems the least amount of access—permissions or privileges—necessary to perform their tasks. In other words, each entity in an information system should have only the minimal privileges required to execute its functions and no more. This minimizes the risk of accidental or malicious misuse of access, whether by human actors or by software.

The Principle of Least Privilege was first formally introduced by Jerome Saltzer and Michael D. Schroeder in their seminal 1975 paper "The Protection of Information in Computer Systems." In this work, they outlined the principle as a fundamental concept in computer security, emphasizing the importance of restricting access to resources to only those necessary for a user or process to perform its tasks, thereby minimizing security risks.

Context and Importance

The Principle of Least Privilege (PoLP) is a foundational concept in software development and information security. In the context of modern technology, software systems often operate with numerous users, services, and processes interacting with each other, each requiring varying levels of access to data, systems, and networks. PoLP ensures that users, applications, and system processes only have the minimal access privileges needed to perform their designated tasks, preventing unnecessary exposure to potentially dangerous or sensitive areas of the system. By reducing the attack surface and limiting the damage caused by compromised accounts or malfunctioning code, PoLP serves as a key defense mechanism in protecting systems from both external and internal security threats.

In today's technology landscape, the importance of PoLP cannot be overstated, especially given the increasing complexity of software architectures and the prevalence of cyberattacks. Privilege escalation attacks, where a malicious actor exploits system vulnerabilities to gain higher-level access, are among the most common and damaging forms of intrusion. By adhering to the Principle of Least Privilege, organizations can significantly reduce the likelihood of such attacks succeeding, as even if a user or service is compromised, the attacker would be constrained to a limited subset of system resources. This principle is particularly critical in cloud computing, microservices, and distributed systems, where the interconnection of many components requires careful management of access control to avoid cascading vulnerabilities and breaches.

Best Practices and Guidelines

Minimize access permissions: Grant users, applications, and processes only the permissions necessary to perform their specific tasks, avoiding broad or unnecessary access rights.

Use role-based access control (RBAC): Implement RBAC to assign permissions based on user roles, ensuring users receive only the privileges relevant to their job functions.

Limit administrative privileges: Restrict the use of administrative or root access to a small group of trusted individuals and require multi-factor authentication for elevated permissions.

Regularly review and audit permissions: Conduct periodic audits to identify and revoke unnecessary or outdated permissions, ensuring access remains aligned with current needs.

Apply the principle consistently across systems: Enforce least privilege across all layers of the software stack, including applications, databases, and infrastructure, to reduce overall security risks.

Common Misconceptions and Pitfalls

- Assuming users know "what" they need: Users may request more permissions than necessary out of convenience or lack of understanding, leading to excessive access.
- Overlooking service and application accounts: Focusing only on user permissions and neglecting service or system accounts can create vulnerabilities with high-level access.
- Failing to regularly review access: Once permissions are granted, they often go unchecked, leading to the accumulation of outdated or unnecessary privileges over time.
- Complexity in implementing fine-grained access control: The fine-grained management required by PoLP can be complex and resource-intensive, leading organizations to delay or simplify its implementation.
- Assuming PoLP is a one-time effort: PoLP is not a one-off task; it requires continuous monitoring, adjustment, and enforcement as systems and roles evolve.

Related Concepts

1. Separation of Duties (SoD): This principle states that no single individual or process should have full control over any critical function or process. By separating duties, it ensures that multiple parties or systems are required to complete tasks, reducing the risk of fraud or errors. It complements PoLP by limiting the scope of authority granted to any single entity.
2. Need-to-Know Principle: This principle asserts that individuals or systems should only have access to information they need to perform their role, which mirrors PoLP by minimizing access to sensitive data or resources. It's commonly used in secure environments like government and military systems.
3. Fail-Safe Defaults: This concept suggests that, in the event of a failure or error, systems should default to a secure state, typically denying access by default and granting it only when explicitly permitted. It reinforces PoLP by ensuring that minimal access is the norm and exceptions are strictly controlled.
4. Defense in Depth: This security principle advocates for multiple layers of security controls, so even if one layer is bypassed, other defenses remain in place. While PoLP focuses on minimizing access, Defense in Depth ensures that multiple independent barriers protect the system, making breaches harder to achieve even when privileges are limited.
5. Principle of Least Astonishment: This guideline suggests that system behavior should be intuitive and predictable, preventing surprises that could lead to misconfigurations or security flaws. In the context of PoLP, it emphasizes designing systems in a way that limits access permissions without creating confusion or unnecessary complexity for users and administrators.

References

- Wikipedia, *Principle of least privilege*, [pub: 24 Dec 2024, cited: 3 Jan 2025]

Separation of Concerns

Definition and Origin

Separation of concerns is a design principle in software engineering that involves dividing a system into distinct sections, where each section addresses a separate concern or responsibility. This helps reduce complexity, improves maintainability, and makes the system more modular by isolating different aspects of functionality (e.g., user interface, data processing, or business logic) so that they can be developed, tested, and modified independently.

The concept of Separation of Concerns was coined by Edgar Dijkstra, a prominent computer scientist, in the 1970s. Dijkstra emphasized the importance of dividing complex systems into smaller, manageable parts, each focusing on a specific aspect or "concern," in order to make the system easier to understand, develop, and maintain. Although Dijkstra introduced the term in the context of programming and software design, the idea aligns with broader principles of modularity and abstraction in engineering.

Context and Importance

Separation of Concerns (SoC) in software and technology refers to the practice of organizing a system or application into distinct modules or layers, where each module is responsible for a specific aspect of functionality, or "concern." This principle is vital for managing the complexity of modern software systems, which often consist of multiple interacting components. By separating concerns, developers can focus on individual parts of a system without being overwhelmed by the entire codebase. For example, in a web application, the user interface, business logic, and data storage concerns can each be handled by separate modules, making it easier to update or replace one without affecting the others. This division improves clarity, reduces the likelihood of errors, and facilitates parallel development by multiple teams.

The importance of SoC in software development extends beyond just simplifying the design process. It enhances maintainability and scalability by isolating changes to specific areas of the system. When concerns are well-separated, developers can make modifications to one part of the system (e.g., improving the UI) without unintentionally introducing bugs in unrelated areas (like database access). Additionally, it improves testability, as each concern can be tested independently, making it easier to identify and fix issues. SoC also supports reusability—since modules are designed to handle specific concerns, they can often be reused in different contexts or projects, saving time and resources. Overall, separation of concerns is a foundational principle that enables efficient development, maintenance, and evolution of complex software systems.

Best Practices and Guidelines

Modularize functionality: Break down the system into distinct, independent modules that handle specific responsibilities (e.g., UI, business logic, data access).

Encapsulate logic: Keep concerns isolated by ensuring that each module only exposes necessary interfaces and hides internal details.

Follow the Single Responsibility Principle (SRP): Ensure each module or class has one reason to change, focusing on a single responsibility to avoid mixed concerns.

Use layers and abstractions: Implement architectural patterns (e.g., MVC, layered architecture) to separate different concerns at various levels (e.g., presentation, application, data).

Promote reusability: Design modules to be reusable across different parts of the application or in different projects by minimizing interdependencies.

Common Misconceptions and Pitfalls

- Over-separation: Splitting concerns too finely can lead to excessive complexity and fragmentation, making the system harder to understand and maintain.

- Ignoring dependencies: While concerns should be separated, overly rigid separation can result in redundant or inefficient code, especially if modules become too interdependent.
- Shallow separation: Simply splitting concerns at a high level (e.g., UI and business logic) without properly addressing sub-level concerns (e.g., validation, error handling) can result in insufficient modularity.
- Overemphasis on separation at the expense of performance: Excessive modularization can lead to performance overhead, such as increased function calls or excessive abstraction, which might impact runtime efficiency.
- Neglecting communication between concerns: Separation of concerns shouldn't mean complete isolation—failure to define clear, efficient interfaces between modules can lead to poor integration and excessive coupling.

Related Concepts

1. Single Responsibility Principle (SRP); Part of SOLID principles, SRP states that a class or module should have only one reason to change, meaning it should focus on a single concern. This principle helps avoid the entanglement of multiple responsibilities, making code more maintainable and modular.
2. Law of Demeter (LoD): Often summarized as "talk only to your immediate friends," LoD suggests that a module should only interact with closely related modules or objects, limiting the scope of communication. This helps keep concerns isolated and reduces unnecessary dependencies.
3. Modularity: A design principle that emphasizes decomposing a system into distinct, self-contained modules, each responsible for a specific function. Modularity directly supports Separation of Concerns by creating boundaries between different system components.
4. Dependency Inversion Principle (DIP): Another SOLID principle, DIP advises that high-level modules should not depend on low-level modules but should depend on abstractions. This principle helps to decouple different concerns in the system by using interfaces or abstract classes, facilitating flexibility and ease of change.

5. Keep It Simple, Stupid (KISS): KISS is a design philosophy that suggests keeping systems as simple as possible. It indirectly supports Separation of Concerns by advocating for the removal of unnecessary complexity, making it easier to separate and manage different aspects of the system.

References

- Wikipedia, *Separation of concerns*, [pub: 25 Dec 2024, cited: 3 Jan 2025]

Single Point of Failure

Definition and Origin

A Single Point of Failure (SPOF) refers to a critical component or part of a system, network, or process that, if it fails, would cause the entire system to fail or become inoperable. It's a vulnerability where the failure of one element disrupts the entire operation, highlighting the need for redundancy or failover mechanisms to ensure continuity.

Context and Importance

In the context of software and technology, a Single Point of Failure (SPOF) refers to any critical component or system that, if it were to fail, could bring down the entire operation or service. This could include hardware components like a server or storage device, or software components such as databases, network infrastructure, or code modules. As systems become more interconnected and complex, the presence of a SPOF can represent a serious vulnerability, making it essential for technology architects to design systems with redundancy and failover capabilities to ensure resilience. For instance, a cloud-based service relying on a single database server without failover mechanisms could experience significant downtime if that server encounters an issue. In such cases, downtime not only disrupts service but could lead to loss of data, revenue, and customer trust.

The importance of addressing SPOFs in software and technology has become even more critical with the rise of mission-critical applications and global-scale systems. As businesses increasingly rely on digital infrastructure for operations, customer interactions, and data processing, ensuring continuous availability and reliability has become paramount. The consequences of a SPOF failure are no longer limited to isolated incidents; they can have far-reaching effects on business continuity, security, and reputation. In industries like finance, healthcare, and e-commerce, where downtime or data loss can result in regulatory fines, loss of sensitive information, or compromised security, identifying and mitigating SPOFs is a key part of risk management and system design.

Best Practices and Guidelines

Identify Critical Components: Regularly assess and identify potential SPOFs within your architecture, including hardware, software, and network dependencies.

Implement Redundancy: Use failover mechanisms, such as load balancing, backup servers, or replicated databases, to ensure availability if a critical component fails.

Design for Scalability: Architect systems to handle increased traffic or workload by scaling horizontally, reducing reliance on a single point.

Monitor System Health: Continuously monitor the performance and status of critical systems to quickly detect and address issues before they lead to failure.

Test Failover Strategies: Regularly test disaster recovery and failover procedures to ensure they function effectively under real-world conditions.

Common Misconceptions and Pitfalls

- Assuming Redundancy Equals Reliability: Simply adding backup components or servers doesn't guarantee fault tolerance if the system design or failover process isn't properly implemented or tested.

- Overlooking Software SPOFs: Focusing only on hardware or network components can lead to neglecting software-related SPOFs, such as single-threaded processes, database bottlenecks, or key API dependencies.
- Underestimating Impact of Latency: In redundant systems, the failover process might introduce performance degradation or delays, which can affect system usability or customer experience.
- Failing to Account for Human Error: Many systems rely on manual intervention for failover, which introduces the risk of human error during critical moments.
- Ignoring Scalability Needs: Failing to anticipate future growth or changes in workload can lead to SPOFs emerging as systems scale, even if initially designed without any apparent risks.

Related Concepts

1. Failover Design Principle: Systems should be designed to automatically switch to a backup in case of failure to avoid a single point of failure (SPOF).
2. Redundancy Principle: Redundant components should be deployed to ensure that if one fails, others can take over without impacting the system.
3. Principle of Least Privilege: Limit access to critical components to prevent a failure from propagating due to unauthorized access or misuse.
4. Availability Heuristic: Emphasizes designing systems with high availability, minimizing downtime and SPOFs by distributing workloads and critical resources.
5. Reliability Engineering Principle: Systems should be regularly tested for vulnerabilities, including potential SPOFs, to ensure robust performance under failure conditions.

References

- Wikipedia, *Single point of failure*, [pub: 10 Dec 2024, cited: 3 Jan 2025]

O. Security & Cryptography

CIA Triad: Confidentiality, Integrity, Availability

Definition and Origin

Steve Lipner defines the CIA Triad as a foundational model in cybersecurity, representing three core principles that ensure the protection of information:

- Confidentiality: Ensuring that sensitive information is accessible only to authorized individuals or systems, preventing unauthorized access or disclosure.
- Integrity: Ensuring that information remains accurate, complete, and unaltered, protecting it from unauthorized modification or tampering.
- Availability: Ensuring that information and systems are accessible and functional when needed by authorized users, preventing disruptions or downtime.

Context and Importance

The CIA Triad (Confidentiality, Integrity, and Availability) is a critical framework for ensuring the security of software and technology systems. As software becomes increasingly integral to nearly every aspect of modern life, the principles of the CIA Triad guide developers, security professionals, and organizations in protecting digital assets. Confidentiality ensures that sensitive information, such as personal data, financial records, and intellectual property, is shielded from unauthorized access. In the context of software, this can involve encryption, access control mechanisms, and authentication protocols to safeguard user privacy and corporate secrets. Breaches of confidentiality can lead to identity theft, financial fraud, or loss of competitive advantage, making it a cornerstone of both software development and cybersecurity.

Integrity ensures that data remains accurate, consistent, and unaltered, which is vital for the reliable functioning of software systems. In the realm of software development, maintaining data integrity prevents errors, corruption, and malicious manipulation of information, ensuring that users and systems receive trustworthy results. Availability ensures that systems and data are accessible and operational when needed, preventing downtime that could cripple business operations. A disruption in availability—whether due to cyberattacks like DDoS (Distributed Denial of Service), natural disasters, or software failures—can result in significant financial loss, legal liabilities, and damage to an organization's reputation. Together, the principles of the CIA Triad form a holistic security strategy that helps protect software and technology systems from a broad range of threats and vulnerabilities, fostering trust, reliability, and resilience in today's interconnected world.

Best Practices and Guidelines

Confidentiality: Implement strong encryption for sensitive data both at rest and in transit; use robust authentication and access control mechanisms (e.g., multi-factor authentication).

Integrity: Use hashing algorithms and digital signatures to verify data integrity; regularly check for unauthorized changes or tampering.

Availability: Ensure redundancy with backups and fault-tolerant systems; implement load balancing and failover solutions to prevent downtime.

Regular Audits: Continuously monitor and audit software for vulnerabilities and potential security breaches to ensure ongoing compliance with security policies.

Patch Management: Apply security patches and updates promptly to mitigate vulnerabilities that could compromise confidentiality, integrity, or availability.

Common Misconceptions and Pitfalls

- Misconception of Equal Priority: Treating all elements of the CIA Triad as equally important for every system; in reality, some systems may prioritize confidentiality (e.g., healthcare) over availability, or vice versa (e.g., emergency services).

- Overemphasis on Encryption: Assuming that encryption alone ensures confidentiality without considering other factors like access control, user authentication, or data exposure through insecure endpoints.
- Neglecting Availability: Focusing too heavily on confidentiality and integrity while overlooking system uptime and redundancy, leading to service disruptions in critical situations.
- Lack of Real-time Monitoring: Believing that static security measures (e.g., firewalls, antivirus) are enough to protect integrity and availability, while neglecting the need for continuous monitoring and response to evolving threats.
- Overconfidence in Security Tools: Relying solely on security tools (e.g., firewalls, antivirus software) to protect the entire system, without considering broader factors such as user behavior, organizational policies, or human error.

Related Concepts

1. Data Protection Laws (e.g., GDPR, CCPA): These laws emphasize the confidentiality of personal data, ensuring that organizations protect user privacy through measures such as consent, data encryption, and access controls. They mandate data protection practices that directly align with confidentiality and integrity standards.
2. The Principle of Least Privilege (POLP): A key principle for ensuring confidentiality and integrity, POLP dictates that users, systems, and applications should only have the minimum access necessary to perform their functions. This limits potential damage from insider threats or external breaches.
3. The Integrity Principle in Software Development (ISO/IEC 27001): This international standard for information security management systems (ISMS) highlights the importance of maintaining data integrity. It ensures systems and processes are in place to prevent unauthorized alteration of information and to detect discrepancies.
4. Availability in Service Level Agreements (SLAs): Service providers often define availability requirements within SLAs, specifying uptime guarantees and response times. SLAs are used to measure and ensure that services remain available and resilient, crucial for mission-critical systems and high-availability software.

5. Zero Trust Architecture (ZTA): Zero Trust principles focus on verifying every access request, assuming no implicit trust, and securing confidentiality and integrity across networks. The approach helps maintain security by continuously monitoring and validating both internal and external interactions.

References

- Wikipedia, *Information security*, [pub: 12 Dec 2024, cited: 3 Jan 2025]

Defense in Depth

Definition and Origin

Defense in Depth is a security strategy that employs multiple layers of protection to safeguard systems and data. Rather than relying on a single security measure, it uses a combination of preventive, detective, and corrective controls (e.g., firewalls, encryption, intrusion detection systems) to reduce the likelihood of a breach and mitigate potential damage. The goal is to create a multi-faceted defense that slows, detects, and responds to attacks.

The concept of Defense in Depth is not attributed to a single individual but rather evolved as part of military strategy and later adapted to information security. The term originally comes from military doctrine, where it refers to using multiple layers of fortifications or strategic positions to slow down or stop an enemy attack.

In the context of cybersecurity, Defense in Depth emerged over time as the complexity of threats increased. It became widely adopted by security professionals and organizations in the 1990s and 2000s as a best practice for protecting systems. While no single person is credited with "inventing" the concept for cybersecurity, it was popularized by security experts and organizations as a comprehensive approach to protecting networks, systems, and data from various attack vectors.

Context and Importance

In the context of software and technology, Defense in Depth is crucial due to the increasingly complex and sophisticated nature of cyber threats. Modern applications, systems, and networks are regularly targeted by a variety of attack vectors—ranging from malware and phishing to advanced persistent threats (APTs) and zero-day exploits. As these threats evolve, relying on a single layer of defense, such as a firewall or antivirus software, becomes insufficient. Defense in Depth emphasizes a multi-layered approach, ensuring that if one security measure fails, others will still provide protection. For example, a combination of network security tools, access controls, encryption, and continuous monitoring can effectively reduce vulnerabilities and provide redundancy in defense mechanisms.

The importance of Defense in Depth within software and technology is also tied to the principle of "fail-safe" security. Even the most robust systems and applications are vulnerable to weaknesses, whether due to flaws in code, human error, or unforeseen vulnerabilities in third-party components. By implementing multiple layers of security—such as securing the application code, network traffic, user authentication, and database access—organizations can significantly reduce the risk of a successful breach. Additionally, this layered approach improves detection and response times. If an attacker bypasses one security layer, subsequent layers increase the likelihood of detecting the intrusion early, allowing for faster mitigation and reducing the overall impact of a security breach.

Best Practices and Guidelines

Layered Security Controls: Implement multiple, complementary security layers (e.g., firewalls, encryption, authentication) to mitigate risks at various points in the system.

Principle of Least Privilege: Limit user and application access to only the minimum necessary resources to reduce potential attack surfaces.

Regular Vulnerability Testing: Continuously test for vulnerabilities (e.g., code audits, penetration testing) to identify weaknesses and address them proactively.

Secure Software Development Lifecycle (SDLC): Integrate security practices at every stage of development, from design to deployment, ensuring secure code and configurations.

Continuous Monitoring & Incident Response: Use real-time monitoring and automated alerts to detect suspicious activities and have an incident response plan in place for quick mitigation.

Common Misconceptions and Pitfalls

- Over-reliance on Perimeter Defense: Believing that securing the network perimeter alone (e.g., firewalls) is enough to protect the system, ignoring internal threats and vulnerabilities.
- Complexity Leads to False Security: Adding multiple security layers without proper integration or management can create false confidence, leading to overlooked gaps or misconfigurations.
- Assuming One Layer Is Sufficient for All Threats: Using the same security measures for all types of attacks, without tailoring protections to specific threats or vulnerabilities.
- Neglecting Regular Updates & Patching: Failing to continuously update security measures or software, leaving systems vulnerable to known exploits and zero-day attacks.
- Ignoring Usability and User Behavior: Focusing only on technical controls while neglecting user training and behavior, which can be a significant factor in security breaches (e.g., phishing).

Related Concepts

1. The Principle of Least Privilege (PoLP): This principle asserts that users and applications should only have the minimum permissions necessary to perform their functions. By reducing the number of privileges, the impact of potential attacks is minimized, aligning with the layered approach of Defense in Depth.
2. Fail-Safe Defaults (Saltzer and Schroeder's Design Principles): This principle advocates for default security configurations that deny access unless explicitly allowed. It ensures that even if security controls fail, the system is still resistant to breaches, which complements multi-layered defenses.

3. Security Through Obscurity (Not a recommended best practice but relevant to understanding vulnerabilities): While not a primary strategy, this principle involves hiding details of a system to reduce its attractiveness to attackers. In a Defense in Depth context, it can be one part of a broader security strategy, but it should never be relied upon solely.
4. Kerckhoffs's Principle: This principle states that the security of a system should not depend on the secrecy of the algorithm but rather on the secrecy of the key or the configuration. In the context of Defense in Depth, it means relying on a combination of diverse security measures (e.g., encryption, multi-factor authentication) rather than a single approach.
5. The Zero Trust Model: The Zero Trust approach aligns with Defense in Depth by assuming that threats can exist both inside and outside the network. It mandates continuous verification of identity and security posture, applying strict access controls, and limiting trust based on the least privileged access at every layer of the network.

References

- Wikipedia, *Defence in depth*, [pub: 8 May 2024, cited: 3 Jan 2025]

Kerckhoffs's Principles: System should be secure even if everything except key is public

---

Definition and Origin

Kerckhoffs's Principle states that a cryptographic system should remain secure even if everything about the system, except the secret key, is publicly known. In other words, the security of the system should rely solely on the secrecy of the key, not the obscurity of the algorithm.

Kerckhoffs's Principle was coined by the Dutch cryptographer Auguste Kerckhoffs in 1883. He articulated the idea in a work on military cryptography, emphasizing that the security of a cipher should not depend on keeping the algorithm secret, but only on keeping the cryptographic key confidential.

Context and Importance

Kerckhoffs's Principle has profound implications for software and technology, especially in the context of cryptography and secure communications. As software systems increasingly rely on complex algorithms and data protection, the principle emphasizes the importance of designing cryptographic systems that are robust even when their underlying algorithms are publicly known. In the age of open-source software and widespread information sharing, ensuring that the security of cryptographic systems depends solely on the secrecy of the key, rather than on the obscurity of the algorithm, has become a cornerstone of trust and reliability. This is particularly relevant for systems like SSL/TLS encryption for web security, where the strength of the system lies in the private keys rather than in the public protocols themselves.

In modern software development, Kerckhoffs's Principle is crucial because it promotes transparency and interoperability. By relying on open and widely scrutinized algorithms (such as AES or RSA), the security of systems is made stronger through public review and improvement, while key management remains the sole point of vulnerability. This principle also supports the concept of security through obscurity, which is widely considered a poor practice. Instead, it advocates for using well-vetted, openly accessible cryptographic methods while keeping key material private. In technology, this has led to the widespread adoption of standards that are independently verified and more resilient to evolving threats, providing users and organizations with higher confidence in the security of their data and communications.

Best Practices and Guidelines

Use well-established algorithms: Rely on widely accepted, publicly scrutinized cryptographic algorithms (e.g., AES, RSA) to ensure transparency and robustness.

Keep keys secret: The security of a system should depend on the confidentiality of the cryptographic keys, not the obscurity of the algorithm.

Avoid security through obscurity: Do not rely on hiding the algorithm or implementation details as a primary defense mechanism.

Regularly update key management practices: Implement secure key generation, storage, and rotation procedures to protect against key exposure.

Embrace open standards: Adopt open standards and protocols for cryptographic systems to encourage external validation and continuous improvement.

Common Misconceptions and Pitfalls

- Misconception: Algorithm secrecy is critical: Believing that the algorithm itself must be kept secret for security, rather than focusing on keeping the key secret.
- Pitfall: Overestimating key security: Assuming that key management (e.g., storage, transmission) is secure without implementing robust practices like encryption or secure key exchanges.
- Misconception: Open algorithms are insecure: Incorrectly assuming that publicly known algorithms are weak or vulnerable, when in fact they are typically vetted and more resilient.
- Pitfall: Relying on outdated algorithms: Using cryptographic methods that are no longer considered secure or have known vulnerabilities, neglecting to update to newer standards.
- Misconception: One-time security: Believing that a system is secure once the key is kept secret, without considering ongoing threats or the need for continuous review and improvement.

Related Concepts

1. Shannon's Maxim (or "The enemy knows the system"): Proposed by Claude Shannon, this principle asserts that the security of a cryptographic system should not depend on the secrecy of the algorithm, but solely on the secrecy of the key. It reinforces the idea that attackers will have access to the public details of the system.

2. The Principle of Least Privilege: This security principle advocates limiting access rights for users, processes, and systems to the bare minimum necessary for them to perform their tasks. While not directly about cryptography, it complements Kerckhoffs's by ensuring that even with the algorithm public, exposure of critical resources (like keys) is minimized.
3. Open Design: Related to Kerckhoffs's Principle, open design emphasizes the idea that the security of a system should not rely on keeping the design secret. Instead, the system's security should withstand external scrutiny, with only the key being kept private.
4. Confidentiality, Integrity, and Availability (CIA Triad): This foundational security model stresses the importance of keeping data confidential (through key secrecy), ensuring its integrity, and maintaining its availability. While the CIA Triad is broader, it aligns with Kerckhoffs's emphasis on key confidentiality.
5. Defense in Depth: This principle advocates using multiple layers of security to protect systems, ensuring that the compromise of one layer (like the algorithm's public disclosure) doesn't result in total system failure. It supports Kerckhoffs's idea by suggesting that the key should be the only weak point in a well-architected system.

References

- Wikipedia, *Kerckhoffs's principle*, [pub: 27 Oct 2024, cited: 3 Jan 2025]

Perfect Forward Secrecy

Definition and Origin

Forward secrecy is a property of secure communication protocols where session keys used to encrypt data are not derived from long-term keys, meaning that even if the long-term keys (e.g., private keys) are compromised in the future, past communication remains secure. This ensures that past sessions cannot be decrypted, even if an attacker gains access to the server's private key later.

Forward secrecy (also known as perfect forward secrecy, or PFS) was introduced in the mid-1990s by Whitfield Diffie and Martin Hellman, the same cryptographers who developed public-key cryptography. They described it as part of their work on key exchange protocols, particularly in the context of the Diffie-Hellman key exchange.

The concept of forward secrecy was further formalized and widely adopted through its inclusion in modern cryptographic protocols, such as TLS (Transport Layer Security) and IPsec, particularly in the 2000s. Although Diffie and Hellman laid the foundation, the specific term "forward secrecy" became more commonly used later as the importance of protecting past communications in the event of key compromise became clear.

Context and Importance

Forward secrecy (PFS) is a crucial feature in modern cryptographic protocols, particularly in the context of software and technology that involves securing communication over the internet. In traditional encryption schemes, session keys are often derived from long-term keys, such as the private key of a server. This means that if the long-term key is ever compromised, an attacker can decrypt all past communications that were encrypted using it. With the increasing sophistication of cyberattacks and the possibility of adversaries acquiring private keys in the future, forward secrecy ensures that even if a server's private key is exposed at a later date, past sessions remain secure. This is especially important for technologies like secure messaging, online banking, and cloud storage, where confidentiality of data, both current and historical, is critical.

The growing need for forward secrecy is driven by the increasing value and sensitivity of data stored and transmitted online. As businesses, governments, and individuals continue to rely on digital platforms for sensitive activities, the consequences of data breaches or surveillance become more severe. Forward secrecy helps mitigate the risks associated with future key compromises, ensuring that hackers cannot decrypt historical data even if they gain access to private keys later. In software development and network security, implementing forward secrecy is seen as a best practice for maintaining privacy and trust in digital services. It is especially significant in technologies such as TLS/SSL (for securing web traffic), VPNs, and email encryption, where robust protection of user data is essential.

Best Practices and Guidelines

Use Strong Key Exchange Protocols: Implement forward secrecy by utilizing key exchange algorithms like Diffie-Hellman (DHE) or Elliptic Curve Diffie-Hellman (ECDHE) that support ephemeral keys.

Enable PFS in TLS/SSL Configurations: Ensure that your web servers and applications are configured to prioritize ECDHE or DHE ciphers for TLS connections, avoiding static RSA or DH keys.

Regularly Rotate Server Keys: Periodically rotate long-term keys and certificates to reduce the impact of potential key compromise.

Disallow Deprecated Ciphers: Disable weak or outdated ciphers such as RSA or DH without ephemeral keys to avoid compromising session security.

Test for Compliance: Regularly audit and test your systems using tools like Qualys SSL Labs to ensure forward secrecy is properly enabled and configured in your infrastructure.

Common Misconceptions and Pitfalls

- Misconception: PFS is Only About Strong Encryption: Forward secrecy focuses on how session keys are generated and exchanged, not just the encryption strength. Using strong encryption without proper key exchange (e.g., RSA without ephemeral keys) does not provide PFS.
- Pitfall: Relying on Outdated Protocols: Some older protocols (like SSL and early versions of TLS) do not support forward secrecy or require manual configuration. Continuing to use these insecure protocols can expose data to potential future breaches.
- Misconception: PFS Makes Data Unbreakable: While forward secrecy protects past communications if keys are compromised, it does not prevent attacks on real-time data or protect against vulnerabilities in other areas of the system (e.g., software flaws).
- Pitfall: Misconfiguring Cipher Suites: Improper server configuration (e.g., enabling weak ciphers or not prioritizing PFS-supporting algorithms) can leave sessions vulnerable despite enabling PFS.

- Misconception: PFS Solves All Privacy Issues: Forward secrecy protects against future key compromise, but it doesn't address other threats like man-in-the-middle attacks, traffic analysis, or weaknesses in user authentication.

Related Concepts

1. Principle of Least Privilege: This principle dictates that a system should only provide the minimum level of access necessary for any entity to perform its tasks. In the context of PFS, it means that private keys should be tightly controlled and not exposed unnecessarily, reducing the risk of compromise.
2. Defense in Depth: PFS is part of a broader security strategy where multiple layers of defense are employed to protect data. Even if one layer fails (e.g., a key compromise), the use of PFS ensures that past communication remains secure, adding an additional protective layer.
3. Security by Obscurity (Avoidance): Relying on "security by obscurity," such as hiding encryption methods or assuming that a protocol will stay secret, is ineffective. PFS avoids this by ensuring that encryption security does not rely on the secrecy of the method, but instead on strong key management and ephemeral session keys.
4. Cryptographic Agility: This principle encourages systems to be adaptable to changes in cryptographic standards and algorithms. PFS aligns with cryptographic agility by enabling the use of modern key exchange mechanisms like ECDHE and allowing older, insecure methods to be phased out as vulnerabilities are discovered.
5. Data Minimization: Data minimization emphasizes only collecting and retaining the minimum necessary data for the shortest time needed. In PFS, ephemeral keys are used for each session, meaning that encryption keys are not stored long-term, which aligns with the principle of not retaining excess data that could later be compromised.

References

- Wikipedia, *Forward secrecy*, [pub: 26 Oct 2024, cited: 3 Jan 2025]

Schneier's Law

Definition and Origin

Schneier's Law states: "Any person can create a system that he himself cannot break." This highlights the inherent complexity and limitations of security systems, suggesting that if a system is designed securely enough that the creator cannot break it, it is likely secure against others as well. It underscores the idea that systems should be evaluated based on the difficulty of breaking them, not on trust in their creators.

Schneier's Law was coined by Bruce Schneier, a renowned security expert and cryptographer. He introduced the concept to emphasize the idea that security systems should be judged based on their resistance to attacks, rather than on the competence of their designers. It reflects his broader views on the nature of security and trust in cryptographic and other complex systems.

Context and Importance

Schneier's Law is especially relevant in the context of software and technology, where systems are increasingly complex, and the threat landscape is constantly evolving. In software development, it's common for developers and security experts to focus on their own understanding of the system's vulnerabilities and exploits. However, Schneier's Law emphasizes that no matter how skilled the developer is, it is impossible for them to anticipate every possible attack vector or security flaw. This underscores the importance of designing systems that do not rely on the creator's ability to predict or prevent attacks, but rather on principles such as strong encryption, transparency, peer review, and the adoption of robust, well-vetted security practices.

In the broader technological landscape, Schneier's Law highlights the need for systemic security approaches in software engineering. Rather than trusting the intentions or expertise of individual developers or teams, organizations must adopt a "trust but verify" model, incorporating techniques like third-party audits, open-source collaboration, and adversarial testing. This is crucial as malicious actors become increasingly sophisticated and capable of exploiting subtle flaws in design. Schneier's Law advocates for creating security measures that are resilient against any attacker, not just those with access to the inner workings of the system, fostering a culture of transparency, continuous testing, and improvement to ensure long-term reliability and trustworthiness in software and technology.

Best Practices and Guidelines

Design for Openness: Build systems that assume external scrutiny, leveraging peer reviews, open-source practices, and transparent development processes to identify flaws.

Avoid Security by Obscurity: Don't rely on the secrecy of the design or implementation to protect the system; instead, ensure security is robust even when attackers understand the system.

Assume Adversarial Intent: Design systems with the assumption that they will be attacked by knowledgeable adversaries, ensuring comprehensive testing, auditing, and vulnerability assessment.

Use Strong Cryptography: Incorporate well-vetted, industry-standard cryptographic algorithms and protocols to safeguard data integrity and privacy.

Continuous Improvement: Regularly update and patch systems, monitor for vulnerabilities, and adopt new security measures to stay ahead of emerging threats.

Common Misconceptions and Pitfalls

- Over-reliance on Expert Knowledge: Believing that only the creator's expertise can secure a system, ignoring the fact that attackers may have different, unforeseen skills and perspectives.
- Trusting Closed Systems: Assuming that secrecy in system design (e.g., proprietary code or algorithms) is a substitute for strong security, which can lead to vulnerabilities being missed or exploited.
- Assuming Security Equals Complexity: Thinking that the more complex a system is, the more secure it must be, when in fact complexity can introduce additional vulnerabilities and make maintenance harder.
- Focusing on Obscure Threats: Prioritizing rare or sophisticated attack scenarios while neglecting common, well-understood risks that can be more easily exploited.

- Ignoring the Human Factor: Underestimating the role of human error, social engineering, and weak implementation practices in compromising system security, despite strong technical designs.

Related Concepts

1. Kerckhoffs's Principle: "The security of a cryptographic system should not depend on the secrecy of the algorithm, but only on the secrecy of the key." This principle aligns with Schneier's Law by emphasizing that a system's security should not rely on the obscurity of its design but rather on strong, resilient elements like keys and secure protocols.
2. Clifford Stoll's Law: "The more complex the system, the more vulnerable it is." This law cautions against over-engineering systems, emphasizing that complexity can inadvertently introduce security weaknesses, mirroring Schneier's idea that security should not depend on the designer's ability to foresee every potential flaw.
3. Conway's Law: "Organizations which design systems are constrained to produce designs which are copies of the communication structures of these organizations." While not directly about security, this principle suggests that the way a software system is structured can reflect the limitations of its creators, implying that secure systems must be built with broad collaboration and independent testing to avoid internal blind spots.
4. Meyers's Law: "You can't protect everything, so prioritize the most valuable assets." This law mirrors Schneier's Law in that it underscores the need to build systems that are resilient, focusing resources on the most critical aspects rather than assuming the system is impenetrable across all areas.
5. The Principle of Least Privilege: "Every module or user of a system should have only the minimum privileges necessary to perform its function." This principle supports Schneier's Law by promoting a security posture where the system is designed with constraints and failsafe mechanisms, so even if attackers gain access, their ability to cause harm is limited.

References

- Wikipedia, *Bruce Schneier*, [pub: 6 Dec 2024, cited: 3 Jan 2025]

Security through Obscurity Fallacy

Definition and Origin

The Security through Obscurity Fallacy refers to the mistaken belief that a system's security can be ensured simply by keeping its design, code, or mechanisms secret. This approach is flawed because it assumes that security relies on secrecy rather than on strong, well-tested security measures. If the system is eventually exposed or reverse-engineered, its security can be easily compromised. True security should rely on robust, transparent methods that withstand scrutiny, not just obscurity.

The term Security through Obscurity is commonly associated with the broader field of information security and has been discussed by various experts over time. While it's difficult to pinpoint a single individual who "coined" the term, it has been frequently critiqued by prominent security professionals and theorists, particularly in the context of cryptography.

One key figure who helped popularize the critique of this idea was Bruce Schneier, a renowned cryptographer and security expert. In his book Secrets and Lies: Digital Security in a Networked World (2000), Schneier emphasizes that relying solely on secrecy as a security measure is inherently flawed. He argues that security should instead be based on well-established, publicly scrutinized methods rather than relying on the hope that no one will uncover the secret design.

Although Schneier is a significant voice in this area, the concept itself has evolved through ongoing discussions within the information security community over many years.

Context and Importance

In the context of software and technology, Security through Obscurity refers to the misguided practice of relying on the secrecy of algorithms, code, or system architectures to protect against threats. Often seen in proprietary systems or closed-source software, the idea is that keeping the inner workings of a system hidden will prevent attackers from exploiting vulnerabilities. However, this approach ignores the fundamental principle of security that relies on transparency and the assumption that adversaries will eventually discover or reverse-engineer hidden components. For example, relying on an unpublished cryptographic algorithm can lead to catastrophic consequences if it is eventually broken, as opposed to using widely vetted, open standards that have undergone rigorous peer review and testing.

The fallacy becomes particularly dangerous in modern technology, where security must withstand scrutiny from diverse adversaries, including skilled hackers and nation-state actors. In software development, transparency and public scrutiny are crucial for identifying vulnerabilities and flaws that may not be apparent in the initial design phase. Open-source software, for example, benefits from the contributions of a large community of developers who can audit and improve the code, leading to stronger, more resilient systems. By contrast, security based solely on obscurity can create a false sense of safety, leading organizations to neglect proper security practices such as regular code audits, penetration testing, and the use of well-known cryptographic protocols. Ultimately, security through obscurity fails to build a robust defense and risks undermining trust in the technology itself.

Best Practices and Guidelines

Use Strong, Publicly Vetted Standards: Rely on widely accepted cryptographic algorithms and security protocols that have been extensively tested and reviewed by the security community.

Avoid Hidden Mechanisms: Do not rely on keeping your system's design, code, or security mechanisms secret as a primary defense; security should be based on sound practices, not obscurity.

Promote Transparency: Encourage open-source development where code can be reviewed, tested, and improved by the broader community to identify vulnerabilities early.

Conduct Regular Security Audits: Continuously assess your system's security with independent code reviews, penetration testing, and vulnerability scanning.

Adopt Defense in Depth: Implement multiple layers of security, including encryption, access controls, and intrusion detection, to mitigate risks, rather than relying on secrecy alone.

Common Misconceptions and Pitfalls

- Secrecy Equals Security: Believing that keeping a system's code or design hidden guarantees protection, when in reality, secrecy alone cannot defend against determined attackers.
- Obscurity Prevents Exploits: Assuming that attackers won't find vulnerabilities simply because the system is obscure, ignoring the fact that systems will eventually be analyzed or reverse engineered.
- Lack of Peer Review is Safe: Relying on unreviewed, proprietary security mechanisms under the assumption that they are secure, while overlooking the value of public scrutiny in identifying flaws.
- Hidden Details Will Never Leak: Assuming that sensitive design elements (like algorithms or protocols) won't be exposed through leaks, reverse engineering, or insider threats.
- Minimal Testing is Sufficient: Relying on "security by obscurity" to avoid thorough testing or independent audits, when a lack of proper validation increases the risk of undetected vulnerabilities.

Related Concepts

1. Kerckhoffs's Principle: This cryptographic principle states that the security of a system should not depend on the secrecy of the algorithm, but rather on the secrecy of the key. In other words, even if the algorithm is publicly known, the system can remain secure as long as the key remains confidential.
2. Shannon's Maxim: "The enemy knows the system." This principle, proposed by Claude Shannon, emphasizes that assuming an attacker knows the system design is a more realistic approach than relying on obscurity. Security should be based on robust, well-understood methods rather than hiding the system details.

3. The Principle of Least Privilege: This security principle advocates that systems should limit access to the minimum necessary resources for users or processes. Relying on security through obscurity could result in overlooking proper access controls and least privilege, which could lead to larger vulnerabilities.
4. Open Security: Open security suggests that security systems should be open for public scrutiny and analysis. Systems based on security through obscurity often avoid this, which can result in critical flaws going unnoticed. Open security promotes transparency and invites third-party experts to identify weaknesses.
5. Eternal Vigilance: This principle stresses the need for continuous monitoring, testing, and updating of security measures. Security through obscurity often leads to complacency, with systems thought to be safe due to their hidden nature, while real-world threats evolve and exploit overlooked weaknesses.

References

- Wikipedia, *Security through obscurity*, [pub: 22 Dec 2024, cited: 3 Jan 2025]

Shannon's Maxim: Enemy knows the system

Definition and Origin

Shannon's Maxim, "The enemy knows the system," refers to the idea that in cryptography and communication, it is assumed that any adversary has complete knowledge of the system's structure and algorithms, except for the secret key or private information. This principle underscores the need for robust security measures, where the security of a system does not rely on the secrecy of its design, but rather on the secrecy of critical elements, such as encryption keys or passwords.

Shannon's Maxim, was coined by Claude Shannon, the American mathematician and cryptographer who is considered the father of modern information theory. He introduced this principle in the context of secure communication and cryptography, emphasizing that one should design systems assuming that an adversary has full knowledge of the public aspects of the system, such as algorithms and protocols, and may only be challenged by the secrecy of certain keys or private data.

The idea is part of his foundational work on cryptography and security, particularly in his 1949 paper Communication Theory of Secrecy Systems.

Context and Importance

In the context of software development and cybersecurity, this maxim underscores the importance of designing systems with the assumption that adversaries may have full visibility into the software's architecture, protocols, and even the cryptographic algorithms used. This is particularly relevant in the age of open-source software, widespread reverse engineering, and advanced hacking techniques. A secure system should not rely on hiding the mechanics of its operation; instead, its security must stem from the strength of its cryptographic algorithms, access controls, and other security measures. By adhering to this principle, developers can create more robust systems that are resilient even in the face of sophisticated attacks where the adversary has a deep understanding of the system's structure.

In software security, the maxim also informs the design of cryptographic systems, authentication mechanisms, and data protection strategies. For instance, modern encryption schemes like AES (Advanced Encryption Standard) and public-key cryptography assume that the underlying algorithms are known to potential attackers. The security of these systems relies not on obscuring how they work, but on the computational difficulty of breaking them without the correct keys. This philosophy helps guide secure software development, where the goal is to ensure that even if an adversary knows the algorithms, they cannot feasibly exploit vulnerabilities. In an era of rapid technological advancement and increasing threats, Shannon's Maxim encourages developers and security professionals to focus on creating systems where the robustness lies in their mathematical foundation and implementation, rather than in obscuring their details.

Best Practices and Guidelines

Design for openness, not secrecy: Assume attackers can understand your system's design, protocols, and algorithms. Focus on securing sensitive data, not hiding system details.

Use strong cryptography: Ensure encryption and authentication mechanisms are based on well-established, peer-reviewed algorithms, not proprietary or obscure methods.

Minimize trust in security through obscurity: Rely on the strength of your security protocols rather than attempting to obscure or hide their workings.

Secure key management: Ensure that private keys, passwords, and other sensitive credentials are the focal points of your security, not the system's architecture.

Regular security testing: Continuously test your system for vulnerabilities, assuming an adversary has full knowledge of the system, and ensure robust defenses against attacks.

Common Misconceptions and Pitfalls

- Misconception: "Security through obscurity is enough": Believing that hiding the system's details is sufficient for security. In reality, strong encryption and secure protocols are more important than secrecy about the system's structure.
- Pitfall: Over-relying on "secure" algorithms: Assuming that proprietary or "secret" algorithms will remain secure, when in fact, security depends on well-tested, publicly scrutinized methods.
- Misconception: "If I hide the code, it's safe": Believing that simply obfuscating or protecting the source code guarantees security, ignoring the fact that the system can still be vulnerable through other means (e.g., side-channel attacks).
- Pitfall: Neglecting key management: Focusing on system design and not securing private keys or credentials, which are the actual points of vulnerability in most systems.
- Misconception: "My system is too niche to be targeted": Assuming that because a system is specialized or less popular, it won't attract attention from attackers, when in reality, adversaries may exploit known weaknesses in any system.

Related Concepts

1. Kerckhoffs's Principle: This principle, closely related to Shannon's Maxim, asserts that a cryptographic system should remain secure even if everything about the system, except the secret key, is known to the attacker. It highlights the importance of key secrecy rather than relying on keeping the algorithm or system design secret.
2. Occam's Razor: In the context of security, this principle suggests that simpler, well-understood solutions are often more reliable than overly complex or obscure ones. Relying on obscure methods for security can introduce vulnerabilities, while simpler, widely vetted methods are often more secure.
3. Principle of Least Privilege: This principle dictates that users and systems should only have the minimum level of access necessary for their function. Even if an attacker knows the system's structure, reducing access limits their potential for exploitation.
4. Defense in Depth: A strategy that emphasizes layering multiple security measures, ensuring that if one part of the system is compromised, others can still provide protection. This aligns with Shannon's Maxim by preparing for the possibility that an adversary understands the system.
5. Fail-Safe Defaults: This principle suggests that systems should be designed with secure defaults that minimize risk, even when attackers know how the system works. For example, system configurations should default to the most restrictive settings and only allow broader access when explicitly authorized.

References

- Wikipedia, *Claude Shannon*, [pub: 25 Dec 2024, cited: 3 Jan 2025]

Saltzer and Schroeder's Principles

Definition and Origin

Saltzer and Schroeder's Principles are a set of design guidelines for creating secure computer systems. They focus on minimizing vulnerabilities and improving system security. The key principles are:

1. Economy of Mechanism: Keep the design simple and minimal to reduce the potential for errors or weaknesses.
2. Fail-Safe Defaults: Default configurations should be secure, with restrictions unless otherwise explicitly specified.
3. Complete Mediation: Every access to a resource must be checked for authorization, ensuring no bypassing of security controls.
4. Open Design: The security of a system should not depend on the secrecy of its design or implementation.
5. Separation of Privilege: Use multiple conditions or factors to grant access, reducing risk by not relying on a single privilege.
6. Least Privilege: Give users and processes the minimum level of access needed to perform their tasks.
7. Least Common Mechanism: Minimize shared resources to reduce unintended interactions or potential exploits.
8. Psychological Acceptability: Security mechanisms should be user-friendly and not impede legitimate use or behavior.

These principles help to create more resilient, secure systems by minimizing risk and complexity.

Saltzer and Schroeder's Principles were coined by Jerome Saltzer and Michael D. Schroeder, two computer scientists who introduced them in their seminal 1975 paper titled "The Protection of Information in Computer Systems". This paper, which appeared in the ACM Computing Surveys, laid the foundation for modern computer security design principles.

Saltzer and Schroeder are widely recognized for their influential work in the field of computer security, and their principles have since become a cornerstone of secure system design.

Context and Importance

Saltzer and Schroeder's Principles, introduced in 1975, were revolutionary in the context of computer security because they offered a structured and systematic approach to designing secure systems. At a time when computer systems were becoming increasingly interconnected and important for handling sensitive data, these principles provided essential guidelines to address the growing security concerns. They emphasized simplicity, robust access control, and the concept of minimizing risk through thoughtful system design. As software systems evolved, particularly with the rise of the internet and networked environments, these principles became a foundational framework for building software that could withstand malicious attacks, unauthorized access, and unintentional vulnerabilities. By focusing on issues like least privilege, fail-safe defaults, and complete mediation, Saltzer and Schroeder highlighted the importance of secure software architecture from the ground up, not as an afterthought.

In today's context, Saltzer and Schroeder's Principles remain highly relevant and are embedded in the design philosophy of modern software and technology. With the increasing complexity of systems—ranging from cloud computing and mobile applications to IoT and AI—these principles provide clear guidance for ensuring that security is an integral part of system development. For instance, "Least Privilege" and "Fail-Safe Defaults" directly inform access control mechanisms in software, ensuring that users and services only have access to the minimum resources necessary to perform their tasks. Additionally, as cybersecurity threats have grown more sophisticated, the focus on "Complete Mediation" and "Separation of Privilege" has become crucial in defending against both external attackers and insider threats. In this way, Saltzer and Schroeder's principles are not just theoretical; they offer a practical framework for developing secure systems that can scale safely in an increasingly hostile digital environment.

Best Practices and Guidelines

Simplify System Design: Keep software and security mechanisms as simple as possible to reduce complexity and potential vulnerabilities.

Apply Least Privilege: Grant users and processes only the minimum level of access necessary to perform their tasks, limiting potential damage in case of compromise.

Use Fail-Safe Defaults: Configure systems with secure defaults, allowing explicit permission for access rather than assuming trust.

Ensure Complete Mediation: Always check and enforce access controls for every resource request, preventing unauthorized access or bypassing.

Design for Psychological Acceptability: Make security features intuitive and user-friendly to encourage proper usage without hindering legitimate tasks.

Common Misconceptions and Pitfalls

- Overcomplicating Security: Believing that more complex security mechanisms always improve protection; simplicity is key to reducing errors and vulnerabilities.
- Assuming Security Through Obscurity: Relying on hiding the system design or implementation to protect security, rather than using robust, open designs with clear access controls.
- Excessive Permissions: Granting unnecessary broad access to users or systems, thinking it improves usability, instead of strictly adhering to the principle of least privilege.
- Ignoring Complete Mediation: Assuming that once a user or system is authorized, access checks are no longer needed, potentially allowing privilege escalation or unauthorized bypass.
- Neglecting User Experience: Implementing complex or intrusive security measures that frustrate users, leading to circumvention or insecure behavior.

Related Concepts

1. The Principle of Least Privilege (POLP) – This principle, also a key part of Saltzer and Schroeder's guidelines, asserts that users and processes should be granted the least amount of access necessary to perform their tasks. It's a fundamental practice in securing both software and system architecture.
2. Law of Least Astonishment – This principle suggests that software should behave in a way that users expect, minimizing surprises or confusion. It ties into Saltzer and Schroeder's "Psychological Acceptability," ensuring security mechanisms do not hinder legitimate use.

3. The Fail-Safe Principle – Similar to Saltzer and Schroeder's "Fail-Safe Defaults," this principle emphasizes designing systems to default to a secure state in the event of failure, preventing unintended access or security breaches when things go wrong.
4. The Open Design Principle – Echoing Saltzer and Schroeder's idea of "Open Design," this concept asserts that the security of a system should not rely on keeping its design secret, but rather on employing strong and publicly vetted security measures.
5. Separation of Concerns – This software engineering principle advocates dividing a system into distinct sections that focus on separate concerns or functionalities. It relates to Saltzer and Schroeder's "Separation of Privilege" by encouraging the segmentation of responsibilities to reduce security risks and limit potential damage.

References

- Wikipedia, *The Protection of Information in Computer Systems*, [pub: 13 Nov 2024, cited: 3 Jan 2025]

Zero Knowledge Principle

Definition and Origin

A Zero-Knowledge Proof (ZKP) is a cryptographic method in which one party (the prover) can prove to another party (the verifier) that they know a certain piece of information, without revealing the information itself. The proof ensures that the verifier learns nothing other than the fact that the statement is true, maintaining the confidentiality of the underlying data.

The Zero-Knowledge Proof (ZKP) concept was introduced by Shafi Goldwasser, Silvio Micali, and Charles Rackoff in 1985. They formalized the concept as part of their work on the foundations of cryptography, specifically in the context of interactive proofs and complexity theory. Their pioneering work earned them significant recognition, with Goldwasser and Micali later receiving the Turing Award for their contributions to cryptography.

Context and Importance

The Zero-Knowledge Principle has become a cornerstone of modern cryptography, playing a critical role in securing digital transactions, identity verification, and privacy protection in software and technology. In an era where data breaches and privacy concerns are rampant, ZKPs offer a way to authenticate users or prove the validity of information without revealing the sensitive data itself. This principle is especially important in decentralized systems like blockchain, where users need to prove ownership or transactions without exposing underlying details, ensuring both security and privacy. For example, ZKPs are utilized in privacy-focused cryptocurrencies, such as Zcash, to allow transactions to be verified as legitimate while keeping sender, receiver, and transaction amounts confidential.

In addition to their role in cryptocurrencies, Zero-Knowledge Proofs are also being increasingly used in various software applications where privacy and trust are essential. ZKPs enable secure online voting systems, private authentication mechanisms, and confidential data-sharing protocols by reducing the need for users to disclose their personal information. They also provide solutions to regulatory compliance challenges, as businesses can prove adherence to policies or regulations without sharing sensitive internal data. As digital privacy becomes a growing concern, the Zero-Knowledge Principle is poised to become even more vital, ensuring that data remains protected while still allowing for necessary interactions, ultimately transforming how trust is established and maintained in the digital world.

Best Practices and Guidelines

Minimize Data Exposure: Only prove the validity of a statement without revealing any sensitive or unnecessary information to maintain privacy.

Use for Authentication: Leverage ZKPs for secure user authentication where sensitive credentials (e.g., passwords) are never transmitted.

Optimize Performance: Ensure efficient implementation of ZKPs to prevent excessive computational overhead in real-time applications like blockchain and online transactions.

Maintain Transparency: While data is concealed, ensure that the process and security of ZKP mechanisms are transparent and auditable by trusted parties.

Ensure Compliance: Use ZKPs to demonstrate compliance with regulations (e.g., GDPR, KYC) without exposing private user data to third parties.

Common Misconceptions and Pitfalls

- ZKPs Guarantee Complete Security: ZKPs enhance privacy, but they don't eliminate all security risks. Other vulnerabilities, such as weak encryption or poor implementation, can still expose data.
- ZKPs Can Be Used for Any Problem: Not all cryptographic problems are suitable for Zero-Knowledge Proofs. ZKPs are ideal for specific scenarios, like proving knowledge without revealing it, but not for every use case.
- ZKPs Are Always Efficient: While ZKPs are powerful, they can be computationally expensive and may introduce performance bottlenecks, especially in large-scale applications or with complex proofs.
- ZKPs Do Not Require Trust: ZKPs provide privacy but still depend on the integrity of the protocol and cryptographic primitives. Improperly designed ZKP systems can still be vulnerable to attacks.
- ZKPs Provide Full Privacy: While they enhance privacy, ZKPs do not guarantee complete anonymity or protection against all forms of surveillance, such as traffic analysis or timing attacks.

Related Concepts

1. The Principle of Least Privilege: This security principle states that a user or system should have only the minimum level of access required to perform its tasks. ZKPs align with this by proving knowledge or authenticity without exposing unnecessary data, minimizing the exposure of sensitive information.
2. Data Minimization (GDPR): Under the General Data Protection Regulation (GDPR), organizations are required to collect only the data necessary for a specific purpose. ZKPs help adhere to this principle by enabling proofs without requiring the transfer of personal data, thus supporting compliance with privacy laws.

3. Confidentiality: ZKPs are a key mechanism for ensuring confidentiality in transactions and communications. This principle, which is central to cryptographic practices, states that sensitive information should not be revealed to unauthorized parties. ZKPs protect sensitive data while confirming its validity.
4. Non-repudiation: In digital systems, non-repudiation ensures that a party cannot deny the authenticity of their actions (e.g., a transaction). ZKPs can prove that a user possesses certain knowledge or has taken an action, without allowing them to later deny it or expose details of the information involved.
5. Transparency and Accountability (Blockchain Transparency): In blockchain and decentralized technologies, ZKPs contribute to the principle of transparency while maintaining accountability. Although they keep transaction details private, they allow public verification of the correctness of operations (e.g., proving that a transaction is valid without revealing amounts or parties).

References

- Wikipedia, *Zero-knowledge proof*, [pub: 25 Dec 2024, cited: 3 Jan 2025]

Zero Trust Principle

Definition and Origin

The Zero Trust Principle, as defined by Stephen Paul Marsh, is a security concept that assumes no entity—whether inside or outside the network—can be trusted by default. Instead, all users, devices, and systems must be continuously authenticated and authorized, and access is granted only based on strict verification, ensuring that security is maintained at all times, regardless of the network's perimeter. This principle emphasizes the need for least-privilege access and constant monitoring to mitigate risks.

The core idea is:
"Never trust, always verify."

Context and Importance

Stephen Paul Marsh's contributions to the Zero Trust Principle emphasize the evolving need for robust, context-aware security models in an increasingly interconnected and complex digital landscape. With the growing adoption of cloud technologies, remote work, and mobile devices, traditional security models that relied on a clear perimeter around corporate networks have become increasingly ineffective. Marsh's interpretation of the Zero Trust Principle underscores that in the modern software and technology environment, security should not be based on the assumption that internal networks or users are inherently trustworthy. Instead, continuous verification and access control mechanisms must be applied to every interaction, regardless of where the request originates. This approach reflects a fundamental shift towards viewing every request—whether internal or external—as a potential security risk, which must be rigorously authenticated and authorized.

In the context of software and technology, the Zero Trust Principle has become crucial for mitigating the risks posed by increasingly sophisticated cyber threats, such as advanced persistent threats (APTs), data breaches, and insider attacks. As organizations adopt more decentralized architectures, like microservices, and integrate various third-party services, maintaining strict control over data access and system interactions becomes paramount. Marsh's framework promotes least-privilege access, meaning users and devices are only granted the minimum necessary access to perform their tasks, reducing the potential attack surface. By enforcing strict access policies and continuous monitoring, the Zero Trust model minimizes vulnerabilities in software systems, ensuring that security is enforced dynamically at all layers—protecting both the data and the integrity of the technology infrastructure. This is particularly vital as organizations increasingly face compliance requirements and need to safeguard sensitive data from evolving threats.

Best Practices and Guidelines

Assume Breach: Treat every user, device, and network request as untrusted until verified, regardless of its origin (internal or external).

Continuous Authentication: Implement continuous and real-time user and device verification, ensuring security is maintained throughout interactions.

Least-Privilege Access: Grant users and systems the minimal level of access necessary to perform tasks, reducing potential attack surfaces.

Micro-Segmentation: Isolate networks and systems into smaller segments to limit lateral movement in the event of a breach.

Comprehensive Monitoring: Continuously monitor and analyze user and device behaviors, ensuring anomalies are detected and addressed promptly.

Common Misconceptions and Pitfalls

- Zero Trust = No Trust: A misconception is that Zero Trust means no trust at all. In reality, it emphasizes verifiable trust, not the absence of it, ensuring continuous authentication and authorization.
- It's Only for External Threats: Zero Trust is not just about protecting from external threats; it also defends against internal risks, including insider threats and compromised credentials.
- Zero Trust is a One-Time Setup: It's a dynamic, ongoing process requiring continuous monitoring, adjustment, and improvement, not a one-time implementation.
- Zero Trust Replaces Firewalls: While it reduces reliance on traditional perimeter defenses, Zero Trust is a complementary strategy, not a replacement for firewalls or other security layers.
- Zero Trust is Only for Large Enterprises: Zero Trust is scalable and can be implemented by organizations of any size, with tailored policies that meet specific needs and resources.

Related Concepts

1. The Principle of Least Privilege (PoLP): This principle dictates that users, systems, and applications should be granted only the minimal access necessary to perform their tasks. It directly complements Zero Trust by limiting potential attack surfaces and reducing the scope of security breaches.
2. Defense in Depth: This security strategy involves layering multiple defenses at different points in the system to ensure that if one layer is breached, others will still provide protection. It aligns with Zero Trust by ensuring that access is continuously verified and that multiple controls are in place.

3. Fail-Safe Defaults (or Default Deny): This principle suggests that systems should be configured to deny access by default, only granting permission after thorough verification. It supports Zero Trust by enforcing strict access controls and minimizing the likelihood of unauthorized access.
4. Separation of Duties (SoD): This principle involves distributing responsibilities and access privileges among different individuals or systems to reduce the risk of fraud, errors, or malicious actions. It aligns with Zero Trust by ensuring that no single user or entity has excessive control over a system or process, minimizing risks.
5. Continuous Monitoring and Auditing: This concept stresses the importance of constant surveillance and logging of activities to detect unusual behavior or security breaches. In a Zero Trust environment, continuous monitoring is vital to verify identities and ensure compliance with access policies in real-time.

References

- Wikipedia, *Zero trust architecture*, [pub: 11 Dec 2024, cited: 3 Jan 2025]

Zimmermann's Law

Definition and Origin

Zimmermann's Law, refers to the idea that technological advancements tend to make surveillance easier and more pervasive over time. Specifically, it suggests that the capabilities of computers to track and monitor individuals double approximately every eighteen months, leading to an increasing risk of privacy erosion. This observation underscores the growing potential for surveillance through technological development and its implications for personal privacy.

Zimmermann's Law was coined by Phil Zimmermann, the creator of PGP (Pretty Good Privacy), a widely used encryption software. He is known for his advocacy for privacy and cryptography. Zimmermann's Law reflects his concerns about the increasing ease and capability of surveillance technologies, particularly in the context of rapidly advancing computer capabilities and their implications for privacy.

Context and Importance

Zimmermann's Law highlights a fundamental tension in the development of software and technology: as technological capabilities grow, so too does the potential for surveillance and the erosion of personal privacy. Zimmermann's observation that "the ability of computers to track us doubles every eighteen months" underscores the rapid advancement of computing power, driven by factors like Moore's Law, which predicts the doubling of transistors on a microchip roughly every two years. This exponential increase in computing power has enabled more sophisticated data tracking, monitoring, and analysis, making it easier for both government agencies and private companies to gather detailed information about individuals' behaviors, preferences, and locations. In the software and tech sectors, this trend has resulted in an arms race between privacy advocates and entities seeking to leverage this technology for surveillance.

The importance of Zimmermann's Law lies in its implications for the ongoing debate about privacy, security, and the ethical use of technology. As software and technology evolve to offer more sophisticated tools for monitoring, it becomes increasingly challenging to safeguard individual freedoms and protect against unwarranted intrusion. Zimmermann, through his creation of PGP, sought to counterbalance this trend by providing individuals with the means to encrypt their communications and maintain their privacy. His law serves as both a warning and a call to action, reminding technologists, policymakers, and citizens that while technology can offer immense benefits, it also introduces significant risks to personal autonomy and privacy. As the pace of technological progress continues to accelerate, the need for robust privacy protections and ethical considerations in software design becomes ever more pressing.

Best Practices and Guidelines

Prioritize Privacy by Design: Incorporate encryption and data protection features into software development from the outset to minimize surveillance risks.

Limit Data Collection: Avoid unnecessary data tracking or collection; only gather what is essential for the function of the service.

Implement Transparency: Clearly communicate to users what data is collected, how it is used, and who has access to it, ensuring informed consent.

Use Decentralized Systems: Favor decentralized or peer-to-peer technologies to reduce the concentration of personal data in centralized databases vulnerable to surveillance.

Regularly Audit Security: Continuously assess and update security practices to stay ahead of evolving surveillance technologies and ensure data protection.

Common Misconceptions and Pitfalls

- Surveillance Is Only a Government Issue: Many believe surveillance concerns are limited to government agencies, but corporations and third-party entities also collect and misuse personal data.
- Encryption Alone Solves Privacy Issues: While encryption is critical, it's only one part of the privacy puzzle. Data collection practices, user consent, and secure software design are equally important.
- More Data Means Better Services: Some argue that collecting more personal data improves services, but excessive tracking increases privacy risks without necessarily enhancing user experience.
- Technology Is Neutral: Zimmermann's Law suggests that technology's natural progression favors surveillance, which means software development must be intentionally designed to protect privacy, not assume neutrality.
- Surveillance Risks Are Static: A common pitfall is assuming that privacy threats remain constant; in reality, as computing power grows, surveillance capabilities continuously evolve and expand.

Related Concepts

1. The Law of Inverse Surveillance (or "Brunton's Law"): This law suggests that as surveillance tools become more sophisticated, tools for resisting surveillance, such as encryption and anonymity technologies, must also evolve at a similar pace to counterbalance them. It highlights the arms race between surveillance and privacy technologies, similar to Zimmermann's Law.
2. Moore's Law: While Zimmermann's Law focuses on the implications of increased computing power for surveillance, Moore's Law explains the exponential growth of processing power. As computing capabilities double every 18 months, this directly contributes to the growing potential for surveillance, tracking, and data analysis.
3. The Principle of Least Privilege: This security principle dictates that software should only give users the minimum access necessary to perform their tasks, minimizing data exposure. It aligns with Zimmermann's Law by advocating for restricting unnecessary data collection and reducing the risk of surveillance or data misuse.
4. Data Minimization Principle (GDPR): This principle, under the General Data Protection Regulation (GDPR), mandates that organizations collect only the data necessary for their stated purpose and retain it for no longer than necessary. It counters the surveillance risk identified in Zimmermann's Law by limiting the scope of personal data collection.
5. The Risk of Centralized Systems: This principle cautions against creating centralized databases or platforms where sensitive user data is stored. Centralization increases the potential for mass surveillance, as highlighted by Zimmermann's Law. Advocating for decentralized systems, like blockchain or peer-to-peer networks, can mitigate such risks.

References

- Wikipedia, *Phil Zimmermann*, [pub: 22 Dec 2024, cited: 3 Jan 2025]

General Principles & Observations

P. Problem Solving

The 5 Whys Principle: Ask "Why?" five times, until the underlying cause is identified

Definition and Origin

The 5 Whys principle is a problem-solving technique used to explore the root cause of an issue by asking "Why?" five times, or as many times as needed, until the underlying cause is identified. Each answer forms the basis of the next "Why," helping to uncover deeper layers of the problem. It is commonly used in lean manufacturing, quality control, and continuous improvement processes.

The 5 Whys principle was developed by Taiichi Ohno, a Japanese industrial engineer and the father of the Toyota Production System (TPS). Ohno introduced the technique as part of efforts to improve manufacturing processes and eliminate inefficiencies. It became a core component of lean manufacturing practices, aiming to identify and address the root causes of problems rather than just treating symptoms.

Context and Importance

In the context of software and technology, the 5 Whys principle serves as a valuable tool for diagnosing issues that arise during development, deployment, or usage of systems. Software development is inherently complex, with many interconnected components and layers of abstraction. When bugs, performance issues, or system failures occur, teams can use the 5 Whys to go beyond the immediate symptom—such as an error message or a failed feature—to identify the core problem. For example, if a program crashes, asking "Why?" multiple times helps determine if the issue stems from faulty code, misconfigured infrastructure, inadequate testing, or a deeper process failure, such as poor communication among team members. This structured approach ensures that problems are addressed at their root, preventing quick fixes that might only resolve the visible symptoms but leave the fundamental issue unresolved.

The importance of the 5 Whys in software and technology lies in its ability to improve quality assurance and continuous improvement. By systematically addressing the root causes of issues, development teams can enhance system reliability, reduce recurring bugs, and streamline processes. Additionally, it fosters a culture of proactive problem-solving and learning, where teams focus on long-term solutions rather than short-term patches. It also aids in post-mortem analysis after incidents or system failures, allowing for actionable insights that can improve future design and development practices. Ultimately, the 5 Whys helps software teams avoid costly rework and technical debt while contributing to better user experiences and more resilient technology products.

Best Practices and Guidelines

Start with the symptom, not the assumption: Focus on the immediate problem (e.g., crash, bug, slow performance) and ask "Why?" to trace the root cause, avoiding preconceived solutions.

Involve the right stakeholders: Collaborate with developers, testers, and operations teams to ensure a comprehensive analysis of the issue from multiple perspectives.

Ask “Why?” up to five times: While five is the common guideline, stop when you reach the root cause; more or fewer iterations may be necessary.

Document each step: Keep a clear record of each "Why?" and answer, which can provide insights for future improvements and prevent repetitive issues.

Focus on systemic causes: Aim to identify process or design flaws that led to the issue, rather than just fixing isolated technical glitches.

Common Misconceptions and Pitfalls

- Over-simplifying the problem: If asking "Why?" just five times will always uncover the root cause, when sometimes more in-depth analysis or additional tools are required.
- Focusing on blame: Using the 5 Whys to assign blame to individuals or teams instead of focusing on systemic issues or process improvements.

- Not involving the right people: Ignoring the importance of cross-functional collaboration; different perspectives can reveal deeper insights.
- Stopping too early: Concluding the investigation after just a few "Whys," without fully exploring potential root causes, leading to incomplete solutions.
- Confusing symptoms with causes: Mistaking surface-level issues (like error codes or UI glitches) as the root cause, rather than exploring deeper system or design flaws.

Related Concepts

1. Pareto Principle: The 80/20 Rule
2. Brooks's Law: Adding manpower to a late project makes it later
3. Conway's Law: Organizations design systems that mirror their communication structure
4. Lehman's Laws of Software Evolution: software must constantly evolve to adapt and remain useful

References

- Wikipedia, *Five whys*, [pub: 11 Dec 2024, cited: 3 Jan 2025]

Chesterton's Fence: Avoid changing the system without first understanding the reasoning behind its existence

---

Definition and Origin

Chesterton's Fence is a principle that suggests one should not remove or alter a system, rule, or institution without first understanding the reasoning behind its existence. The idea is that changes should be made cautiously, acknowledging that there may be hidden wisdom or purpose in established practices, even if their rationale isn't immediately apparent. The concept is named after G.K. Chesterton, who used it in his writing to emphasize the importance of considering the potential consequences of change.

Chesterton's Fence was coined by the British writer and philosopher G.K. Chesterton. The concept is drawn from his 1929 work The Thing, where he discusses the idea of preserving existing systems and structures until their purpose and value are fully understood. The analogy he uses is of a fence or gate that has been erected for some reason—one should not take it down without first understanding why it was put there in the first place.

Context and Importance

In the context of software development and technology, Chesterton's Fence serves as a cautionary principle against hasty innovation and change. In the fast-paced world of tech, there's often a rush to adopt new tools, languages, or frameworks without fully understanding the reasons behind the current practices or technologies in place. Much like Chesterton's analogy of a fence, established technologies or methods may have been developed for valid, though perhaps not immediately obvious, reasons. For instance, legacy systems or older software architectures may seem outdated or inefficient, but they were designed with specific constraints and needs in mind. By quickly discarding them in favor of new trends, developers and organizations risk overlooking critical lessons or functionality that may still hold value in specific contexts.

The importance of Chesterton's Fence in technology lies in the need for thoughtful evaluation before making significant changes to systems or processes. In software, this could mean not rushing to refactor an entire codebase or replace a tool without first understanding its role and why it was chosen in the first place. Sometimes, what appears to be an outdated or inefficient practice might be rooted in deeper trade-offs or constraints—whether technical, financial, or user-driven—that newer approaches may not fully address. Taking the time to examine and understand existing systems can lead to more informed decisions, prevent unintended consequences, and ensure that changes made are genuine improvements rather than reactive overhauls driven by short-term trends.

Best Practices and Guidelines

Understand the Legacy: Before changing or replacing a system, take the time to fully understand the reasons and constraints behind its original design.

Evaluate Risks: Assess the potential long-term consequences of altering existing technologies, especially in terms of stability, security, and compatibility.

Question Assumptions: Don't assume newer solutions are inherently better—challenge the reasons for change and ensure the benefits outweigh the risks.

Iterate, Don't Overhaul: Rather than large, disruptive changes, consider incremental improvements that respect existing systems while addressing their limitations.

Preserve Core Functionality: Ensure that any modifications maintain or enhance the core functionality and goals of the original system, avoiding superficial fixes.

Common Misconceptions and Pitfalls

- "Old means obsolete": Assuming that older technologies or systems are inherently inferior or outdated without understanding the rationale behind their design.
- "Change equals progress": Believing that any change is an improvement, when in fact, hasty changes can introduce instability, complexity, or new problems.
- "We know better now": Overestimating the advantages of new solutions without considering that previous systems may have solved challenges that are not immediately apparent.
- "Innovation for the sake of innovation": Prioritizing the latest trends or tools without assessing their actual need or value in the current context.
- "Failure to recognize hidden tradeoffs": Ignoring the trade-offs or constraints that shaped the original system, leading to changes that fail to account for real-world limitations.

Related Concepts

1. YAGNI: You Aren't Gonna Need It - Yet
2. Law of Demeter: Only talk to your immediate friends
3. Occam's Razor: Simplest explanation is usually correct
4. Spolsky's Law of Leaky Abstractions: All non-trivial abstractions, to some degree, are leaky

5. Principle of Least Astonishment: Software should behave in a way that users find intuitive and expected

References

- Wikipedia, *G. K. Chesterton*, [pub: 28 Dec 2024, cited: 3 Jan 2025]

Divide and Conquer: Break problem into smaller subproblems, then solve and combine

---

Definition and Origin

Divide and Conquer is an algorithmic strategy that solves a problem by breaking it into smaller subproblems, solving each subproblem recursively, and then combining their solutions to solve the original problem. This approach is often used to optimize efficiency, especially in problems that can be divided into independent or nearly independent parts.

The Divide and Conquer strategy, as a formal algorithmic approach, is not attributed to a single inventor or coiner. However, the concept has ancient roots, and it was used long before it was formalized in modern computer science.

The strategy is often traced back to Euclid (circa 300 BCE), who used a similar approach in his algorithm to compute the greatest common divisor (GCD) of two numbers, known today as Euclid's algorithm.

In terms of its formalization in computer science, John von Neumann and Konrad Zuse are sometimes credited for laying down the foundation of algorithm design methods that led to the popularization of Divide and Conquer techniques in the mid-20th century. The technique became widely recognized as a core part of algorithm design, particularly in the 1960s and 1970s, as algorithms like Merge Sort, QuickSort, and Binary Search were developed using this approach.

In summary, while no single person is credited with inventing Divide and Conquer, its development is a cumulative process over many centuries, with key contributions from ancient mathematicians and modern computer scientists.

Context and Importance

In the context of software and technology, Divide and Conquer is a foundational algorithmic technique that has significantly shaped how problems are approached and solved efficiently. The primary strength of Divide and Conquer lies in its ability to break down complex, large-scale problems into smaller, more manageable subproblems. This decomposition makes it easier to apply recursive solutions, where each smaller subproblem can be solved independently and then combined to produce the overall solution. This approach is not only effective for reducing time complexity but also facilitates parallelism, allowing different parts of a problem to be solved simultaneously, which is crucial in modern computing with multi-core processors. Algorithms such as Merge Sort, QuickSort, and Fast Fourier Transform (FFT) leverage Divide and Conquer to improve efficiency, reducing the overall computational burden.

The importance of Divide and Conquer in software development is also reflected in its role in optimizing both time and space complexity. Many problems in fields like sorting, searching, computational geometry, and matrix multiplication are tackled using Divide and Conquer due to its ability to minimize the number of operations needed to reach a solution. In addition, its recursive nature allows for elegant, modular solutions that are easier to maintain and understand. Divide and Conquer also underpins key strategies in data analysis, machine learning, and distributed systems, where breaking down large datasets or tasks into smaller chunks allows for more efficient computation and scaling. As technology continues to evolve with an increasing demand for high-performance software, the Divide and Conquer paradigm remains a cornerstone in the design of algorithms that drive efficiency and innovation.

Best Practices and Guidelines

Identify Independent Subproblems: Ensure the problem can be broken into smaller, independent subproblems that can be solved recursively without overlapping dependencies.

Optimize Base Case Handling: Define clear base cases to terminate the recursion efficiently, avoiding unnecessary computations and preventing infinite recursion.

Balance the Subproblem Sizes: Strive for a balanced split of subproblems to optimize performance and minimize the depth of recursion, reducing time complexity.

Leverage Parallelism: Take advantage of parallel processing or multi-threading when subproblems are independent, improving overall execution speed in modern hardware environments.

Efficiently Combine Results: Design the combining step to be as efficient as possible, ensuring that the time spent merging or combining solutions doesn't negate the benefits of dividing the problem.

Common Misconceptions and Pitfalls

- Overhead from Recursion: Excessive recursion can introduce significant overhead due to function calls and memory usage, especially if the subproblems are not sufficiently reduced in size or are poorly balanced.
- Improper Base Case: Failing to define or improperly implement the base case can lead to infinite recursion or suboptimal performance, increasing complexity unnecessarily.
- Inefficient Merging: The merging step can become a bottleneck if not optimized, especially when combining large amounts of data, negating the benefits of dividing the problem.
- Assuming Parallelism Always Helps: While Divide and Conquer can often be parallelized, not all problems or subproblems benefit from parallel execution due to synchronization overhead or dependencies between tasks.
- Excessive Memory Usage: Recursive algorithms in Divide and Conquer may require large amounts of memory for storing intermediate results, leading to potential memory constraints or inefficiencies, especially with large inputs.

Related Concepts

1. Amdahl's Law: Parallel speedup is limited by sequential portions
2. Big-O Notation: Algorithm efficiency measured by time and space complexity
3. Law of Diminishing Returns: More resources yield smaller improvements
4. Kernighan's Law: Debugging is twice as hard as writing code

References

- Wikipedia, *Divide-and-conquer*, [pub: 13 Dec 2024, cited: 3 Jan 2025]

Hanlon's Razor: Never attribute to malice what can be explained by stupidity

---

Definition and Origin

Hanlon's Razor is a principle that states:
"Never attribute to malice that which is adequately explained by stupidity (or ignorance)."

Hanlon's Razor is a principle that suggests we should not assume harmful intent when something can be explained by simple error or incompetence. It advises against attributing malice to actions that might just be the result of misunderstanding, oversight, or ignorance.

Hanlon's Razor is commonly attributed to Robert J. Hanlon, who reportedly coined the phrase in 1980. It appeared in a collection of humorous "rules" called "Murphy's Laws of Combat." However, the principle itself — the idea of not attributing malice to what can be explained by incompetence — has roots in earlier philosophies and ideas, such as those found in the works of figures like Napoleon Bonaparte and others who emphasized caution in interpreting others' actions.

Context and Importance

In the realm of software development and technology, Hanlon's Razor serves as a useful guiding principle for managing complex systems, teams, and codebases. In fast-paced environments where mistakes, bugs, and communication errors are common, it's easy to assume that negative outcomes arise from intentional sabotage or malicious behavior. However, this can lead to unnecessary conflict, distrust, and wasted time. Adopting Hanlon's Razor encourages professionals to first consider the possibility that errors are due to human fallibility, lack of experience, or miscommunication, rather than deliberate harm. This mindset fosters a more collaborative and solution-oriented approach, where the focus shifts toward identifying root causes and addressing systemic issues, rather than assigning blame.

Moreover, Hanlon's Razor is crucial for maintaining a healthy team dynamic and a productive culture in technology organizations. When team members or stakeholders act with the assumption that others are acting in good faith, even when mistakes occur, it promotes a culture of openness, learning, and continuous improvement. In tech projects, where iteration and problem-solving are key, it’s critical to avoid creating an environment where people are afraid to make mistakes or ask questions. By embracing the idea that mistakes are often a result of ignorance or lack of knowledge rather than ill intent, teams are more likely to engage in constructive discussions, improve their practices, and ultimately deliver better products.

Best Practices and Guidelines

Assume good intentions: Don’t jump to conclusions about malice; first consider that mistakes or issues might stem from lack of knowledge or simple error.

Focus on root causes: Look for underlying systemic issues (e.g., communication gaps or lack of training) rather than assigning blame to individuals.

Encourage open communication: Foster a culture where team members can admit mistakes without fear of negative judgment, leading to quicker resolution and learning.

Prioritize collaboration over criticism: Address problems as a team, emphasizing problem-solving over assigning fault.

Promote continuous improvement: Use mistakes as learning opportunities to improve processes, tooling, and knowledge sharing across teams.

Common Misconceptions and Pitfalls

- Overlooking genuine malice: While Hanlon's Razor suggests assuming ignorance over malice, it can sometimes downplay situations where deliberate harm or sabotage does occur, especially in toxic environments.
- Ignoring recurring issues: Repeated mistakes may lead to the misconception that poor practices are simply due to "stupidity," when they may actually be symptoms of deeper, systemic problems that need addressing.
- Overlooking accountability: Applying Hanlon's Razor too broadly can lead to neglecting necessary accountability for persistent or easily preventable errors, especially in senior roles.
- Underestimating complexity: Mistakes may be more complicated than just incompetence, with factors like organizational constraints or poorly designed systems contributing to errors, which may be overlooked by focusing solely on human error.
- Enabling complacency: Relying too heavily on the "stupidity" explanation might prevent teams from critically assessing their processes and improving them, leading to a culture of complacency rather than proactive learning.

Related Concepts

1. Murphy's Law: Anything that can go wrong, will go wrong
2. Occam's Razor: Simplest explanation is usually correct
3. Conway's Law: Organizations design systems that mirror their communication structure
4. Peter Principle: In a hierarchy, every employee tends to rise to their level of incompetence

References

- Wikipedia, *Hanlon's razor*, [pub: 18 Dec 2024, cited: 3 Jan 2025]

The Law of the Instrument: When you have a hammer, everything looks like a nail

Definition and Origin

The Law of the Instrument, also known as "Maslow's Hammer," is a cognitive bias where individuals rely too heavily on a familiar tool or method, even when it may not be the most appropriate for the situation. It suggests that people tend to apply solutions or approaches they are comfortable with, rather than considering alternative, potentially more effective options. The phrase is often summarized as: "If all you have is a hammer, everything looks like a nail."

The Law of the Instrument was coined by the psychologist Abraham Maslow in 1966. He introduced the concept in a paper titled "The Psychology of Science," where he illustrated how people tend to over-rely on familiar tools or methods, even when they may not be the best fit for the problem at hand.

Context and Importance

In the context of software and technology, the Law of the Instrument highlights a common pitfall in problem-solving and decision-making. Developers and engineers often rely on familiar tools, programming languages, or frameworks simply because they are comfortable with them, even if these tools are not the best fit for a given task. For example, a developer who is proficient in a particular language like JavaScript might attempt to use it for all aspects of a project, even if a different language, such as Python or Go, would provide better performance, scalability, or ease of development. This over-reliance on a preferred tool can lead to inefficient solutions, technical debt, and missed opportunities to leverage more suitable technologies for specific challenges.

The importance of recognizing the Law of the Instrument in technology lies in the potential for innovation and optimization. By acknowledging the bias toward familiar tools, software professionals can more critically assess the requirements of a given problem and choose the most appropriate technologies, frameworks, or methodologies. This mindset encourages experimentation with new tools and approaches, fostering innovation and leading to more efficient, scalable, and maintainable solutions. For instance, while one might be inclined to use an existing monolithic architecture because of familiarity, recognizing when microservices or serverless architectures might be a better fit could significantly enhance system performance and agility. Avoiding the trap of the Law of the Instrument ultimately enables teams to build better products and stay adaptable in a rapidly evolving tech landscape.

Best Practices and Guidelines

Evaluate the problem, not just the tool: Assess the specific requirements of a task before selecting the technology or methodology to ensure it's the best fit.

Stay open to new technologies: Regularly explore and learn about new tools, frameworks, or languages that may offer more efficient or scalable solutions.

Avoid over-reliance on familiarity: Challenge the comfort of familiar tools by considering alternatives that may provide better performance or flexibility for the project.

Prioritize adaptability: Choose technologies that can evolve with future needs rather than focusing solely on short-term convenience or ease of use.

Encourage cross-disciplinary knowledge: Foster a culture of collaboration and knowledge-sharing within teams to broaden the collective understanding of available tools and methods.

Common Misconceptions and Pitfalls

- Assuming familiarity equals efficiency: Relying on known tools doesn't guarantee optimal solutions; what’s familiar may not always be the best choice for the task.

- Overlooking scalability and long-term needs: Focusing on immediate comfort with a tool can neglect future scalability or maintainability requirements.
- Neglecting performance trade-offs: A preferred tool may work well in certain cases but introduce bottlenecks or inefficiencies in others, especially as the project grows.
- Ignoring newer, more specialized tools: Sticking with a familiar stack can prevent teams from adopting more modern or specialized technologies that better address current challenges.
- Believing "one size fits all": Not every problem requires the same solution—what works for one project or domain may not be appropriate for another.

Related Concepts

1. YAGNI: You Aren't Gonna Need It - Yet
2. Hofstadter's Law: It always takes longer than you expect
3. Occam's Razor: Simplest explanation is usually correct
4. Parkinson's Law: Work expands to fill the time available for its completion.
5. Mythical Man-Month: You can't exchange time and people linearly

References

- Wikipedia, *Law of the instrument*, [pub: 19 Sep 2024, cited: 3 Jan 2025]

Mencken Razor: For every complex problem, there is a solution that is simple, clear, and wrong

---

Definition and Origin

Mencken's Razor is a principle that suggests, "For every complex problem, there is a solution that is simple, clear, and wrong." It highlights the tendency to oversimplify complex issues and the risk of adopting misleading or incorrect explanations.

Mencken's Razor is attributed to the American journalist and social critic H.L. Mencken. While he didn't explicitly coin the term in his writings, it is a paraphrase of his perspective on human nature and problem-solving. Mencken often expressed skepticism toward overly simplistic explanations of complex issues, which is captured by the essence of the razor.

Context and Importance

In the context of software and technology, Mencken's Razor serves as a cautionary principle against the temptation to oversimplify complex systems or challenges. The world of technology is inherently intricate, with multiple variables, interdependencies, and ever-evolving constraints. In software development, for example, solutions that appear straightforward—such as "just add more resources" to solve performance problems—often overlook the deeper underlying issues, like inefficient algorithms, poor architecture, or improper data management. Mencken's Razor reminds developers and technologists that while simple answers are appealing, they often fail to account for the full scope of complexity involved, leading to solutions that may be "wrong" or incomplete in the long run.

The importance of Mencken's Razor also extends to the design and implementation of technology systems. In a fast-moving industry driven by rapid innovation, there's often pressured to deliver quick fixes or launch products with simplified solutions to meet deadlines or market demands. However, this can lead to technical debt, security vulnerabilities, and a lack of scalability. By embracing the spirit of Mencken's Razor, software engineers and technologists are encouraged to adopt a more nuanced approach—one that recognizes complexity and seeks well-thought-out, comprehensive solutions rather than settling for easy fixes. This mindset ultimately fosters more sustainable, robust, and resilient technology systems that can evolve and adapt as needed.

Best Practices and Guidelines

Avoid oversimplification: Recognize that complex technical issues rarely have easy, one-size-fits-all solutions.

Dig deeper: Don't settle for surface-level explanations—investigate underlying causes and consider all factors.

Prioritize thoroughness over speed: Resist the urge for quick, simplistic fixes that may overlook long-term impacts.

Embrace complexity: Build solutions that account for future scalability, performance, and maintainability, rather than relying on quick hacks.

Question assumptions: Challenge overly simplistic models and encourage critical thinking to identify potential flaws or missing elements.

Common Misconceptions and Pitfalls

- Assuming more resources = better performance: Simply adding hardware or infrastructure can mask deeper issues like inefficient code or poor architecture.
- Favoring quick fixes over long-term solutions: Rushed decisions often lead to technical debt, making future development harder and more expensive.
- Overlooking edge cases: Simplified solutions often ignore less obvious or rare scenarios, leading to broken systems under certain conditions.
- Believing user-friendly = simple backend: Easy-to-use interfaces don't guarantee robust, efficient systems behind the scenes.
- Neglecting testing and validation: Relying on assumptions rather than rigorous testing can result in faulty or unreliable software.

Related Concepts

1. Murphy's Law: Anything that can go wrong, will go wrong
2. Occam's Razor: Simplest explanation is usually correct
3. Spolsky's Law of Leaky Abstractions: All non-trivial abstractions, to some degree, are leaky
4. Brooks's Law: Adding manpower to a late project makes it later
5. Conway's Law: Organizations design systems that mirror their communication structure

References

- Wikiquote, *H. L. Mencken*, [pub: 8 Nov 2024, cited: 3 Jan 2025]

Occam's Razor: Simplest explanation is usually correct

Definition and Origin

Occam's Razor is a problem-solving principle that suggests when faced with competing hypotheses or explanations, the one with the fewest assumptions should be preferred. In other words, the simplest solution, often with the least complexity, is usually the correct one.

Occam's Razor is attributed to the 14th-century English philosopher and theologian William of Ockham. While he did not explicitly state the principle in the form we use today, his writings advocated for simplicity in explanations. The idea is often summarized by his phrase "Entia non sunt multiplicanda sine necessitate," which means "Entities should not be multiplied beyond necessity."

Context and Importance

In the context of software development and technology, Occam's Razor encourages simplicity in design and problem-solving. Developers often face complex problems, and it can be tempting to implement intricate solutions with numerous features or overly complicated architectures. However, adhering to Occam's Razor means striving for minimalism—focusing on the core requirements and avoiding unnecessary features or complex code that might increase the potential for bugs, maintenance challenges, and technical debt. A simpler, more straightforward solution is not only easier to understand and implement but also tends to be more robust, as it reduces the surface area for errors and allows for easier testing, debugging, and iteration.

Occam's Razor also plays a crucial role in system architecture and decision-making. In rapidly evolving fields like software development, where time-to-market and adaptability are key, unnecessarily convoluted systems can quickly become a liability. By adopting simpler, more efficient designs, teams can more easily pivot, scale, or integrate new technologies without being encumbered by overly complicated frameworks or architectures. Ultimately, following Occam's Razor in technology leads to more maintainable, agile systems that can evolve with changing requirements, providing long-term benefits over more complex alternatives.

Best Practices and Guidelines

Simplify Design: Prioritize straightforward, clear designs over complex, feature-heavy solutions.

Minimize Dependencies: Reduce reliance on external libraries or frameworks unless absolutely necessary.

Focus on Core Functionality: Implement only the essential features needed to meet user requirements.

Avoid Overengineering: Resist the urge to add unnecessary features or complexities that don't directly add value.

Iterate and Refactor: Start simple, then refine and improve incrementally based on real-world feedback.

Common Misconceptions and Pitfalls

- Oversimplifying Complex Problems: Mistaking simplicity for a lack of sophistication, leading to under-designed solutions that miss important requirements.
- Ignoring Scalability: Believing simple solutions are always the best without considering how they might scale or evolve over time.
- Avoiding Necessary Complexity: Over-applying Occam's Razor and avoiding complexity even when it's essential for handling edge cases or long-term maintainability.
- Sacrificing Performance for Simplicity: Opting for overly simple solutions that might compromise performance or efficiency in larger systems.
- Misinterpreting Minimalism: Confusing simplicity with cutting corners—leading to poor user experience or insufficient functionality in the name of simplicity.

Related Concepts

1. KISS: Keep It Simple, Stupid
2. YAGNI: You Aren't Gonna Need It - Yet
3. Law of Demeter: Only talk to your immediate friends

4. Pareto Principle (80/20 Rule); Roughly, 80% of the value comes from 20% of the features.
5. Single Responsibility Principle (SRP): Part of SOLID, a module should have only one responsibility

References

- Wikipedia, *Occam's razor*, [pub: 30 Dec 2024, cited: 3 Jan 2025]

Q. Organizational Dynamics

The Allen Curve

Definition and Origin

The Allen Curve refers to a concept in organizational behavior that suggests a negative relationship between the physical distance between people in a workplace and the frequency of their communication. As the physical distance between individuals increases, the likelihood of communication decreases. It highlights the importance of proximity in fostering collaboration and interaction within teams or organizations.

The Allen Curve was coined by Thomas J. Allen, a professor of management at the Massachusetts Institute of Technology (MIT), in a 1977 paper titled "Managing the Flow of Technology." Allen conducted research on how the physical layout of office spaces affected communication and knowledge sharing in organizations. His findings led to the formulation of the Allen Curve, which quantifies the inverse relationship between physical distance and communication frequency.

Context and Importance

The Allen Curve has particular relevance in the context of software development and technology industries, where collaboration and the efficient exchange of information are critical for innovation and productivity. In these fields, teams often work on complex projects that require constant communication and coordination, whether for coding, debugging, or problem-solving. The Allen Curve suggests that physical proximity can greatly enhance the frequency and quality of interactions among team members, fostering faster decision-making, better problem resolution, and a more cohesive development process. In environments where cross-functional teams, such as developers, designers, and product managers, must collaborate closely, the Allen Curve highlights how spatial arrangements can either promote or hinder communication and knowledge transfer.

In today's increasingly digital and distributed work environments, the relevance of the Allen Curve extends to virtual spaces as well. With the rise of remote work and the use of digital collaboration tools, companies have had to adapt the principles of proximity and communication to virtual settings. While physical distance no longer applies in the same way, the spatial metaphors inherent in digital platforms (such as virtual "office" layouts, channels for communication, and collaborative tools) can still influence interaction dynamics. The Allen Curve's principles are used to design better virtual collaboration strategies—ensuring that teams, even when geographically dispersed, maintain high levels of interaction and engagement. In software and tech industries, where innovation depends heavily on the free flow of ideas and rapid iterations, understanding and applying the Allen Curve's insights can help organizations optimize their team structures, office layouts, and communication strategies for better outcomes.

Best Practices and Guidelines

Foster Proximity: Arrange teams in close physical or virtual proximity to encourage spontaneous communication and collaboration, especially for cross-functional teams working on complex tasks.

Leverage Collaboration Tools: Use digital tools (e.g., Slack, Microsoft Teams, or project management software) to simulate the benefits of proximity, ensuring easy access for team members to interact and share ideas quickly.

Encourage Open Office Layouts: In physical spaces, adopt open office designs or co-working spaces that reduce barriers and facilitate informal interactions, boosting communication frequency.

Facilitate Regular Check-ins: Implement frequent stand-ups, sprint reviews, or virtual "coffee chats" to maintain consistent communication across dispersed teams.

Design for Flexibility: Adapt work environments (both physical and digital) to allow for dynamic, impromptu collaboration, which mirrors the benefits of physical proximity in fostering innovation.

Common Misconceptions and Pitfalls

- Assuming Proximity Equals Productivity: Simply placing team members close together doesn’t guarantee increased productivity or communication—other factors like team culture, task complexity, and individual working styles play a significant role.
- Neglecting Remote Team Dynamics: The Allen Curve is based on physical proximity, but its principles can be misapplied in virtual teams without considering the unique challenges of remote communication, such as time zones and the over-reliance on digital tools.
- Overcrowding Workspaces: In an attempt to encourage proximity, overcrowding workspaces or forcing constant interaction can lead to distractions, burnout, and reduced focus, counteracting the benefits of the Allen Curve.
- Ignoring Informal Communication: Focusing solely on structured communication channels or office layouts without facilitating informal, spontaneous conversations (e.g., virtual "water cooler" chats) can miss a critical element of the Allen Curve's effectiveness.
- One-size-fits-all Approach: Misapplying the Allen Curve by assuming all teams benefit equally from proximity; the needs of highly specialized or independent roles may require different spatial arrangements than collaborative development teams.

Related Concepts

1. Brooks's Law: Adding manpower to a late project makes it later
2. Conway's Law: Organizations design systems that mirror their communication structure
3. Two Pizza Rule: Team should be small enough that it can be fed with two pizzas

References

- Wikipedia, *Allen curve*, [pub: 7 Jul 2023, cited: 3 Jan 2025]

Gresham's Law of Programming

Definition and Origin

Gresham's Law is an economic principle that states, "bad money drives out good money." It means that when two forms of currency with the same nominal value are in circulation, the one perceived as less valuable (or of inferior quality) will be used for transactions, while the more valuable (or higher quality) currency tends to be hoarded or withdrawn from circulation.

Gresham's Law is named after Sir Thomas Gresham, a 16th-century English financier and advisor to Queen Elizabeth I. However, the concept itself was not originally coined by Gresham. The principle was first articulated by Gresham's contemporaries, but it became associated with him due to his involvement in advising the queen on monetary matters. The law was later formalized by economists in the 19th century, particularly in the works of economist Henry Dunning Macleod.

Context and Importance

Gresham's Law can be applied to the field of software and technology, especially when considering the relationship between competing technologies or systems. In a market where multiple technologies coexist, the "bad" or less efficient one can drive out superior alternatives if it is more widely adopted, easier to use, or more aggressively marketed. For example, in the early days of computing, certain programming languages, operating systems, or software standards gained dominance not necessarily because they were the most technically advanced, but because they were more accessible or had better commercial backing. This phenomenon can be seen in the widespread adoption of less technically sophisticated systems that become entrenched due to network effects or vendor lock-in, even though superior options may be available.

The importance of Gresham's Law in software and technology lies in its impact on innovation, competition, and market dynamics. When "bad" technology becomes dominant, it can hinder progress by preventing better solutions from gaining traction. This stifles innovation and locks users into outdated or suboptimal systems. For example, the dominance of a specific programming language or software ecosystem may discourage developers from adopting new, more efficient tools, slowing the overall evolution of the industry. Understanding Gresham's Law in this context encourages companies and developers to recognize the long-term benefits of adopting superior technologies and striving to create environments that reward quality, interoperability, and innovation over convenience or market share dominance alone.

Best Practices and Guidelines

Prioritize Quality over Convenience: Choose and promote technologies that offer long-term benefits, even if they require more initial effort or investment.

Encourage Open Standards: Support open-source and open-standards solutions to prevent lock-in to inferior proprietary systems.

Foster Innovation: Invest in and adopt emerging technologies that improve efficiency and functionality, rather than sticking to outdated solutions due to familiarity.

Monitor Market Dynamics: Be aware of how market forces and user preferences may lead to the dominance of suboptimal technologies and actively advocate for better alternatives.

Educate Stakeholders: Ensure that developers, decision-makers, and users understand the risks of adopting "bad" technologies, and emphasize the importance of selecting tools based on their technical merits.

Common Misconceptions and Pitfalls

- Assuming Popularity Equals Quality: Just because a technology is widely adopted doesn't mean it's the best choice; market dominance can result from factors like marketing, convenience, or legacy systems.

- Overlooking Long-Term Impact: Short-term cost savings or ease of adoption may lead to the use of inferior technologies that become costly or inefficient in the long run.
- Ignoring Network Effects: Relying too heavily on dominant, suboptimal technologies can perpetuate their use, even when better alternatives exist, due to entrenched user bases and ecosystem dependencies.
- Underestimating the Role of Innovation: Focusing too much on "safe" choices (e.g., well-established tools) may prevent companies from exploring or investing in new technologies that could be more efficient or scalable.
- Falling into Vendor Lock-In: Committing to proprietary, less flexible platforms can trap businesses in a cycle of using outdated or inferior technologies due to switching costs or integration challenges.

Related Concepts

1. Conway's Law: Organizations design systems that mirror their communication structure
2. Spolsky's Law of Leaky Abstractions: All non-trivial abstractions, to some degree, are leaky
3. Principle of Least Astonishment: Software should behave in a way that users find intuitive and expected
4. Pareto Principle (80/20 Rule); Roughly, 80% of the value comes from 20% of the features

References

- Wikipedia, *Gresham's law*, [pub: 20 Dec 2024, cited: 3 Jan 2025]

Joy's Law

Definition and Origin

Joy's Law states that "most of the smart people work for someone else." It highlights the idea that innovative talent and technical expertise are often found outside of a company, and that organizations should look beyond their own walls to find valuable ideas and solutions. The law is named after Bill Joy, co-founder of Sun Microsystems, who expressed this insight about the challenges of innovation in the tech industry.

Joy's Law was coined by Bill Joy, co-founder of Sun Microsystems. He expressed this idea in the 1990s, suggesting that valuable talent and innovation often reside outside a company or organization. This observation became an influential insight in the tech industry and beyond, underscoring the importance of collaboration and external talent.

Context and Importance

Joy's Law holds particular significance in the realms of software and technology, where innovation and development are often driven by the collaboration and contributions of talented individuals from various organizations. The law highlights a crucial insight into the fast-evolving tech landscape: no single company, no matter how large or successful, can monopolize all of the brightest minds. In industries characterized by rapid change, companies that limit their talent pool to internal resources risk missing out on critical advancements. Joy's Law thus underscores the importance of tapping into external expertise, whether through open-source projects, partnerships, or acquisitions, to remain competitive and innovative.

In the context of software development, Joy's Law also speaks to the growing importance of community-driven innovation. The success of open-source software is a direct reflection of this idea—projects like Linux, Apache, and Mozilla Firefox have demonstrated that a diverse, global community of developers can produce high-quality, cutting-edge technology far more effectively than a single organization could. By embracing external collaboration and recognizing the value of contributions from individuals working outside the corporate sphere, companies can leverage a much broader pool of ideas, ensuring that their products stay at the forefront of technological advancement. Ultimately, Joy's Law serves as a reminder that fostering a culture of openness and external collaboration is key to driving progress in the software and technology sectors.

Best Practices and Guidelines

Leverage Open-Source Communities: Encourage participation in and contribution to open-source projects to tap into global innovation and diverse expertise.

Foster External Collaboration: Build partnerships with universities, startups, and other organizations to access fresh ideas and specialized knowledge.

Outsource Innovation: Consider collaborating with external contractors or consultants to solve niche technical challenges or drive specialized development.

Encourage Cross-Industry Talent: Actively seek talent from outside your immediate industry to bring new perspectives and approaches to your technology stack.

Adopt a Culture of Knowledge Sharing: Create an internal culture that values learning from external sources and fosters the integration of external ideas into internal development processes.

Common Misconceptions and Pitfalls

- Overestimating In-House Expertise: Assuming that internal teams have all the answers can limit innovation and overlook external, specialized knowledge.
- Underestimating External Collaboration Complexity: Failing to recognize the logistical, legal, and communication challenges that come with working with external contributors or organizations.
- Ignoring Diverse Talent Pools: Relying too heavily on hiring from within the same geographic or industry pool, missing out on diverse perspectives and expertise.
- Overreliance on Open Source: Believing that open-source solutions can always meet specific needs, without considering the limitations or the need for customization.
- Fear of Losing Competitive Advantage: Misconstruing external collaboration as a threat to intellectual property or competitive advantage, leading to overly restrictive or closed innovation strategies.

Related Concepts

1. Linus's Law: Given enough eyeballs, all bugs are shallow
2. Conway's Law: Organizations design systems that mirror their communication structure
3. Parkinson's Law: Work expands to fill the time available for its completion.
4. Spolsky's Law of Leaky Abstractions: All non-trivial abstractions, to some degree, are leaky

References

- Wikipedia, *Joy's law (management)*, [pub: 29 Aug 2024, cited: 3 Jan 2025]

Larman's Laws

Definition and Origin

Craig Larman's Laws are a set of principles aimed at guiding software development practices, particularly in the context of object-oriented design and agile methodologies. They emphasize simplicity, incremental development, and communication. The laws highlight that design decisions should prioritize flexibility, keep complexity manageable, and avoid premature optimization. Some key laws include:

1. Law of Leanness: Focus on delivering only the necessary features.
2. Law of Simplicity: Strive for simple, clear, and understandable designs.
3. Law of Iteration: Embrace frequent iterations and refactoring to adapt to evolving requirements.
4. Law of Communication: Foster constant communication between developers, stakeholders, and users to ensure alignment and shared understanding.

These principles support agile approaches like Scrum or Extreme Programming (XP) by emphasizing adaptability and continuous improvement.

Larman's Laws were coined by Craig Larman, a well-known software engineer and author, primarily recognized for his work in agile development and object-oriented design. He introduced these laws to guide practitioners in applying agile principles and best practices, particularly within object-oriented design and iterative development frameworks. His work, especially in the context of Agile methodologies and UML (Unified Modeling Language), advocates for simplicity, continuous improvement, and effective communication in software development.

Larman's Laws are often found in his books, such as Agile and Iterative Development: A Manager's Guide and Applying UML and Patterns.

Context and Importance

Larman's Laws are a set of guiding principles that have gained significant importance in the context of modern software development, particularly within agile methodologies and object-oriented design. The principles emphasize simplicity, continuous feedback, and iterative improvement, which are crucial in today's fast-paced, ever-evolving technology landscape. In a world where requirements often change rapidly and unpredictably, these laws advocate for flexibility, modularity, and constant communication with stakeholders. By focusing on simplicity and incremental development, Larman's Laws help developers avoid overengineering and complex solutions that may not deliver value in the long term. The emphasis on iteration and refactoring allows teams to adapt and improve the design of software as new insights emerge, ensuring that systems evolve in alignment with user needs and business goals.

The importance of Larman's Laws in software and technology lies in their ability to address common challenges such as scope creep, technical debt, and communication breakdowns. These principles encourage teams to break down large, monolithic designs into smaller, manageable pieces, enabling faster delivery and more responsive adjustments. The Law of Simplicity, for instance, urges developers to prioritize clear and straightforward designs, which leads to easier maintenance and better long-term scalability. By embedding these practices into everyday development processes, organizations can reduce the risk of building overly complex systems and can more effectively deliver high-quality, value-driven software. Ultimately, Larman's Laws help bridge the gap between theory and practice, making agile principles more tangible and actionable in the context of real-world development challenges.

Best Practices and Guidelines

Prioritize Simplicity: Aim for simple, clear designs that are easy to understand, maintain, and extend over time.

Iterate Continuously: Embrace regular feedback and refactor frequently to improve design and adapt to changing requirements.

Minimize Complexity: Avoid overengineering and focus on delivering only what's necessary, reducing unnecessary features and technical debt.

Collaborate Frequently: Foster open communication between developers, stakeholders, and users to ensure alignment and shared understanding.

Embrace Change: Design systems to be flexible and adaptable, allowing for easy modifications as new information and needs arise.

Common Misconceptions and Pitfalls

- Misunderstanding Simplicity: Believing simplicity means cutting corners or avoiding necessary design depth, leading to overly simplistic solutions that are hard to scale or evolve.
- Premature Optimization: Focusing too much on optimizing performance early in development, rather than prioritizing simple, working solutions and iterating based on real user feedback.

- Ignoring Refactoring: Skipping regular refactoring in favor of quick, unrefined solutions that lead to technical debt and increased long-term complexity.
- Overloading Communication: Assuming that frequent communication is always the key, but failing to ensure that discussions are focused, productive, and actionable.
- Over-Designing for Future Needs: Designing overly complex systems based on speculative future requirements, rather than focusing on current needs and iterating as requirements evolve.

Related Concepts

1. SOLID Principles
2. YAGNI: You Aren't Gonna Need It - Yet
3. Law of Demeter: Only talk to your immediate friends
4. Pareto Principle (80/20 Rule); Roughly, 80% of the value comes from 20% of the features.

References

- Wikipedia, *Craig Larman*, [pub: 19 Nov 2024, cited: 3 Jan 2025]

Rothbard's Law

Definition and Origin

Rothbard's Law broadly states, "The more a government interferes in an economy, the more inefficient and distorted that economy becomes." Essentially, it suggests that as governments increase inflationary measures, people will increasingly find ways to protect their wealth, whether through alternative currencies, asset diversification, or other strategies to preserve purchasing power. This concept reflects economist Murray Rothbard's views on the unintended consequences of inflationary policies.

Rothbard's Law was coined by economist Murray Rothbard himself. It is based on his observations and writings about the relationship between government inflationary policies and the public's response to them. Rothbard was a prominent figure in the Austrian School of economics, and he explored this idea within his broader critiques of government intervention in markets and monetary systems.

Context and Importance

Rothbard's Law, when applied to the world of software and technology, provides valuable insight into how technological innovation often arises as a response to government-imposed inflationary policies, particularly in areas like digital currency and decentralized systems. Just as Rothbard argued that inflation prompts people to seek alternatives to traditional financial systems, the rise of cryptocurrencies like Bitcoin can be seen as a direct consequence of excessive government control over money supply. In this context, inflationary policies often erode public trust in central banks and fiat currencies, spurring the development of alternative digital solutions that operate outside the purview of central authorities. These innovations align with Rothbard's view that the more governments inflate, the more individuals and businesses will look for technological means to circumvent or protect against such policies.

Moreover, Rothbard's Law highlights how software and technology can serve as tools for autonomy in the face of increasing state interference. As governments expand surveillance and control over digital platforms, technological advancements like encryption, decentralized finance (DeFi), and blockchain-based applications offer a way for individuals to regain control over their personal data, transactions, and financial systems. In this light, the emergence of technologies such as peer-to-peer networks, open-source software, and privacy-focused communication tools represents a response to the very economic and regulatory pressures that Rothbard described. The law underscores the adaptability of human ingenuity and the capacity of technology to circumvent or neutralize the negative effects of inflationary policies, empowering individuals to navigate and protect their economic and digital freedoms.

Best Practices and Guidelines

Promote Decentralization: Design systems that minimize reliance on central authorities, ensuring greater resilience against inflationary and regulatory pressures.

Prioritize Privacy: Develop technologies that protect user data and ensure financial autonomy, reflecting the need for individuals to evade government surveillance and control.

Encourage Open-Source Innovation: Support transparent, community-driven projects to create alternatives to centralized software and platforms, fostering innovation and circumventing monopolistic practices.

Integrate Cryptographic Solutions: Implement encryption and secure technologies to safeguard transactions and communications from inflation-driven financial instability.

Adapt to Evolving Regulations: Stay agile by building flexible systems that can quickly adapt to shifting government policies, preserving user autonomy even in the face of increased intervention.

Common Misconceptions and Pitfalls

- Underestimating the Impact of Regulation: Assuming that technological solutions like encryption or decentralization will always be immune to government intervention can lead to overconfidence in their effectiveness.
- Overlooking User Adoption: Believing that people will automatically adopt new technologies in response to inflationary policies can ignore the barriers to entry, such as lack of awareness or technical expertise.
- Neglecting Scalability: Assuming that decentralized or alternative systems can easily scale without centralized infrastructure can lead to performance bottlenecks or operational challenges.
- Ignoring Network Effects: Focusing solely on technology's ability to circumvent inflation, without considering the importance of widespread network adoption (e.g., in cryptocurrencies or decentralized platforms), can limit their success.

- Overlooking Security Risks: While decentralization offers freedom, it can also expose users to greater risks if security is not properly implemented, as there's no central authority to oversee protections.

Related Concepts

1. Moore's Law: Computing power doubles approximately every two years
2. Metcalfe's Law: Network value grows with square of users
3. Linus's Law: Given enough eyeballs, all bugs are shallow

References

- Wikipedia, *Murray Rothbard*, [pub: 31 Dec 2024, cited: 3 Jan 2025]

Sayre's Law

Definition and Origin

Sayre's Law is a humorous adage that states: "In any dispute, the intensity of feeling is inversely proportional to the value of the issues at stake." In other words, small or trivial issues often provoke disproportionately intense arguments.

Sayre's Law was coined by political scientist Wallace Stanley Sayre in the mid-20th century. He used it to describe the dynamics of university politics, where relatively minor disputes can lead to heated and disproportionate conflicts. The phrase became more widely known after it was popularized beyond academia.

Context and Importance

In the context of software development and technology, Sayre's Law highlights the tendency for minor technical disagreements or issues to escalate into prolonged, passionate disputes, especially when the underlying stakes seem relatively low. This phenomenon is particularly noticeable in open-source communities, software teams, or tech forums where developers and engineers, often with strong opinions about coding practices, design patterns, or frameworks, can engage in intense debates over topics like programming languages, version control strategies, or user interface aesthetics. For example, discussions about which programming language or tool is the "best" for a particular task can sometimes become all-consuming, despite the fact that the practical difference may be minimal in terms of overall project success. Sayre's Law reminds us that, in these environments, the emotional investment in such arguments often outweighs the actual value of the issue being debated.

The importance of understanding Sayre's Law in the tech world lies in its potential to foster better communication and collaboration. Recognizing that trivial issues can trigger disproportionate reactions helps to mitigate conflict and refocus attention on the larger goals, such as product development, user experience, and innovation. It encourages teams to adopt a more pragmatic approach, focusing on finding the most effective solution rather than getting caught in endless debates over relatively insignificant details. In a field where collaboration and adaptability are key, Sayre's Law serves as a reminder to manage emotions, avoid unnecessary distractions, and ensure that disagreements do not derail progress.

Best Practices and Guidelines

Focus on Outcomes: Prioritize solutions that move the project forward rather than getting bogged down in trivial disagreements.

Keep Discussions Objective: Separate personal preferences from technical requirements to avoid unnecessary emotional investment in minor issues.

Limit Scope of Debates: Set clear boundaries for discussions to ensure they remain productive and relevant to the problem at hand.

Encourage Empathy and Respect: Understand that diverse perspectives exist, and disagreements should be resolved constructively, not combatively.

Resolve Quickly, Move On: If a disagreement is unlikely to impact the project significantly, acknowledge it and refocus on the larger goals.

Common Misconceptions and Pitfalls

- Overvaluing Small Disagreements: Treating trivial technical arguments as if they are crucial can waste time and energy that could be spent on more impactful tasks.
- Equating Passion with Importance: Just because a topic sparks heated debate doesn't mean it's the most critical issue to the project's success.
- Ignoring Bigger Picture: Focusing too much on minor technical details can distract from the overall project goals, such as user needs and functionality.
- Perpetuating "Us vs. Them" Mentality: Engaging in personal or ideological conflicts over minor tech choices can divide teams and hinder collaboration.
- Delaying Decisions: Allowing small issues to linger unresolved can create unnecessary delays, especially when consensus isn't critical for progress.

Related Concepts

1. Brooks's Law: Adding manpower to a late project makes it later
2. Conway's Law: Organizations design systems that mirror their communication structure
3. Parkinson's Law: Work expands to fill the time available for its completion.
4. Pareto Principle (80/20 Rule); Roughly, 80% of the value comes from 20% of the features.
5. Linus's Law: Given enough eyeballs, all bugs are shallow

References

- Wikipedia, Sayre's law, [pub: 11 Jul 2024, cited: 3 Jan 2025]

R. Quality & Standards

Crosby's Laws of Quality

Definition and Origin

Crosby's Laws of Quality, often referred to as Crosby's Quality Management Principles, focus on improving quality within organizations. The key principles are:

1. Quality is Free: The cost of achieving quality is less than the cost of failing to achieve it.
2. Conformance to Requirements: Quality means meeting the specified requirements, not exceeding them.
3. Prevention over Inspection: Preventing defects through process improvement is more cost-effective than detecting them after they occur.
4. Zero Defects: Strive for perfection by aiming for zero defects in all processes.
5. The Price of Non-Conformance: The costs associated with not meeting quality standards (rework, loss of reputation, etc.) are significantly higher than the costs of achieving quality.

These laws emphasize that quality is a management responsibility and should be embedded in every aspect of an organization.

Crosby's Laws of Quality were coined by Philip Crosby, an American quality management expert. He introduced these principles in his 1979 book "Quality is Free: The Art of Making Quality Certain." Crosby was a major proponent of quality management and is well-known for advocating the idea that quality should be understood as an integral part of business operations, and that poor quality leads to higher costs in the long run. His approach emphasized the importance of prevention, cost-effective quality processes, and continuous improvement.

Context and Importance

In the context of software development and technology, Crosby's Laws of Quality are highly relevant, particularly as the industry moves toward agile methodologies and continuous delivery. Software projects often face the challenge of maintaining high quality while managing rapid change and tight deadlines. Crosby's first principle, "Quality is Free," is especially important in this realm, where investing in quality early—through robust testing, code reviews, and automated tools—can save significant time and resources later by avoiding expensive debugging, patching, and customer dissatisfaction. In software development, the costs of poor quality can snowball into severe technical debt, customer churn, and reputational damage, making Crosby's assertion that the cost of quality is lower than the cost of non-conformance particularly pertinent.

Crosby's emphasis on prevention over inspection aligns perfectly with modern software practices like test-driven development (TDD), continuous integration (CI), and continuous deployment (CD). Instead of relying on late-stage quality checks (which can be costly and ineffective), these practices encourage quality to be built into the development process from the start. By adhering to Crosby's principle of "Zero Defects," development teams strive to write clean, error-free code and automate as many testing procedures as possible to catch issues early. This proactive mindset ensures that software products are robust, reliable, and capable of meeting user requirements without costly post-launch fixes. In the competitive and fast-paced technology industry, adopting Crosby's principles can lead to better product quality, increased customer satisfaction, and long-term cost savings.

Best Practices and Guidelines

Focus on Prevention: Build quality into the software from the start through practices like test-driven development (TDD) and continuous integration (CI), reducing the need for later defect detection.

Emphasize Conformance to Requirements: Ensure all software features and functionality meet clearly defined requirements to avoid over-engineering or unnecessary complexity.

Strive for Zero Defects: Aim for flawless code by adopting rigorous testing, peer reviews, and automated error-checking, ensuring minimal bugs and high reliability.

Measure Cost of Non-Conformance: Track and analyze the costs of fixing defects, customer complaints, and rework to highlight the financial benefits of maintaining high-quality standards.

Quality is Free: Invest in high-quality processes and tools up front (e.g., automation, code quality tools) to prevent long-term costs from defects, rework, and technical debt.

Common Misconceptions and Pitfalls

- Quality is not free: A common misconception is that quality costs nothing. In reality, upfront investments in tools, training, and process improvements are required, but these save costs in the long term by reducing defects and rework.
- Zero Defects is unrealistic: Some may interpret Zero Defects as perfection, leading to over-engineering or paralysis by analysis. The goal is to minimize defects as much as possible, not to expect absolute flawlessness.
- Inspection can replace prevention: Relying on late-stage testing and inspections rather than preventing defects early in the development process can lead to higher costs and inefficiencies, contradicting Crosby's emphasis on proactive quality.
- Conformance to requirements means minimal features: Conformance to requirements does not mean delivering the bare minimum or under-delivering; it means aligning the product precisely with customer needs and specifications without unnecessary features or complexity.
- Quality is solely the responsibility of QA: Quality is a shared responsibility across the entire development team, not just QA. Developers, designers, and project managers must all contribute to creating high-quality software.

Related Concepts

1. Pareto Principle (80/20 Rule); Roughly, 80% of the value comes from 20% of the features.
2. Law of Leaky Abstractions: All non-trivial abstractions, to some degree, are leaky
3. Brooks's Law: Adding manpower to a late project makes it later
4. Scout Rule: "Leave the code better than you found it"

References

- Wikipedia, *Philip B. Crosby*, [pub: 16 Oct 2024, cited: 3 Jan 2025]

Deming's 14 Points

Definition and Origin

Deming's 14 Points are a set of principles for transforming business practices and improving quality, developed by W. Edwards Deming. They focus on fostering a culture of continuous improvement, emphasizing the importance of leadership, collaboration, and a systematic approach to quality. The 14 Points are:

1. Create constancy of purpose towards improvement of products and services.
2. Adopt the new philosophy of quality and continuous improvement.
3. Cease dependence on inspection to achieve quality; build quality into the process.
4. End the practice of awarding business based on price alone; minimize total cost.
5. Improve constantly and forever every process for planning, production, and service.
6. Institute training on the job to enhance skills and knowledge.
7. Institute leadership to help people do their best work.
8. Drive out fear, so that everyone can work effectively.
9. Break down barriers between departments to improve collaboration.
10. Eliminate slogans, exhortations, and targets that drive suboptimization.
11. Eliminate numerical quotas for workers and managers; focus on quality.
12. Remove barriers to pride of workmanship and encourage meaningful work.
13. Institute a vigorous program of education and self-improvement for everyone.
14. Put everyone to work to accomplish the transformation with commitment from all levels.

These principles emphasize quality, collaboration, and leadership as key drivers of organizational success.

Deming's 14 Points were coined by W. Edwards Deming, an American statistician, professor, author, and consultant, who is widely regarded as one of the pioneers of quality management and continuous improvement. Deming developed these principles as part of his philosophy to help organizations improve productivity and quality, especially in the post-World War II era.

Deming introduced these points in his influential work with Japanese companies in the 1950s, which played a significant role in Japan's industrial recovery and growth. His ideas laid the foundation for what is now known as Total Quality Management (TQM) and have had a lasting impact on business and management practices worldwide.

Context and Importance

Deming's 14 Points, originally designed to improve quality in manufacturing and service industries, have become highly relevant in the context of software development and technology. In the rapidly evolving field of software, where changes are constant and customer expectations are high, Deming's emphasis on continuous improvement, systematic problem-solving, and collaboration is crucial. Many of his principles—such as "Create constancy of purpose" and "Improve constantly and forever"—align well with the iterative nature of modern software development methodologies like Agile. By applying Deming's focus on quality at every stage of the development process, from design through testing to deployment, software teams can deliver more reliable products, adapt quickly to customer feedback, and foster a culture of learning and innovation.

The principles of Deming's 14 Points also encourage a shift from traditional command-and-control management to a more collaborative, team-oriented approach in the technology sector. For instance, his point about eliminating barriers between departments promotes cross-functional teams, which are integral to successful Agile and DevOps practices. Similarly, "Drive out fear" encourages open communication, empowering team members to speak up about potential issues without fear of reprisal. In the context of software and technology, these principles help establish environments where creativity and problem-solving thrive, ultimately leading to better quality software, faster time-to-market, and a stronger ability to meet customer needs and expectations. Deming's focus on leadership and training also supports the development of highly skilled and motivated teams, which are essential for staying competitive in the tech industry.

Best Practices and Guidelines

Foster Continuous Improvement: Prioritize ongoing refinement of software and processes, embracing Agile, DevOps, and regular feedback loops to enhance product quality and user satisfaction.

Build Quality into the Process: Shift from post-development testing to integrating quality assurance at every stage, reducing defects through proactive design, automated testing, and code reviews.

Encourage Cross-Functional Collaboration: Break down silos between development, operations, and other teams to promote shared responsibility for quality and accelerate problem-solving.

Empower Teams and Eliminate Fear: Create a culture where team members feel safe to experiment, report issues, and contribute ideas without fear of blame or retribution.

Invest in Training and Leadership: Continuously develop skills, leadership capabilities, and knowledge for all team members to ensure adaptability and innovation in a fast-evolving tech landscape.

Common Misconceptions and Pitfalls

- Misinterpreting "Quality" as Just Bug-Free Code: Focusing solely on eliminating defects can overlook broader aspects of quality, such as usability, security, and performance, which are also crucial in software development.
- Overlooking the Importance of Leadership: Failing to emphasize the role of leadership in fostering a culture of continuous improvement, empowerment, and communication can hinder the successful implementation of Deming's principles.
- Misapplying "Constancy of Purpose" as Rigidity: Interpreting constancy of purpose as a strict adherence to initial goals without flexibility can lead to stagnation. Adaptation to changing customer needs and market conditions is essential in tech.
- Confusing "End the Practice of Inspection" with "No Testing": Some may misinterpret Deming's point on inspection to mean no testing. However, it's about building quality into processes rather than relying solely on inspection after the fact.
- Ignoring Cross-Functional Collaboration: Still operating in isolated silos between development, QA, and operations can undermine the effectiveness of Deming's principles, as collaboration is key to optimizing the entire software lifecycle.

Related Concepts

1. The Law of Continual Improvement (Kaizen): Improvement constantly and forever
2. Pareto Principle (80/20 Rule); Roughly, 80% of the value comes from 20% of the features.
3. Conway's Law: Organizations design systems that mirror their communication structure
4. Principle of Least Astonishment: Software should behave in a way that users find intuitive and expected

References

- Wikipedia, *W. Edwards Deming*, [pub: 28 Dec 2024, cited: 3 Jan 2025]

Juran's Quality Principles

Definition and Origin

Juran's Quality Principles are a set of guidelines that emphasize the importance of quality management in organizations. They focus on three key areas:

1. Quality Planning: Identifying customer needs and setting measurable goals to meet those needs.
2. Quality Control: Monitoring and measuring performance to ensure the process remains consistent and within established standards.
3. Quality Improvement: Continuously improving processes to enhance performance and achieve higher levels of customer satisfaction.

These principles emphasize the importance of a systematic approach to achieving and maintaining quality in products and services.

Juran's Quality Principles were coined by Joseph M. Juran, a pioneering figure in quality management. Juran was a key contributor to the development of modern quality control methods and is known for his work in promoting the concept of quality management at a strategic level. His principles, which include quality planning, quality control, and quality improvement, are central to his broader philosophy of managing quality throughout an organization. Juran's ideas were influential in shaping the field of quality management in the 20th century.

Context and Importance

In the context of software and technology, Juran's Quality Principles remain highly relevant as they provide a structured approach to ensure that products meet user expectations and function reliably. As software development increasingly becomes more complex, with frequent updates, multiple platforms, and a variety of user needs, these principles help guide organizations in delivering high-quality software consistently. Quality Planning, as outlined by Juran, is crucial in the tech industry where early-stage planning determines key requirements, features, and potential risks. By properly defining these elements from the start, software developers can prevent errors and minimize costly changes later in the development cycle. Quality Control also plays a pivotal role in ensuring that code, design, and architecture meet established standards through continuous testing, monitoring, and debugging to avoid defects. With fast release cycles in Agile and DevOps environments, quality control ensures that incremental changes do not compromise the overall system's stability.

Moreover, Quality Improvement in software and technology aligns with the industry’s focus on continuous iteration and enhancement, especially in the face of changing user demands and emerging technologies. Juran’s emphasis on improvement encourages teams to adopt a mindset of ongoing refinement—whether through feedback loops, user testing, or technical debt management. This focus on quality improvement also supports innovation, enabling organizations to evolve their products in response to both customer feedback and advancements in technology. By embedding Juran's principles into software development processes, companies can foster a culture of excellence, ensuring that their products not only meet current user needs but are also adaptable and resilient in the face of future challenges. Ultimately, these principles help tech organizations deliver high-quality, customer-centric software that drives long-term success.

Best Practices and Guidelines

Plan for Quality Early: Define clear requirements, customer needs, and measurable goals during the planning phase to ensure alignment with user expectations and minimize defects.

Implement Robust Quality Control: Continuously monitor, test, and validate software to maintain consistency, prevent regressions, and ensure adherence to quality standards throughout development cycles.

Focus on Continuous Improvement: Regularly assess processes and outcomes, gather user feedback, and refine software to address evolving needs and improve performance over time.

Involve All Stakeholders: Ensure collaboration between developers, testers, designers, and customers to foster shared ownership of quality across the entire development process.

Prioritize Root Cause Analysis: Address underlying causes of defects or failures systematically, rather than just fixing symptoms, to prevent recurring issues and improve software stability.

Common Misconceptions and Pitfalls

- Quality Is Only the Developer's Responsibility: Quality should be a shared responsibility across the entire team, including product managers, testers, and designers—not just developers.
- Testing Alone Ensures Quality: Quality requires more than just testing; it involves careful planning, design, and continuous improvement throughout the entire software lifecycle.
- Quality Control Is a One-Time Activity: Quality control should be ongoing, integrated into every stage of development, rather than seen as a final step before release.
- Fixing Defects in the Short Term Is Enough: Focusing only on fixing defects without addressing root causes may lead to recurring issues and technical debt, hindering long-term software quality.
- Improvement Happens Automatically: Continuous improvement requires active effort, regular reviews, and intentional adjustments, not just waiting for issues to resolve themselves over time.

Related Concepts

1. Brooks's Law: Adding manpower to a late project makes it later
2. Pareto Principle (80/20 Rule); Roughly, 80% of the value comes from 20% of the features.
3. Conway's Law: Organizations design systems that mirror their communication structure
4. Law of Leaky Abstractions: All non-trivial abstractions, to some degree, are leaky

References

- Wikipedia, *Quality by design*, [pub: 8 Sep 2024, cited: 3 Jan 2025]

Sturgeon's Law

Definition and Origin

Sturgeon's Law states that "90% of everything is crap." It suggests that the majority of works in any field, including art, literature, and entertainment, are of low quality, but the remaining 10% can be exceptional.

Sturgeon's Law was coined by science fiction writer Theodore Sturgeon in 1957. He was responding to critics of science fiction who dismissed the entire genre as "garbage." Sturgeon famously argued that, just like any other field, 90% of science fiction was indeed subpar, but the remaining 10% was valuable and worth recognizing.

Context and Importance

Sturgeon's Law is highly relevant to the world of software and technology, where the proliferation of tools, applications, and products often leads to an overwhelming quantity of low-quality or poorly designed offerings. In the tech industry, for every innovative, game-changing application or platform, there are countless others that fail to meet user needs, are riddled with bugs, or are simply poorly executed. This phenomenon is especially pronounced with the rise of app stores, open-source software, and the ease of digital development, which allows anyone to create and distribute software. Sturgeon's observation helps frame the reality that not all technologies or software are created equal, and users must sift through a large amount of "crap" to find the products and services that truly stand out.

The importance of Sturgeon's Law in software development and technology also lies in its reminder that quality is often the exception rather than the rule. It encourages both consumers and developers to set realistic expectations and avoid blanket judgments based on limited experiences. For developers, it suggests the value of persistence and refinement, emphasizing the need for rigorous testing, thoughtful design, and user-centric innovation. For consumers and businesses, it underlines the necessity of critical evaluation when selecting tools, technologies, or platforms. In both contexts, Sturgeon's Law calls attention to the importance of discernment, not only in recognizing the gems among the "crap" but also in acknowledging that even the best products require continuous improvement to maintain their value.

Best Practices and Guidelines

Prioritize Quality Over Quantity: Focus on identifying and adopting the top 10% of tools, platforms, and applications that meet high standards, rather than being overwhelmed by the vast array of options.

Iterate and Improve: Recognize that even successful software is rarely perfect initially; continuous refinement is key to improving product quality and staying relevant.

Conduct Rigorous Testing: Ensure thorough testing and validation to filter out poorly designed or faulty products, minimizing reliance on trial and error.

Embrace User Feedback: Actively collect and incorporate feedback to identify flaws, prioritize enhancements, and gauge the real-world value of a product.

Maintain Realistic Expectations: Accept that not every technology or software will meet your needs perfectly; patience and discernment are required to find the right solutions.

Common Misconceptions and Pitfalls

- Misconception: More options lead to better outcomes – Sturgeon's Law highlights that a large quantity of software or tech products doesn't necessarily mean higher quality; often, more choices result in a greater volume of mediocre or poorly executed solutions.

- Pitfall: Assuming all products are worth trying – With the abundance of software on the market, it's easy to assume that every new app or tool is potentially useful. In reality, most offerings fail to deliver long-term value or function as expected.
- Misconception: Innovation guarantees quality – Just because a product is new or uses cutting-edge technology doesn't mean it's well-built or effective. Innovation doesn't always equate to quality or reliability.
- Pitfall: Overconfidence in rapid development – The rush to release products quickly can lead to incomplete or unstable software. Sturgeon's Law reminds us that speed can often result in subpar quality if proper testing and refinement are skipped.
- Misconception: Popularity equals excellence – High download numbers or widespread adoption do not always reflect the quality of a software product. Popularity can be influenced by marketing, trends, or timing, not necessarily functionality or user experience.

Related Concepts

1. Murphy's Law: Anything that can go wrong, will go wrong
2. Pareto Principle (80/20 Rule); Roughly, 80% of the value comes from 20% of the features.
3. Brooks's Law: Adding manpower to a late project makes it later
4. Lehman's Laws of Software Evolution: software must constantly evolve to adapt and remain useful
5. Law of Leaky Abstractions: All non-trivial abstractions, to some degree, are leaky

References

- Wikipedia, *Sturgeon's law*, [pub: 27 Nov 2024, cited: 3 Jan 2025]

S. Data & Information

Benford's Law: First digits in data sets follow predictable pattern

Definition and Origin

Benford's Law, also known as the First-Digit Law, is a statistical principle stating that in many naturally occurring datasets, the leading digit (the first non-zero digit) tends to be small. Specifically, the digit 1 appears about 30% of the time, while larger digits like 9 appear less frequently (around 5%). This counterintuitive distribution applies to a wide range of data, including financial figures, population numbers, and physical constants.

Benford's Law was first discovered by the mathematician Simon Newcomb in 1881. He noticed that the first pages of logarithm tables (which were frequently used for calculations) were more worn than the later pages, suggesting that numbers starting with smaller digits were used more often.

However, the law is named after Frank Benford, a physicist who independently rediscovered the phenomenon in 1938. Benford confirmed and extended Newcomb's work, showing that the pattern applied to a wide range of datasets beyond logarithms. Hence, the law is often referred to as Benford's Law, though both Newcomb and Benford contributed to its understanding.

Context and Importance

In the context of software and technology, Benford's Law plays a crucial role in data analysis, fraud detection, and anomaly detection. Since many naturally occurring datasets tend to follow the first-digit distribution described by Benford's Law, it can be used as a benchmark to identify irregularities in digital data. For example, in the field of financial software, Benford's Law is often applied to flag potentially fraudulent activities, such as manipulated accounting or tax evasion. If a dataset significantly deviates from the expected distribution of first digits, it may signal that the data has been fabricated or altered. Software tools can automate this process, helping auditors, analysts, and investigators spot inconsistencies in large datasets, such as financial statements or transaction records, with high efficiency.

Moreover, Benford's Law has gained importance in the development of machine learning algorithms and data cleansing tools. Many machine learning models rely on vast amounts of real-world data, which is often messy or inconsistent. Understanding the natural distribution of numbers can help software developers identify outliers, correct data errors, and improve model accuracy. In image processing, for example, Benford's Law can be used to check the authenticity of images, as digitally altered images might not conform to the expected statistical patterns. Overall, the application of Benford's Law in software development enhances the reliability of data-driven systems, making it a valuable tool for both data validation and security.

Best Practices and Guidelines

Validate Data Integrity: Use Benford's Law to detect anomalies in datasets, helping identify potential data manipulation or errors.

Automate Fraud Detection: Implement algorithms in financial software or transaction monitoring systems to flag suspicious patterns that deviate from expected first-digit distributions.

Ensure Data Quality: Leverage Benford's Law to clean and validate large datasets before they are used in machine learning models or analyses.

Monitor for Data Consistency: Regularly apply Benford's Law to ensure consistency and authenticity in datasets, especially in areas like digital forensics and image verification.

Understand Limitations: Be mindful that Benford's Law doesn't apply universally—use it as one of many tools for data analysis, not as a sole diagnostic.

Common Misconceptions and Pitfalls

- Not Universal: Benford's Law doesn't apply to all datasets. It's most effective with large, diverse datasets and may not work well with constrained or artificially bounded data.
- Overreliance for Fraud Detection: Deviations from Benford's distribution don't automatically indicate fraud—other factors like data sources, context, and reporting practices should also be considered.
- Assuming Perfect Fit: Expecting datasets to perfectly follow Benford's Law can lead to false positives. Many legitimate datasets may show minor deviations without being manipulated.
- Ignoring Data Scale: Benford's Law is scale-invariant, meaning that the distribution of first digits is the same regardless of the magnitude of numbers. Failing to account for this could lead to incorrect interpretations.
- Misapplying in Small Datasets: Benford's Law is most reliable with large datasets. In small or highly homogeneous datasets, the first-digit distribution may not align with Benford's expectations, leading to misanalysis.

Related Concepts

1. Pareto Principle (80/20 Rule); Roughly, 80% of the value comes from 20% of the features.
2. Zipf's Law: The N-th entry is often approximately inversely proportional to N
3. Central Limit Theorem: Distribution of sample means approximates a normal distribution as sample size increases.

References

- Wikipedia, *Benford's law*, [pub: 17 Dec 2024, cited: 3 Jan 2025]

Chekhov's Gun: Nonessential elements of a story must be removed

Definition and Origin

Chekhov's Gun is a literary principle stating that every element introduced in a story must be relevant and serve a purpose. If an object, character, or detail is mentioned early on, it should be used or have significance later in the narrative, avoiding unnecessary or extraneous elements.

Chekhov's Gun was popularized by the Russian playwright Anton Chekhov. Although he didn't use the exact term "Chekhov's Gun," he famously expressed the principle in his writing advice. One of his well-known quotes on the subject is:

"If in the first act you have hung a gun on the wall, then in the following one it should be fired. Otherwise, don't put it there."

This idea emphasizes narrative economy, ensuring that everything in a story serves a purpose.

Context and Importance

In the context of software development and technology, Chekhov's Gun can be interpreted as a principle of avoiding unnecessary complexity or features in a system. Just as in storytelling, every feature or element introduced in software should serve a clear purpose or function. For instance, if a developer adds a new module, button, or functionality, it should be relevant to the user's experience or to the broader goals of the software. Features or components that are added without clear utility can lead to bloat, increased maintenance costs, and a confusing user interface. By applying the Chekhov's Gun principle, developers can create more efficient, streamlined systems that prioritize functionality over superfluous design or options, leading to better performance and user satisfaction.

Furthermore, in software engineering, Chekhov's Gun also underscores the importance of simplicity in both code and architecture. Unused or unnecessary code not only creates confusion and potential bugs but also makes it harder to maintain and scale the software over time. This principle encourages developers to be deliberate in their design choices, removing any "guns"—features, lines of code, or design patterns—that don't directly contribute to the final product. As software projects grow, keeping the codebase lean and purposeful is crucial to long-term success. By ensuring that every component is intentional and functional, software teams can avoid wasting resources, reduce technical debt, and maintain a clear vision for the product's evolution.

Best Practices and Guidelines

Prioritize Relevance: Only introduce features, components, or code that have a clear purpose and contribute directly to the software's functionality or user experience.

Minimize Bloat: Avoid adding unnecessary features or code that do not add value, as they can complicate maintenance and performance.

Maintain Simplicity: Keep the codebase lean and focused by removing unused or redundant elements to reduce complexity and potential for errors.

Plan for Purposeful Integration: Ensure that every introduced feature or module will be used later in the software's lifecycle, avoiding unused "dead code."

Review and Refactor Regularly: Continuously assess your software to remove or refactor elements that no longer serve their intended purpose, ensuring long-term clarity and efficiency.

Common Misconceptions and Pitfalls

- Assuming Everything Must Be Used Immediately: Chekhov's Gun doesn't mean every introduced feature must be immediately relevant; it just shouldn't be pointless. Features may be important later but should still have a clear role.
- Overengineering for Future Use: Designing complex systems or adding features "just in case" they're needed later can lead to unnecessary complexity and wasted resources.

- Ignoring Scalability: A feature may seem essential now but might become irrelevant or redundant as the software evolves. Not revisiting features as the system scales can lead to inefficiency.
- Confusing "Useful" with "Familiar": Developers might add features that feel intuitive or familiar without considering whether they truly contribute to the user experience or overall functionality.
- Neglecting Maintenance: Just because something was initially necessary doesn't mean it remains relevant. Failing to revisit and remove unused code or features over time leads to codebase bloat.

Related Concepts

1. DRY: Don't Repeat Yourself
2. KISS: Keep It Simple, Stupid
3. YAGNI: You Aren't Gonna Need It - Yet
4. Law of Demeter: Only talk to your immediate friends
5. Single Responsibility Principle (SRP): Part of SOLID, a module should have only one responsibility

References

- Wikipedia, *Chekhov's gun*, [pub: 11 Dec 2024, cited: 3 Jan 2025]

Data Quality Laws: Accuracy, Completeness, Integrity, Validity, Timeliness, Uniqueness

---

Definition and Origin

Data Quality Laws refer to key principles that ensure data is reliable, useful, and effective for decision-making. Here's a concise definition of each:

- Accuracy: Data should be correct and free from errors, reflecting the real-world scenario it represents.
- Completeness: All required data is present, with no missing or incomplete information.

- Integrity: Data should be consistent and maintain relationships across different data sets without contradictions or corruption.
- Validity: Data should conform to the defined formats, ranges, and values, aligning with the intended rules or standards.
- Timeliness: Data should be up-to-date and available when needed for decision-making.
- Uniqueness: Data should be free from duplicates, ensuring each record is represented only once.

Context and Importance

In the context of software and technology, Data Quality Laws are fundamental to ensuring that the systems, applications, and platforms built around data can function effectively and reliably. Software applications, whether they involve data analysis, artificial intelligence, or business operations, rely heavily on high-quality data to generate meaningful insights and perform optimally. If the underlying data is inaccurate, incomplete, or inconsistent, it can lead to faulty predictions, wrong decisions, system malfunctions, or even security breaches. With the increasing reliance on data-driven decision-making, these quality standards must be strictly adhered to in software development, database management, and system integration to ensure that technology can be trusted and provide real value.

The importance of Data Quality Laws extends beyond just operational efficiency. In the tech landscape, where user expectations are high and regulatory requirements are becoming more stringent, maintaining high-quality data can significantly impact user satisfaction, compliance, and business success. For example, inaccurate data in a customer relationship management (CRM) system can lead to poor customer service, while data integrity issues could breach privacy laws and damage an organization's reputation. By adhering to principles like accuracy, completeness, and timeliness, companies can enhance the reliability of their products and services, improve customer trust, and ensure they meet legal and ethical standards. Ultimately, these laws help tech companies optimize their software systems and maintain long-term success.

Best Practices and Guidelines

- Accuracy:

- Use automated data validation tools to check for errors during data entry and processing.
- Implement data quality checks to cross-verify against trusted sources or benchmarks.

- Completeness:
  - Set mandatory fields and ensure data collection forms are comprehensive, preventing missing critical information.
  - Establish validation rules that flag incomplete records and enforce full data capture.
- Integrity:
  - Maintain relational data integrity by using foreign keys, constraints, and referential checks in databases.
  - Perform routine data consistency checks to ensure relationships between datasets remain intact.
- Validity:
  - Define and enforce strict data entry rules, including acceptable formats, ranges, and values.
  - Implement real-time validation to ensure data conforms to predefined criteria before entering the system.
- Timeliness:
  - Automate data synchronization and updates to ensure real-time data availability.
  - Set clear timelines for data updates and review processes to keep information relevant and current.
- Uniqueness:
  - Implement de-duplication algorithms to identify and remove duplicate records in databases.
  - Use unique identifiers for each record to prevent redundancy and ensure singular representation.

Common Misconceptions and Pitfalls

- Assuming Data Quality is a One-Time Task: Data quality is an ongoing process, not a one-time fix. Continuous monitoring and improvement are required as data evolves.
- Neglecting the need for completeness: Incomplete datasets are often overlooked, but missing information can lead to faulty insights and decision-making.

- Overlooking integrity in data relationships: Focusing on individual data fields while ignoring how they relate to each other can lead to inconsistent or unreliable data.
- Ignoring data validity rules: Data that doesn't follow specified formats or business rules might still be accepted, causing issues in analysis or system processing.
- Assuming timeliness is automatic: Even accurate and valid data becomes obsolete if not updated regularly, leading to outdated insights or decisions.
- Prioritizing Quantity Over Quality: Focusing on gathering large volumes of data without addressing its quality can result in overwhelming systems with unreliable or irrelevant information, hindering effective use.
- Overlooking Data Governance: Failing to establish proper data governance structures can lead to inconsistent data management practices, making it harder to enforce quality standards.

Related Concepts

1. Conway's Law: Organizations design systems that mirror their communication structure
2. Pareto Principle: Roughly 80% of effects come from 20% of causes
3. Principle of Least Privilege: Restricts user access to the minimum necessary permissions to perform required tasks.

References

- Wikipedia, *Data quality*, [pub: 20 Dec 2024, cited: 3 Jan 2025]

Pollyanna Principle: Maintain an optimistic outlook, even in the face of challenging circumstances

---

Definition and Origin

The Pollyanna Principle refers to the idea of maintaining an overly optimistic or positive outlook, even in the face of challenges or negative circumstances. It is named after the character Pollyanna, from Eleanor H. Porter's novel, who is known for her unwavering, sometimes unrealistic, optimism. In a business context, it describes the tendency to focus on the positive aspects of a situation or outcome while downplaying or ignoring potential risks or downsides.

Context and Importance

The Pollyanna Principle in the context of software and technology refers to the tendency within technology companies, particularly in the 1980s and 1990s, to emphasize overly optimistic messaging about their products, innovations, and future potential. IBM, as a major technology leader at the time, often presented its advancements with a sense of unrelenting positivity, sometimes glossing over technical challenges or limitations. This attitude, while promoting confidence and enthusiasm within the company and its customer base, also risked creating unrealistic expectations. In the fast-evolving world of software and technology, such optimism could lead to misalignment between what was promised and what was actually deliverable, impacting trust and long-term success. This phenomenon is often observed in the marketing of new software or technological innovations, where potential benefits are highlighted while risks or developmental roadblocks are minimized.

The importance of recognizing the Pollyanna Principle in today's software and technology sectors lies in the balance between innovation and realism. While optimism can drive progress and inspire both teams and consumers, over-promising without acknowledging potential pitfalls can lead to disappointment and damage a company's credibility. In industries like software development, where products often involve complex technical hurdles and evolving customer needs, a more transparent and balanced approach is crucial. Modern companies are increasingly aware that managing expectations—while still communicating the value of new technology—helps build trust and ensures sustainable growth. By avoiding the pitfalls of the Pollyanna Principle, technology firms can foster more honest dialogue with their users, adapt more quickly to challenges, and ultimately deliver more reliable and effective products.

Best Practices and Guidelines

Balance Optimism with Realism: Promote innovation and progress, but acknowledge challenges, limitations, and potential risks in technology projects.

Set Clear, Achievable Expectations: Ensure that marketing and communication about software products are aligned with what can realistically be delivered.

Encourage Transparency: Be honest about potential hurdles, including technical debt, development timelines, and user experience issues.

Foster Continuous Feedback: Regularly assess user feedback and incorporate it into product iterations, avoiding the assumption that initial features will always meet customer needs.

Learn from Failure: Acknowledge mistakes and setbacks as opportunities for improvement, rather than minimizing or ignoring them.

Common Misconceptions and Pitfalls

- Overestimating User Adoption: Assuming that new features or technologies will be instantly embraced by users without considering learning curves or resistance to change.
- Underestimating Complexity: Ignoring the technical challenges and resource demands of scaling or maintaining software, leading to unrealistic timelines and overpromised capabilities.
- Neglecting Long-Term Sustainability: Focusing on short-term success or hype while overlooking ongoing support, maintenance, and updates that are critical for sustained user satisfaction.
- Overlooking Risks: Downplaying or ignoring potential security vulnerabilities, data privacy concerns, or compliance issues that can arise during development or deployment.
- Ignoring Market Realities: Believing that innovation alone will guarantee success, without properly accounting for competition, market readiness, or customer needs.

Related Concepts

1. Brooks's Law: Adding manpower to a late project makes it later

2. Conway's Law: Organizations design systems that mirror their communication structure
3. Hofstadter's Law: It always takes longer than you expect
4. Pareto Principle (80/20 Rule): The idea that 80% of outcomes often come from 20% of efforts.
5. Spolsky's Law of Leaky Abstractions: All non-trivial abstractions, to some degree, are leaky

References

- Wikipedia, *Pollyanna principle*, [pub: 14 Dec 2024, cited: 3 Jan 2025]
- Wiktionary, *IBM Pollyanna Principle*, [pub: 27 Sep 2024, cited: 3 Jan 2025]

Law of Argumentative Comprehension: Understanding an argument requires recognizing its structure and evaluating its premises

---

Definition and Origin

The Law of Argumentative Comprehension refers to the principle that, for an argument to be fully understood and evaluated, one must accurately grasp the intended meaning, context, and logical structure of the argument. This involves not only recognizing the claims being made but also understanding the reasoning and evidence supporting those claims. In essence, it emphasizes the importance of interpreting an argument in its full complexity before assessing its validity or strength.

The Law of Argumentative Comprehension is not typically attributed to a single philosopher or theorist as a formal, widely recognized concept within the field of logic or philosophy. It appears more as a general principle of critical thinking, emphasizing the need to fully understand an argument before evaluating it. This idea is rooted in basic principles of logical analysis and argumentative clarity, which are foundational to thinkers like Aristotle and later philosophers, but it doesn't have a specific inventor or coiner. The principle aligns with the broader concept of "charitable interpretation," a term often associated with philosophers like Donald Davidson, who stressed the importance of understanding an argument in the best possible light before critiquing it.

Context and Importance

In the context of software development and technology, the Law of Argumentative Comprehension underscores the importance of thoroughly understanding the rationale behind design decisions, code implementations, and system architectures before making assessments or suggesting changes. As technology solutions grow in complexity, it is vital for developers, engineers, and architects to not only understand how systems function but also why specific approaches were chosen, including the trade-offs involved. This comprehension is essential during code reviews, technical discussions, or when integrating new technologies, as decisions often carry far-reaching consequences on maintainability, scalability, and performance. Without fully understanding the underlying argument or reasoning behind a solution, developers may misinterpret the intentions or overlook key factors, potentially leading to inefficient or misguided improvements.

Furthermore, the Law of Argumentative Comprehension plays a critical role in collaborative technology environments, where teams must communicate complex technical ideas clearly and effectively. In a field where rapid iteration and adaptability are crucial, miscommunication or a shallow understanding of the reasoning behind certain choices can result in errors, wasted resources, and missed opportunities. This principle encourages individuals to actively seek out the full context of decisions—whether they be in user interface design, security protocols, or system architectures—so that they can contribute meaningfully to the discourse and build on existing knowledge in a way that advances the collective goals of the team or organization. By ensuring that everyone involved is on the same page and genuinely comprehends the arguments at play, software projects are more likely to succeed with higher quality outcomes.

Best Practices and Guidelines

Understand the Rationale: Before critiquing or altering code or design, ensure you fully grasp the reasoning behind the choices made, including trade-offs and constraints.

Seek Full Context: Consider the broader context—such as system requirements, user needs, and future scalability—before making judgments about technical decisions.

Clarify Assumptions: Identify and clarify any implicit assumptions that may influence the design or implementation to avoid misinterpretation or gaps in understanding.

Engage in Active Dialogue: Encourage open discussion with team members to ensure that all perspectives are considered and the argument behind each decision is fully articulated.

Adopt a Charitable Interpretation: When evaluating others' work, interpret their decisions in the most constructive way possible, focusing on understanding their reasoning rather than rushing to critique.

Common Misconceptions and Pitfalls

- Overlooking Context: Assuming that an argument or decision is purely technical without considering broader context, such as business requirements, user needs, or legacy system constraints.
- Misinterpreting Intentions: Rushing to critique or dismissing a design or solution without fully understanding the intended goals or challenges the original team faced.
- Focusing Only on the Surface: Evaluating solutions based on superficial aspects (e.g., code style or small details) while ignoring the deeper reasoning or trade-offs involved.
- Assuming Simplicity: Believing that a complex system or design could have been simpler without understanding the underlying complexities or compromises required to meet specific needs.
- Ignoring Historical Decisions: Failing to appreciate the historical context and prior decisions that shaped the current approach, leading to misjudgments about why certain choices were made.

Related Concepts

1. Broken Windows Theory (i.e. Entropy): visible signs of disorder and neglect in an environment encourage further disorder and more serious crimes.
2. Principle of Least Astonishment: Software should behave in a way that users find intuitive and expected
3. Scout Rule: "Leave the code better than you found it"

References

- Wikipedia, *Argument technology*, [pub: 21 Aug 2023, cited: 3 Jan 2025]

Papert's Principle: People learn best when they are actively engaged in the process

---

Definition and Origin

Papert's Principle, derived from the work of Seymour Papert, emphasizes the idea that people learn best when they are actively engaged in the process of constructing their own knowledge, rather than passively receiving information. This principle advocates for learning environments where individuals, particularly children, can explore, experiment, and interact with concepts in meaningful ways, often through hands-on activities and problem-solving. It aligns with constructivist theories of learning, where knowledge is built through experience and reflection.

Papert's Principle is closely associated with Seymour Papert, a renowned educator and researcher in the field of artificial intelligence and learning theory. He is best known for his work in constructivism and for developing the Logo programming language, which was designed to help children learn through exploration and problem-solving. While the term "Papert's Principle" is not a formalized concept with a specific definition in his work, the principle reflects key ideas from his writings, particularly those in his seminal book Mindstorms: Children, Computers, and Powerful Ideas (1980), where he outlined how learning is enhanced through active engagement and self-directed discovery.

Thus, Papert himself is considered the originator of the core ideas that underpin what is often referred to as "Papert's Principle."

Context and Importance

Papert's Principle has profound implications for the field of software and technology, particularly in the context of educational tools and digital learning environments. In the late 20th century, Papert envisioned a world where children could use computers not just for passive consumption of information, but as powerful tools for creation, exploration, and problem-solving. He developed the Logo programming language with this vision in mind, allowing young learners to control a "turtle" to draw shapes on the screen, promoting experiential learning through coding. Papert believed that when children interacted directly with technology, they could engage in deeper cognitive processes, connecting abstract concepts to real-world applications. This perspective challenged traditional, teacher-centered methods of instruction and encouraged a shift toward student-centered, project-based learning, facilitated by technology.

The importance of Papert's Principle in modern software and technology is especially relevant in today's digital age, where interactive and adaptive learning platforms have become integral to education. Technologies such as coding games, simulation software, and educational apps align with Papert's vision by providing students with opportunities to learn by doing, fostering creativity and critical thinking skills. The rise of platforms like Scratch, an educational programming language developed by the MIT Media Lab (also influenced by Papert's work), exemplifies how technology can empower learners to create their own projects and explore complex ideas in an intuitive, hands-on way. In an era of rapid technological change, Papert's principles continue to advocate for the use of software and technology as tools not just for information retrieval, but for deep, personalized, and active learning that equips students with the skills needed to navigate and innovate in an increasingly digital world.

Best Practices and Guidelines

Encourage Active Engagement: Design software and technology tools that allow users, especially learners, to actively create, experiment, and solve problems rather than just consume information.

Foster Exploration: Provide open-ended platforms where users can explore and discover concepts at their own pace, promoting curiosity and self-directed learning.

Facilitate Iteration: Enable learners to test, revise, and improve their work, reinforcing the importance of trial and error in the learning process.

Promote Personalization: Tailor technology to accommodate individual learning styles and interests, allowing users to pursue topics and projects they find meaningful.

Support Collaborative Learning: Design tools that encourage collaboration and knowledge-sharing, allowing learners to work together, exchange ideas, and build collective knowledge.

Common Misconceptions and Pitfalls

- Assuming Technology Alone Drives Learning: Believing that simply providing access to software or technology will automatically lead to meaningful learning, without considering how users interact with or engage with the tools.
- Overloading with Complexity: Designing tools or platforms that are too complex or overwhelming, which can hinder exploration and creativity rather than promote it.
- Neglecting Guidance and Support: Focusing on self-directed learning without providing adequate scaffolding, mentorship, or resources to help learners navigate challenges.
- Underestimating the Role of Social Interaction: Ignoring the importance of collaborative and social aspects of learning, which can limit the full potential of technology as a tool for shared knowledge-building.
- Treating Learning as Linear: Assuming that learners must follow a fixed, linear path through software or content, which contradicts the principle of exploration and flexible, personalized learning.

Related Concepts

1. Engelbart's law: Technology should be used to extend human capabilities.
2. Fitts's Law: Time to target depends on distance and size
3. The Principle of Constructivism: Learners build their own understanding through experiences.

References

- Wikipedia, *Papert's principle*, [pub: 30 Mar 2021, cited: 3 Jan 2025]

Zipf's Law: The N-th entry is often approximately inversely proportional to N

Definition and Origin

Zipf's Law is a statistical principle that suggests in many types of data (such as word frequencies in a language), the frequency of an item is inversely proportional to its rank. In simpler terms, the second most frequent item occurs half as often as the most frequent one, the third most frequent item occurs a third as often, and so on. This creates a power-law distribution where a few items are very common, and many items are rare.

Zipf's Law was coined by linguist George Zipf in the 1940s. Zipf observed this pattern in the frequency of words in natural languages and found that a small number of words are used very frequently, while many words are used much less frequently. He formalized this relationship in his work on statistical linguistics and later applied the principle to various other domains.

Context and Importance

Zipf's Law has important implications in software and technology, especially in the context of data analysis, search engines, and natural language processing (NLP). In the world of digital communication, such as web searches, social media, or user-generated content, a small subset of keywords or phrases tends to dominate traffic or interaction, mirroring Zipf's distribution. For example, in search engine queries, a few high-volume keywords (like "weather" or "news") are queried much more often than the vast majority of less common terms. Recognizing this pattern helps developers and data scientists design algorithms that prioritize the most relevant content or optimize search results, making systems more efficient and user-friendly.

Furthermore, Zipf's Law also informs resource allocation and storage efficiency in software development. For instance, in databases or content delivery networks (CDNs), knowing that a small percentage of data will be accessed far more frequently than the majority allows engineers to optimize caching strategies, improve load balancing, and enhance overall system performance. Zipf's Law is also central to machine learning models, where understanding the distribution of word frequencies or user interactions can help fine-tune algorithms for more accurate predictions, recommendations, or automated responses. In essence, Zipf's Law underscores the unevenness inherent in data, guiding the creation of systems that better handle the complexity and scale of modern digital environments.

Best Practices and Guidelines

Optimize for frequent items: Design algorithms and systems (e.g., search engines, recommendation engines) to prioritize high-frequency data or queries, ensuring faster responses and better user experience.

Efficient data storage: Implement caching strategies for high-traffic items, reducing load on databases and improving system performance.

Load balancing: Distribute resources in proportion to demand, allocating more capacity to the most frequently accessed data or services.

Reduce complexity: Simplify models by focusing on the most common elements, such as frequent words in NLP, to improve processing efficiency and accuracy.

Scalable systems: Build flexible architectures that can easily scale to handle both the common, high-demand items and the long tail of infrequent requests.

Common Misconceptions and Pitfalls

- Overemphasis on the tail: Focusing too much on rare items in a dataset can lead to inefficient resource allocation, as they contribute minimally to overall usage or performance.
- Assuming perfect adherence: Not all datasets strictly follow Zipf's Law; assuming it always applies can lead to misguided design choices or inaccurate predictions.

- Ignoring temporal variations: The distribution of data may change over time (e.g., trends in search queries), so relying solely on Zipf's Law may result in outdated assumptions.
- Neglecting contextual factors: Zipf's Law reflects frequency, not relevance—high-frequency items may not always be the most meaningful or contextually appropriate for a given task.
- Underestimating rare events: While rare items may seem insignificant, neglecting them entirely can lead to missed opportunities or poor user experience, especially in personalized recommendations or anomaly detection.

Related Concepts

1. Pareto Principle: The 80/20 Rule
2. Amdahl's Law: Parallel speedup is limited by sequential portions
3. Metcalfe's Law: Network value grows with square of users
4. Little's Law: Average items in queue equals arrival rate times waiting time
5. Law of Diminishing Returns: More resources yield smaller improvements

References

- Wikipedia, *Zipf's law*, [pub: 31 Dec 2024, cited: 3 Jan 2025]

ABOUT THE AUTHOR

Quinn Smith holds a BSc in Computer Science from the University of South Africa and has over 20+ years in software engineering.

Social media:

- LinkedIn: https://www.linkedin.com/in/smithquinn

Fun fact:

He finds that writing offers a more effective and precise means of expressing his thoughts and ideas. Verbal communication often leads to ambiguity and misunderstandings, making written expression a clearer and more reliable outlet for conveying concepts.

www.ingramcontent.com/pod-product-compliance
Lightning Source LLC
LaVergne TN
LVHW052211200926
848481LV00001B/77
* 9 7 9 8 3 4 8 5 5 5 7 6 4 *